Land, Food, Freedom

# LAND,

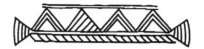

# *FOOD,*

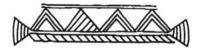

# FREEDOM

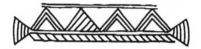

## STRUGGLES FOR THE GENDERED COMMONS IN KENYA 1870 TO 2007

### LEIGH BROWNHILL

**Africa World Press, Inc.**

P.O. Box 1892

Trenton, NJ 08607

P.O. Box 48

Asmara, ERITREA

# Africa World Press, Inc.

P.O. Box 1892
Trenton, NJ 08607

P.O. Box 48
Asmara, ERITREA

Book and cover design: Saverance Publishing Services
Cover artwork: Seth Tobocman

Library of Congress Cataloging-in-Publication Data

Brownhill, Leigh.
  Land, food, freedom : struggles for the gendered commons in Kenya, 1870 to 2007 / Leigh Brownhill.
    p. cm.

Includes bibliographical references and index.

  ISBN 1-59221-690-0 (hardcover) -- ISBN 1-59221-691-9 (pbk.)  1. Women peasants--Kenya--Political activity--History. 2.  Peasantry--Kenya--History. 3. Land tenure--Kenya--History. 4. National liberation movements--Kenya--History. 5. Kenya--History--Mau Mau Emergency, 1952-1960--Women. I. Title.

HD983.B76 2009
333.2--dc22

                                      2009003427

# ❧ CONTENTS

# ॐ GLOSSARY

All terms are *Gikuyu* unless otherwise indicated

| | |
|---|---|
| ahoi | tenant |
| anake | age-set |
| askari | *Kiswahilili* = guard |
| athomi | mission converts |
| baraza | *Kiswahilili* = meeting |
| ene | customary owner |
| githaka | land belonging to the subclan |
| gutumana wira | cooperative labour usually involving ten or more people |
| harambee | *Kiswahilili* = "let's all pull together," self-help groups |
| irua | rite of passage, usually involving male and female circumcision |
| ituika | generational handover ceremony |
| itura (pl. matura) | a homestead group |
| karing'a | pure |
| kaya | *Giriama* = shrine, customary seat of government, sacred grove |
| kiama | council |
| kiama kia atumia | women's council |
| kipande | *Kiswahilili* = registration card |
| kiraho | *Kiswahili* = oath |
| mabati | *Kiswahili* = iron sheets |
| Maendeleo ya Wanawake | *Kiswahili* = Progress for Women club |
| maisha | *Kiswahili* = life |

| | |
|---|---|
| mbari | clan |
| mganga | *Kiswahili* = 'witch doctor' or herbalist |
| mitaro | terraces |
| moran | warrior |
| mugunda wa mathaga | land allocated to a daughter by her parents |
| muthoni | in-law |
| mwalimu | *Kiswahili* = teacher |
| mwendia ruhiu | a man without his own home |
| mwene | landowner |
| mzee | *Kiswahili* = old man |
| Ngai | God |
| ngwatio | collective work group |
| njama ya ita | war council |
| Njuri Ncheke | *Meru* = supreme council |
| nyapara | farm supervisor |
| posho | *Kiswahili* = maize mill |
| riika (pl. marika) | age-grade |
| shamba | *Kiswahili* - farm or garden |
| tha | blessings in land |
| uhuru | *Kiswahili* - freedom |

# PART I

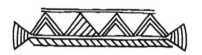

# GENDERED COMMONS, GENDERED COMMONERS

# ～ INTRODUCTION sub ～

*In a revolution, when the ceaseless slow accumulation of centuries burst into volcanic eruption, the meteoric flares and flights above are a meaningless chaos and lend themselves to infinite caprice and romanticism unless the observer sees them always as projections of the sub-soil from which they came. The writer has sought not only to analyse, but to demonstrate their movement, the economic forces of the age; their moulding of society and politics, of men in the mass and individual men; the powerful reaction of these on their environment at one of those rare moments when society is at boiling point and therefore fluid* (James, C.L.R., preface to *The Black Jacobins*, 1989, pp. x-xi).

## INSPIRATIONS AND ORIGINS ✗2

I begin this study of social movements in Kenya over the long 20th century (Arrighi 1994) by referring to C.L.R. James' examination of the 1791 Haitian revolution. In his 1938 *The Black Jacobins*, James explained the dynamics of Haitian revolutionaries' successful fight against European slavers and Napoleon's navy in order to better equip revolutionaries of the mid-20th century for their fight against colonialism. My analysis of Kenyan peasant women's struggles for subsistence is informed by James' historical materialism and his focus on the unwaged as agents of revolution. In this brief introductory chapter, I examine elements of James' work that provide theoretical and methodological foundations for my study. These few pages are followed by a more thoroughgoing discussion of theory in Chapter One, which in turn sets the stage for the presentation of the substantive data and analysis in Chapters Two to Eleven.

C.L.R. James, after Karl Marx, argued that power relations are laid bare during times of revolution. If "the observer sees them always as projections of the sub-soil from which they came," then revolutions can reveal the demands and capacities of those who are usually silenced. The words of those in power are typically committed to the historical record. But in times of revolution, the voices and accounts of the exploited and those opposed to dispossession are also heard. These voices appear in official, scholarly and popular texts as well as in memoirs, memories and oral histories of participants and observers. Revolutionaries of the past, according to James, "have given us an example to study" ((1938) 1989: 375) and thus provide us with an opportunity to better understand the dynamics of transformation in current struggles.

The study of Africans' revolutionary movements was one of James' many special gifts to 20th- and 21st-century humanity. James' classic 1938 study of the Haitian revolution, *The Black Jacobins*, reflects his view that Africans have historically led the way in struggles for freedom against slavery, colonialism, racism and capitalism. James showed how, between 1791 and 1803, African and Mulatto captives organized to win a war against Napoleon's navy and become the first slaves in the Western Hemisphere to free themselves from captivity and create an independent republic. From whence did their remarkable capacities arise? According to James, the Haitian revolutionaries worked and lived together in gangs of hundreds on the huge sugar plantations that covered what was then called San Domingo's North Plain. They were "closer to a modern proletariat than any group of workers in existence at the time, and the rising was, therefore, a thoroughly prepared and organised mass movement" ((1938) 1989:86).

Haitians rose up against what was, in James' estimation, the most advanced capitalist production system in the world. European merchants and planters had constructed a Caribbean sugar industry that involved slave ships, auctions and markets, plantations, huge barracks, sugar mills and the newest factory technology. All components were seamlessly integrated into emerging global commodity markets via well-established transportation, financial and communications circuits.

Within six weeks of their publication, pamphlets from the streets of Paris produced during the French Revolution were delivered to the "new world" by sailors on slave and merchant ships plying the Atlantic. The famous call, "Liberty, Fraternity, Equality," was taken up by the captives and carried into the Haitian Revolution. A tremendous incentive to the antislavery struggle of Africans in San Domingo was the French Jacobins' move to abolish slavery, or private property in people. The same Atlantic-wide network used by French slave masters to organize exploitation was used by the Jacobins, black and white, to extend the French Revolution to Haiti.

In *The Black Jacobins*, James brought to bear upon emerging mid-20th century anticolonial and Pan-African liberation struggles an analysis of an historic revolution of the *unwaged*. This analysis affirmed and elaborated Marx's central discovery that the organizational capacity of capital bequeathed a revolutionary potential to *waged labor*. In 1867 in Volume One of *Capital*, Marx wrote that

> One capitalist always kills many. Hand in hand with this centralization, or this expropriation of many capitalists by few, develop, on an ever-extending scale, the co-operative form of the labor-process, the conscious technical application of science, the methodical cultivation of the soil, the transformation of the instruments of labor into instruments of labor only usable in common, the economizing of all means of production by their use as means of production of combined, socialized labor, the entanglement of all peoples in the net of the world-market, and with this, the international character of the capitalistic regime. Along with the constantly diminishing number of the magnates of capital, who usurp and monopolize all advantages of this process of transformation, grows the mass of misery, oppression, slavery, degradation, exploitation; *but with this too grows the revolt of the working-class, a class always increasing in numbers, and disciplined, united, organized by the very mechanism of the process of capitalist production itself.* The monopoly of capital becomes a fetter upon the mode of production, which has sprung up and flourished along with, and under it. Centralization of the means of production and socialization of labor at last reach a point where they become incompatible with their capitalist integument. Thus integument is burst asunder. The knell of capitalist private property sounds. The expropriators are expropriated (Marx 1867/1967): I, 763, *emphasis added*).

James recounted how Haitians turned their organization, unity and discipline deriving from the regime of capitalist sugar production and the triangular trade toward the task of expropriating the slaveowners of their property in the industrial sugar plantations and, most remarkably, of their property in the captives themselves.

James offered several entry points into the study of revolutionary social change that I take up here. I study the "sub-soil" from which revolutionary movements in Kenya arose by focusing on the indigenous subsistence political economy. This rural, peasant reality is quintessentially a world of women and unwaged work. I examine how colonial and corporate capital "organized, united, disciplined" the exploited, both waged and unwaged, to resist in specific instances in Kenya between 1870 and 2007. I consider the extent and the shape of Kenya's integration into a process of "globalization from below." And I do so in order to make more prominent the strengths of previous social movements. These are a legacy that is invaluable for the success of current mobilizations.

This study focuses on Kenyan women's engagement in social movements for the defense and control of the commons. There are several other studies of Kenyan women's mobilizations in the 20th century (Abwunza 1997; Khasiana and Njiro 1993; Likimani 1985; MacKenzie 1990, 1991; Pala et al. 1978; Presley 1992; Wipper 1977). However the present analysis makes three new departures.

First, I periodize 20th-century social movement history in Kenya within a global context characterized by "waves of corporate amalgamation" (Nitzan and Bichler 2002). I trace the connection between the expansion of global circuits of capital and global circuits of struggle (Dyer-Witheford 1999) as they are expressed in the Kenyan case. I do this by identifying changes in the "male deals" (defined in Chapter One) that brought into collaboration certain African and European men for the purposes of building the hierarchical relations of colonial rule.

Second, in keeping with James' call for the recognition of women's power (1976/1984), this study provides a *sustained* focus on women's social movement activities over more than a century. This is in contrast to the majority of published accounts, which treat as episodic the engagement of Kenyan women in political change. This sustained focus allows for an analysis of change in peasant women's movements and in their life-centered organizational capacities.

Third, this study embraces a "subsistence orientation," or a perspective that centers activities and social relations that support life for all. In the analysis of capital and anticapitalist resistance, a subsistence orientation turns the focus away from industrial and agricultural waged laborers and toward unwaged commoners, especially rural women. By shifting the focus to the resistance and organization of gendered commoners, the subsistence perspective reveals what has eluded many other analysts, that is, the centrality of women to the struggle for land, food and freedom in Kenya. This subsistence perspective offers a framing of Kenyan social movements as struggles for the liberation of *all peoples* from hunger, violence and exploitation.

In Kenya there has been an almost unbroken century-long chain of social movements against capitalist enclosures. I show that in these social movements, Kenyans have persistently defended and elaborated their life-centered subsistence political economies. Subsistence social relations make up the "sub-soil" out of which revolutionary movements have arisen. The defense of subsistence relations is one common goal in Kenyan uprisings and social movements throughout the century. A key finding of this study is that Kenyan social movement activists have in fact harbored and transferred vital, actually existing, subsistence alternatives to corporate rule from the precolonial past into 21st-century social movements.

Many outstanding Kenyans contribute to transformational world social movements. Kenyans' prominence in global movements in the 21st century is in part due to the wide relevance of the life-supporting capacities, practices and social relations they have defended and reshaped over a long 20th century. Peasant women in rural and urban areas are the frontline food farmers, preparers and traders whose daily work sustains people in the subsistence realm and in the cash economy. The work of feeding people brings many women farmers and traders into direct confrontation with the commodifying regime of capital. Because this study takes the view from below and is concerned with commoners' *power* against capital, it foregrounds peasant women's engagement in social movements for subsistence.

In the history of resistance in Kenya, peasant and dispossessed women are consistently prominent over a whole range of revolts, demonstrations and insurrections. Women's daring actions, their names and sometimes their own words are recorded in official, popular and scholarly sources. There are, however almost no written sources that systematically document or explain women's prominence. Much of the broad literature on women and gender relations in Kenya does recognize women's accomplishments and points to women's collectivity as a strength. The present analysis identifies the source of that strength and collectivity and traces the changing organizational forms within which Kenyan women, with men, have used and elaborated their collectivity over the 20th century. A subsistence orientation and attention to the global political economy facilitate an understanding of the specific shape, significance and continuity of Kenyan resistance to enclosure and exploitation.

This book was crucially shaped by the memories shared with me by elderly Kenyan women who have participated in historic uprisings and revolutionary movements. Oral history interviews provide rich details of many of the events examined here. And, critically, oral history interviews offered new perspectives on these events, which are reflected neither in official accounts nor in most scholarly studies. The insiders' view of Mau Mau has also been recorded in biographies, autobiographies, scholarly analyzes and police and court records. The present study builds on this rich and varied literature to analyse fifteen uprisings and social movements over the course of the century, with particular attention to the views, demands and experiences of women activists themselves.

The pervasive silences around both subsistence and women's activism in Kenyan popular struggles are striking. Kenyan women's demands and actions for land, food and freedom have been hidden, while activist women and their communities have sometimes been met with violent reprisal by state and private armed forces. Social movements seeking access to and control over the necessities of life have repeatedly arisen in Kenya. This long struggle for freedom has taken many different forms over the past century. What is new in the 21st century is the thoroughgoing integration of the subsistence struggles of Kenyan women into a global "movement of social movements."

This book examines social movements in which peasant women were prominent in an effort to better understand first, the transformation of Kenyan society between 1870 and 2007 and second, current global struggles. The chapters that follow consider changes in the organization of social movements on the one hand, and the organization of capital on the other. These chapters delineate three "cycles of struggle." By means of these cycles, Kenyan social movements have contributed to the development of global social movement networks at the same time as corporations have proceeded over the 20th century to amalgamate first by industry and sector, and then nationally and globally (Nitzan and Bichler 2002:16). Although these successive 30- to 60-year cycles have featured varying configurations of popular and corporate social forces, I will argue that the central issue over which the classes struggle remains constant: *fertility*, here used to refer broadly to land, labor and all of the capabilities and productive powers of the exploited class, especially its women. This perspective allows me to show that East Africans' subsistence demands and capabilities are key contributions to the construction, on a global scale, of new alternatives to corporate rule.

Connecting Kenyan struggles to changes in the global political economy of capital enabled me to see the ways that the expanding organization of capital itself contributed to Kenyan insurgents' move from local defensive actions against colonialism to engagement in global processes of social transformation. This international political economy approach also provides a means of recognizing the centrality of African women's subsistence concerns to the current process of globalization from below.

## OVERVIEW OF THE CHAPTERS

The chapters of this book are organized into three chronological parts, which coincide with three cycles of struggle mentioned above, each characterized by distinct male deals. Although processes of enclosure, resistance and subsistence elaboration were unfolding simultaneously during each of the three cycles of struggle, the weight or importance of one or another process was clearly greater in particular cycles than in others. Part II examines enclosures; in Part III resistance is emphasized; and Part IV focuses on a resurgence of the subsistence political economy. In this way the chapters emphasize the predominant process when analyzing each of the three cycles, while also giving attention to the three simultaneous moments of enclosure, resistance and the building of subsistence. Part I considers the theoretical approach employed in this study. A more detailed overview of the chapters in Parts II, III and IV follows.

### *Part II: 1870-1929 (Chapters Two and Three)*

Part II introduces the historical background to the century's "fight for fertility" (defined in Chapter One). It examines localized uprisings against early British *enclosures* and associated male deals with African traders in the period 1870 to 1929.

Chapter Two (1870 to 1900) begins with an overview of indigenous subsistence land and exchange relations in the period. It then turns to an examination of the changes wrought by the incursion into central Kenya of British missionaries, adventurers and the traders of the Imperial British East Africa Company.

Chapter Three shows that the struggles of the early 20th century (1900 to 1929) involved three main categories of gendered ethnicized class actors: (1) European colonialists, (2) African collaborators with the British and (3) peasant women with the alliance of waged and unwaged men for the defense and elaboration of the subsistence political economy. Relations among these three sets of actors are analyzed in the uprisings of Mekatilili wa Menza (1913) and Mary Muthoni Nyanjiru (1922). The chapter argues that Kenyan peasant women, in particular, organized actions against the trade and labor policies of the British, and against the newly appointed African "chiefs" who implemented these policies. For the rest of the century, social movements in Kenya built on these early mobilizations by women and their male allies. These movements were designed to break up the male deals between African and European men.

### *Part III: 1930-1959 (Chapters Four, Five, Six, Seven and Eight)*

Part III considers the national and regional scope of social movement *resistance* to the chiefs' male deals in the period 1930 to 1959. The analyses offered here demonstrate that this was a period of intense resistance that centered around a campaign for indigenous and anticolonial control over fertility, which was at the heart of subsistence. Chapters Four through Eight concentrate on social relations in the 1930s, 1940s and 1950s. The chapters on the 1930s and 1940s provide analyses of the mobilizations that led up to and culminated in the armed gendered class struggle known as the Mau Mau war. After 60 years of British rule, the colonized threw off colonialism in a decade of armed struggle (1952-1960).

Chapter Four (1930-1949) argues that the new male deals of the 1930s and 1940s were aimed at capturing the labor and land of African women. This argument is pursued through an analysis of two instances of contested gendered enclosure: (1) the 1934 Carter land commission and (2) the female-circumcision policy of Meru District Officer, H.E. Lambert.

Chapter Five (1930-1949) examines resistance initiated by peasant women that was joined by men who had broken with the male dealers. I conceptualize these *relations of solidarity for the defense of subsistence* as "gendered class alliances." In the independent school movement, the Murang'a women's terracing strike and the Olenguruone struggle, peasants and waged allies attempted to throw off relations of colonial exploitation. Each uprising or movement contributed to the mobilization by the late 1940s of a coordinated armed struggle for independence.

Chapter Six (1950-1952) considers how, in three uprisings in the early 1950s, insurgents built ever-more inclusive and militant gendered class alliances. With the 1950 general strike, the 1951 women's cattle dip protest and the 1952 outbreak of armed struggle, peasant commoners launched the Mau Mau war for independence. They focused on breaking the control that foreign and local male dealers asserted over Africans' land, labor and the fruits thereof. They did so especially by building alliances among exploited women and men aimed at defending and extending indigenous subsistence practices and relations.

Chapter Seven (1953-1956) shows that in the mid 1950s colonialists adopted as a counterinsurgency strategy the forced privatization of land in the African reserves that had, since colonial incursion, been maintained under common and customary tenure. The commodification of land and the subsequent introduction of cash cropping in peasant farm areas were meant to break and overcome the Mau Mau collective defense of subsistence land relations. Mau Mau collectivity involved swearing an oath to "fight to the death." This unity constituted its strength. The chapter examines two British policies meant to break that unity and to impose a commercial organization of labor and land: (1) the enclosure of Kikuyu civilians, mainly women, children and elders, in concentration camps in 1953; and (2) the privatization of customary common lands as required by the 1954 Swynnerton Plan, which in effect abolished women's customary entitlements.

Chapter Eight (1957-1959) argues that by the late 1950s the Mau Mau struggle was characterized by the emerging processes of globalization from above and from below. These processes are revealed through the analysis of two British counterinsurgency strategies against Mau Mau: the formation of *Maendeleo ya Wanawake* women's "development" clubs in the concentration camps and "rehabilitation" through torture of Mau Mau prisoners in British custody. *Maendeleo ya Wanawake* clubs became, in the 1960s, a model for "women in development" programs, which I suggest were (and continue to be) central to the project of corporate globalization from above. Popular outrage at the British abuse of Mau Mau prisoners provided a flashpoint for international unity and mobilization. Prisoners and international activists coordinated to mount pressure on the British government to end the war and the colonial occupation of Kenya.

X3
L *Part IV: 1960-2007 (Chapters Nine, Ten and Eleven)*

Part Four analyzes Kenyans' *elaboration of subsistence* relations within global social movements against corporate male deals in the period 1960 to the present. Chapters nine and ten bring the analysis into the 21$^{st}$ century by focusing on fights for fertility in the post-1963 independence period. The chapters draw on five case studies to show that Kenyan peasants have elaborated and extended the subsistence political economy in the postcolonial era. This "subsistence resurgence" constitutes Kenyans' major contribution to the process of "globalization from below," defined in Chapter One.

Chapter Nine (1960-1979) shows that in the 1960s and 1970s subsistence relations proliferated. Notable were relations of collective farming and cooperative labor. The subsistence resurgence is demonstrated through analysis of the growing women's group movement and the *harambee* (self-help) movement. In these movements Kenyan peasant women secured greater control over their own fertility, as expressed through the production and use of life goods such as food, shelter, fuel and biodiversity.

Chapter Ten (1980-2007) argues that between 1980 and 2007 Kenyan social movement activists have engaged in an accelerated and expanding process of globalization from below as they resist corporate globalization from above. Globalization from below has involved the intensified involvement of Kenyan subsistence movements in global anticapitalist movements. This argument is pursued through an examination of three struggles between 1980 and 2007: the Freedom Corner hunger strike, the land occupation movement and the struggle for the drafting of a new constitution. Analysis of these movements sheds light on the significance of more recent processes, including challenges to the neoliberal agenda of the G-8 carried out through the World Trade Organization.

Chapter Eleven concludes the book by considering the many significant ways in which Kenyan peasant women have contributed to the mobilization of social movements for subsistence over the long 20th century. The chapter considers how gendered class alliances and the creative amalgams of indigenous and exogenous social forms were used to break "male deals" during three successive cycles of gendered, ethnicized class struggle. The subsistence-oriented demands of 21st-century Kenyan social movements are assessed in terms of their potential for the strengthening of Kenyan and global movements for the gendered commons.

~ CHAPTER ONE ~

# THEORETICAL APPROACH: THE SUBSISTENCE PERSPECTIVE

## ARGUMENT —sub

The purpose of this book is to show how peasant women within Kenyan "social movements," those organized challenges to exploitation by the unwaged, have successfully mobilized and expanded Kenyans' capacities to provide the essentials of life to all. Toward the end of the first decade of the 21st century, peasant women's special life-centered subsistence capabilities proved critical to the efficacy of social movement activism and the survival strategies of ordinary people, as these unfolded under the brutal conditions of global corporate rule.

What explains the success with which exploited Kenyan "gendered commoners" challenged British colonialism, beginning with the "Mau Mau" - or those youth men who raided British caravans and famine relief convoys in the 1880s - and culminating with the Mau Mau of the 1950s, who brought Kenya to independence in 1963? How can we understand the persistence of precolonial indigenous spiritualisms and cultural practices such as female genital mutilation in the general population and within various 21st-century social movement organizations?

This book examines the strengths of Kenyan social movement organizations by considering how activists constructed creative amalgams of what are referred to here as "indigenous and exogenous social forms." That is, as activists were forced into a colonial framework (building roads, learning to read, being confined to reserves), they brought together aspects of their own indigenous cultural practices and selected capitalist practices, relations and networks to form new organizational forms. These hybrid organizational forms were fired in the furnace of Africans' resistance to colonialism and thus were made as weapons in the fight against exploitation. The chapters that follow identify and analyze the organizational forms employed in Kenyan social movements over the long 20ᵗʰ century.

One example of such creative amalgams was Mekatilili wa Menza's "taxing" of the Giriama peoples in her efforts to raise funds to hold a six-week congress in the Giriama's sacred forest shrine. The British poll and hut taxes were universally hated by the colonized. Mekatilili spoke against colonial taxes while collecting her own, which people reportedly gladly paid. Mekatilili had called the congress to discuss ways to counter colonial incursions and to strengthen community control over resources. Another example of these hybrid organizational forms was the simple use of the telegraph by African clerks in the 1920s to send anticolonial activists' petitions and grievances to the Colonial Office, the League of Nations and the governments of various countries.

Through struggle, Kenyan activists maintained life-centered capabilities by defending selected precolonial practices and social relations. They also reconfigured precolonial practices by selectively adopting those aspects of exogenous social forms that contributed to strengthening the life-sustaining capacities of their indigenous social forms.

The organization of Kenyan social movements changed over the century, concomitant with changes in the relations of local and global capital. As the scope of colonial enclosures widened, so too did the scope of commoners' activism. Through the century, Kenyan activists engaged in the defense of indigenous subsistence political economies and incorporated specific aspects of exogenous - colonial or capitalist - social forms into their strategies of resistance and everyday practices of survival. In so doing, Kenyan social movement actors have kept alive some of the life-supporting capabilities and values of the precolonial indigenous subsistence political economy. At the same time they have transformed localized precolonial practices to make them more inclusive and applicable under changed circumstances, for instance in urban slum communities.

This book analyzes, in particular, the gendered and ethnicized class character of Kenyan social movements and underlines the *subsistence content* of the relationships being wrought in the process of globalization from below. The study contributes to the project of demonstrating how capital has organized, united and disciplined the exploited, both waged and unwaged, to resist their exploitation; and how, in the instances presented, peasant women have been at the forefront of these persistent, effective and increasingly global movements against capitalist enclosure. Kenyan commoners' world historic struggles provide critical examples for activists, scholars, commoners and others, of the reconstruction and defense of a life-centered subsistence political economy capable of sustaining entire communities.

The "gendered commons" is used here to refer to those places in the world in which people live "in common" within elaborated subsistence relations. These "places" are sometimes understood legally as "commons," trust land, state land or lands with other similar formal designations. But often the gendered commons are built upon private land, such as in slums and in rural farmlands, where occupants do not have secure rights. That is, though the occupants may not own the land, they do their best to collectively organize their security, the common use of resources and access to basic requirements.

These are social relations among women and men struggling for universal access to the earthly commons. The terms "gendered commons" and "gendered commoners" denote the organizational strengths of Kenya's social movements for land, food and freedom. By understanding the powers, actions and demands of those who have risen up against injustice, we can better prepare ourselves to win the continuing global struggle against capital, and to nurture that "other world" that has already been born. In the 1930s C.L.R. James studied the "sub-soil from which [the Haitian revolutionaries] came" in part to inform and inspire the nascent anticolonial movement. In the same vein, this book seeks to contribute to 21st-century global struggles for the gendered commons in Kenya and globally.

# GENDERED, ETHNICIZED CLASS ANALYSIS –sub

This book undertakes a gendered, ethnicized class analysis of Kenyan social movements. There are three main features of this extended class analysis that are delineated here. First, the conceptual category of the "exploited class" is broadened beyond waged workers to include all those (peasants, students, children, housewives, indigenous people and others) whose unpaid labor and resources are channeled into and undergird the market economy. The typical resources that capital alienates from unwaged workers include labor power, nature, public space, indigenous knowledge and time.

Second, gendered, ethnicized class analysis provides tools with which to examine the social relations through which capital organizes the exploitation of the unwaged. The relation of capital to the unwaged is not as clearly defined, nor as easily regulated, as are the "transparent" contractual relations between worker and boss. I employ the concepts of "fight for fertility," "male deal" and "housewifization," defined below, to examine these social relations through which unwaged labo r and the commons are channeled into the capitalist market economy.

Third, the revolutionary significance of the life-sustaining activities and resistance of unwaged exploited people is recognized. Because the unwaged, by definition, live at least partially outside the commodified realm, many maintain potentially transformational subsistence or life-centered capabilities. These include collective, organic food production, harvest sharing and subsistence trade. Such capabilities, and the cooperative form of labor involved in each, contribute to mobilization not only to challenge exploitative relations but also to replace them with life-centered social relations. In 21st-century Kenya, peasants maintain many indigenous communal relationships to land, labor and harvests.

I will define and discuss the key concepts that make up the framework of gendered, ethnicized class analysis.

## SUB — THE SUBSISTENCE PERSPECTIVE

Karl Marx noted in 1881 that an archaic form of communal life in Russia had survived into the capitalist era. He observed that peasants in Russia's "rural commhues" had maintained the crucial intellectual and material means with which to reinvent communal life to replace the capitalist system. Marx wrote of Russian rural communes to Vera Zasulich:

> But where are the tools, the manure, the agronomic methods, etc., all the means that are indispensable to collective labour, to come from? It is precisely this point which demonstrates the great superiority of the Russian "rural commune" over archaic communes of the same type. Alone in Europe it has kept going on a vast, nationwide scale. It thus finds itself in historical surroundings in which its contemporaneity with capitalist production endows it with all the conditions necessary for collective labor. It is in a position to incorporate all the positive acquisitions devised by the capitalist system without passing through its Caudine Forks. The physical lie of the land in Russia invites agricultural exploitation with the aid of machines,

> organised on a vast scale and managed by cooperative labour. As for the costs of establishment - the intellectual and material costs - Russian society owes this much to the "rural commune," at whose expense it has lived for so long and to which it must still look for its "element of regeneration." (Marx 1881/2004:346)

Like the Russian communes of the 1880s, the very different cooperative social relations that persist in Kenya into the 21st century provide a starting point for the reinvention of a commoning society. This study shows that Kenya's gendered commoners' capacities to organize, to resist and to replace capitalist relations of exploitation arose, in particular, from their engagement in life-centered or "subsistence" social relations and practices. These subsistence capacities are central to the present study and therefore require some discussion.

This understanding of the social relations of subsistence differs radically from that of many other writers. "Subsistence," in much economic, sociological and development literature, is understood as self-provisioning, or production of only enough food for a family or small group to survive, involving minimal trade and allowing life to be sustained at only the most basic level. A distinction is typically made between "peasants," who practice subsistence agriculture, and "farmers," for whom agriculture is primarily a business (Shaffer 1982:170; Redfield 1965).

Subsistence farming also involves trade and "business." This kind of trade is organized by farmers themselves, often involves direct producer-consumer interaction and often is carried out in conjunction with allied traders. Subsistence trade is here considered a key source of the strength and continuity of life-centered relations that link the survival mechanisms and the social movements of rural and urban dwellers.

Robert Bates examined the 1980 and 1984 famines in Kenya and defined a "subsistence crisis" as a shortage of maize, the staple food crop (1989:93). Bates' narrow definition suggests subsistence means "ability to survive," even if only with the least nutritious and unvaried diet. Ronald Seavoy asserted that peasants "prefer indolence more than enjoying an abundance of goods and services that money can purchase" (2000:3) Peasants' "subsistence labour norms" constitute, for Seavoy, a "subsistence compromise" in which "indolence" is assigned "a higher social value than money acquisition or material abundance" (p. 3). Peasants, in this view, are willing to risk hunger and starvation rather than exert the effort required to produce surplus crops.

For John Schaffer, Robert Bates and Ronald Seavoy, as well as many others, subsistence is equivalent to privation. For them, development means the commercialization of agriculture (Bates 1989, 1981/2005) which would "extinguish subsistence" (Seavoy 2000:252). Since Seavoy believes that peasants prefer "indolence" to hard work, he predicts that "force may be necessary to suppress peasant discontent in order to sustain the process of development" (p.109). He goes further to advise that police and soldiers in peasant nations "must be prepared to enforce commercial policies on peasants with the maximum amount of violence if necessary" (p.113). He concludes by advocating "huge amounts of coercion":

> Development economists must understand that economic development will not occur unless the commercialization of agriculture is the first priority of governing elites of peasant nations and that the full power of central governments must be mobilized to initiate and sustain the process. The real problem is how to extinguish subsistence agriculture. This requires a revolution. Managing and enforcing the agricultural revolution is a complex and high risk political process and economic policies will not initiate or sustain the revolution. The only way the commercial revolution will succeed is by central governments and its agents administering huge amounts of coercion (p.252).

The understanding of subsistence advocated in this book directly contradicts that of Seavoy, Bates and other similarly-oriented writers and policy makers. Far from the coercive policies of commodification that these analysts promote as a means of eliminating subsistence, this study suggests that the political project of defending and elaborating subsistence society is critical to the building of alternatives to socially and ecologically destructive global corporate capitalism.

Commodification is the subsumption of use values into the cash nexus as direct commodities at sites of waged and unwaged exploitation. Unpriced goods and services, or use values, are appropriated from the subsistence political economy where, in many societies, peasant women predominate as producers and maintain significant control over their labor and its products. Capital's simultaneous reliance upon and destruction of the social relations and the products of subsistence political economies is inseparable from its conception as a system. Rosa Luxemburg noted in 1913 that

The historical process of the development of capitalism on the world stage in all of its colourful and moving variety takes place first in the exchange relation of capital with its non-capitalist environment as it confronts the difficulties of a barter economy, secure social relations and the limited demand of patriarchal peasant and artisan production. . . . Capital uses heroic means to conquer the feudal barter economy at home and the subjugation and destruction of the traditional communities overseas, laying open the doors to commodity exchange and production (1951/ 1964:92).

From its "rosy dawn," capital has required, for its expansion and survival, the raw materials and labour of the subsistence political economy or what Luxemburg calls the "natural economy" (Luxemburg 1951/1964:369-370). Capital is a parasite upon subsistence. Capital is dependent on the commons and the gendered commoners. In contrast, the commoners have historically been (and have the capacity to be) autonomous from capitalist relations. Subsistence is the "medium and soil" within which capitalism survives. Capitalists at the same time destroy this medium and soil (Akhter 2001:175). This "using up" proceeds more rapidly, especially under neoliberal laws, than does renewal and replacement.

In the logic of profit, human life itself is valued only as a means of production for capital (Marx 1867/1976; McMurtry 1999). What appears on corporate accounting sheets includes only a tiny fraction of the actual resources, destruction and wastage of corporate activity (Waring 1999; Benjamin and Turner 1992). Left off of the ledgers are those "externalities" so critical to both capitalist exploitation and to the survival of life on earth. These externalities are the environment and the entire sphere of social reality I here call "subsistence." Corporations are, quintessentially, externalizing machines. Miles states that, with commodification,

> purchases and the value of the expanding commercial production register as increases in wealth while displaced/superseded subsistence production and its loss is never counted. Neither is the cost of migration of individual community members or whole families in search of survival, nor the ecological and health damage often consequent on large scale chemicalized monocropping, industrial production and resource extraction (Miles 2001:858).

Subsistence is here defined as being a set of practices *against* commodification. Life is the primary goal of subsistence activity. In the commodified political economy of capitalism, profit is the central and highest goal and life is "only a coincidental side-effect" (Bennholdt-Thomsen and Mies 1999:20).

Bennholdt-Thomsen and Mies offer a definition of subsistence that this study embraces as

> freedom, happiness, self-determination within the limits of necessity - not in some other world but here; furthermore persistence, stamina, willingness to resist, the view from below, a world of plenty. The concept of self-provisioning is, in our opinion, far too limiting because it refers only to the economical dimension. "Subsistence'" encompasses concepts like "moral economy," a new way of life in all its dimensions: economy, culture, society, politics, language etcetera, dimensions which can no longer be separated from each other (1999:19).

The subsistence perspective is grounded not in market measures, but in an analysis of the ways in which people make their living and the ways in which they interpret the meaning of life. Subsistence producers are not "engaged in hopelessly outdated production or a backward lifestyle in any sense, but instead they are directly concerned with the production of food and life rather than with the acquisition of money to buy food and live" (Akhter 2001:174-175). Subsistence political economies are those historically rooted social systems of production and exchange that are primarily focused on and value the sustenance of *life for all*, now and in future generations (Bennholdt-Thomsen and Mies 1999).

Subsistence, or the life-centered political economy, can be illustrated by reference to the commons. If commons are spaces, goods and institutions being shared by commoners, then the social relations of universal sharing can be called "commoning," or what I call subsistence social relations. Linebaugh and Rediker emphasized the noncapitalist and noncommodified character of the commons:

> the commons were more than a specific English agrarian practice or its American variants; the same concept underlay the clachan, the sept, the rundale, the West African village, and the indigenous tradition of long-fallow agriculture of Native Americans - in other words,

it encompassed all those parts of the Earth that remained unprivatized, unenclosed, a noncommodity, a support for the manifold human values of mutuality (Linebaugh and Rediker 2000:26).

Social relations of the commons are noncapitalist. As colonial capitalist relations incorporated indigenous political economies, subsistence commoners retained elements of their noncapitalist social relations. In addition, as we shall see, many commoners borrowed elements of capitalist social forms and incorporated them into the life-centered practices and social relations of resistance and survival. In the process, many commoners became anticolonialist and *anticapitalist*, especially as they resisted capital's appropriation and destruction of the commons through processes of enclosure. A subsistence perspective, then, focuses on the struggles undertaken to defend and extend these anticapitalist, life-centered commoning social relations.

Subsistence is ancient; but it is also contemporary, ever-evolving and capable of incorporating the highest technology and most elaborated social networks. In a capitalist world, to subsist is to resist. And resistance to enclosure changes the character of subsistence. At the same time, capital continues to incrementally or cataclysmically extract land, labor and resources from the subsistence sector. The loss of these life goods also transfigures subsistence relations and practices. Therefore, the subsistence political economies that persist at the beginning of the 21st century can be said to share at least five major features:

*First*, they are rooted in selected precapitalist social relations.

*Second*, they exhibit social relations that are different from precapitalist social relations. Capitalist encroachment results in a reduction of subsistence-oriented resources and, consequently, the transformation of cooperative social relations among commoners.

*Third*, resistance to enclosure has also changed preenclosure subsistence relations. This is particularly the case as those who resist enclosure incorporate aspects of the commodified political economy into indigenous social relations of resistance and survival. These "creative amalgams" of indigenous and exogenous social forms transform and may at the same time reinforce the continuity of these transformed indigenous relations and practices.

*Fourth*, subsistence political economies of the 21st century are virtually all besieged by global capitalism.

*Fifth*, the introduction of a single global capitalist market provides new pathways of communication that offer new opportunities for dissent and greater possibilities for coordinated actions for a global life-centered political economy that draws on the best of what all peoples have created in the process of struggle.

This study's focus on social movements *for subsistence* distinguishes it from most other studies on Kenya. I analyze subsistence as a positive force, unlike many who see subsistence and peasants as necessarily poor, backward, reactionary and patriarchal; and those who see subsistence only as an anachronism in a journey to "full" capitalist development. The framework provided by gendered, ethnicized class analysis reveals the significance of Kenyan women's activism in the historical nexus of struggle between the subsistence and commodified political economies.

A related distinguishing feature of this book concerns my treatment of the 1950s Mau Mau war. Of the 15 instances of struggle analyzed, it is unquestionably the most important in terms of its duration, intensity, numbers of people involved and impact on the ethnicized, gendered class politics of the 20th century as a whole. While this book is not exclusively a study of Mau Mau, it is the first study to frame the analysis of Mau Mau in gendered subsistence terms. This framing includes, but goes beyond, the elaboration of a list of what Mau Mau women did in the 1950s. It focuses analysis more fundamentally on the forces that shaped the gendered, ethnicized class relations of conflict and of alliance that were operative in this most explosive decade in Kenya's long 20th century.

In sum, my book counters the commercializing prerogatives of those such as Seavoy and Bates who denigrate and seek to extinguish subsistence relations. And it applies and confirms Vandana Shiva, Maria Mies and Veronika Bennholdt-Thomsen's feminist subsistence perspective through a gendered, ethnicized class analysis of case studies of women's involvement in Kenyan subsistence-oriented social movements (Mies and Shiva 1993; Bennholdt-Thomsen and Mies 1999). This application of the subsistence perspective yields a dynamic picture of gendered social relations embedded in a subsistence political economy. I now turn to a discussion of the remaining concepts central to this study.

## — CIVIL SOCIETY AND THE GENDERED COMMONS

The term "civil society" has been used popularly in Kenya as elsewhere to connote the legitimate participation of citizens in debates about the organization of society. In the 19th century the term referred only to the involvement of *property owners* in public affairs. Nevertheless, many activists still use the term civil society positively to affirm a grassroots political stand against neoliberal globalization from above (Bond 2006; Fisher and Ponniah 2003).

John McMurtry broadened and specified the conception of the civil commons. According to him, civil commons refers to "any co-operative human construct which enables the access of all members of a community to life goods." "Life goods" are values and services the absence of which diminish life's full range of expression (McMurtry 2001:820). Drawing on McMurtry, Terisa Turner and I have written that the civil commons has

> innumerable expressions, from vernacular language itself to public health care, regulated clean air and water, universal education, public art and architecture, open environmental spaces, nutritious food, adequate shelter and affective interaction. It is within the civil commons that women create and socialize human beings, the most critical "product" of human labour from the perspective both of capital and citizenry (Turner and Brownhill 2001c:806).

Civil commons echoes Linebaugh and Rediker's characterization of the commons as "a support for the manifold human values of mutuality" (2000:26). The gendered commons, in turn, is an extension of McMurtry's civil commons and builds on the lively discussion of the commons of which McMurtry and Linebaugh and Redicker's work is a part.[1]

*Gendered commons* is the term I have designated to emphasize the facts that commoners are gendered and that women and men have specific and varied relations to one another and to the production and use of life goods. The term gendered commons has two referents. First, it refers to a *space*, the earthly commons, that is shared among commoners, men and women. Second, it refers to the *processes of struggle* through which the earthly and civil commons are wrested from the control of capital by commoners and made into "a common treasury for everyone to share" (Bragg, citing Rosselson 1981/1993).

Gendered commons are "spaces of negotiation" between and among women and men seeking to defend and redefine a life-centered political economy. Efforts to reinvent the gendered commons involve the renegotiation of selected indigenous social relations by those most directly affected. Both subsistence and gendered commons are feminist concepts. Feminism is understood to mean the recognition of and the fight against women's exploitation.

Gendered commons can be said to exist wherever every person born has uncontested access to all life's necessities and all that is required for the development of the full range of human expression. In practice, of course, the earth is not being fairly shared among its inhabitants. Earth, and human society, are dominated by captains of industry who destroy and pollute land, air and seas far beyond the geographically delimited plots on which their private property stands. The process of the construction, defense and reconstruction of the gendered commons stands against this destruction. This process can be best discerned in the social movements of women and men struggling to create what Veronika Bennholdt-Thomsen and Maria Mies call a subsistence-oriented society (1999). This struggle for the gendered commons is characterized, in Kenya, by men's alliances with women in subsistence-oriented social movements aimed at ending capitalist exploitation and enclosure.

## sub- MALE DEALS AND ENCLOSURES

Movements for the defense of the gendered commons are at the same time movements against enclosure. Enclosure is the process by which capital privatizes and commodifies land, labor, social relationships and other life goods from the common or public realm. In the process of corporate expansion and amalgamation, private firms commodify, within and across national boundaries, nature (land, water) unpaid labor, built space, social services, food and producer-controlled trade. The process results in an undermining of gendered class entitlements to the commons and an erosion of democracy and human security. The deterioration is even more consequential because all these supposedly "free" inputs to capitalist production are in practice the products, primarily, of women's labor, of female fertility (Benjamin and Turner 1992). Three conceptual tools of gendered class analysis - the *male deal, housewifization* and *globalization from above* - are useful in examining the anatomy of the process of enclosure.

The processes of enclosure and commodification require force on the one hand and compromise on the other (Seavoy 2000: 113, 252). Capital bargains with a few among the dispossessed to establish what Turner has called a "male deal" (Turner 1994:20-21). In Kenya male deals involved cross-class and cross-ethnic collaboration of African men and colonialists. Asians in Kenya also made such deals with British colonists. Male dealers served as intermediaries to channel exploited Africans' land and labor into the commodified economy.

In Kenya, three types of male deals were constructed by the British over the 20th century: the traders', the chiefs' and the corporations' cash crop male deals. The type of male deal that colonialists required in order to organize the exploitation of land and the population changed as struggle introduced changes into the organization of corporate and state activities. The traders', chiefs' and corporate cash crop male deals, and the context within which they emerged, are further detailed below.

Enclosures have long been associated with the narrowing of women's rights and entitlements (Federici 2004; Merchant 1980; Rogers 1980). This was certainly the case in Kenya in the 20th century. The male deal allowed a small number of European and African men to dispossess large numbers of men and almost all women of their customary entitlements to land. A process Maria Mies (1986) called "housewifization," in which husbands took charge of women's land and other sources of fertility, facilitated capitalists' access to a whole range of productive resources.

Housewifization involves the dispossession of women of land, professions and other means of production and their enforced service to men. Housewives are no longer relatively autonomous women with specific entitlements to the means of survival and social efficacy. They depend on husbands for access to means of survival. And the products of the housewife's labor can be disposed of by the husband without consultation. One of the housewife's most important "products" is her own labor power, that of her husband and the future labor power of her children (Mies 1986:110). The male deal and housewifization make up interlocking components of the processes of gendered class formation.

sub — ## GLOBALIZATION FROM ABOVE, GLOBALIZATION FROM BELOW

At the global level, activists engage in a process of extending subsistence life-centered relations across borders by engaging in *globalization from below*. In 1999 Dyer-Witheford wrote that

> globalization, rather than simply representing an inexorable deepening of capitalist control, constitutes a defensive corporate response to series of interweaving challenges that in the 1960s and 70s plunged the international structure of accumulation into crisis. Moreover, while the immediate impact of this riposte was profoundly to disarray oppositional forces, it has also opened unforeseen opportunities for their new cooperation and alliance. Not the least of these is the use of global capital's own means of communication and transport to connect a proliferat-

ing array of countermovements whose own world-encircling activities of resistance and reconstruction I term "the other globalization" (1999:131).

Globalization from below or "the other globalization" is here understood as the development of democratic international alliances and linkages aimed at articulating alternatives to corporate globalization. It is the process by which localized "fights for fertility" (defined below) and regional subsistence struggles are strengthened and linked to their counterparts in other parts of the world.

The term globalization is used here to refer to the phase of global corporate amalgamation beginning in the 1970s and continuing into the 21st century. As it is not only corporations but also social movements that have engaged in processes of globalization, I characterize corporate globalization as "globalization from above" and popular globalization as "globalization from below." Globalization from above involves the freedom of capital to speculate and to move products, investments and profits across borders. This freedom is, at the same time, an "unequal freedom" (McMurtry 1998a), in which labor is increasingly restricted by being forced into insecure, dangerous, unprotected work; migration, refugeeism and unemployment.[2] Structural adjustment and the entire policy framework of the World Trade Organization "routinely subordinate social, environmental and cultural considerations to transnational trade and profit" (Miles 2001:864).

Corporate globalization intensifies the exploitation of unwaged labor including that of women, indigenous people, peasants and others who live largely outside of the commodity-cash nexus. Their exploitation is increased with globalization from above because corporations are, under the neoliberal regime, permitted to seek new sources of profit in the relatively "untouched" spaces of nature, built space, social services and unwaged work itself (Benjamin and Turner 1992). This increased integration of common resources and unwaged workers into global circuits of capital provides a framework for the emergence of new forms of gendered, ethnicized class struggle.

## THE FIGHT FOR FERTILITY

As noted above, gendered ethnicized class analysis provides tools for understanding the anatomy of popular struggle by the unwaged. The *fight for fertility* is one such conceptual tool.

The concept of the fight for fertility highlights distinctions amongst the parties engaged in gendered class conflict. In this fight, three parties struggle for control over fertility: women themselves, their own menfolk (husbands, chiefs, politicians) and foreign capitalists. Fertility is here defined very broadly as the capacity for autonomous production of children, food and other crops, animals, cultural expressions and social networks. Land, labor, indigenous knowledge, bodies and time itself are all important aspects of fertility. All are subject to contention. Who controls them and for what purposes? Women are endowed with the unique capacity to bring forth life. Human beings and human labor power are prime values in subsistence social relations. Human labor power is also the most strategic commodity under capitalism. The fight for fertility in Kenya is a fight centered primarily around (1) the control of land, (2) the control of women's agricultural labor and (3) the control of women's reproductive capacities.

Among those who may appear to be fighting enclosure are some who attempt to become the new beneficiaries of the old exploitative system. Hence women in the ex-colonies have, in the past, been "sold out" after independence when specific men have seized the colonial mantle and proceeded to dominate women and society as a whole (Campbell 2003; Randall 2003). In contrast, other men break with the male deals and join women in "gendered class alliances" for the defense and elaboration of the subsistence political economy and against the imposition of commodified social relations. These alliances often take place between women and the men of their sons' and grandsons' generations. Younger men are more likely to break with the male deal because the resources and relationships young men need in order to marry and to prosper are diminished by the male deals struck by their elders.

In sum, the fight for fertility involves three parties. It involves those women who struggle to control their own fertility in its manifold expressions for the purpose of enhancing life for all. Women struggle with those local menfolk (often family members) who seek power over women's time, labor, bodies, productivity and other aspects of fertility. Local men either act in accord with women's interests in gendered class alliances, or they work against women's interests in male deals with capital. Women in the fight for fertility must also contend with the second partner in the male deal, capitalists themselves, in the person of colonialists, agents of transnational firms and others who seek to gain control over the commons and women's specific capacities.

## TYPES OF MALE DEALS

Analyzing the subsistence character and content of Kenyan social movements requires consideration of the international political economy within which Kenya's class conflicts have taken shape. Accounts by Colin Leys (1971), Immanuel Wallerstein (1976) and Fredrick Cooper (1981) provide analyses of East Africa's staged articulation into world capital flows. Nitzan and Bichler's compelling explanation of the "concrete historical trajectory of corporate amalgamation" (2002:57), and Nick Dyer-Witheford's (1999) interpretation of "cycles of struggle" helped to further specify the periodization of waves of corporate incursion and of Kenyan anticapitalist resistance developed in this study.

The history of colonial and corporate ascendancy in Kenya is marked by the cementing of specific, successive male deals between selected African men on the one hand and colonial and postcolonial capitalists on the other. This book details how male deals facilitated corporate access to Kenyans' subsistence resources. The British made male deals first with African traders (1870s), then with appointed chiefs (1920s) and finally with export cash crop farmers (1960s). Each new male deal was introduced as a mechanism for restructuring corporate activity. That is, as corporations amalgamated and restructured their production and trade systems "from above," they were simultaneously required to reorganize relations with labor "on the ground." In the Kenyan case, this reorganization of labor was facilitated by the construction of new male deals, each of which was focused on the transferring of specific types of resources from African commoners into corporate market channels, often through state institutions. These new male deals, in turn, gave rise to the emergence of new forms of social movement organization.

The first was the *traders' male deal,* in which British caravan leaders, such as agents of the Imperial British East Africa Company, made trade pacts with particular East African men. These traders exported food and luxury goods via British caravans and organized labor from among the commoners whenever the British required it. Between 1870 and 1900 these African traders became wealthy and powerful by channelling life goods out of their communities. The export of food reserves contributed to the famine of the late 1890s that killed tens of thousands of people.

Beginning in 1902 the British augmented their fledgling colonial governing apparatus by appointing African men from among the earlier traders and missionary adherents to act as chiefs, subchiefs and headmen. These men implemented colonial law on a local level, collected taxes and supplied white settlers with labor. African traders maintained their power into the next period, but most no longer had such exclusive, high-level access to the centers of colonial power. Asian merchants, who were originally brought from India by the British to construct the railroad, made increasing inroads into control over domestic trade, especially because of colonial restrictions on Asian ownership of land.

The second male deal, then, was the *chiefs' male deal,* which emerged in its fullest form at the end of the 1920s. Chiefs took on the task of compelling commoners to make themselves available for compulsory unwaged public service, such as road building, and both waged and unwaged labor on the European settler plantations located near the "native reserves." Many white settlers were drawn to Kenya by low-priced, fertile land and the promise of cheap and abundant labor supplies. Because many African men were engaged in migrant waged labor for white settlers in more distant locations, the chiefs mainly forced peasant women to work, and these women soon had many grievances against the chiefs and settlers.

By 1929, the colonial government hierarchy was undergirded with a vast infrastructure of African officials. They included not only chiefs, subchiefs and headmen, but also senior chiefs and low-level administrative officers, agricultural assistants, clerks and guards. Chiefs and senior chiefs were intimately involved in consultations with the British administration via several committees of inquiry into such matters as the boundaries of reserves, the extent of new enclosures and the laws governing customary land tenure. Chiefs' centrality to the processes of enclosure of land and labor put them on the front lines of the most explosive conflicts of the century.

The third male deal is the *corporate cash crop male deal,* constructed in the 1960s on the basis of massive new land privatization exercises started in the 1950s. This male deal gave global (especially U.S. and European) agrochemical companies direct access to the labor of millions of small farmers in Kenya, most of whom were housewifized women. In the 1960s and 1970s hundreds of thousands of men, who owned as few as two acres of land each, contracted to grow export cash crops, mainly coffee and tea. Disadvantageous contracts bound men and their families into state-supported corporate circuits. These peasant husbands channelled the crops produced by their wives and children into volatile global markets via state-run cooperative societies.

The corporate cash crop male deal remained, at the turn of the 21$^{st}$ century, the central mechanism through which corporations tried to extend their control over land and labor. But other mechanisms used by capital in the past to pacify the population remain in use. The continuous reemergence of famine and food crises, which characterized British colonial occupation of Kenya in 1890s, remains a hallmark of 21$^{st}$-century corporate globalization. The cash crop male deal provoked a transformational politics of resistance beginning in the 1980s. "Coffee wives," or peasant women married to men who had taken loans to start tiny coffee plantations, began a large-scale "return to subsistence" in the mid-1980s as a means of surviving structural adjustment and famine. In the 1990s slum dwellers mobilized to defend their urban neighborhoods. By 1999 pastoralists, the landless and the unemployed began to occupy and reappropriate enclosed land for the purpose of establishing subsistence farms. In the new millennium Kenyan peasant women, who never surrendered in their fight for land, food and freedom, were engaged in a wide array of movements at local, national and global levels to defend and elaborate a life-centered subsistence political economy.

## Notes

1.  See, for example, the website www.commoner.org.uk for an e-journal, *The Commoner*, dedicated to debates about the contemporary and historic commons; and *Canadian Journal of Development Studies*, Special Issue 22, 2001, on "Gender, Feminism and the Civil Commons."

2.  See Roxana Ng (2002:74-81) where she focuses on migrant workers in Toronto, some of whom were pushed out of their own countries by the enclosing processes of corporate globalization.

# PART II

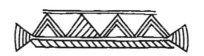

# KENYA
# ON THE EDGE
# OF EMPIRE,
# 1870 TO 1929

~ CHAPTER TWO ~

# KENYAN COMMONS, BRITISH ENCLOSURES, 1870 TO 1900

## INTRODUCTION

In 1870, East Africa fell largely outside the sphere of British colonial influence. It was merely on the edge of Britain's empire, a faraway shore somewhere between Capetown, South Africa, and the Indian subcontinent. In 1870 it was Arab merchants and traders who had a more immediate grip on the land and peoples of the region. Wealthy sultans based themselves in luxurious homes within the small cities they constructed in Zanzibar, Mombasa, Lamu, and elsewhere along the East African coast. They organized the capture, transportation, auction and export of slaves, spices and sundry tropical commodities.

Because the British sought to suppress the slave trade after it had been outlawed elsewhere in the British empire, the Arab settlements in East Africa provided perfect justification for Britain's incursion. In suppressing the slave trade, the British military paved the way for the settlement of government officials, religious missionaries and explorers and traders of many kinds. By 1885 Kenya was "on the map" of empire. British colonial officials proceeded to reshape indigenous social organization to more closely suit the needs of colonialists and settlers. In 1895 London declared Kenya a "protectorate" and imposed an alien system of tax collection, labor recruitment and land privatization. Throughout the period, Kenyans protested each of these impositions.

In order to establish the dynamic context out of which grew peasant women's and men's resistance to colonial exploitation in Kenya in the 20th century, this chapter outlines characteristics of the indigenous subsistence political economy. It briefly considers the state of subsistence in East Africa in the period between 1870 and 1900. Subsistence trade, land tenure relations and gendered land use among indigenous groups of central Kenya are examined.

# KIKUYU COMMONING AT THE TURN OF THE 20ᵀᴴ CENTURY

*As the Kikuyu put it, githaka ni ngwatira - land is a loan* (Muriuki 1974:76).

Universal access to land was an important organizational feature of central Kenyan societies before the colonial occupation in the 1880s. Access might have to be negotiated, but unless one was a very antisocial, uncooperative or violent person, he or she would not be denied access to land. This section addresses central features of Kikuyu land tenure relations and gendered uses of land.

Kenyan historian Godfrey Muriuki has suggested that a Kikuyu matriarchy was "superceded by a patrilineal and patrilocal social and political organization" by the middle of the seventeenth century (Muriuki 1974:44). Yet elements of a matriarchal Kikuyu society, some of which are reviewed below, remained in land tenure practices through the 20ᵗʰ century.

Between 1700 and 1900 the Kikuyu migrated south across the ridges emanating from Mount Kenya. In the Murang'a and Nyeri areas to the north, rights to land were acquired through first occupation. In Kiambu to the south, where some Kikuyu moved later, land was purchased from the Ndorobo and Athi peoples who lived by hunting, gathering and honey production in the forests (Kershaw 1997; Muriuki 1974).

In Kiambu, "protracted ceremonial negotiations" helped the Kikuyu land buyers to "be sure in their assumption of the land" since it was only then that "they knew that the [Ndorobo] ancestors had adopted the Kikuyu as descendants and owners" (Kershaw 1997: 20-21). Such land transactions, like the indigenous caravan trade, represented far more than the exchange of goats for land. The buyer and the seller became kin. They shared rights and duties. These land relations demonstrate the gendered cosmology of land transactions in which indigenous people defined relations of obligation and mutual aid. Kin were not required to be of the same "ethnic group." Rather it was their sharing of land that connected them.

Such fluid relations of ethnicity contrast with the rigid "tribal" boundaries imposed by the British at the end of the 19th century when the classical trope of divide and rule was employed to enable colonial dominion. The migration of the Kikuyu into the Kiambu area slowed in the late 1860s and early 1870s. By 1880 hardly any land at the higher, wetter altitudes was available for sale, and most Ndorobo by this time had taken up farming and "become Kikuyu" (Kershaw 1997:44).

Collective land rights prevailed in uncultivated land and "areas of uncleared forest, market sites, dancing grounds and public meeting places; salt licks, mineral springs, deposits of sand, clay and iron ore; and sacred groves and trees" (Mackenzie 1998:27). Use of such land was negotiated with clan elders. Elders granted wide privileges to all who asked in order to preserve and strengthen the unity of clans and the larger community.

According to Kershaw, two interpretations of the unity among *mbari* [clan] members were in use among the Kikuyu in the early 20th century.

> In the first, the unity would mean equality in terms of possession of the land: all members had equal right to it, regardless of the varying contributions they had made to the purchase of the land. In the second, symbolic unity went hand in hand with economic inequality: the amount of each member's contribution [to the original purchase] determined the rights of *mbari* members in the land. The first interpretation tended towards communal, the second towards individual ownership of land (Kershaw 1997:27).

The proponents of each of these two interpretations were increasingly at odds in the colonial period, as land shortages eroded the social bases of collective rights. As white settlers enclosed more land tensions rose.

Kikuyu women possessed extensive entitlements to land, circa 1870, before European occupation. Women's precolonial entitlements were predicated on their membership in the Kikuyu community through birth, adoption, marriage or other means. Some Kikuyu women remained single, lived with their parents and bore children through specially sanctioned sexual partners. This subsistence land relation involved women bringing a husband onto her own farm on her parents' land. Mackenzie calls this relation *mwendia ruhiu*, meaning marriage to a man without his own home (Mackenzie 1998:xiii, 32-34). In such cases women maintained rights over any children they mothered. The children of these marriages inherited land from their mother's parents.

Sometimes fathers gave daughters a wedding gift of *mugunda wa mathaga*, a piece of land,[1] instead of the more customary gift of goats (Fisher 1954 in Mackenzie 1998:36). Land was given to women as gifts and entitlements from natal and affinal kin. Kikuyu women could also be given land as *tha*, or blessings, from both kin and strangers (Kershaw 1997).

A woman was entitled to marry a man from another *mbari*, or even from another ethnic group altogether. She would normally move to her husband's father's land and her husband's mother would allocate land to her. Daughters could also marry *ahoi* [tenants] on their parents' land, and thereby stay in their natal home with their husbands (Kershaw 1997). Even in the Kikuyu origin myth, Wamuyu, the youngest daughter of Gikuyu and Mumbi, the mythical founders of the Kikuyu, "did not get a husband." She "later bore children while still in her father's home and her children became the tenth clan of the Agikuyu" (Gakuo 1992:34). Both polygyny and monogamy were operative among the Kikuyu at different times in response to demographic changes (Kanogo 2005).

Widows were normally incorporated into their husbands' *mbaris*. Young women might be married to their husband's brother. Women past childbearing age were more likely to simply continue to live in their deceased husband's home. Widows past childbearing age might also become "female husbands." To do so they would marry a younger woman who would live in the homestead of the "female husband." The wife was allowed to take sexual partners and her children were incorporated into the female husband's household and the dead husband's *mbari* (Mackenzie 1991).

Customarily during times of famine, girls and women from food-deficit areas were adopted into families in food-surplus areas. Adoptees often had the same access to family land as had any other daughter. The pawning of women and children during famine was very common. Muriuki reports that "No stigma was attached to the pawnship and the system was commonly practiced by the Kamba, the Kikuyu and the other Mount Kenya peoples, but it was only practiced during famine time. In any case, it fulfilled an important function by ensuring that a family did not starve. Pawnship was certainly not regarded as slavery, indeed it was a stage towards full adoption" (Muriuki 1974:85). In the 1890s adoption and pawnship were commodified by an upsurge of slave trading. I am not suggesting here that pawnship entailed a "right" to land in the same sense that inheritance, for instance, gives an heir the right to land. It was one way that women did get access under duress instead of starving or being sold into slavery.

Although the precolonial land rights of Kikuyu women were dependent upon their relations with men, in practice, few if any women among the Kikuyu could have been considered landless before the European scramble for Africa. Kikuyu indigenous land relations secured *for all* access to land and other life goods. However colonialism increased inequalities among the Kikuyu, especially by the co-optation of selected African men into the colonial project as traders, missionary adherents and chiefs. While many people lost their land to white settlers, a few African men were accumulating large parcels.

This increasing inequality led to heightened tensions between the two visions of customary Kikuyu unity. Those whose notion of Kikuyu unity stood on a moral grounding of equality in the control of resources were to see their "solidarity of equals" undermined. The land claims, positions of political power and growing capacity to read and speak English gave the emerging African elite a new source of support for their own vision of unity premised on the "solidarity of unequals," whereby some men had greater authority over land than other men (Kershaw 1997).

By the end of the 1890s conflict over access to land was rife (Bates 1989:28). Male deals between British traders and local African men set the stage for the large-scale channeling of food, labor and land from the indigenous life-centered political economy into the British commodified political economy. The British gained a foothold in central Kenya when they took over East Africans' indigenous trade routes and slave traders' caravan trails. Kikuyu territory lay at the western periphery of the area through which groups of indigenous Kamba men traveled in the long-distance caravan trade. The next section details the contours of this precolonial indigenous subsistence trade system and considers the traders' male deals that facilitated British takeover of indigenous trade.

## LONG-DISTANCE SUBSISTENCE TRADE: CARAVANS, MARKET PEACE AND OATHS OF FRIENDSHIP

The early 19th-century indigenous African caravan trade between coastal and highlands Kenya was integrated into global commodity circuits via the Arab and Indian merchants of Mombasa. East Africans' indigenous trade was never a purely commercial activity. Rather, Africans' long-distance overland trade was one mechanism through which indigenous trading partners built the gendered commons to secure a livelihood for all. This precolonial subsistence trading system focused more on the construction of relations of cooperation in the building of regional food security than on the profits to be gained from the exchange of commodities. "Profits" in this trade could be assessed by measuring the well-being of the people served by the food-centered exchanges on which the precolonial indigenous caravans depended.

Thomas Spear's description of East African trade in the 19th century underlines the complex regional interdependence that characterized subsistence trade relations:

> The exchange of foodstuffs and local products occurred at local and four-day markets where people brought their own food surpluses or craft products and exchanged them with those of their neighbours. Such markets were overseen by the elders, while warriors maintained the market peace. Regional trade was conducted at border markets sited between adjacent peoples. The neutrality of such areas was established before trading began by oaths sworn by the two parties. Kikuyu and Maasai each took peace oaths before opening a border market, and Oromo and Giriama sacrificed a goat and swore an oath of friendship before they commenced trading (Spear 1981:115).

Such peaceful relations and long-term economic integration belie the legitimizing colonial myth of "perpetual warfare" between "hostile tribes" before the intervention of Pax Brittanica. British explorer William Astor Chanler wrote in 1896 that markets in Meru

> consisted of openings in the plantations, beaten hard by many feet. Thither came the women of neighboring districts of the Embe country daily, and expended many hours in exchanging their produce one with the other. One old woman would bring a large bag ... of cassava; another manioc, another yams; while a fourth would bring bananas (Chanler 1896:239).

Violence and theft in the subsistence markets were rare. "The fact that women carried on a considerable portion of market trade in itself imposed a degree of order, since men were generally reluctant to inject violence into activities in which women were substantially involved" (Ambler 1988:86). Spear noted that Kikuyu women traders frequently traveled to Maasailand and "were protected by mutual oaths sworn between the two peoples which remained in force even when the men were fighting one another"

(Spear 1981:115). Life-centered trade relations were valued and protected by oaths, especially when women were involved.

It was only in the 1860s that the "larger, better financed, and more heavily armed Swahili caravans from the coast" supplanted Kamba and Giriama traders on the highlands-coastal caravan routes (Spear 1981:122). At this point, trade relations began to shift from cooperation to conflict, and from serving regional subsistence needs to serving commercial projects for coastal merchants and foreign traders. Swahili caravans were organized specifically to extract exportable commodities, from slaves to ivory and rhinoceros horns, from the East African countryside. Their interest in subsistence food supplies was limited to the provisioning of the caravan porters, who could number in the hundreds, or even thousands. Swahili caravans were larger and traveled farther than the Giriama food-centered caravans. But as the Swahili depended less on local relations of kin or peace oaths than the Kamba and Giriama did, the Swahili traders were more willing to use force to obtain food supplies.

By the 1870s Swahili traders had largely replaced the negotiated trade relations of the indigenous caravan trade with a new system. Swahili trade involved the establishment of a few trading posts operated by selected African men. These men both hosted the Swahili caravans as they passed, and acted as wholesalers who collected goods to supply the caravan traders. These relations laid the groundwork for the first of three types of male deals utilized by the British in the colonization of Kenya beginning shortly thereafter, in the 1880s.

The Swahili caravan leaders sought food to sustain trade missions that concentrated on the accumulation of exportable luxury items and slaves. This shift from food-centered trade to the traffic in human and luxury commodities introduced a fundamental change in indigenous trade patterns. Indigenous traders were edged off the established trade routes, as their food supplies came to be the target of raids by hungry Swahili porters. The old long-distance trade among Africans thus became more localized, but no less complex. Subsistence trade was diversified, dispersed and highly networked. Markets were integrated into a household exchange system involving barter, gifts and tributes from tenants, bridegrooms and others. Indigenous subsistence markets were often located strategically between areas of distinct production to facilitate trade of different kinds of goods (Ambler 1988:87).

With the predominance of Arab and Swahili traders on the caravan routes, the local needs of producing communities began to be superseded by the appetites of the caravan traders. In the 1870s British explorers, missionaries and finally agents of colonial capital began to ply these same routes and to employ the same force to obtain supplies. The amount of British caravan traffic moving into the interior increased rapidly in the 1880s and 1890s. With it rose the demand for Africans' food crops and labor. The British then imported human and animal diseases and in myriad ways disrupted indigenous social networks of survival.

The first contacts, conflicts and collaborations between Kenyan commoners and European colonialists revolved around control over food, labor, livestock and land. These productive resources, or expressions of fertility, were used and shared by the indigenous people within sophisticated relations of community and family. At the same time the British required these life goods as inputs into their own commodifying regime. To secure steady supplies of food, labor and other necessities, the British sought out local male allies who acted as trade wholesalers. From the beginning of the British colonial occupation, the fight for control over fertility involved three parties: the imperialists, African peasants or gendered commoners, and a small group of African traders, or middlemen, who facilitated colonial enclosure of the gendered commons.

The reports of colonial adventurers and officials of the time (Frederick Lugard, John Boyes, Francis Hall, John Ainsworth) suggest that there were probably no more than 25 Kenyan men with whom the British made important trade pacts in the 1880s. During the 1890s, the status of these men was enhanced by the British because Queen Victoria had declared Kenya her Protectorate on July 1, 1895. In consequence it was not only trade that tied men like the Kikuyu trader Wan'gombe to Ainsworth and other early British colonial officials. It was, in addition, a matter of the British instrumentalizing the African "big men" to collect taxes and provide labor.

Ties between African men and European capitalists were to prove useful to both sets of men as they mutually supported each other's separate claims to land. Between 1895 and 1900, Kikuyu land relations, and those throughout East and Central Africa, were significantly reorganized (Wright 1993:23). One result of colonization was new division along ethnic lines. The British introduced an apartheid-like, segregated hierarchy of Europeans, Asians and Africans. Along with these divisions, the European occupiers blocked cooperation among indigenous peoples living in different geographical regions by separating them into "reserves." The British established belts of white settlement between long-standing neighbors, such as the Kikuyu and Maasai peoples of the highlands and Rift Valley. The Maasai were forcibly moved to a hostile environment, and the Kikuyu land was subject to extensive and successive enclosures.

The purpose of presenting an outline of precolonial indigenous sub-sistence land and trade relations is to establish a touchstone or baseline for examining African and European claims to land and efforts to control labor. From this grounding in the gendered commons of the precolonial era, we proceed in the next section to examine the political economy constructed by capital through the exploitation of famine-struck, dispossessed Africans.

## THE FAMINE FROM EUROPE AND THE INCORPORATION OF KENYA INTO THE BRITISH EMPIRE

Devastating famines and pestilence accompanied British colonial occupation of Kenya. These disasters made landgrabs relatively easy for the British, who alienated large expanses of the most fertile land to sell and give to the Europeans invited to settle in Kenya after 1900. British, German and Italian occupiers brought into East Africa large numbers of cattle from India and Aden in the early 1890s. This influx of new cattle brought with it new diseases and contributed to an Africa-wide epidemic of rinderpest that killed most of the cattle on the continent (Reader 1998:583).

With nearly 100 percent of their cattle dead from pleuropneumonia and rinderpest, many Maasai survived by camping outside the Imperial British East African Company station at Dagoretti at the outskirts of Nairobi. Young men who were strong enough worked for the Europeans in exchange for food (Mungeam 1966b). The main work of the Maasai *morans*, or warriors, was to raid nearby Kikuyu villages and farms. Between 1895 and 1900 thousands of Kikuyu people died of starvation. Some estimate that in northern Kikuyuland, between 10 and 70 percent of the population starved to death. In the southern Kikuyu areas, closest to the station of the Imperial British East Africa Company, up to 90 percent of the people perished (Mackenzie 1998:59). The Kikuyu called the calamity the *Ng'aragu ya Ruraya*, or the "Famine from Europe" (Clough 1990:11).

Just as the British occupation of and imposition of "free trade" upon Ireland, India and China had been accompanied by increasingly horrific famines between the 1840s and the 1870s (Davis 2001; Woodham-Smith 1962), so too did the colonization of Kenya entail a deadly visitation of hunger between 1895 and 1901. Pastoralists lost their herds and therefore their means of subsistence. They fled to agricultural communities for help. Food surpluses dwindled. Famine followed. Men raided for food. Elders pawned women and children into food surplus areas, with the hope of redeeming them after the famine ended. Some women survived by taking refuge near dry riverbeds and eating the shoots and tubers growing there.[2]

During the "Famine from Europe," for the first time there were home-less single (or widowed) women roaming around with no support networks. If not captured into the slave trade, the lucky ones moved to the Muslim Swahili quarters in the small but growing towns of Kitui, Machakos, Mombasa and Nairobi. After the famine, *ahoi,* or tenants, could not afford to marry but instead concentrated on increasing their herds (Kershaw 1997). In this way one avenue of women's access to land was narrowed.

Throughout Eastern and Southern Africa, the 1890s famines pushed indigenous populations into migration, disintegration and recombination and recovery, as drought subsided and refugees returned to their com-munities. In Kenya, Kershaw noted, that in the time of the Famine from Europe, 1895-1901, groups of young Kikuyu men camped in the forest and attacked government caravans carrying relief food. They were known as "Mau Mau" (Kershaw 1997:17). In the 1950s, the term Mau Mau again entered the popular lexicon to denote the Kenya Land Freedom Army in its fight for independence.

In Kenya in 1895, some Kikuyu men had accumulated enough wealth through their trade with the British caravans to stockpile food and thereby to maintain a presence in famine-struck areas when most of the popula-tion had fled (Ambler 1988:149). With the country emptied, these wealthy Kikuyu took their pick of prime farmland and vistas and claimed the land as their own. Ambler noted that "the famine accentuated the distance between rich and poor" (p.148). British colonialists had created the context for famine: disease, pestilence, drawing off of food surpluses and the related hierarchization of a relatively egalitarian society.

In another early act of incorporating Kenya into Britain's fast-expand-ing global empire, colonial officers who were stationed in Mombasa trans-ported men from famine-struck areas of India to East Africa as inden-tured railway laborers. Between 1895 and 1903, some 32,000 Indian men crushed stones, hewed wood and laid ties on Kenya's railway, the original "Lunatic Express" (Gregory 1971:52; Miller 1971).[3]

For most Kikuyu, European settlement meant famine, disease and enclosure of Kikuyu territory. Soon the colonial government designated forest commons as "crown land." All Africans were confined to "native reserves." Africans were made "tenants at the will of the crown." This was in addition to the many conflicts resulting from land grabs during the 1890s famines. Conflicts involving land claims and counterclaims made at the turn of the century were to reemerge in succeeding generations. In 1934 members of the Kenya Land Commission collected evidence of the lasting impact of the famine on land access in Kikuyu territory (Ambler 1988:148). And during interviews she conducted in Kiambu in

1956, Kershaw learned of elders' continuing debates over the processes through which their clans had gained access to land in the 1890s (Kershaw 1997:61).

Due to the large number of famine deaths, the commons became a space of *new* gendered, ethnicized class relations. The subsequent social and economic disruption resulted in the introduction of landlessness among Kikuyu women. Colonial incursion entailed, among other gendered processes, an increase in inequality in Kikuyu society. This applied especially to women, whose *actual productive capacities* remained crucial for colonial and African survival, but whose *customary indigenous rights* were abrogated. The British were keen to assist their main trading partners among the Kikuyu in acquiring greater shares of land and control over greater amounts of labor. This suited both the wealthy African traders and the British whose food supply needs they met.

Although British policies and practices of enclosure emphasized the exacerbation of inequalities, the British did not necessarily want to completely undermine Kikuyu unity. For it was the great collective energy of Kikuyu women's amassed labor that made possible the production of enormous quantities of food. The British could not have explored Africa nor laid a railway line without the tremendous collective force of the porters and railway crews who toiled under slave-like conditions for six years. In the same way it was only the collective work of large numbers of Kikuyu men and women on settler plantations and on road- and bridge-building projects that made possible the expansion and maintenance of a colonial society in Kenya. Underlying all of this labor was the food supply produced by rural peasant women.

The colonial government and white settlers used the subsistence political economy as a crutch to prop up their own fledgling commodified political economy. Zeleza argued that the colonial state in Kenya

> neither had the power nor the will to "destroy" the peasant economy. Indeed, because settler capital was so weak, the state needed the continued existence of a peasant sector that was productive enough to generate surplus, some of which could be appropriated by the state itself to be used for the running of the administration, to subsidize settler production, and for the rest to provide for such conditions that the maintenance and reproduction of the working class would be ensured (Zeleza 1989:161).

To gain control over labor in the Kenyan highlands, in the absence of an open slave market, the British established male deals with local men. In the beginning these earliest of male deals centered on the control over women's labor, food and products. These movable products were first subject to colonial control. It was after these movables were captured and channeled into the support of the colonial system that the system grew strong enough to undertake larger-scale enclosures. Later, in the early 1900s, the immovable product most prized by the indigenous people, the land, was subjected to colonial control. This enclosure was effected through force of arms and by means of the more formalized male deals that were constructed by the British with the colonial hierarchy of chiefs, subchiefs and headmen in the first three decades of the 20th century.

After the Famine from Europe, African men fought the British and each other for control over land. Women appeared in colonial records peripherally, for the most part, as the daughters or wives of men who had greater or lesser degrees of control over territory. But Kikuyu women were never peripheral in the indigenous subsistence political economy. One measure of the value placed on women's work was the fact that African big men remained big by *marrying* many wives. These women then cultivated the fields and produced children. They also worked together and with others to brew the beer for entertaining and growing tons of food for local needs and long distance trade. The men then sold the food to colonial caravan leaders and British officers in the fortified stations of the Imperial British East African Company. Their wealth also allowed African big men to support hunters and other men to supply British demands. Polygamy and the export of locally-produced food and other commodities characterized the gendered and ethnicized class relations of the traders' male deal. This male deal constituted the central mechanism through which women's fertility and the life goods of the community as a whole were channeled into the colonial political economy in late 19th-century Kenya. We now turn to an analysis of Africans' resistance to these new processes of colonial expropriation.

### Notes

1. *Mathaga* is a kind of plant. This suggests that *mugunda wa mathaga* is "a garden of a certain kind of plant or tree" or perhaps, a garden bordered by this particular plant.

2. Adagala and Kabira relate how women domesticated arrowroots and other tubers by surviving along riverbeds during times of famine generations ago (1985: 23).

3.  It was thought to be impossible or crazy to even try to lay a railway line through the rugged East African terrain, especially over the escarpments of the Rift Valley. There were also wild animals (several railway workers were killed by lions), severe weather conditions, water shortages, insects and, of course, indigenous people who attacked the railway camps and sabotaged the railroad tracks at every opportunity.

# ∼ CHAPTER THREE ∽

# TRADERS, CHIEFS AND HUSBANDS: NEW MALE DEALS AND THE BRITISH ENCLOSURE OF KENYAN LAND AND LABOR, 1900-1929

## INTRODUCTION

In the early 20th century, there were two major political mobilizations in Kenya. Women, and especially old women, directly defied the authorities and mobilized movements to confront colonial rulers. The significance of the actions of Mekatilili wa Menza (1912-1914) and Mary Muthoni Nyanjiru (March 16, 1922) arises from their dramatizing the mechanisms of colonial enclosure. Also of significance is the fact that women were so prominent in these historic acts of resistance. This prominence is consistent with indigenous practice among both the Kikuyu and the Giriama (Ahlberg 1991; Brantley 1986). Women elders ruled over food gardening and women's initiations (Hobley 1910/1971; Kenyatta 1938/1953; Wane 2000). Female seers and women's secret societies were two additional social forms embedded in indigenous societies, out of which women's political legitimacy was drawn (Kinyatti 1986; Presley 1992; Brantley 1986).

Women's political action in these instances was new insofar as (a) the unifying forces of colonial taxation, forced labor and land alienation had organized men to join women in a coordinated rejection of colonialism; and (b) the indigenous resistance was focused against both European occupiers and the local African men who collaborated with them. These two features of the organization of resistance - gendered class alliances among activist women and men, and actions targeting the male deal - were innovations that were elaborated in subsequent social movements through the course of the century.

# "ANY WOMAN" COULD HAVE ORGANIZED THE RESISTANCE: MEKATILILI MANYAZI WA MENZA AND THE 1913 GIRIAMA UPRISING

Throughout the 1800s the Giriama people, one of nine groups within the Mijikenda community of Kenya's coast, successfully resisted enslavement by Arab merchants, plantation owners and slave traders. They did so, in part, by living in "isolated groups of huts, hidden away in the bush" (N. Leys 1924:127). Some Giriama had been sold into slavery for the payment of a debt and taken to Zanzibar and beyond to India and the Arab world. And a few Giriama became wealthy slaveowners themselves. But most remained free farmers, cattle herders and traders within the ten-mile-wide strip of territory adjacent to the Indian Ocean coast. Fred Morton noted that

> In the early colonial period, the Kenya coast was a difficult place in which to live, by any standards. Beginning with the Anglo-Mazrui War of 1895-96, general tragedies followed in line like a litany: floods in 1897, famine in 1898-99, smallpox in 1899, then relief until drought and pleuropneumonia among sheep and goats led to the 1909-10 famine, which was soon followed by the 1912-13 famine, the Giriama rising of 1913-14, and, during the First World War, forced conscription into the Carrier Corps, drought and influenza (Morton 1990:175).

When the British arrived in Mombasa in the mid- and late-19th century, officials sometimes railed against slavery. At the same time, they respected Arab slaveowners' private property rights, even when those rights extended to the ownership of human beings. For instance, the British paid up to $25 to slaveowners to "redeem" runaways and set them free (Cooper 1980:48-50). Lord Lugard, while working for the Imperial British East Africa Company (IBEAC), started a scheme around 1902 to allow runaways on Kenya's coast to purchase their own freedom by working for his company. Most runaways preferred to simply run farther away from their ex-masters. Many fled to Giriama communities, became farmers and stayed out of towns where they might meet the slave catcher (Leys 1924:127).

The experience of enslavement and the fight against slavery injected into the Giriama people some of the qualities of Maroon societies such as those created by African captives in the Caribbean basin in the period 1500 to 1833. The Giriama fought off slavers and protected runaways. They joined together in secret societies to maintain their antislavery struggle. In the mid-1800s, as the community absorbed runaways and others, the Giriama expanded their territorial boundaries in order to acquire sufficient resources for the subsistence of all. They became a highly self-sufficient people who maintained trade relations with other Mijikenda groups, Indian middlemen, Arab merchants and indigenous neighbours farther into Kenya's interior. Most of the agricultural products exported from Malindi were produced not by local slaves, who came from Southern and Central Africa, but by free Giriama women (Brantley 1986:335; Cooper 1980; Wright 1993). Their grain "was shipped, mainly to Arabia, from the mouth of the river, in dhows" (Leys 1924:127).

By 1903 Britain abolished slavery in Kenya and runaways were free from threats of recapture. In 1912 when the British started to recruit, impress or simply force Giriama into labor on colonial plantations and roads, the Giriama were militant in their refusal to submit. Mekatilili was the "everywoman" who raised the specter of renewed slavery, but now in the guise of forced labor, to unite her people.

C. W. Hobley was subcommissioner of the Coast Province from 1912 to 1921. He knew first hand about the "serious political agitation" that went on there in 1913 and 1914. He wrote later that the Giriama "knew the power of Government, but always seemed to think that by the adoption of a persistent *non possumus* [Latin = we cannot] attitude they could wear us down so that we should become tired, thus relaxing our efforts. This policy had succeeded with the Arabs for centuries past, and so why should it not succeed with us?" (Hobley (1929/1970:166). In his 1913 "October Report" to Hobley, district commissioner Arthur Champion wrote that "Every Giriama is much more afraid of the *Kiraho* [oath] than of the government; the WaGiriama boast openly that the government are afraid to fight them and for that very reason have never done so" (KNA: CP 5/336-I, Champion, "October Report," cited in Brantley 1986:343). Giriama resistance to the British moved from the "attitude of *non possumus*" to active, widespread civil disobedience and armed uprisings in the period June 1913 to October 1914.

In 1912 under Champion's commission, the British set up tax collection stations in Giriama districts and initiated road-building programs.

They then demanded laborers for road-building projects and new white-owned plantations. They restricted the indigenous palm wine trade and clamped down on the illegal trade in ivory. Champion's porters raped Giriama women. Long-standing Giriama reluctance to submit to British authority was hardened.

In June 1913 Hobley toured Giriamaland and reinforced the call for laborers on European plantations at the coast. He also contravened the customary authority of the elders by urging the Giriama to defy the medicine men, who were respected indigenous leaders and healers. He warned that he would send in a military patrol of 40 men if the people refused to obey the appointed colonial headmen and native councillors. Finally, Hobley threatened the 20,000 Giriama living north of the Sabaki River with dispossession. The British desired "closer administration," meaning more effective capacity to count huts and collect taxes; it also meant inducing "the able-bodied males of the tribe to leave home in search of work" (Leys 1924:131). Hobley told them they were only "tenants at the will of the crown," and that they would have to be moved (Bradley 1973:78; Leys 1924:128-129; Morton 1990:179). Norman Leys provided the following explanation of the dislocation of the Giriama in 1914:

> the Giriama in particular were notoriously averse from wage-earning. And in their case the high direct taxation that in the case of other tribes compels men to leave home to seek work failed to have that effect. Living as they do only some thirty or forty miles from a natural harbour, they can, or could, until the "move" under discussion, grow grain for export, which Indian middlemen collected and shipped. That was the sole reason the tribe was concentrated [by the government] in the less fertile land south of the river rather than on the more fertile northern bank. The usual reason for moving a tribe, to give the land evacuated to Europeans, does not apply in this case. It is true that a [European] syndicate does own an immense area north of the Sabaki and that the Giriama feared that it would be given more land. But the real reason for the move was not to make more room but to increase the supply of laborers. This case of the Giriama disproves the common allegation that the tribes in Kenya cannot be got to engage in production for export themselves but must become wage-earners in order to become useful citizens of the world. It also proves that the Government does not, to say the least,

smile encouragingly on Africans who prefer to grow crops for export on land in their own occupation rather than work for wages (Leys 1924:130-131).

Giriama widow Mekatilili Manyazi wa Menza was present at one of Hobley's public meetings. She also lived north of the Sabaki River and took a direct interest in Hobley's warnings. Some remember her as a prophet and a warrior. To Hobley, she was "half-mad," and a "witch" (Hobley 1929/1970:165; Hobley 1910/1971). In fact, Mekatilili was an ordinary woman who gained the support of the majority of Giriama women, elders and youth in the fight against British rule. She called for the restitution of the elders' power in the fight against land alienation and labor impressment.

Mekatilili drew on the tradition of the Giriama woman prophet, Mepoho, who lived in the early 19th century. Mepoho told of white men who could travel as fast over the land and in the sky as the Arabs had traveled on the water. When the white men arrived, she predicted, the soil would go bad; mothers would not bear healthy children; boys would become disobedient of their elders; girls would marry young; and elders would no be longer able to rule (Brantley 1986:338-339). Mekatilili and many other Giriama saw that each aspect of Mepoho's prophecy was coming true.

Mekatilili first mobilized Giriama women. She employed the developed indigenous trade networks and markets to quickly gather together a large number of women, who agreed with her plan to unite the youth and elders and "save their sons and daughters" from the Europeans (Brantley 1986:339). Mekatilili's women collected five rupees from each elder and three rupees from each young man. The money was used to facilitate a planned congress at the Giriama's sacred *kaya* (shrine) west of Mombasa. The elders, who wanted to retain their customary authority, backed the women's effort. Many young men joined because they were key targets of colonial labor recruiters. The British restrictions on regional indigenous trade introduced earlier in 1913 directly affected young men and without an independent source of livelihood, they were subject to impressment into colonial labor gangs. These youth resisted paying taxes to the British. They readily gave their money to Mekatilili's women and supported her call for a popular assembly.

Within a month of Hobley's threat to abrogate the northern Giriama's land rights, Mekatilili, with considerable "energy and powers of oratory" (Brantley 1986:343), had organized a Giriama-wide assembly at the *kaya* west of Mombasa. From early July to mid-August 1913, thousands of Giriama converged at the *kaya*. These included young men, elders and women. Many women went to the *kaya* meeting alone. Some had run away from their husbands to attend (Brantley 1986:339). No British-appointed headmen attended. The decisions taken in the six-week long congress were sealed with oaths.

Mekatilili led some of the early discussions at the *kaya*, where she demanded an end to British impressment of labor and decried the erosion of the authority of the traditional elders. She argued that the headmen received wages in exchange for following British orders. Mekatilili reasoned that if the headmen gave up their salaries, the government would have no grounds on which to send the young men to work on the Europeans' plantations or government road-building projects. She is reported to have told those assembled that "Every elder must pay it back. And if they dare not send it themselves [I myself will] take it to "Bibi Queen," the mother of the Europeans. We are not to fear the Europeans" (KNA:CP 9/403, "Nziji wa Yaa's Statement," November 14, 1913, cited in Brantley 1986:340).

Having raised the issues at hand, Mekatilili took no further leading part in the events that followed, according to the statements of eyewitnesses. Oathing ceremonies were conducted by elder women and men: one oath carried the penalty of death if broken; another, the mother's oath, caused male offenders to become deaf or mute and women offenders infertile. Brantley stated that

> the terms of the oaths indicate the degree to which there was dissatisfaction among elders, women and young men. Each oath was sworn, using medicines, sacrifices and ceremony, cursing anyone who did not obey its proscriptions to be 'caught' by its penalty. ... [the elders'] oath was thus aimed at headmen, sworn against Giriama who refused to pay council fees to the elders instead. Included in this oath was anyone who showed the police or hut-counters where people lived, any who attended or witnessed at the headmen's courts, any who counted more than one wife for tax purposes, anyone who helped construct government roads and buildings and anyone who provided information about ivory. They swore against men appearing in shirts and trousers, calling them by the contemptuous term "*korobi*" or "call boys." Since the women had convinced the gathering that headmen had received money to obtain laborers, the elders swore against government headmen who refused either to give up their salaries or their own sons in response to the demands (Brantley 1986:341).

The results of the oathing ceremonies organized at the *kaya* meetings of July and August 1913 were immediate: "British administration simply ground to a halt. The oaths were secret, anyone who told of them faced death. Champion could not get porters; headmen's councils did not meet; no one paid taxes. Even loyal headmen were afraid" (Brantley 1986:343).

In November 1913 Hobley personally oversaw the interrogation of chiefs in the *kaya* and extracted from them Mekatilili's name. In acquiescing to Hobley's armed retinue, the men who implicated Mekatilili broke the oaths they had taken. In doing so, the British imposed (and many local men accepted) a male deal through which Mekatilili was offered up to the British in exchange for saving the chiefs in the *kaya* from being killed by Hobley's police. She was arrested soon thereafter. In her testimony before government officials on November 14, 1913, Mekatilili stated that

> there was a meeting at Makambweni where a large number of women were present. I called it. ... Any woman could have gathered the meeting together. No special power is required. I am not a *mganga* [witch doctor] and have no medicine. We told Ngonyo that the Europeans in Mangea wanted labor to work at the monthly wage on the grounds that the government paid salaries to headmen (KNA:CP 9/403, "Mekatilili's Statement" 1913, cited in Brantley 1986:339).

Hobley recalled that Mekatilili toured Giriamaland,

> preaching active opposition to Government. This resulted in daily attacks on Government servants, a general refusal to pay taxes, and the tribe was on the verge of open rebellion. It was, however, averted by a stupendous effort at a memorable *durbar* [Indian court] in the center of the district. Katilili [Mekatilili] was arrested, and the elders of every section took an oath of peace and good behaviour according to their ancient ritual. Matters thus quieted down for a time, but the under-current of opposition was always there and ready to crop up again at a favourable opportunity (Hobley 1929/1970:165-166).

The next favorable opportunity arose the following year. Hobley recalled the fighting that broke out in 1914, a year after Mekatilili and Wanje, one of three male Giriama chiefs appointed at the *kaya* in 1913, were exiled:

A sudden call for transport porters came in from military headquarters, and this demand was transmitted to the various districts by the officer who was in acting charge of the province. Knowing the Giriama situation, it was his intention that no contribution should be sought from that tribe, but, through an oversight in his office, the Commissioner of that district was asked to supply a contingent. He therefore called upon the elders to comply, and this proved to be the match which fired the magazine. Whether Ngonyo [a wealthy ivory trader who lived near Mekatilili] gave the signal will never be known, but someone did. The young bloods massed with great rapidity, a few wretched police were killed and wounded, and their next move was an attack on the temporary post on Mangea Hill (Hobley 1929/1970:166-167).

Even in the town of Malindi, where 'urbanized' Giriama resided, only three recruits responded to the call for porters. The government then "raided the town by night under the guise of martial law and rounded up two hundred Africans" (Martin 1973:78). Meanwhile, more soldiers were sent into the rural area to subdue resistance and "pacify" the "hostile Giriama." Hobley and the administration also took the opportunity to move against the Giriama north of the Sabaki River and forcibly evacuate them (Leys 1924:128-129). Davis noted that it was during "another La Nina drought in 1914" that "the British moved savagely against a subgroup of Mijikenda squatters, the Giriama, killing 250 people and destroying 70 percent of their dwellings" (Davis 2001:203). Hobley wrote 15 years after the uprising that

the Giriama for the first time in their history were learning obedience, the tax revenue was increasing, roads were being made, travel in the district was becoming easier and, if the Public Works Department had given a greater measure of support to the water conservation scheme, greater progress would have been made. But at any rate the struggle with the Giriama can, from this period, be considered to have concluded, and it was only owing to the occurrence of the [first world] war that it was so protracted (Hobley 1929/1970:168).

Mekatilili and other women's involvement in Giriama resistance provides insight into the gendered class relations of colonial rule and opposition to it.

Women initiated a rebellion and men joined to break with the male dealers among the Giriama who were collaborating with the British. Mekatilili's uprising involved the coordination of gendered class alliances among some 10,000 Giriama dispersed across a wide region. Together the militants of 1913 worked to resist British authority over the Africans' labor and land. Mekatilili built on indigenous practices of collectivity, including women's secret societies, to gather women and their allies together for the protest.

Mekatilili did not need to rely *only* on calls for the revival of ancient customary political organization or kin networks, which had both been somewhat strained or diluted with the migration out of the original *kaya*. The First World War, labor impressments, trade restrictions and taxes had impacted all Giriama and created new common conditions of dispossession against which large numbers of people resisted. In addition, the Giriama were connected to one another across great distances by their own trade networks. Mekatilili's movement, grounded in indigenous relations of trade and kinship, drew on old customs to respond to exogenous elements of the colonial social order (war, taxes, labor demands and trade restrictions) and to organize the power to break the male deals between the British colonialists and collaborating Giriama men.

Though Mekatilili's movement did not succeed in its aim of ending British demands for taxes and laborers, the Giriama people remained fiercely independent and autonomous throughout the 20th century. The Maroon-like character of Giriama society has persisted into the 21st century. Giriama women maintain their customary dress, language and customs within a life-centered subsistence political economy. Insofar as the Giriama threw off the relations of slavery that underpinned integration of precolonial peasants into the global capitalist economy, they created, like the Maroons, the Haitians and other Caribbean peoples, what could be called a postcapitalist commoning society.

# MARY MUTHONI NYANJIRU: THE 1922 CURSE OF NAKEDNESS AGAINST FORCED LABOR

The 1922 uprising in which Mary Muthoni Nyanjiru was central was, like Mekatilili's uprising, a fight for fertility involving colonialists, African collaborators with the British and an alliance of exploited women and men. The fight erupted when the exploited protested the arrest of a spokesman for the movement opposing forced labor policies imposed by the British and implemented by African chiefs. Nyanjiru's action involved a two-day protest in Nairobi on March 15-16, 1922, in which 8,000 people demanded the release of the political prisoner, Harry Thuku. It ended with the British massacring some 150 demonstrators. Thuku, a prominent landowning Kikuyu activist, established the East African Association in 1921. Thuku and the other founders were opposed to African chiefs and headmen in the Kikuyu Association (KA). The KA chiefs collaborated with the British administration and settlers, especially with respect to the recruitment of African women from reserves for forced labor on the Europeans' coffee estates. Many Kikuyu knew Thuku as the "Chief of Women" because of his public speaking tours during which he protested the colonialists' use of the forced labor of women. Thuku's stance against forced labor reinforced women's refusal to leave their own fields to cultivate the fields of the European occupiers.

Kikuyu women had long been responsible for the daily subsistence needs of their families and the community at large. One of the reasons that women objected to forced labor was that the labor-intensive coffee harvest season on settlers' estates coincided with the busiest times within their own subsistence planting, weeding and harvesting cycle. Men's customary agricultural pursuits had focused on ritual and famine crops (Fisher 1954; Kershaw 1953/1972). As land and men's labor were diverted into export cash crop production for white settlers, men's ritual and famine crop production suffered decline. As a result, women's production of food crops gained greater strategic urgency. Changes in the allocation of land, labor and the kinds of crops that were grown undoubtedly had an immediate and cumulative negative impact on indigenous food security.

Women focused even more strictly on the production of indigenous food crops and famine crops in the absence of so many of their menfolk who were pressed into waged labor. African rural women were, in consequence, viewed by the British as "conservative," "ignorant" and "backward." In much the same way, the colonists viewed the indigenous farming techniques that women persisted in using as inferior. These techniques included their collective work, which ensured enough food for all and the indigenous practice of cultivating scattered plots of land. The scattered plot system meant that, for example, riverside land was equally divided so that all had a share of this particularly fertile land. The British thought this was "inefficient" because women spent "too much time" walking between their scattered plots and therefore less time cultivating, weeding or harvesting. Women's so-called conservatism led them to retain these indigenous practices and specialized cropping systems at a time when thousands of labor-hungry white settlers sought to commercialize agriculture and export as fast as possible in the period between 1895 and 1930. Although the British claimed to have come to East Africa to "abolish slavery," they reinstituted it under the name of compulsory or forced labor and thereby sought to establish their farms as profitable enterprises.

At a public meeting in Dagoretti outside of Nairobi on June 24, 1921, Thuku and other young Kikuyu men railed against the district commissioners and chiefs who ordered poor African elders and fathers to send their daughters and wives out to work on the European farms. In the previous month, 60 girls had been taken to a European estate and had not returned. In addition "a list was produced of the names of girls who had been violated while so out at work on farms and were pregnant, with the names of their native seducers in some cases" (W. Ross 1927: 225-226). The Governor, Sir Edward Northey, wrote to the Colonial Office in London in October 1921 and ordered an investigation into the rapes while preempting the investigators' report by alleging that the girls had been willing accomplices and not victims (Wipper 1989:303).[1] Thuku was arrested on March 14, 1922 for his antigovernment speeches and held at the central police station in Nairobi.

Officials of the East African Association, the nationalist organization that Thuku headed, rallied African workers in Nairobi to go on strike. On March 15, transport workers, domestic workers and government employees deserted their workplaces and gathered in front of the police station where Thuku was being held (Buell 1928/1965:375). Mary Muthoni Nyanjiru and her stepdaughter, Elizabeth Waruiru, were among the city's female workers who came out to demonstrate. Nyanjiru was a Kikuyu woman who had moved from the village of Weithaga in the reserves to Nairobi some time in the first part of the 20th century (Wipper 1989:318). James Njorage, member of the directing committee of the East African Association, administered secret oaths to the women of the Association on the evening of March 15 outside the police station. The oath, in which women vowed to succeed in their mission or die trying, was taken by Mary and Elizabeth, and up to 200 other women (Spencer 1985:43, interview with Elizabeth Waruiru on October 11, 1973, cited in Wipper 1989:318).

The crowd outside the police station on March 15, 1922 dispersed that night but gathered again on the following morning (Buell 1928/1965:375). As the crowd grew, a deputation of the East African Association, including Jomo Kenyatta, held a meeting with Acting Governor Sir Charles Bowring in his office (Singh 1969:15). Forty armed African guards stood watch over the demonstrators, who were for the most part sitting on the ground in groups. Reverend Wright, Vicar of All Saints Anglican Church, walked through the crowd speaking to the protesters who waited to hear from the East African Association leaders. He noted that the demonstrators were peaceful and that several times groups of people held prayers. As the protest continued, the women moved toward the front of the crowd and gathered near the police guards (Rosberg and Nottingham 1966:51).

The Acting Commissioner of Police, J.C. Bentley, arrived at the lines at around 10:45 a.m. He estimated that there were from 7,000 to 8,000 people present. Demonstrators continued to arrive from all directions (Wipper 1989:314). Around noontime, Jomo Kenyatta addressed the strikers. He announced that the East African Association deputies had reached a compromise with the governor: Thuku could not be released, but the governor had promised Thuku a fair trial. Kenyatta urged the demonstrators to disperse. As some stood to leave, others argued with Kenyatta and the East African Association deputation and accused them of having been bribed by the administration.

Mary Muthoni Nyanjiru stood at the front of the crowd near Kenyatta. When the demonstrators began to leave the police lines, she threw her dress over her shoulders and exposed her naked body. Nyanjiru shouted, "You take my dress and give me your trousers. You men are cowards. What are you waiting for? Our leader is in there. Let's get him!" (Rosberg and Nottingham 1966:51-52).

The 300 women ululated loudly. The strikers were galvanized by Mary's actions and the women's call to battle. Those men who were beginning to disperse returned. A large section of the crowd rushed forward towards the armed guards. Nyanjiru stood only a few feet away from the guards, who had been on duty for 18 continuous hours. The guards kneeled and engaged their rifles at the command of the superintendent of police, Captain Carey. The strikers pressed up to the armed guards, who then opened fire. White settlers and game hunters who had gathered on the verandah at the nearby Norfolk Hotel joined in the massacre by shooting demonstrators in the back as they fled (H. Thuku 1970:33). Mary Muthoni Nyanjiru was one of the first to be killed. Estimates of the death toll range from 26 to 150 (Singh 1969:16). At least four women were killed.

The fight against forced labor was extolled in a popular song sung by women workers:

> When Harry Thuku left, that is the time I started scratch-
> ing my buttocks.[2]
> When he came back the scratching stopped.
> Let the white man face that,
> Because he is the one who forced Harry Thuku to go to
> Europe [in exile].

The chiefs were directly condemned in song:

> Philipo [or any other chief], let him be cursed.
> It is they who have caused to be taken away the chief
> of the girls who live in the coffee (cited in Wipper
> 1989:304).

The government forbade the singing of this song because it attacked the chiefs. Other songs were soon written, including those that immortalized Mary Muthoni Nyanjiru. The "Thuku uprising," as it came to be known, served throughout the 20th century as a reminder of the power of the "curse of nakedness," a deeply rooted practice of women exposing their naked bodies to protest and banish anything or anyone who caused harm to them or their communities.

In 1996 I spoke to Ruth Wangari wa Thung'u, who joined the independence movement with an oath in 1946, about what influenced her to join the independence struggle and to continue, into the 1990s, to engage in protest against injustice. Wa Thung'u recalled learning about Muthoni Nyanjiru as a child in the 1920s:

> When people went and were put in jail, that is when Muthoni and her counterparts thought of going to the jail to see the people who were imprisoned. Just like we see now, how people have been imprisoned and how we are going to court and being refused to see those people and we say we are going to go by force. There is nothing else that happened because they had gone, they were naked, they were just shot. They were seeing those were policemen who were refusing them to go. But the women wanted to show that they were able because this country was theirs and they were not afraid (Ruth Wangari wa Thung'u, First Woman interview, July 24, 1996).

Ruth Wangari wa Thung'u herself employed the same curse of nakedness in Nairobi in 1992, as we shall see in Chapter Ten.

The protestors at the police station in Nairobi in March 1922 were brought together by the admixture of four significant forces:

*First*, they had been drawn to Nairobi for labor in the formal and informal sectors of the colonial urban economy. They lived together in the slums of the town and shared common workplaces and living conditions. The colonists themselves had brought these particular people together.

*Second*, many of the workers or their relatives in the rural areas had worked on plantations as forced laborers on enclosed African land.

*Third*, many of the protestors were members of unions and the East African Association. These exogenous organizations - or those imposed by the colonial powers - were adapted to the realities of local kin-based associations. Their members transformed indigenous social forms - kin-based networks - by drawing together people across ethnic boundaries to fight for wages, work conditions and wider rights. Previously, the significant areas of interethnic relations had focused on land-sharing, barter and marriage. To this was added the shared resistance to colonial labor exploitation.

*Fourth*, indigenous social forms bound together many of the protestors. These included kin and trade networks that linked urban workers with the rural peasantry. The use of oaths during the demonstration is one indication of the blending of indigenous practices with political associations that arose from the conflict between the colonizers and the colonized.

Finally, Mary Muthoni Nyanjiru employed the customary curse of nakedness. She mobilized the protestors and cursed the African men who were collaborating with the British. African collaborators included both the soldiers who did the actual killing, and men such as Kenyatta, who had acquiesced to the governor's deal. In this act of identifying and opposing African male dealers, Nyanjiru's uprising was similar to Mekatilili's in 1913. Women and men in each case had considered not only the British to be enemies, but also the African male dealers who sided with the British. This recognition and condemnation of the collaboration of male dealers was to be a feature of Kenyan fights for fertility for the rest of the century.

The Nyanjiru protest focused international attention on Kenyan labor conditions. The activities of religious and anticolonial groups in Britain, as well as continued pressure from within Kenya, forced the government to reduce Africans' taxes, maintain wage levels and stop the implementation of the 1924 Masters and Servants Ordinance, which allowed for the easier removal of squatters from settler farms. Only in 1932, two years after Britain had signed the international Forced Labor Convention which outlawed compulsory labor, did the Kenyan colonial officials pass the Compulsory Labor (Regulation) Ordinance. Like the international convention that preceded it, the colonial Kenyan ordinance ostensibly banned the use of forced labor. But it permitted compulsory military service, convict labor and "communal services" for emergencies and for works of public importance (Bush 1999:63; Singh 1969:43).

By 1924, with Thuku in exile and Nyanjiru dead, the East Africa Association members began to call for the creation of independent schools. They also demanded the return of alienated land, the abolition of the *kipande* registration card for men, the abolition of taxes for women and the reinstatement of elders, rather than British-appointed chiefs, as arbiters of local conflicts. The Association's aims were remarkably similar to those discussed at the six-week Giriama *kaya* assembly of 1913. Both groups made wide-reaching demands that in effect challenged the entire edifice of colonial rule. A governmental crackdown on interethnic organizing followed Nyanjiru's martyrdom. In 1925 the Deputy Chief Native Commissioner, Colonel Watkins, told the East African Association members that the organization could no longer operate with government sanction because it admitted members from all ethnic groups. The government expressly forbade cross-ethnic alliances, and reported that if the Kikuyu wanted to form an exclusively Kikuyu organization, the government would be prepared to allow its activities (Singh 1969:25). Leaders of the association decided to change only the name and continue to organize on a cross-ethnic basis.

In the event, the Kikuyu Central Association, which was the product of this name change, was heavily dominated by Kikuyu men from Murang'a. Women were not allowed to join. Gender segregation in this official nationalist organization was in part in keeping with earlier customary forms of gender-specific councils of elders. But it was out of step with women's own colonial-era organizing, in which they almost always sought to unite with men, as exemplified by Mekatilili's campaign and most of the other instances of struggle examined here.

In the 1930s and 1940s, Kikuyu women responded to their exclusion by forming and participating in anticolonial political organizing within the Mumbi Central Association (MCA). The Mumbi Central Association was a radical revision of the Kikuyu women's council (*kiama kia atumia*). These council's customarily both united and disciplined women. "Among the Kikuyu there is a council, or *kiama*, of old women in every district; they collect goats periodically and present them to the elders of ukuru, or priestly class. They occasionally fine troublesome women, and the fine, usually a goat, has to be obtained by the culprit either by extra work or by begging one from her father. The men fear the women's *kiama*, as it is believed that the members of it have the power to bewitch people" (Hobley 1929/1970:274). Presley argues that the MCA "used as a wedge for entry into the activities of the Kikuyu Central Association" (Presley 1992:7). Women later used their collective energies in the MCA to mobilize thousands of women for the establishment and running of independent schools and churches, a subject to which we turn in Chapter Five.

# CONCLUSION: HIGH POINTS IN THE STRUGGLE FOR SUBSISTENCE, 1870 TO 1929

The fights for fertility analyzed here dramatize the power of gendered class alliances in which women and men drew strength from indigenous and colonial social forms to withdraw labor and cooperation from an exploitative colonial system. These alliances protested tax and labor laws because these facilitated British appropriation of labor from the subsistence realm. Women were effective in organizing the defense of subsistence in large part because they had recognized customary rights within this indigenous political economy. It follows that the greater the opportunity for unity between women and men, the more effective was the resistance to enclosures. In the event, some African men cooperated significantly in the further reduction of women's circumscribed precolonial land rights. As the colonial era proceeded, such men facilitated British expropriation of land and therefore contributed to rising inequalities among Africans in terms of their access to land.

In 1913, as a world movement petitioned for legislation against forced labor, Mekatilili defended herself in court. She insisted she was not an *mganga*, a witch doctor. "Any woman could have gathered the [1913 protest] meeting together. No special power is required" (KNA:CP 9/403 cited in Brantley 1986:339). Perhaps no special magical power or medicinal knowledge was necessary. But the power of "any woman" to call a meeting of her peers, community members and the public is special, and significant. It requires that the community recognize women's entitlements. The practical exercise of that entitlement, in Mekatilili's case, was a radical expression of democratic indigenous relations.

In the face of the famines brought on by the British in asserting physical control over East Africa, the subsistence political economy rebounded in the 1900 to 1929 period. Indigenous women were particularly active in the maintenance and elaboration of subsistence relations, networks and practices against the constraints imposed by the colonialists. Indigenous rural women predominated in the reserve areas, after men were drawn away into migrant labor. Gendered class relations of subsistence commoning were modified by the conditions of colonial capitalism and by the process of commodification itself. Rural land-poor women and wives of migrant laborers did their husbands' work as well as their own. Despite the extra workload, women who were engaged in this food-centered political economy were able to feed the majority of indigenous people as well as the occupiers. One way they did so was through collectivizing their own labor in work groups of many descriptions.

At the turn of the century, the British began to appoint chiefs and headmen from among their loyal Kikuyu trade partners. The newly appointed chiefs and headmen curtailed the land rights of male tenants and their own kinswomen. The chiefs were called upon to testify at numerous British inquiries into native land tenure. This opened the door to the reconfiguration of common land use and wrote into the colonial record a narrowed set of indigenous entitlements.

The rural food-centered political economy, generated very significantly by the labors of farming women, was integrated into the commodified economy growing up around it. As land-poor men were dispossessed of land, they left the reserves for waged work or were drafted into military service. Many of the people who lived in the towns for part of the year relied on food supplies from their rural homes. By 1917, three years after 350,000 East African men had been impressed into military service, and with land relations in a state of flux, many African farmers suffered crop failure in a long drought (Van Zwanenberg 1975:10). Widespread famine was averted by the return of the soldiers and the rains in 1918. In spite of land alienation, social disruption, famine and drought, for much of the first 30 years of effective British rule, from 1899 to 1929, subsistence commoning remained the predominant mode of production throughout the colony of Kenya.

How did colonialism reconfigure relations among African men and women, wealthy and poor? Many authors have dealt with this question. But none have employed a subsistence perspective to examine East African anticolonial struggles. How did new social forms introduced by colonists decompose indigenous collectivities? How did subsistence actors draw upon collectivities of the past and the new divisions of labor of the colonial era in the struggle to survive and transform the colonial commodified political economy? Most importantly, given this subsistence grounding, how and to what extent did subsistence producers adapt, maintain and reinvent life-centered activities for the purpose of resisting enclosure and strengthening the life economy of the gendered commons? In Part III, we begin to answer these questions with reference to the anticolonial Mau Mau war and the social movements that contributed to African preparations for that war.

### Notes

1.  The far-fetched allegation of women being "willing accomplices and not victims" was echoed as recently as 2004 in the British government's response to the Maasai women's mass rape case against the British army which does training in Maasai territory (Walter 2003:23).

2.  A form of censure, insult or curse, similar to, but not as serious as the "curse of nakedness." Women usually sang the song and scratched their buttocks when their white boss came around (Wipper 1989).

# PART III

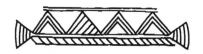

# LAND,
# FOOD,
# FREEDOM,
# 1930 TO 1959

# LAND, FOOD, FREEDOM I: CHIEFS' MALE DEALS IN THE STRUGGLE FOR THE COMMONS, 1930 TO 1949

## INTRODUCTION

C hapter Four addresses the chiefs' male deals that characterized the process of commodification in the 1930s and 1940s. By 1930 the British had constructed a strictly regimented hierarchy of African officials, which rested upon the principles of indirect rule (Lugard 1965). "Briefly stated, the essence of Indirect Rule is that the administration of African territories must be based upon African institutions managed by Africans with the advice of British officials" (Matthews 1937:433). Indirect rule was typically employed in communities where strong centralized indigenous authority structures predated colonial incursion. The British co-opted these central authorities to assist in ruling the African peoples on behalf of the British. In Kenya, very few communities had such centralized authorities. In their absence, the British appointed African "chiefs" who became directly a part of the colonial regime of rule.

The British established 24 native reserves in 1926 and therein delineated the "African territories" within which African chiefs might manage their own institutions. The other main objective of creating the reserves was to ensure the protection of lands under the control of Europeans, the "White Highlands," and to limit those lands available to Africans for settlement and cultivation (Ghai and McAuslan 1970:90). A number of further legal measures were taken in the 1930s to better secure Europeans' land rights and to provide means through which African labor would be made available to Europeans. The creation of chiefs facilitated the implementation of almost all such ordinances, by-laws and other legislative decisions. As Perham noted in 1935,

> I think we must admit that even the best-informed and most sympathetic government cannot ask the co-operation of an African chief without modifying his position. It wishes him to act, and to act quickly, in collecting tax, producing labor and clearing roads. It wants him to be constantly accessible, and not to keep disappearing in order to make rain, to visit ancestral graves, or to consult diviners. In the native administration ordinances, we can read a list of the duties which native authorities have to perform. If you run your eye down the list you will see mention of sanitation, noxious weeds, the regulation of gambling, prohibiting the cutting of trees, restricting the carrying of firearms, exterminating tsetse fly, with many other duties which the chief at first either does not understand or of which he cannot approve. In order to induce him to use his authority we tend to rely, more or less consciously, upon the hold we have over him through his dependence upon us for his position and salary. He, on his part, must endeavour not to strain an authority which at that very moment is being undermined as a result of our influence. The old authority of the chieftanship, in fact, tends to drain away from below while we pour in our new authority from above (Perham 1935:11).

This chapter argues that in their efforts to recover from the world depression (the "dirty thirties"), British administrators in Kenya concentrated on constructing male deals with select African men in order to recapture the labor and land of African women that had been "freed" from colonial control in the early 1930s, when settlers couldn't afford labor and much farmland was returned to food crops for local consumption. The British made these new male deals with chiefs and other low-level African colonial officials who had been recently incorporated into the British administrative structure. Welbourn noted that

> in Kikuyu they [the British] imposed senior chiefs onto a social system which had never previously known them; and in general chiefs found themselves in the almost

impossible position of having to mediate the instructions of central government to tribesmen who denied their right to rule and despised them for their ignorance, or neglect, of custom (Welbourn 1971:329).

Two male deals associated with the British attempts to capture and enclose African land and women's fertility are examined in this chapter: the 1934 Kenya Land Commission, known as the Carter Commission, and H.E. Lambert's pro-female circumcision policy in Meru. Both are examples of the projection of colonial power into the rural areas.

The Carter Commission – with its official and unofficial members, its Committee of Inquiry, its public hearings, its 1,000-page Report and its official policy impacts – presented the formal face of British power in Kenya. This *formalism* can be compared to the *ad hoc* nature of policies enacted by many local British administrators, especially when it came to incorporating indigenous institutions into the regime of colonial rule. To learn of their subjects' political institutions, colonial officers employed ethnographic and anthropological methods. In March 1934 Margery Perham spoke to a joint meeting of the Royal African Society and the Royal Society of the Arts in London where she defended indirect rule in Africa. Notes of the meeting record comments from the floor, including from a Dr. C.K. Meek, who said that

> anthropology is neither an esoteric science solely concerned with the past nor yet a panacea for all present ills. It merely endeavours to tell you as much as possible about the people you are trying to govern. ... Every intelligent Administrative Officer in the Colonial Service is necessarily an anthropologist (cited in Perham 1935:23).

H.E. Lambert was one such administrator. He, as many other colonial officials before him, was a self-styled anthropologist whose investigations of indigenous institutions were motivated by a drive to find African allies through whom the British might assert power at the local level. Lambert also used his ethnographic insights to draft policies that he thought were well-adapted to local customs and practices, and therefore more likely to be accepted by the people in his jurisdiction. I focus here specifically on his efforts to increase population growth among the Meru, an ethnic group whose slow rate of recovery from famines, indigenous practices of abortion and relatively late marriages imperiled nearby white settlers' access to sufficient, cheap labor power.

Whether on a formal or *ad hoc* basis, the exercise of colonial power in the 1930s and 1940s led to the establishment of legal frameworks that shaped land and labor struggles well into the 1960s (Ghai and McAuslan 1970:91). African chiefs were central to the extension of colonial rule and were targets of anticolonial activism.

# THE 1934 REPORT OF THE CARTER COMMISSION: A MALE DEAL FOR THE APPROPRIATION OF AFRICAN LAND

Chiefs were appointed and given nominal powers in the African reserves. At the same time, European settlers pursued greater powers in the government to make decisions regarding finances, labor and land policies. In the 1920s and 1930s settlers increased their representation on the Legislative Council and, moreover, on the many select committees to which the Legislative Council referred much of its important business (Ghai and McAuslan 1970:59). This "business" of the settlers often concerned the land and labor of Africans. It was in this context of rising settler influence over local administrative policies and rising demands by aggrieved Africans that the Kenya Land Commission was appointed in 1932 to consider the issue of land in the African reserves and in the White Highlands.

The 1932 to 1934 Kenya Land Commission included Morris Carter, former chief justice in Uganda, a former Kenyan district commissioner, Rupert Hemsted, and a white settler, F.O.B. Wilson. The Committee was originally called into being in 1930 by Lord Passfield, then secretary of state for the colonies under the Labor government in London. By the time the Commission was constituted in 1932, the Labor government had fallen. The commissioners reflected settlers' interests instead of Passfield's original emphasis on the strengthening of Kikuyu land rights through compensation for any further land alienation with "land of equal value and extent" (CO 533/395; cited in Mackenzie 1998:83).

The stated purposes of the Kenya Land Commission's investigation of land tenure in Kikuyuland were "to consider the needs of the native population, present and prospective, with respect to land, whether to be held on tribal or an individual tenure"; to "determine the nature and extent of claims asserted by natives over land alienated to non-natives and to make recommendations for the adequate settlement of such claims whether by legislation or otherwise"; and to "define the area, generally known as the Highlands, within which persons of European descent are to have a privileged position" (Kenya Land Commission, Report, 1934:1-2; cited in Mackenzie 1998:230 fn 159).

The Carter Commission, as it came to be called, was the most thorough and influential of the numerous land inquiries organized by the colonial government over the first half of the 20th century (Ghai and McAuslan 1970:91). These included Hobley's 1910 inquiry, Beech's 1912 study, Ainsworth's 1920 report and the 1929 Maxwell Commission. These land inquiries were designed, in the main, to address Kikuyu protests of land loss and to establish legally defensible rationales for European alienation of indigenous peoples' lands. At the beginning of the century, colonists asserted that the indigenous people did not own the land. Rather, the British believed, "natives" only recognized rights of use, or usufruct. It was not, from this perspective, necessary for the British to purchase the land or to compensate those evicted. Administrators argued that although indigenous people occupied the land, they themselves recognized no kind of exclusive ownership. Hobley's 1910 inquiry into Kikuyu land tenure offered a broader interpretation of Kikuyu land rights. He advised that the Kikuyu did need to be compensated for the "ground value" of land alienated from them, not only for the rights of use (Hobley 1910/1971). Although the government agreed in principle, the compensation was never paid.

Beech's 1912 inquiry examined the complexity and nonexclusivity of Kikuyu land tenure systems. He found that indigenous land relations embraced both individual rights to land as well as universal rights of access. Furthermore, although no woman seemed to be able to inherit or own land, "there are elaborate rules as to a woman's *life interest* in lands, just as certain duties with regard to cultivation are her privileges, and hers alone" (Beech 1917:56). The flexibility of Kikuyu land rights was vividly demonstrated with regard to dispute resolution, wherein Beech found that there were no hard and fast rules determining who had rights to a particular plot of land. Instead, in the Kikuyu judicial system, consisting of a court of elders, the Kikuyu "adhere to general principles, and then treat each case as it arises" (Beech 1918:142-143). The flexibility of customary law characterized not only Kikuyu land tenure systems but every other social practice that impinged upon the use and allocation of land, including marriage and circumcision.

However, this flexibility was not conducive to the rigid and static "traditions" that the British sought to delineate in order to legitimize their expropriation of Kikuyu land. In 1920 John Ainsworth undertook the next study of Kikuyu land tenure. He convened two meetings with African headmen, a European interpreter and several other Europeans. From this brief assessment he concluded that, contrary to Beech's findings, "the Akikuyu had *no definite customs* dealing with the occupation of land and ... this was due very largely to the absence of any regular form of tribal control or organization" (Ainsworth 1920:10 *emphasis added*; cited in Mackenzie 1998:72). Women's land rights did not arise at all in Ainsworth's meetings, nor in his report.

In 1929 yet another study of Kikuyu land tenure was published by the Maxwell Commission, whose members included Chief Native Commissioner G.V. Maxwell, Kikuyu Province District Officer S.H. Fazan and the prominent white settler archaeologist L.S.B. Leakey. The Maxwell Commission investigated Kikuyu land tenure systems in order to make "recommendations as to what rules should be enacted to govern the occupation rights of tribes, clans, families or individuals in each or any area, due regard being had to Native Law and Custom" (Colony and Protectorate of Kenya 1929:5).

Kikuyu chiefs, headmen and elders in Karatina, Murang'a, Kiambu, Embu, Chuka and Meru were interviewed during public meetings over 17 days in 1929. The men who testified in Kiambu, Murang'a and Nyeri, Mackenzie pointed out, emphasized those components of land tenure "that privileged male authority over the land. Thus, they initiated a dominant discourse within Kikuyu society, wherein the interests of women, and the landless, were unrepresented and in which far less maneuverability, flexibility and complexity in dispute resolution was acknowledged" (Mackenzie 1998:76). Kiambu men, in particular, argued in favor of individual title deeds. In opposition to the Kikuyu Central Association, associations of the wealthy chiefs, such as the Kenya Loyal Patriots (the successor to the Kikuyu Association) and the Progressive Kikuyu Party, advocated individual titles to land, as they had during previous land commission investigations. The African men who gave testimonies to the commissioners had their own land claims to defend. Muriuki argued that

> the newly-created chiefs were at the forefront of this demand for individual ownership, as they were anxious to safeguard their recent acquisitions, some of which had been acquired by sharp practice, or by the buying out of poor relatives and neighbours. ... It is clear, therefore, that it was the chiefs, supported by like-minded individuals, who deliberately altered the traditional system of *mbari* [clan] ownership of land and the redemption of land sales to suit their own ends (Muriuki 1974:80).

To build the institutions of indirect rule, the Maxwell Commission hoped to blend aspects of indigenous tenure with principles of ownership based in British law, a process they likened to producing "the cultivated variety of the native plant" (Colony and Protectorate of Kenya 1929:43). The Commission aimed to appease Kikuyu chiefs and other large land-owners but to maintain a veneer of "tribal custom" to secure land for most of the remaining Kikuyu. Settlers and administrators relied upon the subsistence political economy of the indigenous peoples for food and for labor power production. Elizabeth Colson noted that

> in the years between World War I and World War II, the principle of indirect rule through traditional authorities dominated the political scene in most British colonies and in the Belgian Congo. This principle led to the recognition of chiefs and rulers where none had existed in the earlier periods. This had its parallel in the respect paid to supposed customary rules of tenure (Colson 1971:197).

In 1932, when the Carter Commission began to collect its evidence on Kikuyu land tenure for a further official report to the government, there was already a crisis in Kikuyuland involving declining access to land for existing families. Increasingly, there was no land at all available for sons and daughters who were ready to marry.

Beginning in 1919 the children born of the survivors of the Famine from Europe (1895-1901) began to be initiated through circumcision. Within a few years, by the early 1920s, Kikuyu initiates throughout the colony were eager to be allocated land by their parents or clan so that they could marry. Many *ahoi*, or tenants of African landowners, were already so land-poor that they could not allocate to their sons and daughters land sufficient for their subsistence. *Ahoi* were also under increasing pressure to move out to make room for the landowners' own descendants. Many small landholders who could provide plots to their children knew that their grandchildren would not have sufficient land. Only the large landowners were able to provide to children and grandchildren land adequate to subsistence needs (Kershaw 1997:98). By the 1930s, land litigation was common.

Kiambu's senior chief, Koinange, testified before the Carter Commission that when the Europeans had arrived and asked for land, the Kikuyu had not yet recovered from the Ruraya famine and associated diseases:

> Because we were few in number, we did not, at the time object, as we were thinking that all would be well and trusting in the Government: while we found that the Europeans who came on to our *githaka* [clan land],

as we thought simply as *ahoi*, that is, people who came as temporary occupiers, had turned themselves into the owners and the real owners into the tenants (Kenya Land Commission, Evidence, 1934: 128; cited in Mackenzie 1998:85).

The Kikuyu squatters on white settler farms were in an even more precarious and contradictory position by the 1930s. There was plenty of unused and unoccupied land on many settlers' gargantuan estates, some of which extended to hundreds of thousands of acres. Lord Delamere was granted, at no cost, a leasehold of 156 square miles, while Colonel Grogan was given a free grant of about 300 square miles of forested land (Ross 1927:243).

The Kikuyu Central Association, discussed in Chapter Three, sent members to testify before the Carter Commission. They pointed out that the settlers had far more land than they could use and argued that

> if, owing to "the ignorance of administrators," land thought to be unoccupied was given to settlers, then by the same principle, the uncultivated four and a half million of the five million acres given to under 2,000 Europeans should "revert to the natives of the soil" (Kenya Land Commission Evidence 1934:198-203; cited in Mackenzie 1998:88).

Many newlywed sons and daughters of the squatter laborers had already begun to occupy such land. Some had the permission of their white bosses to cultivate and keep cattle on unused settler land. But none of the squatters, young or old, had any security on the land they occupied. The situation in Olenguruone, as will be seen in Chapter Six, exemplified one approach – government-run settlement schemes – that the government employed in an ostensible effort to resolve the land problem and maintain limits on Kikuyu access to land.

Europeans' exclusive rights to land in the Highlands were preserved in the commissioners' report, which noted that

> squatters ... have no right to the land .... But they have a temporary right to use land while in employment. In our view care should be taken to ensure that the essence of the contract is a labor contract rather than a tenancy agreement (Kenya Land Commission, Report, 1934:497; cited in Furedi 1989:24).

The policies which arose out of the Carter Commission's recommendations included the Marketing of African Produce Ordinance of 1935. This Ordinance put new controls on the marketing of African crops produced in the reserves. Africans could no longer sell to whomever they chose. Ghai and McAuslan noted that

> until 1934 Africans had sold their maize crop to itinerant traders but rules made in that year required traders to display their prices at all times, and limited trading to the hours between sunrise and sunset which restricted such forms of trading, and gave the KFA [the settlers' Kenya Farmers Association] a chance to establish itself as a buyer in the reserves. This it was eager to do as African sales on the home market imperilled the profitability of European maize growers and the uniform pool price system operated by the KFA for them. The requirement of sales in a market to licensed buyers only helped complete the process begun in 1934 (1970:93).

The Marketing of African Produce Ordinance allowed the white settlers' Kenya Farmers Association to "maintain and extend its monopoly position as the buyer of maize in Kenya, and compel the African producer to share the burden of the less profitable export market" (Ghai and McAuslan 1970:93). This Ordinance was central to the new era of state intervention, via the chiefs' male deal, in African agriculture and marketing.

Another result of the Carter Commission's report was the enactment of the Resident Labor Ordinance of 1937. Resident laborers, or squatters, had been attracted to the White Highlands not by the pitiable wages to be earned, but rather by the abundant land that settlers made available to laborers for grazing and gardening. Many squatters owned dozens or even hundreds of animals and cultivated vast stretches of land. Squatters utilized more land in the White Highlands for their subsistence production and trade than the white settlers did for their commodified activities (Furedi 1989). Most squatters earned far more from independent sales of milk, meat and produce than they earned from wages. Their animals and gardens also supplied laborers' food needs and items required for trade and ritual purposes. Europeans came to see the extensive squatter utilization of land in the Highlands as a threat to settler control over markets and as a possible threat to settler landownership claims. The 1937 Resident Labor Ordinance aimed to restrict African land use on white settler farms in order to secure European market control and private property rights.

The Ordinance limited squatter livestock to 15 heads and restricted the land each laborer could cultivate to two acres, with one additional acre for each wife after the first. It also allowed settlers to demand 240 to 270 days of labor from each squatter, up from 180 days. The policy was implemented unevenly throughout the Highlands. Over 100,000 Kikuyu refused to sign the new contracts. They were evicted. Stories and songs told of the great *Kifagio*, or "sweep" of African resident laborers and their livestock from the white settler farms in the late 1930s (Kanogo 1987; wa Kinyatti 1980).

White settlers called on racist stereotypes of the "backwardness" of Africans and their "primitive," "lazy" and haphazard cultivation techniques. Settlers pointed to the problems of soil erosion in the reserves as evidence of the damage that would be done to the colonial economy should the Kikuyu be given secure and permanent access to prime agricultural land in the Highlands. The British ignored the fact that the reserves within which the Kikuyu farmed were too small to allow for the shifting cultivation that had previously been the method of maintaining soil fertility.

L.S.B. Leakey was one of the settlers who, despite his adamantly pro-settler politics, contradicted the stereotypical view of Africans as "backwards" and their agriculture as "primitive." He stated to the 1934 Commission that

> the Kikuyu formerly, and to a great extent still (where they have not done as they are told), planted maize and beans and sweet potatoes and other crops mixed up together. The Kikuyu country is hills and valleys, and they cultivate a great deal on the slopes. Under those conditions, the beans come out first and were harvested first, the maize second, and the sweet potatoes remained covering the ground during the dry season. To-day the Agricultural Department suggests that they will get a better yield per acre from their land if they plant maize separately, beans separately and potatoes separately. ... The net result ... is that the maize is harvested just when the dry season is well on and there is enough sun to ripen it, and it is pulled up by the stalks. Then very often in the dry season you get one of these very heavy thunderstorms, and the soil is washed out into the river, and that is a result of the natives following the methods of the Agricultural Department (Kenya Land Commission, Evidence 1934:676-677, cited in Mackenzie 1998:92-93).

Given Leakey's fierce defense of white settlement in Kenya, his positive opinion about Kikuyu farming methods holds special weight. Even he could recognize the benefits of the indigenous agricultural systems. Despite Leakey's input, and voluminous testimony from Kikuyu, the Commission argued that it would not accept that individual Kikuyu "owned" their land unless they could prove that they had *exclusive rights* to use and ownership of the land. This concept of landownership, drawn from English property law, was totally incompatible with Kikuyu land tenure regimes. Consequently all Kikuyu claims to landownership were nullified. The Kikuyu, as other indigenous people in Kenya, remained "tenants at the will of the Crown."

To address the question of the insufficiency of land in the reserves to support the populations they contained, the commission recommended policies for the intensification of agriculture and the adoption of European cultivation methods, seeds and tools. The commissioners held firmly to the belief that it was not land shortage but incompetent farming that caused food shortages in the Kikuyu reserves. The environmental policies that reflect this understanding of ecological degradation are treated later in Chapter Five.

The Carter Commission compensated the Kikuyu for the loss of a portion of their land by adding 16,520 acres to the Kikuyu reserves and paying Local Native Councils some £2,000 (Mackenzie 1998:95). Final authority over reserve land was vested not in individuals, nor the elders, *ene* [customary owners], families, clans or subclans; but rather in the fictional notion of the Kikuyu "tribe." The British recognized no indigenous authority other than the corporate ethnic group, the Kikuyu "tribe" they themselves had created.

There were no indigenous authorities who were even nominally in charge of all the Kikuyu. There were respected elders' councils, both women's and men's. There were also indigenous judicial systems, war councils, clan organizations, age-grades and special "offices" such as that of healer, potter, blacksmith and seer. But none of these ultimately held power over other people. At most, they guided the actions and decisions of others. The egalitarian nature of the land tenure system held the key to the stability – that is, the relative egalitarianism – of the society as a whole. Popular commitments to the complex and overlapping bundles of entitlements to resources customarily held by all Kikuyu were, in effect, the real sources of authority over land. These entitlements were vested in each Kikuyu and implemented through community-minded relations of reciprocity and mutual support.

The only African authorities the colonial administration did recognize were their own appointees. The men who joined the colonial administration as functionaries had helped to channel land from Kikuyu commoners to the white settler population. These men also often accumulated great wealth and acquired large tracts of land. These male dealers must have been seriously disappointed when the Carter Commission failed to grant private land titles to them. In a sense, the Kikuyu male dealers and the Kikuyu commoners were left to their own devices, to struggle along with one another; to litigate and conflict and waste their energies on boundary disputes. By maintaining the fiction of the Kikuyu as a "tribe" that shared one expanse of land, the government intended that the customary practices of universal access to land would prevent the emergence of a growing landless class and allow the Kikuyu to reproduce themselves and be available for waged (or forced) labor. Too many dispossessed people posed an imminent danger to colony, as the Mau Mau were about to prove.

British officials selectively granted African men land titles and licenses to produce coffee in order to maintain the collaboration of those who acted as the colonialists' indirect rulers. In this way, the Native Grown Coffee Rules of 1934 opened the door for a few African men in Kisii and in Meru to apply for licenses to grow coffee (Ghai and McAuslan 1970:93). This was a significant first step toward the commodification of Africans' land and labor for the production of coffee on small peasant farms. We shall learn more about this when discussing postindependence developments in Part IV of the book.

In the short term, white settlers had their own insecurities assuaged by the Carter Commission. Their titles to land were upheld by the Commission against the claims of the Kikuyu they had dispossessed. The administration succeeded only partially in "recapturing" the labor force by enforcing landlessness among those whose labor was required on settler farms, and thereby narrowing the possibility of Africans' self-sufficiency. The emergence of an independent African peasantry that could compete with white farmers was foreclosed for the moment. The reserves, when crowded with people on plots of land insufficient to support a family, provided a ready source of male migrant labor. The smaller the farms in the reserves, the more the women who lived there would be forced to offer their own labor and that of their children on the white settlers' farms that abutted the Kikuyu land unit. Peasant women left in the reserve had now a triple workload. They did their own work, the work of their migrant menfolk and work, often unwaged, for local white settlers.

The Kenya Land Commission overrode the land rights of the majority of Kikuyu people. It facilitated colonial enclosures not only in the reserves but in the White Highlands as well. The Commission entrenched ethnic hierarchies, with Europeans' rights prioritized over Africans'. Colson showed that

> the newly created system was described as resting on tradition and presumably derived its legitimacy from immemorial custom. The degree to which it was a reflection of the contemporary situation and the joint creation of colonial officials and African leaders, more especially of those holding political office, was unlikely to be recognized (Colson 1971:197).

The impact of the new land regime on women was especially unrecognized. Reconfigured gendered class divisions among the Kikuyu left women particularly vulnerable to landlessness. Many of the customary means through which women got access to land were left out of the "tradition" and "immemorial custom" that made it into the Land Commission's report. Without land, women were exposed to greater violence, exploitation and control by both African and European men. Many such processes of ethnicized gendered class conflict over land were to play out in a series of struggles that grew in militancy until the climactic outbreak of the Mau Mau war in 1952.

Kikuyu women's fertility-related concerns were at the heart of another controversy in the 1930s: H.E. Lambert's efforts to intervene in and control the timing of the female circumcision ceremonies among the Kikuyu's neighbors, the Meru.

# H.E. LAMBERT IN MERU BETWEEN THE WARS: THE BRITISH ENFORCE MUTILATION OF GIRL CHILDREN

> Nowadays *kirigu* is used in Kikuyu as a term of contempt for an uncircumcised married woman; it expresses, of course, her real status in the tribal system, in which there is a greater differentiation between the circumcised and the uncircumcised than between the married and the unmarried (Lambert 1956/1965:4).

H.E. Lambert was one of a long line of colonial officials who worked to militarily control the colonized people and the land. All, in differing degrees, tried to regulate the social order of the indigenous people. Earlier officials such as Hobley and Routledge had taken an interest in the customs of the people they dominated; at first only land tenure practices appeared to have any policy implications for the British. But the population of European settlers had increased from less than 100 in 1902 to 12,000 in 1926 (Ghai and McAuslan 1970:36). Most white settlers, especially plantation owners, required quite large numbers of laborers on a permanent and casual basis. For instance in 1924, the 1,715 Europeans who occupied farms in Kenya employed 87,000 Africans (Ross 1927: 89).

Many coercive state policies were used throughout the period to "encourage" Kenyans to join the workforce. Kenya was in fact known to have one of the most coercive labor policies in British Africa (L. Thomas 2003). As early as 1913 with Mekatilili's uprising, Kenyans engaged in anti-forced-labor movements. After the high death toll from combat, influenza and other illnesses during the First World War, the administration was keen to ensure a high birth rate. In this context the age of initiation, marriage and the "right to procreate" among the indigenous people had become important policy issues for the colonialists in Kenya.

The organization of African women's reproductive labor changed as colonial enclosures proceeded. Land alienation drastically reduced the resources available to Africans by the 1920s. In the 1930s, one response to the shortage of land among the Meru, a group closely related to the Kikuyu, was the delay of marriages. Those elder women and men who had the power and authority to call for *irua* [circumcision] ceremonies could delay the initiations of whole age grades because of drought conditions. Parents had little land to give in the reserves, and in the White Highlands, Africans had no legal claim to any land, but only occupied the land on a contractual basis. The white settlers had every power to evict workers, and by the late 1930s, they had begun to do just that.

In the 1930s men of 28 years old were still considered "boys" by their elders because they had not been initiated (First Woman interview, Ruth Wangari wa Thung'u, July 24, 1996). And because they were not circumcised, they were not eligible for marriage. This was equally the case for Meru girls. Girls faced additional complications. While premarital sex was not sanctioned, premarital pregnancy was shunned. In part, it was shunned because an uncircumcised girl was considered ill-prepared for childbirth. The Meru practiced female circumcision as a prenuptial rite whereas the rest of the Kikuyu had, at least in the past, circumcised girls before the onset of menstruation. An uncircumcised mother was derided all over Kikuyuland, especially among the Meru. In Meru, girls had a greater chance than their Kikuyu "cousins" of getting pregnant while uncircumcised, because Meru girls were not initiated until well after they had begun to menstruate. It was therefore said to be fairly commonplace for Meru girls to abort if they were impregnated before their circumcisions.

Indigenous control over initiations was totally integrated with larger economic considerations, especially food production, wherein women had decision-making power. Vast quantities of food such as porridge and beer were needed during initiation ceremonies (Thomas 2003:29-30; Wane 2000:60). Women produced porridge and beer in groups. Much of the singing, dancing, food preparation and ceremonial activity relied upon the collective labor of women. Each initiate had at least one woman fully devoted to caring for and advising her during the recovery months. These advisors generously fed new initiates wholesome foods during a healing period that could last three months. The advisors trained the young women in the rights and responsibilities of adulthood.

If one included the time spent in events that were accessories to the circumcision itself, the initiation process took between three months and two or more years. The withdrawal from the labor pool of thousands of initiates and their advisors across Kikuyuland for several months was a disturbing prospect for white settlers. They relied completely upon the availability of an abundant supply of free labor. The white settlers saw free labor in two lights. First, Kikuyu women's labor had to be free from reliance upon subsistence entitlements and autonomous, collective self-reliance in order to be available on the labor market. Second, colonial law allowed white settlers to exploit African labor freely, in that they paid little or nothing to African workers.

If initiation was the process through which the youth were made full members of society, it also signaled their eligibility for marriage and their right to enjoy new entitlements to land. Initiation required sufficient food for the ceremonies and sufficient land to allocate to the new adults upon their marriages. During drought or war, initiations were postponed. Drought conditions and famine constituted an inauspicious setting within which to encourage the expansion of cultivation or population. While famines were rather infrequent, white settler encroachment on land was persistent, and in the 1920s and 1930s it was increasing. Government and settler alienation of indigenous landholdings made it more and more difficult for African parents to ensure that they had enough land to allocate to the next generation. All these considerations led to later initiation, marriage and childbirth.

The increasing severity of female circumcision with the incursion of Europeans is noted by Lambert and Bunche; more women died from associated infections and more women developed extensive scar tissue, which led to infant and maternal mortalities. Operations were more extensive, mutilation was more horrible; premarital pregnancies and abortions were more frequent. In the mid-1930s for the first time, the dancing and playing that followed women's circumcision ceremonies began to involve the initiates hitting and kicking members of the older age-grade (Bunche 1941). The changes were a signal that violence and competition had entered the society along with the violence of the colonial land alienation. When access to land was no longer assured to everyone, the solidarity and collectivity that had featured in previous relations among age-grades began to break apart. Worse, infant and maternal mortality were on the rise.

> At the same time female genital mutilation was politicized. Protecting the rite of female circumcision became a central element of African resistance. According to Bunche, it should be reiterated that the determination of the Kikuyu not to permit any modification of this sacred ritual is largely the product of their bitter reaction to the English land policy. The Kikuyu Central Association was organized to protect land rights, but it has become almost fanatical in its devotion to the symbolic ritual of circumcision, and especially female circumcision. This is the barricade over which they must battle the invading European.
>
> The fact is that the white influences have made the operation more severe and dangerous than formerly. It has already been noted that the cutting is more severe than in earlier times. Initiations are no longer easily held at central places, because native squatters are now often found off the reserves on white men's estates; because girls move into the towns with their parents; and as a result of the increased mobility of the population due to cars, buses, and railroads. Thus, instead of the operations being performed by a select group of skilled operators, they are now frequently crudely done by bungling hands, with harmful results to the initiates (Bunche 1941:64).

With brutal sincerity the Colonial Office announced its intention to improve maternal and infant health in order to encourage "the creation of a healthier and better-developed stock" (Lord Passfield, Secretary of State for the Colonies, London, to Governors, East African Dependencies, March 8, 1930, PRO, CO/822/27/10, cited in Thomas 2003:53). Missionaries, in particular, took up the task of improving maternal health by starting a campaign in 1929 to abolish female circumcision. Efforts by colonialists to ban the rite in most of the colony were abandoned in Meru District in the 1930s and 1940s. The state had tentatively begun to back the missionaries' clitoridectomy ban in the Local Native Councils in Central Province in 1929. The state, however, turned a blind eye to the experimental social engineering embodied, at the same time, in the proclitoridectomy, pronatalist policies of Meru District Commissioner H.E. Lambert.

Colony-wide, there had been steady decrease in the population of Africans between 1890 and the mid-1920s. The decline is easily explained with reference to European interventions, which involved famine, disease, "pacification" and punishing raids, the First World War, more famine and disease, and land alienation (Van Zwanenberg 1975:10). During his second term as district commissioner of Meru, however, Lambert argued that it was because Meru girls were initiated so "late" and practiced abortion that the Meru population growth was so slow (Thomas 2003:13-14). In the 1930s and 1940s Lambert worked with local African appointees to devise a means not to abolish but to *lower the age of female circumcision.*

To stop the practice of abortion and to encourage an increase in the population, Lambert took the extraordinary step of encouraging Local Native Councils, headmen and chiefs to ensure that the circumcision of girls took place before they reached puberty (Thomas 2003:27). This way, young women would be eligible for marriage at an earlier age. If a woman were circumcised and then impregnated out of wedlock, instead of aborting the fetus, she was much more likely to marry the man who had impregnated her and to give birth to the child. Lambert used this policy as part of the imperial effort to secure labor supplies and, in some instances, to punish those women who resisted labor recruitment and military impressment.

In order to carry out this policy, Lambert began to engage indigenous institutions in colonial administration. He constructed relations of collaboration with loyal Africans who could implement colonial policies. He focused on the incorporation of Meru men's councils known as *kiama* or *njuri* into the local colonial hierarchy. Lambert combined "the indirect-rule principle of working through local authorities with his commitment to applied social anthropology," to argue that indigenous men's councils, especially the Supreme Council, or the *Njuri Ncheke*, should be adapted and used to administer colonial law (Thomas 2003: 43-44). Lambert required all African headmen and police to become members of the Supreme Council and in turn gave the Supreme Council sole power to elect African members of the Local Native Council, a body that worked with the government, directly under the district officers' control. Members of the *Njuri*

*Ncheke* were to play an important part in carrying out Lambert's circumcision policies.

As district commissioner, Lambert was in charge of the appointments of African civil servants, including Local Native Council (LNC) members, chiefs and headmen. Lambert had veto power over all LNC decisions and had the authority to dismiss and replace chiefs and headmen who acted against his directives. The African men appointed as native councillors and chiefs enriched themselves and their relatives through patronage. In exchange for preferential access to trade licences, new seed varieties, loans and other benefits, African officials became the "toys" of the District Commissioner. They implemented his policies without question (Thomas 2003:37).

Throughout the 1930s and 1940s, British-appointed Meru headmen and chiefs used Lambert's policy ever more decisively as a weapon against those involved in the African struggle for land. Forcible mutilation was a means by which to challenge and impinge upon African women's unity with one another and therefore their capacities to call men into line and to control Meru land and the distribution of that land to daughters and daughters-in-law. Thomas stated that "Police from district headquarters, accompanied by a *mutani* certified to perform the less severe procedure, carried out *Kigwarie* [forced circumcisions] by traveling from one area to another. ... After gathering all the girls in a field, the police would place them in a line and select for excision those whose breasts had begun to develop" (Thomas 2003:45). Some policemen actually took part in the operations, others stood aside to watch and then inspected each girls' genitalia to ensure that they had been "cut" according to LNC regulations.

Meru District Officer M.R.R. Vidal noted in 1923 that in much of the district, initiation had been postponed for several years because of drought conditions (Meru, AR, 1924, KNA, DC/MRU/1/1/1; cited in Thomas 2003:27). In 1924 the Meru reaped a bountiful millet and bean harvest and so began to plan the next initiation ceremonies. Given that Meru marriages were set to resume in one to three years after the 1924 initiations, Vidal was hopeful that fewer women would abort and more men would become labor migrants as they sought to earn enough money to afford the heifer, bull, ram, ewe and drum of honey required for bride-price (Thomas 2003:30).

Vidal wrote of his concern about labor shortages but did not appear to have taken any action to correct what he saw as a less-than-optimal situation of low population growth. Lambert, however, took a keen interest in bringing African women's labor power-producing capacities directly under colonial control. For Lambert the "social order" was of concern insofar as the customs surrounding marriage and reproduction contributed to or blocked the growth of the labor force. Thomas argued with reference to the "politics of the womb" that

> colonial rule in Asia and Africa fueled these reproductive concerns by situating the definition and maintenance of racial, cultural, and sexual boundaries as important state projects. Pro-natalist political agendas and racial purity initiatives circulated between colonies and metropoles via official, missionary, and reformist channels. Through colonial concerns about race and sexuality, reproduction was cast as a crucial site of state intervention and popular debate (Thomas 2003:11).

Lambert's forced circumcision policy was well under way in 1939 at the outbreak of the Second World War. When military recruiters arrived in Meru province seeking men for the Carrier Corps, uncircumcised and unmarried Meru girls resisted the men's impressment and confounded the recruiters' efforts. The girls undertook a campaign of teasing and goading the young men, their peers, for allowing themselves to be taken away to carry the loads of the white men (Thomas 2003:21). Carrying loads on the head was work done only by women.

But the gendered transgression involved in men's service in the Carrier Corps was not the only consideration in the young women's anticolonial, anti-impressment protest. When elders, women and children had been left by men serving in the First World War, a famine had ensued due to drought, the confiscation by the government of large numbers of heads of livestock and inadequate labor in the subsistence realm. At the end of the First World War the British expropriated 2 million acres of land from the Nandi without compensation, for the settlement of demobilized British soldiers (Ross 1927:81). African men returning from the war brought influenza, sexually transmitted diseases, plague and yaws into the reserves and deadly epidemics ensued. Of the 350,000 East African men impressed into the carrier corps in the First World War, 46,618 were officially recorded as killed in action and another 40,645 were untraced at the end of the war. At least 144,000 Kenyans died in the war and from associated famine and diseases (Van Zwanenberg 1975:10). These considerations, well within the living memory of the Meru at the time, impelled the girls' efforts to keep men away from the military recruiters.

In response to the girls' teasing, a number of young men fled the area, hid in the forest and thereby avoided military impressment. The headman responsible for filling the recruitment quota sought a resolution to the young men's flight by punishing the girls. He had all the young women forcibly mutilated. H. E. Lambert lauded the Meru authorities who "initiated the young ladies," and noted that, with the women confined to their huts recovering from the mutilation, the "young gallants" then "crept cautiously back" to their homes from their hiding places (Meru District Annual Report, 1939, KNA: DC/MRU/1/1/4; cited in Thomas 2003:21). Colonial control over female initiation meant that circumcisions were scheduled to raise the birthrate and fulfill colonial labor requirements, no longer to fulfill the training aspects that prevailed under women's collective control. European and African male control also meant that the mutilations were used as collective punishment.

Many Meru men and women were totally opposed to the colonial intervention in female excision. The surprise attacks of the circumcisers meant that parents had no time to put together the feasts that were normally required, nor to stock the extra food and other supplies necessary for the initiates' healing. Girls sang a derisive song about the policemen, *Kiberenge*, who enforced these mutilations before the girls were betrothed, as was the custom:

> Ah, ii, *Kiberenge* should be cursed
> *Kiberenge* be cursed, ii
> And even if he screams
> He has forced girls without young men to be circumcised.
> (Thomas 2003:47)

During Lambert's tenure in Meru, he appointed Methodist missionary E. Mary Holding to investigate "indigenous women's institutions" in order to determine whether they too could be incorporated into colonial administration (Meru District, AR, 1939, KNA, DC/MRU/1/1/4; "Notes of a Meeting Held at the District Commissioner's Office, Meru, on 23 April 1940," KNA, VQ/11/2; cited in Thomas 2003: 43-44). Holding's detailed anthropological account was ignored, however, when Lambert learned that in some areas "women's cults" were defying LNC resolutions against the more severe forms of circumcision. Lambert demanded that these cults be banned by the *Njuri Ncheke*. Lambert's policy was again defied by young women in other parts of the district who underwent second excisions, "or were being forcibly excised a second time by mothers-in-law and 'midwives' immediately following childbirth" (Meru District, AR, 1940, KNA, DC/MRU/1/1/4; cited in Thomas 2003:44). The second excision was unwelcome by some initiates, fiancés and fathers who had come to prefer the minor form of mutilation (Thomas 2003:48).

With widespread women's defiance apparently being instigated by the very women's institutions that he sought to co-opt, Lambert dropped the idea of engaging women's institutions in colonial administration. He wrote that women openly rejected the authority of the Local Native Council: "to more than half the tribe – the females – it means nothing" (Lambert 1947: 34; cited in Thomas 2003:44). Meru women opposed the Local Native Council as stringently as they opposed the colonial rulers to which the Local Native councillors reported.

The colonial reconfiguration of female circumcision, like the rite itself, was embedded in changes to broad systems of land control, use and entitlement. The Meru men who accepted and implemented Lambert's female initiation policy were also among the first Africans to gain the right to produce coffee and to register titles to their land. Before anyone else, these men bought into the commodified economy and, in exchange, agreed to enforce policies that protected both African men's newly acquired rights and the colonists' labor supplies. Their buy-in violated customary practice by usurping women's control over female sexuality.

The "fight for fertility" raged. Meru male dealers exacerbated the human rights abuses that were implicit in the rite in the first place. While female genital mutilation always narrowed women's range of human expression and experience, initiation normally took place within a context defined by and designed to support the social group engaged in the rite of passage.

The Kikuyu indigenous worldviews on female circumcision are varied. There are very many interpretations of the meaning and significance of cliterodectomy, within and across ethnic groups, with much overlap and a significant measure of diversity. The following description focuses on the collectivity of women's land and labor as these relate to cliterodectomy among the Kikuyu in the early 20th century. This is one historically based interpretation, supported by others' analyses that have generated new understandings and raised new questions. It is informed by oral histories containing many Kikuyu women's and men's ideas on the subject (First Woman interviews, Molo, July 9, 1998; Men of Mungiki, July 23, 1998).

Berman and Lonsdale saw Kikuyu female initiation as a form of self-control, a way of "buying maturity with pain" (1992:390). The perspective developed here suggests that female circumcision was a militant proof of the initiates' collective commitment to the protection of the land on which their blood fell. The ideal situation, in which a woman showed no fear or pain and made no sound during the cutting process, was also a display of the fearlessness with which women sealed their promise to guard their land with their very lives. The fields in which circumcisions took place were the proving grounds of Kikuyu womanhood. There girls became full adults and were assured husbands, land and families. Kikuyu female circumcision took place on specific grounds, in named rivers, at precise hours. The rite might at one time have signified women's sacrificial willingness to die in defense of their land that, with their labor, gave rise to the possibility of life.

Those Meru women who were forcibly mutilated in the 1930s and 1940s were to be integrated not into their indigenous subsistence community but into the colonialists' commodified political economy as unwaged producers of labor power. Lambert did not intend that the Meru should reproduce in order to cultivate their own land and strengthen their indigenous political economy. The greater the Meru population grew, in fact, the smaller would be the percentage that could subsist within the bounds of the Meru reserve. The Meru were instead supposed to acquiesce to land alienation and work for wages to survive. The sum total of Meru women's and men's lives, in Lambert's worldview, was reduced to the provision of service to the colonial export economy.

In the fight to control this aspect of African women's fertility, Lambert required the collaboration of Meru male dealers. In their usurpation of control over women's fertility, their acceptance of private landownership and their production of export cash crops (often using unwaged female labor), Lambert and the Meru male dealers made a template for the counterinsurgency policies that were subsequently recast during the Mau Mau war to quell demands for "land for all."

The Meru circumcision case was a fight for fertility. Women fought to control their own labor and lives and to maintain the subsistence political economy and their place in it, complete with men's labor and presence. Many Meru men responded to the women's anticolonial stance by joining in the women's resistance to military impressment. Male dealers colluded to mutilate the women and force the men into the British military's carrier corps. Some 45 percent of these men could expect to die.

Lambert, military recruiters, labor recruiters, white plantation owners, local Meru chiefs and circumcisers constituted the bloc of foreign and local men who were engaged in this male deal. Women's direct labor and their reproductive capacities were explicitly at the center of this struggle. Local male dealers had their own interests at stake when they agreed to change customary practice and allow men to largely control the initiations of women. Women had formerly had exclusive control over these ceremonies, their timing and their effectuation, including the actual operation of genital mutilation. The African and European men in this deal each had their own land and property to protect. Meru chiefs had worked hard for a decade or more to stop the practice of women receiving *tha*, or blessings in land from male relatives or clan members. Only if women had alternative sources of livelihood could landowners justifiably refuse to share their land. Chiefs and headmen therefore pushed men to accept waged labor and pushed women toward marriage, and the care of children and employed men.

Then, with exclusive rights to their land, Meru large landowners finally got permission from the government to plant coffee trees. This high-value crop had previously been reserved exclusively for Europeans. This was part of the pay-off for the forced circumcisions of several age-grades of young women in Meru in the 1930s and 1940s.

The female circumcision crisis that unfolded in Meru in the late 1930s demonstrated the high degree to which peasant women's resistance to colonialism was integrated into colony-wide struggles against the war, exploitation and land loss. In the Meru reserves in 1939, resistance took place at the site of production of the men who were to be impressed into military service. Meru women used the unifying force of the generational system of socialization in practice at the time to engage in antiwar and anticolonial activities. The Meru women's ridicule was an exercise of their persuasive public power over Meru men. The young women's motivation was to stop the women, children and elders from being deprived of the young men's companionship, labor and protection.

As reported earlier in this chapter, men joined this act of women's resistance by escaping the recruiters. This gendered class alliance, which was as much in opposition to European recruiters as it was to the African chiefs who actually called the men out, was broken by the capture and mutilation of the women. The male deal between Lambert and the Local Native councillors, chiefs and headmen secured men's labor for war service. It also sought women's domesticated and housewifized submission to colonialism. After all, women had to do their own work and to do the work of their menfolk impressed into the military. Furthermore, with the state's need for increased food supplies to feed the military recruits and prisoners of war, African women were pushed in large numbers into employment on both Africans' and Europeans' farms. Many, as we shall see, took up this opportunity to increase their own independent production and trade and to strengthen the regional subsistence political economy. And settlers then worked to control the local trade of produce grown on Africans' farms.

Lambert, with his loyal African chiefs in the Local Native Councils in Meru, had been able to seriously disrupt indigenous women's control over the processes of fertility that accompanied female circumcision. These processes included unity among women, rules on premarital sex play, abortion, marriage, procreation and, finally, land allocation and the attendant cultivation that newly married women expected to undertake as their means of subsistence. Colonial male dealers used forced genital mutilation to punish girls who goaded Meru men into resisting the draft at the outset of the Second World War and to quell the solidarity and strong community-mindedness of the people. Although by the end of the 1940s the male dealers appeared to have won this round of the fight for fertility in Meru, the following decade revealed that the colonial victory was as short-lived as it was unstable.

Meru male dealers established great wealth for themselves in the interwar years, based largely on their exclusive claims over large tracts of land, control over female labor, and business opportunities afforded by their involvement in service to the colonial administration. They were consistently challenged by those who were dispossessed and exploited in the process of the male dealers' accumulation of wealth. But they used their association with the British to protect their claims and their spoils. They maintained a measure of economic and political power well into the independence era in Kenya.

# CONCLUSION

The men who drafted the Carter Commission Report interpreted Kikuyu land rights through the testimonies of African landowners and European experts and officials. The 1934 *Kenya Land Commission Report* extinguished Africans' rights to all land outside native reserves. Private titles, sought by wealthy Kikuyu chiefs, were denied to Africans. The commissioners addressed Kikuyu land grievances by adding just a few thousand acres to enlarge the native reserves. In doing so, the commission protected the exclusive rights of Europeans to own land in large areas of the colony.

The 1934 *Report* recognized overcrowding as a problem in Kikuyu reserves, especially in Kiambu. The commissioners recommended that with the "correct use of the land" and changes in tenure regimes *within* the reserves, the size of the existing land unit would be sufficient (Kenya Land Commission, Report, 1934:362). The *Report* silenced multiple, overlapping and nonexclusive rights of access to land (Mackenzie 1998:96). It supported the principle of allocation of land through male clan members. Kikuyu women's precolonial power was lodged in their access to land. The Carter Commission undermined that power and set the stage for a more militant struggle by women for land and freedom.

In Meru, the British directly distorted women's fertility rites in an attempt to gain control over the whole people's labor power. The Meru circumcision crisis shows how British officials employed indirect rule in practice. Administrators built an African administrative hierarchy at the village level to enforce colonial law. In Meru, these laws included the promotion of female circumcision at an early age and the enclosure of women's fertility within colonial control.

The colonial state's efforts to moderate Kikuyu land claims and to enforce female genital mutilation, as means of controlling land and labor supplies, took place in an atmosphere of intensifying social upheaval. In July and August 1939 unionized waged workers staged the first general strike in Kenya (Singh 1969:84-85). A second followed in 1947. The 1950 general strike merged with other, more militant anticolonial politics to produce the Mau Mau uprising of 1952.

In 1939 Kenya was a colony in turmoil within a world about to descend into ethnic and resource war. Britain itself was about to be devastated, put into debt and lose its colonies. The United States was to become the dominant world player and replace the United Kingdom as the world's preeminent imperial state. The Second World War was a watershed for the struggles of the colonized. The impressment of colonized men into military service and their deployment globally set the stage for the worldwide eruption of liberation struggles. Soldiers from the various colonies met each other and worked together. They saw the fallibility of European men. They wielded weapons against the white man. They intermingled with African American antiracist soldiers in the U.S. Army in Europe. Those colonized men who escaped the massive death roll were neither compensated with pensions nor granted demobilization benefits (Shiroya 1985).

The upshot of these experiences for the Kenyan recruits who survived were great expectations for social justice and autonomous citizenship in a postwar Kenya. Demobilized African soldiers got no benefits. They were instead faced with high inflation and a second colonial occupation with a soldier-settlement scheme that encouraged a massive European influx between 1945 and 1950.

Whereas Kenyans had their own grievances to address, they did so in a context of rising global anticolonial struggle and sentiment. East African soldiers serving in India and Burma during the Second World War met Indian men who had been promised national independence in return for their military service to the crown. India gained independence in 1947. This had a deep impact on Kenyans, especially the soldiers. The Pan-African Congress met in 1945 in Manchester, England. Pan-Africanism was another global movement with which the Kenyan struggles were linked. Jomo Kenyatta participated in the Congress and provided one direct link between local and Pan-African anticolonial movements.

The establishment of an apartheid regime in South Africa in 1948 was also a spur to Kenyan anticolonial activism. There were many white South Africans in Kenya, and many others who admired and wished to emulate the racist South Africans and their Rhodesian counterparts. For Kenyans, then, there was a real threat that the European settlers would achieve their own self-rule in Kenya if the Africans did not do it first. India's independence and China's 1949 revolution provided a context within which the British faced serious, multiple challenges to their hegemony.

The Carter Commission and H.E. Lambert's circumcision policy illustrate the ways that land and labor lay at the center of the fight for fertility. The British male deals with Kenya's new hierarchy of chiefs in the 1930s marked a new era of colonialism. The state incorporated in the civil service some hundreds of African men as chiefs, subchiefs and headmen in the native reserves. These men parlayed political appointments into control over vast tracts of land and command over the labor of women within their entire location. The White Highlands European settler population was, at the same time, growing in number and political influence in the 1930s and 1940s. The plans, policies and laws concerning land use in colonial Kenya were mostly drawn up by white settlers, to suit the white settlers' private enterprise.

With regard to labor legislation, there was much disagreement and debate among settlers and administrators in Nairobi and in London. During the 1930s and 1940s the official government position was *not* to force or encourage the entry of Africans onto the labor market. Under these circumstances, the settlers' demand for labor was met in extrajudicial ways. In the rural African reserves, the British set up their administrative centers adjacent to white settled areas. The settlers demanded labor and British officials facilitated the supply, to varying degrees and by differing means.

This chapter has shown how *experimental* and *ad hoc* were the labor and population policies invented by colonial officials like H.E. Lambert. The Colonial Office implicitly trusted the "man on the spot" (Perham 1935:16) and so turned a blind eye to such experiments. Lambert's procircumcision bylaws would have been repugnant to the British public had it been better informed. Kenya colony was to become a major focal point for anticolonial activity precisely due to the impunity with which British officials and settlers alike were given scope to mutilate and torture Africans in the name of labor discipline.[1] By 1959, the British public would be informed of clear cases of torture and brutality against African women and men in Kamiti and Hola prisons and in "rogue" interrogation centers run by racist white settlers during the Mau Mau war. Before turning to those events, we consider in Chapter Five the anticolonial organizations and uprisings of the 1930s and 1940s. These provided the context and the organizational backdrop for the launching of the guerrilla struggle in 1952.

## *Note*

1.  "The ruthlessness of some of the members of this early group of settlers is almost unbelievable at the present day. One of them supervised his laborers from a chair at the door of his hut by firing a rifle in the direction of any whom he thought to be slacking" (Ross 1927:98).

~ CHAPTER FIVE ~

# LAND, FOOD, FREEDOM II: GENDERED CLASS ALLIANCES IN THE STRUGGLE FOR THE COMMONS, 1930 TO 1949

## INTRODUCTION

In the 1930s and 1940s Kikuyu reserve and squatter populations actively resisted a whole spectrum of new colonial enclosures. These enclosures ranged from land alienation in the reserves, to trade restrictions and the banning of indigenous initiation rites. Land, trade and the age-grade system were central to the Kikuyu social organization. They were sources and expressions of fertility, the external control of which was contested in increasingly networked uprisings during the period.

This chapter examines three of the very many "fights for fertility" that played out in the decades leading up to the Mau Mau war: the independent school movement; reserve women's uprisings in 1947 and 1948; and the Olenguruone settlement scheme struggle of 1941 to 1950. It is important to stress that these examples of resistance took place within a context of generalized anticolonial insurgency during the period (Furedi 1989; Stichter 1982). Trade unions were very active, for instance; and the first general strikes by waged workers were staged in 1939 and 1947 (Singh 1969). The waged workers in the umbrella labor organization, the East Africa Trade Union Congress, made alliances with unwaged rural people.

This chapter focuses on the ways in which unwaged, peasant women and men constructed "gendered class alliances" or cross-gender *relations of solidarity for the defense of the commons.* In all three instances reviewed here, Kikuyus and other peoples fought against British and African male dealers to maintain community control over different aspects of fertility, including knowledge, land and women's reproductive capacities. During this 20-year period, anticolonial activists increasingly wrestled with the question of who within the "community" should or could legitimately exercise control over fertility. The chapter considers how activist women in Githinguri, Murang'a and Olenguruone answered that question.

In the 1930s there began a new cycle of struggle in Kenya that was characterized by European colonizers reconfiguring the structures of state power by constructing new male deals with appointed African chiefs. This reconfiguration involved new levels of state control over "all aspects of ownership and use of land," both in the reserves and the White Highlands, especially during the Second World War (Ghai and McAuslan 1970:97). The previous chapter dealt with two examples of male deals used to assert colonial control over Africans' land and labor power. This chapter examines aspects of the growing resistance to the chiefs' male deals.

In the 1920s and 1930s the Kikuyu community was undergoing several internal changes involving three related kinds of transition. First, in the mid-1920s, there was a sudden increase in the numbers of youth seeking initiation into adulthood through circumcision. Second, by being initiated, they opened the way for their parents to become elders. Third, these changes coincided, in the early 1930s, with the start of a customary generational transition of political power. The relationship between these rituals of transition in the Kikuyu social organization and the struggle against enclosure is outlined below.

In the mid-1920s the oldest children of the postfamine baby boom began to come of age. This was the new generation born of the survivors of the 1890s Famine from Europe. As the years progressed, increasingly large sets of initiates were ready to be circumcised, become adults, marry, procreate and cultivate land. This meant new pressures on communities to maintain control over agricultural lands and the foods produced thereon, so as to reserve surplus for fees and ceremonial feasts. Once the initiations began, they would continue for some years until the youngest of the first postfamine generation were initiated. Soon after initiations, many new initiates' marriages would follow, necessitating more surplus production for bridewealth payments and ceremonial feasting.

When parents had at least one circumcised child, they were eligible to advance in the four elders' age-grades. The rites often involved the payment of fees and the organization of feasts of livestock, beer and other foodstuffs.

A confrontation was pending: at the same time that the colonialists were tightening their grip on the Africans' land and labor, indigenous peoples were requiring more surplus, and control over that surplus, in order to stage their community-wide ceremonies. The most significant of these was the generational handover of political power, known as the *ituika* ceremony.

The Kikuyu maintained a system of rule based on "the principle of the alternation of patrilineal generations" (Prins 1970:42). Each Kikuyu man belonged to one of two "tribal halves," "generations" or moieties. These were known as the Maina and Mwangi generations. If a man was in the Maina generation, his sons belonged to the Mwangi generation. These sons, then, were in the same "generation" as their grandfathers. These generations were not bound by time or age. Each generation contained men of every age, from infant to elder. Thus I use the term moieties, rather than generations, to more accurately capture the meaning of this kind of political organization. One moiety ruled over land and legal matters during its tenure, which might last from 14 to 40 years. Its members then handed over power to the alternate moiety, as described below.

In the early 1930s the Kikuyu began the first rites in a complex ceremony in which the ruling moiety handed over power. The handing-over ceremony took several years to complete. It began with the collection from men of all ages of sheep and goats for feasting, sacrifices and payments. Then the ceremonies were held throughout Kikuyuland. This process of power succession required the settlement of all outstanding legal claims and the righting of all wrongs (Lambert 1956/1965:59). Laws passed by the departing elders were invalidated, and the new ruling moiety either had to change or reinstate the laws (Middleton and Kershaw 1953/1972). The *ituika* ceremony

> formalized the alternating succession of ritual authority between the two generations that were equally represented in all age sets. Authority was transferred only to those who had reached senior elderhood, who were thus already qualified to judge matters of law. It is generally said that this happened every 30 or 40 years (Berman and Lonsdale 1992:345).

The timing of these handovers seemed to coincide less with biological epochs and more with major climatic changes: "the chronology of the last three supposed *ituika* follows that of famine" (Berman and Lonsdale 1992:346).

Prins claimed that the government outlawed the ceremony, and that the *ituika* due around 1925 was never held (Prins 1970:48 fn 2). Missionary writer Father C. Cagnolo wrote that the ceremony was actually begun in the early 1930s and members of the incoming generation-set had started to pay the required fees (Cagnolo 1933:121). But the ceremony was never completed because the government banned it before it was done. It is clear that the British would have strongly objected to that aspect of the *ituika* ceremony that involved the abolition of all laws passed by the outgoing moiety and the renegotiation of legal statutes by the incoming moiety. For the outgoing moiety in 1930 was the same set of rulers from which were drawn many of the chiefs and traders of the early colonial era. A renegotiation of land and legal relations among the Kikuyu would have threatened the land and legal arrangements of the British. The aborted hand-over ceremony of the early 1930s was revisited later, in the 1950s, but on a new political footing.

Lonsdale disputes the fact that the *ituika* was banned by the government. He claims that the Kikuyu themselves changed the nature of the ceremony. He does note that there was a changeover of personnel in the customary councils of elders:

> The late 1920s are remembered as a period of wholesale turnover in Kiambu's community council, or *kiama*, elders; the incomers were KCA [Kikuyu Central Association] men, sympathetic to the property interests of the young. The [1929 female circumcision ] crisis had given the party an entry to Kiambu for the first time; it gained members ridge by ridge, *mbari* by *mbari* [clan by clan] (Berman and Lonsdale 1992:394 , text in square brackets added).

These generational transitions affected all adults, from the new initiates to the most senior elders. It was in this fluid social and political context that the instances of resistance analyzed here marked the start of a new phase in the anticolonial struggle. From the local, defensive actions of the early 20th century, anticolonial activists moved toward regionally coordinated resistance.

# THE 1929 CIRCUMCISION BAN: PRELUDE TO THE INDEPENDENT SCHOOL MOVEMENT

> Since *irua* means not merely the circumcision but the entire process of initiation and teaching, and is the basis of the important age-groups, the Kikuyu regard any effort

to modify the custom as a vital attack upon the foundations of their society. It would be true that the abolition of the circumcision ceremony without provision for an acceptable substitute, would bring about the collapse of the age-group structure and hence of the social stability of the tribe (Bunche 1941:63).

In Chapter Four we learned how the Meru district officer, H.E. Lambert, promoted early female circumcision. Meanwhile in Nyeri, Kiambu and Murang'a, missionaries launched a campaign to eradicate the rite. Several protestant missionary societies, including the Church of Scotland Mission, the Presbyterian Church of East Africa, the African Inland Church and the Anglican Church, had opposed female genital mutilation since the early 1920s with little success. But in 1929 missions took a new approach. All African church elders, mission workers and parents of children in mission schools were to be banned from the churches and schools unless they affirmed their denunciation of the rite by signing the following statement:

Do you say with truth you have given up the matter of circumcision and that you are not a member of KCA and will not become a member unless the mission allows you to do so, should the association come into agreement with the Mission? Yes or No? (KNA: Native Affairs File on Female Circumcision, 1928-1930; cited in Mukaru-Ng'ang'a n.d.:7).

From the start of the missionaries' campaign to abolish female circumcision, male-dominated nationalist organizations such as the Kikuyu Central Association (KCA) advocated the continuation of the rite. KCA men, however, appear to have been more concerned about controlling women's sexuality and morality than about the continuation of the initiation rite itself. According to Lonsdale, the KCA president was "quite willing to discuss clitoridectomy" with the missionaries if the British banned prostitution. "Until whites cleaned up Nairobi their attack on female initiation could only encourage the heathendom they affected to despise" (Berman and Lonsdale 1992:391).

The missionaries' campaign led to a mass departure of Africans from protestant mission churches and schools throughout the territory. Within weeks of the missionaries' 1929 announcement, school attendance had dropped by 90 percent in outlying rural mission schools. Church congregations fell by 70 to 80 percent. Kikuyu women were most adamantly in favor of the continuation of the rite, and were energetic in the campaigns that followed. Using the organization of the European churches and schools for themselves, the antimission activists ensured that the protest quickly circulated across Kikuyuland. Out of the antimission protest emerged a regional independent education system that grew in strength throughout the 1930s and 1940s.

The 1929 female circumcision affair was at root a struggle for control over Kikuyu land and Kikuyu women's capacities to produce. In this classic fight for fertility, missionaries acted as agents of colonial capital. They found very few indigenous men with whom to forge male deals in support of the missionaries' anticircumcision policy. Kikuyu opposition was complete; the male dealers could not prevail. The Kikuyu left the European churches and schools and persisted in performing female circumcisions. In fact the missionaries found themselves faced with unbreakable indigenous community cohesion, rural women's strong solidarity and a coordinated political movement for the return of alienated lands. Those men and women who united in a gendered class alliance against colonial control "won" this fight for fertility in 1929.

Why were Kikuyu women and men so vehemently opposed to the missionaries' efforts to ban female circumcision? Four reasons are suggested here: (1) women's eligibility to marry depended upon circumcision and the associated teachings; (2) women's land rights were conferred mainly through marriage; (3) Kikuyu women (and men) wanted to maintain women's labor in the household and Kikuyu community; and (4) as Ralph Bunche noted, the age-grades formed through circumcision were "the means whereby the entire tribe is united and solidified" (Bunche 1941:49). To what extent did peasant women struggle within the community to gain control over their own resources and productive capacities? Let us briefly consider how "community solidarity" was redefined during the period.

Kershaw wrote specifically about the unity forged among Kikuyu men in the process of acquiring and stewarding land. Two kinds of unity or "solidarity" can be detected in this process: "solidarity of equals," wherein everyone benefits equally, and "solidarity of unequals," wherein everyone toils together but only a few benefit directly.[1] This concept of solidarity is equally relevant to the gendered relations of female circumcision. The Kikuyu were united against missionaries who demanded that Christian Africans reject circumcision and the struggle for land. At the same time, the Kikuyu were overwhelmingly in favor of the continuation of female genital mutilation and saw defense of it as a component of the anticolonial struggle. This unity in defense of clitoridectomy can be understood as a solidarity of unequals between women and men.

Kikuyu women and men upheld the circumcision customs that cemented community cohesion. Built into this cohesion was a distinct inequality between women's and men's customary land rights. Female circumcision has historically been bound up with this gendered inequality. A Kikuyu woman could customarily get access to land after being circumcised and married. Since circumcision was a central mechanism for safeguarding access to land for women, *even in unequal relations with their own menfolk*, women's defense of circumcision must be understood as part of their demand for land rights. The "choice" for women at that time was to either unite as a community to defend the rite that had long been central to women's access to life goods and community entitlements, or to join with European men, who were already implicated in expropriating much Kikuyu land, in a campaign to end the rite, with no alternative proposed. This was no choice at all.

But as women's fertility, or their total capacity to produce, came more and more to the forefront of the anticolonial struggles of the 1930s and 1940s, some Kikuyu women did take steps to address the gendered hierarchy embodied in the Kikuyu solidarity of unequals. In the independent school movement, as we will see, women began in earnest to address girls' education with woman-only initiatives. In the 1930s and 1940s peasant women's challenges to the customary status quo of male control did not come in the form of movements to eradicate circumcision, but rather in other arenas, such as the education of girls, the oathing of women and, after Mau Mau, the direct occupation of land by landless women. Not surprisingly, these feminist efforts came mainly from landless, peasant and dispossessed women within the anticolonial movement and rarely, if at all, from among the wives of chiefs and big landowners. From the 1930s onward, peasant and landless women's challenges to male control over land, labor and sexuality within the Kikuyu community became important components of Kenyan fights for fertility.

# INDEPENDENT SCHOOLS AND THE INDEPENDENCE MOVEMENT, 1930 TO 1952

While most Kikuyu mission adherents deserted the European churches and schools in 1929, a number of the wealthy traders and chiefs returned in the early 1930s when the missions relaxed their stance on female circumcision. However, the majority of the people refused to return. Presley found that "the two factions created by the controversy persisted into the Mau Mau rebellion; that loyalists were members of families that sided with the missionaries in the 1930s and that the Mau Mau rebels were children of the antimissionary faction" (Presley 1992:94). The "antimission" Kikuyu who established independent schools called themselves *karing'a* [Kikuyu = pure] or "independents" (Mukaru-Ng'ang'a N.D.:7). The Karing'a School movement was the more independent of two education associations that arose in the 1930s. The Kikuyu Independent School Association (KISA) sought government funding, while Karing'a schools remained autonomous and self-funded. In both cases, the leap from the independent school movement to the independence movement was a short one.

Since precolonial days female circumcision and education had gone hand-in-hand. Both were of primary interest to rural Kikuyu women. Girls were taught specific skills, customs and ways of relating throughout their childhoods, and especially during the intense period of training for adulthood during what could be a years-long initiation process. Missionaries had begun literacy education in the Kikuyu area in the 1890s. But for the most part, Kikuyu parents forbade their girls to attend mission schools. They instead learned from their mothers, older sisters, aunts, grandmothers, agemates and, crucially, from the female counselors who took them through the stages of initiation over a period of many months, in what was thereafter a life-long relationship. With the help of older women in the independent school movement in the 1930s, many girls resisted their parents' prohibition on formal education (Kabira and Ngurukie 1997).

Rahad Nduta Gachoka remembers the trouble she had in attending school in the late 1930s:

> Yes, I went to school. But to do this I had to run away from home. We girls were not allowed to go to school. Girls were not allowed to go to school by their fathers. It was taken that if a girl went to school then that one has "disappeared." The parents must accept that she has become a prostitute. Like we went from home, three of us, three daughters of Mr. Kamiti, our father. We left from home and what was said then, was that "All of Kamiti's beer has been poured out" (First Woman interview, Rahad Nduta Gachoka, May 26, 1994).

The "beer" that had been "poured out" when the three girls left their father's home without permission was the gift of beer that a groom would bring to the parents of the bride during bride-price negotiations (First Woman interview, Karimi Nduthu, May 28, 1994). Since the daughters had disappeared, people believed that their father would get no bride-price. It was assumed that the girls had run away into prostitution. This absent bride-price denied the girls' brothers the wherewithal to offer bride-prices for their own wives.

Before the 1930s, many young, dispossessed women, especially Maasai women, fled abusive marriages or pawnship to live in the towns and there engaged in prostitution to survive (White 1990a). Urban prostitution had only in the previous 20 years opened a new "profession" for young women, one that had never existed before in Central Kenya. In contrast, some women from rural areas fled to the cities but remitted their earnings to their extended communities in the countryside. Perhaps it is because prostitution was the most notorious instance of young women's abandonment of their family homes under early colonial rule that parents or the older generations so frequently associated girls' education with prostitution.

Rahad Gachoka stated that when she and her sisters escaped from their father's house, they "got assistance" from the *nyapara*, the African supervisor on the European's farm (First Woman interview, Rahad Nduta Gachoka, May 26, 1994). The *nyapara* was not the only man who helped the three sisters: "those men who were the age of my father could not agree to their daughters going to school. But men of a younger age accepted the idea of girls going to school. They had come to know the value of education" (First Woman, Gachoka, May 26, 1994). Despite the fact that Gachoka's uncle was not educated in the colonial schools and had not converted to Christianity (although "he did wear a shirt and trousers"), he did support women being educated. Their uncle welcomed the three sisters into his home, where they lived while attending Kijabe mission school. This kind of alliance between women and young men characterized much of the anticolonial politics of the time.

The 1929 movement against the missions and for the establishment of independent schools, then, was the first chance for large numbers of girls and young women to legitimately break in to the school system. The independent school movement created a context within which girls' education was acceptable to those parents who were concerned that their daughters maintain customary practices and relations.

The independent school movement was not only an opportunity for Kikuyu girls. Rahab Wabici, a women's leader within the Kikuyu Central Association and a teacher, stated that in the independent schools, "We did not have tribal boundaries. We had Luo girls, Kambas and Taitas" (Kabira and Ngurukie 1997:7).

Kikuyu women drew legitimacy from customary rights over the education of girls to engage in the selective and creative appropriation of the colonial apparatus of formalized public education. They were involved in school organization, teaching and curriculum development. Kikuyu women employed their significant organizational powers to build a colony-wide education network. This network extended further, as communities raised funds to send students to Uganda, Tanzania or the United Kingdom for higher education. Women in the independent school movement were central to the collection of money, sometimes holding secret fund-raising events (Kabira and Ngurukie 1997:7). In 1931 the government imposed a ban on money collections by the KCA, but could not stop parents and informal networks from raising funds.

> Members of the fledgling schools donated land, build-
> ing materials, and labor, however, and thus offset the
> edict's effect to some extent. Teachers were paid modestly,
> between 14 and 100 shillings a month, and sometimes
> they were paid in kind. Money was raised from building
> funds, school fees, donations, sporting events, raffles and
> dances (Natsoulas 1998a:290).

The global depression and the missionaries' anticircumcision decree had limited the expansion of mission schools during the 1930s, but the independent schools flourished. There was a massive demand among the Kikuyu for education for both boys and girls. By 1937 there were 54 Kikuyu-operated independent schools with 7,223 students (Natsoulas 1998a:292). One year later there were 62 independent schools in the Kikuyu reserves (Bunche 1941:52).

Presley shows that the Kikuyu "were fully aware that the western elements [of the education system] could provide the necessary tools for young Kikuyu to cope with Europeans - government officials or private employers" (Presley 1992: 99). The various land tenure commissions and inquiries that had taken place and continued to be organized were examples of the kinds of fora into which educated Kikuyu could intervene if they had reading, writing and English language skills. The benefits of education for the Kikuyu struggle to defend their land were clear from the examples of Jomo Kenyatta and Peter Koinange. Both men had been sent abroad for higher education and became important contributors to the independent school movement. Their fare and maintenance abroad were funded by *harambees*, or community-organized fund-raisers, and Kikuyu Central Association subscriptions.

Numerous Gikuyu-language songs were sung about the education of Kikuyu children in the independent schools. "Inheritance of Gikuyu," written by an anonymous songwriter in the 1940s, stressed that education was for *all* children, and the purpose of education was clearly stated:

Parents, help your children
Until all of them become wise,
So that they may help you
In the fight for our land. (Kinyatti 1980:25)

In 1936 government officials took measures to try to control independent schools. They sent inspectors to schools to assess curricular standards.
They set standards for teacher qualifications. Inspectors were empowered
to close down schools found wanting. In 1938 and 1939 the Karing'a
association opened three new schools without government approval. The
government threatened to close the schools down. The association made
appeals to the Colonial Office in London, which sympathized with the
association's educational endeavors and pressured the colonial government
in Nairobi to authorize them. With the Colonial Office behind them, the
independent school associations began to receive more support from the
local colonial government officials. The District Education Board began to
give refresher courses to teachers. By the end of the 1930s, the government
had reluctantly accepted the independent schools as an important part of
the Kenyan educational system.

After years of petitioning the government to establish a teachers'
training college, the independent school associations founded Githinguri
College in 1937. Peter Koinange, son of Senior Chief Koinange, was
appointed principal. The history was set down in songs such as "We are
Building Our Own School":

Go to Githinguri to see the school of Kenyan people
It is in a four storey building.
The builders are Kenyan
The chief overseer is a Kenyan
The building committee is Kenyan
And the money has been contributed by Kenyans.
(Kinyatti 1980:21)

The Kenya Teachers College at Githinguri was opened in January 1939.
Lonsdale succinctly encapsulated the amalgamation of the indigenous
and the colonial at Githinguri. The opening of the college was "blessed
by an elder with ritual leaves in one hand and a microphone in the other"
(Berman and Lonsdale 1992:399).

Presley points out that women in the independent school movement
supported the founding of the school and demanded that girls be admitted. This was one of Kikuyu women's many efforts to secure more accessible

and broad-based educational opportunities for girls, including English-language training. Presley documented women's activism for education:

> A group of women activists took the initiative in 1947 when they founded a girls' wing at the Githinguri school. They financed the girls dormitory and named it *Kiriri* (girls' sleeping place in the mother's house). The women decided to build *Kiriri* without men's help. They traveled from village to village collecting donations. ... The course of instruction, set by the women founders, included writing, the domestic arts, and instruction in English and Swahili. ... Women activists also took the lead in selecting the girls for admission. Those girls who passed the secondary school exam were screened by the women's committee. More than sixty female students were enrolled in *Kiriri* from 1947 until the British closed the school early in the Mau Mau emergency because they believed it was a hotbed of nationalism (Presley 1992: 101-102).

The development of independent schools took place in an environment of increasing indigenous militancy. In 1946 hundreds of Kikuyu across the colony began to take an oath of unity for the purpose of driving the Europeans out of Kenya. A participant, Ruth Wangari wa Thung'u, stated in a 1996 interview:

> I first heard and knew of the Mau Mau in 1947. This was the first time I took the oath. I took the oath at a place called Darugo in Gatundu Division, and on the day I took the oath, Kenyatta was there. I took the oath at the independent church at that place because that was where the oath was administered. By the time I took the oath, in this period I was in school. On that particular day, on the night of which I took the oath, we had spent the whole day having athletics at school then it was announced that that night there would be a meeting. At that meeting people were informed about Mau Mau as a liberation movement. Those who felt interested joined the movement and that is how we took the oath.
>
> It was at this juncture that I knew that come rain or shine, even if we were all to die in the Mau Mau war, we had to fight it. At the time when we were being

administered the oath we were told that even if you are to die you are to take a handful of soil and eat it or hold it with your hand because you are dying for the sake of your country. The person who passed the details of this particular meeting was a certain Reverend Wanyoike, who after preaching, announced that there would be a meeting and that Kenyatta would be attending. So, I remained for the meeting even though I didn't know what kind of meeting it was going to be because of my like of attending this type of political meetings. Most people did this but the few who didn't do this, the few who were not interested in these meetings they went home. Later on, these were among the people who had not taken the oath (First Woman interview, Ruth Wangari wa Thung'u, July 24, 1996).

Priscilla Wambaki, who was treasurer of the Githinguri girls dormitory project, stated that some of the girls from Githinguri "decided to take guns to the forest to be with the men to become freedom fighters" (from an interview with Priscilla Wambaki, Ngenda, May 16, 1979, cited in Presley 1992:102). When the government declared a state of emergency in October 1952, it also closed down all independent schools (Rodney 1973: chp 6.4). Many were razed and others became detention centers for those arrested during the tumultuous decade to follow.

The Christian church, established in Kenya as an element of colonial rule, had long been operated on the basis of hierarchy, obedience and deference to authority. It was adopted and appropriated by the Kikuyu as a site for a completely different expression of spirituality and social communion. Lonsdale characterized the incorporation of Christian theology into Kikuyu religious expression by the independent church congregations:

In one of their hymns they sang: "Lord, forgive us, we are not rejecting you but the thumbprint." Theologically unadventurous, the aims of the *aregi* [the independents] were those of the *kirore* [mission church members], to progress in a productive and educational idiom at once British and Kikuyu. Moreover, they knew how to assemble the necessary resources, both the popular support that made suppression impossible and, in the case of KISA, even grudging official approval (Berman and Lonsdale 1992:398).

In the independent school movement, Kikuyu women found a new opportunity for unity on a large scale (Kabira and Ngurukie 1997:33). The construction of the girls' dormitory at Githinguri and the national campaign that movement women organized to raise the funds constituted an important new kind of networking activity. While Mekatilili and Mary Muthoni Nyanjiru had been involved in money-collection for the protests in which they were respectively engaged, the scope and reach of fundraising within the independent school movement was a new departure. The colony-wide money collection replicated and echoed the colonial campaigns to impose uniform policies on all areas of the country. As the colonialists pursued policies of labor regulation and land rights for whites across the colony, so too did Kikuyu women independent school activists work on a colony-wide basis to pursue Africans' educational opportunities and land rights. A gendered class alliance was evident to the extent that men allied with women in building the girls' dormitory and extending education to all girls.

It is difficult to say how many girls were enrolled in independent schools in Kenya in the 1930s and 1940s. It is even harder to discern which girls were there against their parents' wishes. It is clear, however, that girls asserted themselves in new ways in this period. The fleeing of Kikuyu girls from their fathers' homes was, under precolonial conditions, unusual. And it was unprecedented for groups of sisters and friends in any number to flee, live elsewhere and therein disobey their parents and forsake the benefit of the support of their kinship networks. This new rebelliousness of daughters was enabled in part by the existence, on the one hand, of the independent schools, and on the other hand, by the support, encouragement and alliance of young female students, older women activists and men "of a younger age" (First Woman interview, Rahad Nduta Gachoka, May 26, 1994).

In sum, the gendered class character of the independent school movement suggests that Kikuyu women strove to educate their daughters to be effective, skilled defenders and innovators of women's customary rights to land. By the end of the 1940s, peasant women's collective work groups, age-sets and local kinship organizations were integrated into colony-wide networks of resistance. These networks were capable of raising funds for particular projects, such as the building of the girls' dormitory in Githinguri. Women of the independent school movement educated their daughters as part of the defense and delineation of their rights in land. Women's activism in the independent school movement was duplicated in other arenas, notably in the parallel independent church movement. In Murang'a in the mid-1940s, colonial demands on Kikuyu women's agricultural labor sparked another dramatic instance of peasant women's resistance.

## THE 1947 MURANG'A WOMEN'S TERRACING STRIKES

In the 1940s the colonial government introduced a number of measures designed to curb soil erosion in the overcrowded African reserves. White settlers and agricultural officers were quick to blame Africans' cultivation techniques for the decline of soil fertility (Carey 1953:16). But much of the problem can be traced to colonial intervention, in the form of the delimitation of reserve boundaries, which decreased the amount and the quality of the land available to Kikuyu farmers, and the promotion of particular marketable crops, such as wattle trees, the bark of which is used in the leather tanning process. The government also required steady sources of food for the military. During the war, "the main efforts of the administration were directed to getting the reserves to produce as much food as possible, irrespective of the long-term consequences" (Ghai and McAuslan 1970: 110).

Overcrowding in the Kikuyu reserves meant that more of the steeper hillsides were being brought under cultivation for longer periods with fewer fields being left fallow. Monocropping systems introduced by the government agricultural department reduced the use of plants that served as ground cover in the mixed cropping system of the Kikuyu (Kenya Land Commission, Evidence, 1934:676-677, cited in Mackenzie 1998:92-93). The introduction of new seed varieties, such as English potatoes, eclipsed such crops as sweet potatoes. This switch introduced a food with lower nutritional value and eliminated vital sources of food for goats, who instead of eating the remains of the sweet potato leaves and stalks in the dry season after its harvest, filled their bellies on grasses and green leaves and stripped the ground bare (Mackenzie 1998). Wattle plantations also wreaked environmental havoc.

In the 1920s and 1930s the colonial administration encouraged African production of wattle. These fast-growing trees have many uses, including the production of mimosa flowers, tannin-filled bark and the tall, straight trunks themselves, used in house construction and charcoal-making. Wattle trees can be used in ecological conservation measures, for instance, to control salinity, regenerate road verges, stabilize the soil and to provide shelter belts, visual screens and wildlife habitats.[2] But in the 1920s the colonial government promoted wattle only for its use in the settlers' tanning mills. The results were devastating to the soil.

Wattle was the only major cash crop Africans were allowed to cultivate on plantation scale before the Second World War. Many men got involved in its production. In the 1920s wattle was the monopoly of the chiefs, headmen and mission converts, or *athomi*. In the 1930s peasants with smaller plots of land also began to cultivate wattle. Many growers saved money and time in sowing the wattle by broadcasting the seeds directly onto uncleared land. The plant thrived even in unprepared soils, or soils in which grasses, thorns and bushes grew wild. Because its roots were shallow, they caused the topsoil to dry out. And if planted too closely together, as was likely with broadcast planting, undergrowth was prevented from growing and soil erosion soon followed. Wattle plantations quickly stripped the soil of nutrients and groundcover. Continuous production led to sheet and gully erosion and loss of soil fertility, especially as rivers carried top soil and the rough waste from the wattle harvest downstream to lower elevations (Mackenzie 1998:152-153).

By the early 1940s, gully erosion due to wattle production was severe. Ten-foot-deep fissures opened up on hillsides. Gully erosion was nearly impossible to stem. By the late 1940s, the government stopped supporting the expansion of African wattle plantations. They cited environmental concerns, but these concerns coincided with renewed interest by white settlers in the production of wattle on their own estates.

In 1946 the Fort Hall Betterment Scheme was devised by European administrative staff and white settlers. A central feature of the scheme was the construction of bench and narrow-base terraces on the hillside farms of the Kikuyu reserves. Terraces can help with soil erosion on hillsides. They are also a method of land capitalization (Tiffen et al. 1994:158). Bench terraces consist of a series of level platforms about four to six feet wide built along the contour lines of hillsides at vertical intervals of between eight and twelve feet. Bench terraces require a large amount of cutting and digging of the soil as do narrow-base terraces. Both types require extensive labor inputs for construction and for annual repairs. This earth-moving was to be accomplished with rural residents' unwaged compulsory manual labor.

The colonial administration called on Kikuyu elders and chiefs to recruit labor by calling together communal work groups, or *ngwatio*, which were customarily self-organized for projects that benefited an entire community. Unlike customary communal work, the terracing campaign was imposed from above for purposes disputed by those carrying out the hard labor. By incorporating "tradition" into the implementation of colonial policies, the agricultural planners intended that the difficult terracing work would be more readily accepted by the Kikuyu as part of the improvement of the land.

That the betterment campaign targeted the labor of peasant women is clear. Because most men were away from their home districts, the communal labor fell to women. The wives of chiefs were exempted from the hard labor. Peasant women worked under the supervision of European Agricultural Officers, African chiefs, men called levellers" and often, armed policemen (Ruthenberg 1966).

Although the colonialists had no wage bill, their expenditure on propaganda, equipment and the salaries of European and African officers who directed women's labor in terracing ranged into millions of sterling pounds per annum by 1945 (Kenya 1945, Appendix III). The administration rationalized the cost by arguing that "the only alternative to incurring the expenditure and proceeding with the work is to write off the area and to move the whole population elsewhere" (Kenya 1945:30).

Kikuyu chiefs competed with each other to see who could enforce the terracing of more land. Chief Erastus of Maragua Location was accused by residents of imprisoning women and impounding their goats when they refused to provide communal labor (Mackenzie 1998:163). The British rewarded men who oversaw the most work, and dismissed those who were unwilling or unable to compel women to work. As with the enforcement of female genital mutilation in Meru, terracing became a weapon with which to punish any offense. Leslie Brown, an agricultural officer in central Kenya at the time, stated in a retrospective interview that

> the Administration ... liked to regard soil conservation as a punishment, and when some location was backward over tax paying and given to drunkenness and crime I was often required to go and lay on some soil conservation there. I usually made a token effort to do some but this was obviously not a sound point of view which should not have prevailed (cited in Throup 1988:143).

A European staff member in the Agriculture office reported in 1947 that "only constant pressure keeps work going" ("Knight's report," April-June 1947, cited in Throup 1988:151). By the end of 1946, Murang'a women dug some 6,900 miles of terraces (Mackenzie 1998:163). By 1948, that figure was 10,000 miles (Throup 1988:151). The amount of food that was not produced by that labor is only one measure of the opportunity cost of acquiescing to chiefs' commands, a cost that was to become too high by 1947. The loss of land and labor, and the degree of compulsion that chiefs used in what was widely regarded as forced labor, were the sources of massive resistance.

As early as 1946, soldiers returning from the Second World War objected to their wives being forced to dig terraces. The wives of many soldiers refused to participate in the work. Soon this refusal was taken up on a wider scale. Ex-soldiers used the vernacular press to publish letters and reports against the slave-like conditions to which women were being subjected (Mackenzie 1998:163). At the same time, farm women in Nyeri refused to participate in compulsory cattle dipping meant to inoculate animals against common diseases. They attacked the European district commissioner and Chief Nderi who were encouraging the dipping campaign. The commissioner finally revoked the compulsory dipping order (Throup 1988:157).

On July 20, 1947, just a month after he had been elected president of the Kenya African Union,[3] Jomo Kenyatta spoke at a rally in Murang'a to a crowd of 10,000 about the government's soil conservation program. He praised the principles of conservation and those who undertook the labor of constructing terraces to "protect" hillsides from overly intensive use. The crowd reacted angrily. Most people in the district were already outraged about the labor demand, the slave-like conditions, fines, compulsion and the land loss entailed in terracing. Some women, such as many soldiers' wives, were already "on strike," while many others were contemplating it. The crowd was not pleased to hear Kenyatta praising the soil conservation campaign (Mackenzie 1998:163).

When he heard the disapproving reaction of the crowd, Kenyatta changed his approach. He condemned the use of the forced labor and the tactics employed to compel women to work. He suggested that men do the work instead (Berman and Lonsdale 1997:421). The meeting ended with a resolution that women should no longer comply with the administration's requests for contributions to the communal labor gangs organized for terracing. The next day most Murang'a women refused to answer the chiefs' and headmen's calls for compulsory labor. Some women destroyed terraces, while some men "roughed up" agricultural officials (Berman and Lonsdale 1992:421). The administration compromised and allowed that terracing could be done on an individual basis, with each family terracing its own plot of land. If terracing work were not begun within 15 days, the government warned, residents would be fined. Still, no work was done. Terracing work throughout Kikuyuland ground to a near halt throughout the following year (1948).

Women in Chief Waruhiu's division in Githinguri also stopped work. His had previously been the site of extensive progress in terracing. Waruhiu, who was fiercely loyal to the British, enthusiastically used "indigenous authorities to mobilise the peasantry for terracing" (Throup 1988:158).

This progress gained Waruhiu many enemies. His subsequent murder in 1952 was the opening shot in the Mau Mau war for liberation.

Another significant source of opposition to terracing came from those who were *ahoi*, or tenants of African large landholders. The mid-1940s to the early 1950s were particularly unstable years for Kikuyu tenants, as large landholders sought in many instances to clear their land in order to either sell or to allocate the land to family members, rather than allowing those from outside the family to continue to use the land. Redemption of tenants' plots was common and the tenants were loath to do anything that would increase the value of the land for coffee production and therefore increase their chances of dispossession. In some areas, very large numbers of people were tenants. Kershaw found that in 1950 as much as 45 percent of the population of the village of Igi in Kiambu were tenants, while the rest were the land holders (Kershaw 1997:72).

The digging of terraces was one of the ways that tenants saw their own interests in land being reduced. First, terraces actually reduced the amount of cultivable land. Second, some wealthy men started planting cash crops such as coffee and tea on the terraces. Jean Fisher found that in Murang'a in particular, "people are reluctant to expend money and energy on *mitaro* [Kikuyu = terraces] because the land may be redeemed at any time" (Fisher 1954:257). Peasant women also understood that "the digging of *mitaro* is only another ruse of the Europeans to get Kikuyu land - when the land begins to improve as a result of the *mitaro*, then the European will claim it!" (Fisher 1954:258).

In addition to all of these reasons for Kikuyu women's opposition to terracing was the fact that it was the government that had ordered it. Women were keenly aware of how agricultural labor was organized customarily since it was they who did it. They were therefore alive to every colonial intervention and, as in other instances, were ready to actively defend their rights.

In her extensive 1954 report on Kikuyu "domesticity and husbandry," Jean Fisher presented several reasons for Kikuyu women's opposition to the digging of terraces. Besides not knowing why the terraces were being dug, and disputing the value of terraces for their purported purpose, Kikuyu women told Fisher that digging terraces was very hard work. The women were not opposed to doing hard work, such as the clearing and hoeing that was necessary for cultivation, but they argued that terraces were not necessary for the production of crops. Those men who had not migrated for work and were resident in the reserves often refused to help dig terraces because "the gardens are of the women" (Fisher 1954:257).

Also, when the work of terracing was made the responsibility of each individual family, the terms on which women were able to get the help of their friends and neighbors for the construction of terraces on their land followed the customary practices of collective work. These practices required that the person whose land was being worked provide food and beer to their helpers. Previously such work groups contributed to bush-clearing, hoeing, planting, cutting reeds, weeding and thatching (Fisher 1954:235). With the colonial intervention, digging of terraces was added to the labor performed in cooperation. Not only was terracing considered extra, unnecessary work, but it was very labor-intensive and so required the heavy use of cooperative labor and therefore heavy expenditure. This meant that, as Fisher found, "the preparation of food and beer for the helpers makes much extra work, and a considerable amount of money may be spent in buying food for them" (Fisher 1954:257).

On April 14, 1948, more than 2,000 Kikuyu women demonstrated in front of the district commissioner's office in Murang'a against the Local Native Council's orders for terracing work to resume (Mackenzie 1998:164). The next month women in the same area also refused to engage in the government's grass-planting work. The chief had several women protestors arrested. When news of the arrests reached the surrounding areas, several hundred women again gathered at the district headquarters. This time they were armed with sticks and denounced the chiefs and the district administration loudly. Police beat them back and arrested dozens more. When their case came to trial on May 8, another large crowd of rural women protested outside. They were again dispersed with police truncheons (Mackenzie 1998:164).

The Murang'a women's terracing strike showed that gendered commoners' demands were opposed not only to the colonial government and settlers, but also to the politics of moderate African anticolonialists. Lonsdale notes the generational character of the division: "Another of Kenyatta's old KCA friends, Jesse Kariuiki, berated the young men for causing trouble between their political leaders and government. If they were 'worth calling men' they must stop complaining about women's oppression, 'give up pickpocketing in Nairobi' and dig ditches themselves" (Berman and Lonsdale 1997:421). While Lonsdale's generational differences were part of the division between commoners and moderate men such as Kenyatta, I suggest that it was rather the aims and objectives of each group which most sharply distinguished them from one another.

Soldiers' wives and other peasant women went far beyond the political demands of the Kenya African Union (KAU). The KAU men, such as Kenyatta, did in the end support the peasants' resistance against ter-

114

racing. But he and the organization he headed never fully embraced the Kikuyu commoners' radical rejection of the colonial economy. Moreover, the KAU'ssupport for the subsistence political economy extended only as far as their promotion of selected customary rites and relations that, to the exclusion of other rights, acted as a means of dispossessing women and concentrating power in the hands of fewer, wealthier African men. The KAU demand for title deeds for African landowners is one example of the stance of the organization against customary communal entitlements and for the concentration of power in wealthy men's hands. The question of "title deeds for some" versus "land access for all" was to constitute a major distinction among the anticolonial activists. And this was a highly gendered distinction, as land titles were almost always registered in men's names.

In this and in many similar instances in the 1930s and 1940s, African nationalist men made outright attempts to assert power over African women's fertility. This was not the whole story, however. Many men in the movement against colonialism supported women's autonomous initiatives as we have seen in the Murang'a terracing strike and the building of the girls' dormitory at Githinguri. The 1940s marked a period during which Kenyan men divided into two camps: loyalists versus freedom fighters. And among the freedom fighters was another division still. Some became male dealers who aimed to take control over land and female labor themselves; others acted as allies of women who were fighting for subsistence and the rights of universal access to life goods.

The unity of women and men during this period was noteworthy. Mass gatherings and rallies, at which protest songs were composed and performed, were evidence of growing connections between the various local resistance movements emerging at the time. The experience of the Murang'a women's terracing strikes was discussed at meetings, *barazas* (public meetings) and in public places. News of other women's struggles against terracing circulated throughout the colony. In the late 1940s the central Kenyan villagers also began to receive regular news of the resistance of people in the settlement scheme of Olenguruone in the Rift Valley near the settler town of Elburgon. With the Olenguruone struggle, the colony-wide network of local social movements was given a focal point that precipitated unified action for liberation from colonial rule in the 1950s.

# COORDINATED REGIONAL RESISTANCE AT OLENGURUONE

Until the late 1920s the white settled areas had provided a kind of frontier for many Kikuyu. The forest reserves, where the government hired men as foresters, sawyers and tree planters, were another option for land-less Kikuyu who migrated to find new land to cultivate. As a result of the 1937 Resident Native Laborers Ordinance that was passed after the Carter Commission's Report of 1934, the flow of Kikuyu to the White Highlands had begun to reverse itself. White settlers moved to reduce the numbers of Africans who had access to the fertile lands that allowed them to carry on an independent peasant livelihood. Tens and then hundreds of thousands of Kikuyu were evicted from the highlands under this Ordinance.

At the same time, as we have seen, African chiefs and large landown-ers in the reserves were trying to evict *ahoi*, or tenants, from their land. These big men petitioned against the return of thousands more landless Kikuyu families to the reserves. They appealed to the government to make more land outside the reserves available for the settlement of the landless. European district officers in the Kikuyu reserves concurred. The Colonial Office in London was also convinced that sending Kikuyu squatters back to the overcrowded reserves would exacerbate an already difficult situation. They urged the Kenyan administration to make suitable arrangements for their resettlement.

The Nairobi government succumbed to these pressures and established, in 1940, the Olenguruone settlement scheme. They set aside an area of land for the planned construction of a new village with strictly delineated rules dictating who would live where and what could be cultivated and how. With plans in the works for other settlement schemes at Makueni and Shimba Hills, the government hoped to deflect pressure exerted by Europeans and African elites, as well as to provide a token spillway for the fast-growing population of landless Africans. Olenguruone would not settle all the landless, only some 3,000. But it was viewed as an experi-mental first step in what was hoped to be a means of satisfying Africans' demands for land by opening up difficult and sometimes waterless terrain for African use.

With options closing around them, many Kikuyu headed into the reserves of other communities. They made new subsistence niches for themselves within the political economies of their hosts. Hundreds of Kikuyu families evicted from the highlands or squeezed out of the over-crowded Kikuyu reserves had settled within the reserves of other ethnic groups, including the Maasai, Embu, Meru, Kisii and Kamba (Kanogo 1987:108). Those who ended up at Olenguruone were originally from Kiambu, but had moved to Maasailand around 1930.

The relations of the Kikuyu with their hosts in Il Melili, Maasailand, were probably typical of interethnic relations in other reserves. The Il Melili Kikuyu exchanged labor and foodstuffs for the right to cultivate land. Marriage, trade, adoption and other reciprocal relations between the Kikuyu and their Maasai hosts were common (Kanogo 1987:108). After a decade of continuous utilization of land in Il Melili, the Kikuyu considered themselves owners and not tenants of the land in the Maasai reserve (Kanogo 1987:110). They operated within the customary land tenure system of the Kikuyu. They had no title deeds, but assumed, without Maasai interference, ownership of the land they occupied.

There were thousands of Kikuyu ex-squatters roaming between the reserves, the towns and the White Highlands seeking land on which to cultivate and survive. But European settlers were concerned less about these landless wanderers than about the independent Kikuyu cultivators in Maasailand. Europeans around Elburgon in the vicinity of the Maasai reserve were concerned that squatter laborers would find the option of moving into Maasai territory more appealing than accepting labor on white settler farms (Throup 1988:122). Neither the government nor the white settlers could countenance independent African farmers negotiating cross-ethnic alliances for social and economic activities outside of the control of settlers, chiefs and the colonial administration. Such alliances implied settlers' loss of control over labor and chiefs' loss of authority over subjects.

Therefore, the first settlement scheme, meant to accommodate dispossessed ex-squatters who were in need of land, provided instead the means by which the government could break up the independent Kikuyu community at Il Melili. The move was meant to arrest the development of reciprocal relations among Kenyans and begin to eliminate the option of "interpenetration" of the Kikuyu into other groups' reserves. The government presented the Il Melili Kikuyu as "landless" even though they had long been happily established in Maasailand (Kanogo 1987:109). The Chief Native Commissioner called the Il Melili Kikuyu "trespassers" in Maasailand and insisted that their removal to Olenguruone was "most generous treatment" by the government (Furedi, 1989:81).

In 1940, the government made an official request to the Kikuyu at Il Melili that they move to the new settlement scheme at Olenguruone. The settlement scheme site was bordered by a thick forest reserve to the west, the Mau Escarpment to the north, which made up the steep wall of the Great Rift Valley, and the Maasai reserve to the south and the east. The nearest town was Elburgon, some 15 miles (21 km) to the north, in the heart of white settler land and the home of the largest squatter market in the region.

Colin Maher was the head of the Soil Conservation Unit in Kenya between 1938 and 1950. He designed a means which purported to "scientifically" measure the carrying capacity of soils in Kenya and in this way determined the number of people who could be supported on the land at Olenguruone. In order to continue to deny Africans access to the vast amounts of land alienated for (but unused by) the European settlers, colonial technocrats such as Maher recommended wholesale dislocation of populations along with strictly enforced measures of land reclamation, including terracing, grass planting and culling of cattle.

Maher saw African agricultural and livestock practices as inherently destructive. These views were widely shared by settlers, administrators and missionaries (Carey 1953:16). Walter Carey, Maher and other such influential Europeans in the colony were able, through incessant repetition of the fallacies of poor Kikuyu land practices, to override the opinions of men such as Leakey who had rebutted the denigration of Kikuyu indigenous knowledge. The Europeans had an overriding interest in protecting their own claims to land.

From the start the Olenguruone settlers and the government had differing perceptions of the terms on which Il Melili Kikuyu were to move to the new settlement area. According to the settlers at Olenguruone, the European officer-in-charge of the Maasai reserve had informed the Kikuyu in the presence of two Kikuyu chiefs, Josiah Njonjo and Koinange, that the Il Melili settlers were to be given ownership of land in Olenguruone with no restrictions on its use (Kanogo 1987:111). Chief Njonjo had openly told the Kikuyu that those who had owned land in the reserve before going to the White Highlands would be eligible to own land in Olenguruone. Njonjo had personally interviewed the Il Melili Kikuyu to determine who was eligible. The government denied that any such rights were promised or to be expected by the settlers. The Il Melili settlers refused to leave their farms in Maasailand and in 1941 the government burned down their huts and moved them to Olenguruone by force (Furedi 1989:81).

When the Il Melili Kikuyu arrived at Olenguruone, they began farming according to their customary practices, including shifting cultivation, intercropping and the rotation of stock and crops. In this way, Throup observed, "the Olenguruone Kikuyu maximised the economic potential of the area and minimised the danger of land degradation" (Throup 1988:127). Olenguruone settlers had been resettled in an inhospitable climate. Only one crop a year could be grown and marketing costs were high because of the mountainous terrain and the distance from markets. Yet under the assumption that they had finally been given compensation for the expropriation of their original land, the Olenguruone settlers successfully adapted to their new environment.

The Kikuyu settlers had begun to cultivate their land in Olenguruone in 1941. For the first year of their occupation, the government left the Olenguruone settlers to cultivate as much land as they could clear. Through hard work and the application of precolonial agricultural practices, the Kikuyu farmers worked out a successful mixed crop and livestock farm system in the difficult environment.

During 1942 Colin Maher introduced his rules and regulations. He had designed exacting regulations for the production of subsistence and cash crops in precise quantities on the land he had demarcated for their use. Central to his regimen was that farmers would dig terraces on the steep hillsides, which made up a good part of the acreage in the location. Other regulations included the allotment of 8-acre plots to each male head of household. This entailed a drastic reduction in the area utilized by the farmers. Only 2.5 acres of the 8-acre plots were to be cultivated at any one time.

Aggravating the small size of plots, Maher recommended limitations on the numbers of livestock and the expansion of grass planting. What most infuriated the settlers was the manner in which the British sought to manipulate social relations among the Africans. Kanogo asserted that the scheme regulations "demanded a complete reorganization of people's agricultural practice and social set-up" (Kanogo 1987:112). Plots at Olenguruone "would be inherited by the eldest son of the wife on that plot and not according to Kikuyu custom" (Kanogo 1987:113). Sons were disinherited by the rule and second or third wives were also dispossessed of their means of subsistence in old age. The government then stipulated that

> the size of plots or allowance per peasant cultivator... should be such that they could support a peasant cultivator with a normal [nuclear] family. The government could not undertake to provide plots for abnormal families, who have to find means of augmenting the subsistence obtained from their plots (KNA AN 32/70, Native Agriculture, Olenguruone, Item 6H, February 1946:1).

A government-run Olenguruone subcommittee of the African Settlement Board recommended secondary industries that could provide Africans with the necessary additional income to "augment the subsistence obtained from their plots." Some of these included spinning and weaving, fruit canning and jam making (KNA AN 32/70:6). The women of Olenguruone took up none of these.

Regulations stipulated, in addition, that when adult sons married, they and their brides should move out of the settlement. The government accepted Maher's regulations and his "scientifically" assessed analysis of the carrying capacity of the land as a means to justify interventions to

regulate Africans' production (Tiffen, 1994:14). Maher greatly overesti-
mated the capacity of the soil in Olenguruone to sustain cultivation and
pastures (Throup 1988: 127).

The Olenguruone settlers persistently rejected Maher's regulations.
They argued that the land was theirs and they could decide what to cultivate and how. The government vowed to impose Maher's regulations
even if it meant evicting every settler from the scheme. The outright, total
refusal on the part of Olenguruone women to terrace one inch of soil was
a thorn in the side of Olenguruone planners:

> The matter of planning land use is not plain sailing, as a
> statement must be made on economic, agricultural and
> social policy. For example, the steeper lands above 12%
> could be used for grass or for arable crops by gradual or
> immediate development of bench terraces. On a slope of
> 25% an acre of bench terraces requires 300 man days and
> there is no doubt that these difficult Kikuyu people could
> not carry out this amount of work without a great deal of
> pressure (KNA, AN 32/70, November 23, 1946).

Olenguruone, with its rebellious and fiercely independent Kikuyu settlers, came to be known among colonialists as "the 'Sherwood Forest' of
western Kenya" (Throup 1988:123). It was believed to be a key location
on stock theft routes, where bandits redistributed stolen settler livestock
among poor Africans.

Beginning in 1942 when the government's intentions became clear,
Olenguruone residents began to administer an oath of unity to all men,
women and children on the scheme. With the involvement of the Kikuyu
Central Association, which was operating illegally at the time, the oath
was also taken by squatters on farms surrounding Olenguruone, and then
by Kikuyu in the reserves, especially in southern Kiambu from whence the
Olenguruone residents had originated. Squatters in the southern half of
the White Highlands were especially active in support of the Olenguruone
people. They organized massive labor strikes and refused to sign new contracts with settler bosses. By 1946, all Olenguruone residents had taken the
oath. The oath bound them to defy government regulations and to resist
the threat of eviction from the scheme.

In late 1946, the Olenguruone people organized a meeting in Naivasha
on the day of the arrival of the under-secretary of state for the colonies, Mr.
Creech-Jones. The meeting was attended by several hundred squatter representatives who adopted Olenguruone as their rallying cry against settler

exploitation (Kanogo 1987:117). A colonial official noted that 97 men from one farm had been arrested following the meeting, "for a deliberate flouting of the law of the land" (Kanogo 1987:117). The support network of Olenguruone residents was widespread and strong, but their material resources were waning. By 1944 the settlement area was not able to provide sufficient food to sustain the residents (Throup 1988:126). Squatters in the Nakuru and Naivasha Districts supplied the Olenguruone Kikuyu with food.

The steadfast intransigence of the Olenguruone Kikuyu forced the government to give narrow concessions in 1946. Major F.W. Carpenter, the district commissioner of Nakuru who was responsible for the administration of Olenguruone, held a meeting on October 16, 1946, to address concerns over the land in the scheme. The colonial development planners tried to diffuse rebellion by granting more land. Carpenter informed the 700 members present that "junior wives of polygamous households were to be granted their own shambas and married sons of Olenguruone residents, who had legally entered the settlement, were to be allowed to remain, to be treated as separate families and to be given their own five-acre shambas" (Throup 1988:128). Polygamous men were to have their holdings increased; yet the families were still restricted to the cultivation of only 2.5 acres at a time (Kanogo 1987:116). This concession did not divert the energies of the resistors. The government warned that if the Olenguruone settlers continued to ignore regulations, they would be evicted.

It became clear to the government that "the point at issue was that they wished to be regarded as compensated by land in Olenguruone for land taken away from them many years ago by the European. It seems clear to me that a political end would thereby be achieved and that with such a precedent larger claims by Kikuyus generally would again be pressed" (KNA, AN 32/70, December 10, 1946). In order to avoid this eventuality, the government stressed that the rules and regulations were the basis for government allocation of land to Africans in the schemes, and that if the rules were abrogated, settlers would be forced out.

Beginning in February 1947, the government began to carry out evictions that had been threatened since 1943. The district commissioner ordered settlement leaders to report to his office in Nakuru to discuss the imminent evictions. Instead, the resisters set out to see Jomo Kenyatta in Githunguri (Throup 1988:130). The following week, residents demonstrated outside of the Settlement Office. They chanted "The Settlement Officer must go!" and demanded that Europeans leave Kenya (Throup 1988:130). When 25 residents were served with summons in March 1947, they went into hiding in the homes of squatter supporters on nearby farms. By June, Olenguruone settlers who had been to the reserves came back and reported that the very terracing regulations that the Olenguruone residents had successfully rejected were being forced upon residents of the reserves. At that point, women in the Kikuyu reserves were on strike and had succeeded in arresting terracing work through their unity.

A new Olenguruone "oath of defiance" was devised by Olenguruone activists who began to administer it to women and men throughout the reserves and White Highlands in 1948 and 1949. Olenguruone women, such as Wanjiru Nyamarutu, were actively engaged in administering the oaths in Nakuru and Njoro. Nyamarutu was later to become a Mau Mau general (Kanogo 1987:143-145).

Over six days in July and early August 1948 the government demolished the houses and workshops of those who had been individually prosecuted. One man, Waweru, left a note pinned to his door:

> I want to inform you British that you are not to spoil the boundaries of Olenguruone *shambas* [farms]. If you just think since you came to Kenya you have never seen an African with a gun. I am the one to inform you that the Kikuyu have more power than you have with guns. Just wait until the year 1949 you will have to be sorry for the rules which you are giving us now and when it will be my turn to order you in the same way (KNA, Olenguruone Evictions, 1948, L&O/1/195/48, August 3, 1948).

The officer in charge of the demolitions reported in a telegram that

> most adult men ran away and left *shambas* when demolition party arrived... At *shamba* of Gathungu Karuga wives danced and sang derisively about gov't pulling down huts. A wife of Samuel Koina Getebi when questioned by Potgeiter said it was good of the gov't to get rid of the rats and bugs in the house (KNA, Olenguruone Evictions, 1948, Kenya Police, Signals Branch).

Between October and December 1949, the administration demolished all of the shops and houses. They cut down maize fields and confiscated more than 900 head of cattle and 2,500 sheep. Still the residents refused to leave. They hid maize, peas and potatoes from the police and built hollows in the ground in which they lived, covered by bamboo roofs (Kanogo 1987).

On January 17, 1950, the first convicted resistors were transported from Olenguruone to the Yatta Detention Camp. On their way through Karatina, a radical center of African resistance to colonialism, the prison trucks stopped to refuel. Crowds of Karatina residents surrounded the trucks and attempted to free the Olenguruone prisoners, who were well-known throughout the region by this time. Police beat them back. The Olenguruone people's story was told in songs that quickly circulated through the colony.

The song "Death of a Patriotic Woman" was sung throughout the 1950s to memorialize the imprisonment of some of the women and children of Olenguruone. Those who witnessed the transportation of the rebellious Kikuyu between January and March 1950 broadcast the news of the arrests and repeated in song the story of the captives' journey. The Olenguruone people were transported far away from their homes on trucks into inhospitable terrain. They were then forced to dig pit latrines and build roads with small shovels, picks and their bare hands. The song also recalls the fact that by 1950 in colonial East Africa, telephone lines connected commoners and were used as tools for the building of a regional network of resistance. The telephone made real, at least for an instant, the connection between the struggles of all the Kikuyu peoples.

> A telephone call reached us from Githinguri
> It was Jomo finding out
> If we had arrived.
> We told him of our great sorrow
> Because of the death and burial of Josephine.
>
> Great love I saw there among women and children:
>
> If a bean fell to the ground,
> They split it among themselves.
> Bitter tears were shed by women and children
> because they were tormented
> As they dug latrine pits. (Kinyatti 1980:56-57)

From February to mid-March 1950, there were twice weekly arrests of 50 people in Olenguruone, to be imprisoned at the Yatta Detention Camp. The prison convoys avoided Karatina on their subsequent trips. Before the last Kikuyu left Olenguruone in March 1950, they spread arsenic on the soil of those few residents who had agreed to follow the government's production regulations (Throup 1988:133).

Ben Kaurugo was a teacher in Olenguruone. In 1996 he and his wife Naomi hosted a First Woman team at their modest Ruiru home. During our interview, Kaurugo related his own experience of the evictions:

One day seven white men came to my school, all armed, and guarded by the black soldiers. And all the other teachers ran away but I was left there to confront the armed soldiers and white men. I was handed a book to put a signature, saying that I had agreed for the children to be taken to Yatta [Detention Camp]. I refused. The white man grasped my hand and wanted to force me to put my signature, but there was a strong young man called Kamau Wathaie who grabbed my hand so fast that I did not sign the paper.

So I was told, "Since you have refused to sign, we are going to arrest you." And I said, "I cannot leave the children. So if you want to arrest me, carry me away together with the children." Soon, in all this confusion, I heard people behind me singing (First Woman interview, Mwalimu Ben Kaurugo, June 7, 1996).

Mwalimu Ben,[4] as he is known, was arrested with the children. They were all later released. Ben soon thereafter joined the forest fighters and became an officer in the Kenya Land Freedom Army. In the 1940s and 1950s Ben and Naomi Kaurugo composed many songs about Olenguruone and subsequent struggles. Their songs built morale and unity among the insurgents. Their music and lyrics circulated widely throughout the colony. They informed, encouraged, and emboldened the gathering forces of Mau Mau. The song "The Olenguruone Struggle"[5] conveyed a sense of the Kaurugos' militancy and gendered and generational unity of the Olenguruone settlers:

Great were the cries among the Olenguruone children
Because of their suffering under torrential rains and horrible cold.
Children and mothers were crying together
Because their homes were burnt down. ...

Schoolchildren were left alone in the yard
After their mothers and fathers were arrested
And taken to Yatta and Nakuru

And all because of their own own land.

Teacher Kaurugo was also arrested
But he firmly told the police:
'I will never leave the children orphaned
Meet me then at the school
And they and I can go to jail together.'(Kinyatti 1980:53-54)

Olenguruone opened the floodgates for a massive escalation of Kenya's anticolonial struggle. Olenguruone activists cemented the solidarity of a widely dispersed and diverse set of local and national movements and organizations. The strugglers in Olenguruone also started the practice of giving oaths of unity to women and men, young and old. This was a new departure. Women not only took the oaths with the men, contrary to custom, but also began to administer oaths to both women and men. Women's militance was clearly and vocally exercised in Olenguruone and in the vast network of supporters. Mass oathing soon came to signify the total refusal of the population to submit to colonial rule in any form. Oathing also validated and encouraged women's identification and pursuit of their own demands within a militant colony-wide liberation movement.

# CONCLUSION

Between 1930 and 1950, Githinguri, Murang'a and Olenguruone women used their power over food, land, sexuality and their own labor to defend customary bundles of entitlements. This defense led them to challenge not only the colonial officials and collaborating chiefs, but also the anticolonial men such as Kenyatta, who appeared to be too little opposed to women's forced labor and loss of land rights. African women's land and labor had become central to mechanisms of imperial control. African women wielded immense potential power with their collective labor and their capacity to withdraw that labor. Rural women emerged as central actors in the networks of resistance.

Women and men worked together in gendered class alliances that laid the groundwork for a more thoroughgoing militancy during the Mau Mau war of the 1950s. These alliances produced tremendous unity and momentum among anticolonial activists and their movements. The instances analyzed above are only three examples of the many uprisings and struggles in which women engaged over the period. Women's organizations of resistance to a wide array of colonial policies and practices become more networked and militant over the 20 years to 1950.

Peasant women and men in each of these three cases together defined new, and redefined old, community institutions, such as education, initiation and oathing in a networked movement of social movements. Peasant women's concerns with circumcision, childbirth, marriage, food production, food preservation and trade made them aggressive in the defense of their land rights. All of these rites and relations were being consciously reshaped during the period by women and men, African and European, wealthy and dispossessed. Wealthy African men accorded themselves greater rights than they had ever had under customary tenure. The landless demanded a return to the practices of universal access to land and an expansion of women's land rights.

Women activists often defined the values and undertook autonomous action within Kenyan social movements. In the period reviewed, reserve and squatter Kikuyu began to find their local fights for fertility overlapping in a colony-wide and indeed a worldwide anticolonial movement. Helping to cement this unity were the indigenous social forms as they manifest themselves variously at the time. These included age-sets, intergenerational authority, collective work, food sharing, land sharing, markets, trade, dance, oaths of unity and song.

Just as the British written word inscribed female landlessness into the record of colonialism in various Kikuyu land inquiries, Kikuyu songs were the envelopes within which word of the struggles in disparate locations were carried from village to distant village. New songs were composed and sung as a means of communication and as expressions of resistance and the defense of subsistence. Mau Mau women were famous songwriters of the period and often sang in large groups on an impromptu basis. They adapted traditional and Christian songs to address the issues of the day.

In the derisive tone taken by many who defended white settlement in Kenya in the 1950s, a British member of parliament, C.J.M. Alport, proposed using song to propagandize Africans against Mau Mau and in support of the restoration of colonial rule:

All those who know Africa will, I am sure, agree with me that the main way in which ideas and impressions and news was spread from tribe to tribe and within a tribe was through the medium of dance and song. It may be that certain Africans would prefer to get their ideas in a normal European way, but there are an immense number who would get those ideas more quickly and clearly if they were conveyed in what I would call the African medium (Alport 1954:245).

Alport's proposal to employ "the African medium of song and dance" is yet another instance of the colonial practice of trying to use African custom to further the exploitative goals of imperialism. The main difference between the colonial and the indigenous practices of amalgamating African and European social forms was that the British attempted to produce these cultural amalgams in order to rule more effectively. In contrast, the African anticolonialists created amalgams in order to dissolve colonial rule.

Settlers and government officials had imposed on Kenyans the technologies and social hierarchies associated with early-20th-century capitalism. Aspects of the colonial political economy that contributed to widening the scale of Kikuyu anticolonial organizing over the period included the railroads and telecommunications system, as well as forced labor practices and labor migrancy, with its concomitant diffusion of Kikuyu into an East African-wide diaspora. There were ethnicized gendered class struggles at every point of the colonial "circuit of capital":[6] factories, farms, markets, railways, roads, schools, churches, villages, towns, forests, fields, rivers and hills. All of these spaces were the contested terrain of the colonial conflicts in Kenya. Each provided overlapping colony-wide networks. In these networks traveled laborers, unionists, politicians, social movement activists and those evicted in large numbers from the Rift Valley in the late 1930s and finally from Olenguruone in the late 1940s. The refugees and migrants carried with them stories of their suffering and resistance. They composed prayers and songs that bore testimony to these momentous events.

Motivated by attacks on land rights, the movements, strikers and strugglers of the period asserted a pan-Kikuyu and pan-African unity and solidarity. The missionaries' ban on female circumcision, the agricultural officers' insistence on terracing and the colonial settlement board's imposition of rules to govern families and farming at Olenguruone were threats to Kikuyu land rights. In organizing against these threats, Kenyans first mobilized popular support for an autonomous indigenous education and church system. The independent school movement was situated within and contributed to a wider, incipient liberation movement. Beginning in 1942, unity for this purpose was built and supported by Olenguruone oaths and antiterracing resistance. The challenge of defending the indigenous gendered commons (both the land itself and rights of universal access) had, by 1950, brought together hundreds of thousands of people across genders, generations and geographic locations for the purpose of recovering land and freedom and ejecting colonialists from Kenya.

## Notes

1. See the Appendix at the end of the book for a discussion of two opposing concepts of Kikuyu unity: solidarity of equals and solidarity of unequals.
2. See http://www.worldwidewattle.com/schools/uses.php.
3. The Kikuyu Central Association had been banned by the government. The Kenya African Union was a more politically moderate organization founded to replace the banned KCA.
4. *Mwalimu* means teacher in Kiswahili.
5. Composer unknown. This song may have been written by Ben and Naomi Kaurugo, both of whom are now deceased.
6. Nick Dyer-Witheford (1999) defines the "circuits of capital" as those integrated sites necessary for the generation of profit; including sites of production, consumption, social reproduction and nature. Waged and unwaged workers are exploited throughout this circuit. When the exploited unite, they are capable of turning the circuits of capital into circuits of struggle.

## ~ CHAPTER SIX ~

# LAND IS A BIRTHRIGHT: THE EMERGENCE OF MAU MAU, 1950-1952

## INTRODUCTION

This chapter begins with an examination of the nine-day general strike of 1950 that drew together numerous social forces and set the stage for the Mau Mau war. The chapter examines how landless rural and urban insurgents built on the gendered class alliances of the 1930s and 1940s to turn their collective energies toward breaking the male deals between the British and African chiefs. Renewed colonial efforts to alienate land in the soldier settlement scheme and assert new controls over urban and rural labor in the early 1950s facilitated a convergence of a multitude of localized African struggles. This chapter examines gendered class relations among African commoners during the 1950 general strike in which the main actors were trade unionists and market women. The 1950 general strike demonstrates the centrality of unwaged African women's labor to the subsistence of the community, to the continuation of the colonial economy and in particular to the pursuit of an increasingly militant anti-colonial struggle.

The chapter then turns to an analysis of the 1951 cattle dip protests by Murang'a peasant women and finally to a consideration of the earliest Mau Mau actions that led to the declaration of a state of emergency on October 20, 1952. The combination of a mobilized African population, new colonial restrictions on African trade and rising settler racism had created an explosive atmosphere in the colony.

In order to contextualize the events leading up to the momentous outbreak of the Mau Mau war in 1952, it is necessary to review some of the major changes that took place in the years immediately following the Second World War. These changes centered around the generational politics of land use. This introductory discussion inquires into the deep indigenous and exogenous roots of the conflict at the heart of the liberation war. I find new evidence of women's centrality to generating, organizing and sustaining the armed liberation struggle and the Kenya Land Freedom Army, better known as Mau Mau. Women's centrality to Mau Mau is explained with reference to the customary land relations that were revived, on a new footing, to unite militant anticolonialists for the liberation war.

Women were thoroughly integrated into the entire organizational network of Mau Mau. To a significant extent this diffuse network of Mau Mau committees and battalions overlapped with and was appended to women's long-established colony-wide trade, church, school, kin, age-grade, political and social networks. What has not been sufficiently explained are the origins of women's power, both within Mau Mau and in the face of African and British male dealers of the most brutal variety. This chapter begins to address this question by considering the patriarchal, but potentially egalitarian, democratic governing system of the Kikuyu. The following section outlines the postwar political economy within which the Mau Mau politics of land reappropriation were formed, and outlines elements of customary Kikuyu land politics. The remaining sections of the chapter analyze three instances of resistance that laid important organizational groundings for Mau Mau.

## WOMEN AND THE INDIGENOUS ORGANIZATION OF TRADE, GENERATIONAL POWER AND RESISTANCE

During the Second World War the colonial government encouraged Africans to clear and cultivate as much land as possible and to sell the produce to the government for the war effort (Ghai and McAuslan 1970:110). Chiefs were natural trading partners for the British. They had land and controlled the unwaged labor of many wives, daughters, servants, tenants and others. The chiefs became deeply involved in new business dealings with the British during the early 1940s. Many African farmers expanded food production during the period. But not all African farmers sold their crops to the government.

While a few prominent chiefs expanded the acreage they had under commodity production, a completely different expansion of food production began in the White Highlands. During the war, the government passed ordinances requiring white settlers to produce crops for the government. These included the Defense (Agricultural Production) Regulations of 1940 and the Increased Production of Crops Ordinance of 1942 (Ghai and McAuslan 1970:98-99). Maize, oats, barley, beans and coffee came under new marketing controls.

By 1939, a full eighth of the Kikuyu population was resident on the White Highland farms (Anderson 2005:23). These workers had begun to practice, on the alienated lands, many of the customary rites of clearing, planting and sharing land. With the war, many Kikuyu squatter men were conscripted into the army and women were left on the white-owned estates to support their families. Women worked together in order to do their own work and the work of the absent men. Sometimes with the permission of the white settler, but probably more often without, Kikuyu squatter women increased the acreage they had under food crops for their own use.

Some settlers who had not joined the army acted as wholesalers of squatters' produce. In the early 1940s they paid 4.90 shillings for a bag of squatters' maize and turned a big profit by selling the maize to the government at the "European rate" of 9 shillings a bag (Van Zwanenberg 1975:216). Many Kikuyu women in the White Highlands not only decided what to grow, but they often bypassed settler and government buying centers, revitalized precolonial trade routes and traded on their own accounts (Brownhill 1994). In the process of organizing this "own account" trade, women formed new collectives of producers and traders (Robertson 1997).

Kikuyu women's wide trade networks connected rural areas far and near with the urban centers. While a few African big men wholesalers in Kikuyuland and in the settled areas made more money than did the rest of the small producers, all Africans were paid at a rate lower than that paid to European producers. Consequently while chiefs and other African wholesalers turned a small profit, the autonomously organized subsistence marketing networks gained something more. They reconstructed precolonial interethnic alliances among women to transport foods from surplus to deficit areas or to local markets for distribution. These networks were vital both for survival and eventually for the launching of the independence war.

After 1945, the colonial government opened more African land for a new wave of European soldier settlement (Ghai and McAuslan 1970:101-102). These new settlers expected that cheap waged labor would be readily available. In addition, to provide the new settlers with a preferential place in local markets, the government introduced new restrictions on Africans' production and trade (Ghai and McAuslan 1970:113). Many Africans were devastated by these moves. Even loyal chiefs lost their businesses.

Demobilized African soldiers, who had been promised land, loans and expanded freedoms, were also bitterly disappointed with the actual postwar dispensation. Frustrations rose as prices and taxes increased while wages and opportunities for Africans decreased (Shiroya 1985).

The 1950s opened amid these and other new tensions. For instance, across the continent in Accra, Ghana, the Trade Union Congress initiated a general strike in January 1950, prompting the British to declare a state of emergency which lasted an entire year (Sutherland and Meyer 2000:30-31). The Colonial Office in London, as well as administrators and white settlers throughout the British empire, were alert to African anticolonial agitation as well as to the racist, separatist politics arising among white settlers in South Africa and Rhodesia.

In the 1950s activists in Kenya launched an ultimately successful armed struggle against the British and the African chiefs who collaborated in colonial rule. The tens of thousands of activists involved in the independent school movement and the Olenguruone struggle of the 1930s and 1940s were particularly well-prepared for the Herculean task of ending British colonial occupation. With the experience of these colony-wide mobilizations behind them, seasoned fighters faced the challenge of drawing together the diverse movements for a concerted assault on empire. What organizational forms helped unite Mau Mau for the armed struggle?

In 1950 rural women continued to organize within the independent school movement, traders' and other work networks, the nationalist organizations and the networked social movement that grew up around the support of the Olenguruone resisters. When the government ended its encouragement of African surplus food production, many chiefs and other large landowners lost their businesses. A few big men gained new privileged access to domestic and export markets, especially with the lifting of restrictions on African coffee production in 1943.

Peasant women farmers and traders in the reserves and White Highlands, however, had been less thoroughly integrated into the commodified colonial market, and so were not as negatively affected as were those large traders usurped by white settlers' extended control over markets. Peasant women continued, as during the war, to build regional food-centered trade relations that served simultaneously as channels for the circulation of news, songs and stories of struggle. Peasant women farmers and traders built on informal but widespread and long-standing networks. Others had their own organizations. British-appointed chiefs established the Kikuyu Loyal Patriots group. Members sought to defend and extend their own power and wealth by supporting British policies and pushing for title deeds to their own land.

The Kenya African Union (KAU) remained the moderate national-ist home of many large landholding men such as Jomo Kenyatta. KAU leaders campaigned for constitutional change to allow for the indepen-dence of the colony, and presented themselves as best-suited to take on the task of ruling the country. And because many of the poorest activists espoused demands for immediate independence, the KAU big men also worked to limit the incorporation of new members into the anticolonial struggle. They opposed mass oathing campaigns and gave KAU loyalty oaths only to "trusted household heads" (Lonsdale 1997:422). It was from among this group of moderate nationalists that most of the ruling elite at independence would be drawn.

Trade unions remained very active in the period. They pressed for the rights of workers and the unemployed and had members who took a more militant approach to the liberation of the colony. A group calling itself the *Anake wa 40* (the "40 Group," or perhaps more accurately, the "Warriors of 1940") was central to the move toward an armed struggle in Kenya. *Anake wa 40* was made up of men who had served overseas in the Second World War. They supported the Murang'a women's antiterracing strikes of 1947 and 1948 (Lonsdale 1997:421).

The *Anake* were landless and poor working men. They were artisans, trade unionists and junior members of the KAU. But the *Anake's* politics diverged from the moderate stance of Kenyatta and other large land-holding men (Lonsdale 1997:422-423). Against the express commands of the KAU leaders, the *Anake wa 40* began their own secret committee to administer oaths of unity including the Olenguruone and KAU oaths. The *Anake* opened the membership of the organization; they did not limit themselves to the inclusion of landholding men. They ran a mass oathing campaign that embraced the innovations introduced by the Olenguruone Kikuyu; that is, the *Anake* oathed men *and women*, especially from among the poor.

According to Frank Furedi, the *Anake wa 40* provided a "rough model" of what appears to have been a proliferation of autonomous or rogue oathing committees, which were believed to have been started by squatters in the White Highlands. Furedi noted that

> the new separate young men's committees reflected the grassroots pressure for action. The function and aims of these committees were not clearly worked out and they evolved in response to events. Unlike the old KCA [Kikuyu Central Association], the committees had a limited para-military dimension, such as providing guards for oathing

ceremonies. From the outset the activists demonstrated a determination to use force, if necessary, to achieve their aims. The Forty Group in Nairobi – an organization that sought to adapt the role of the warrior to the demands of political resistance – provided a rough model for the committees. The committees [in the White Highlands] had a direct if informal link with Nairobi. In Kariobangi [a Nairobi neighborhood], one of the strongholds of the Forty Group, resided many ex-squatters from the Highlands. These ex-squatters, who had friends and relations on the European farms, serves as ideal go-betweens (Furedi 1989:109-110).

The *Anake*, and perhaps these other young men's oathing committees, simultaneously drew on and transformed the Kikuyu age-grade conception. *Anake* were, in the customary age-grade system, those in the second grade of warriors, on their way to elder status, who had been circumcised for at least six and a half years, but were still unmarried (Prins 1953/1970:51-52). Certainly not all of the men in the *Anake wa 40* fell strictly into this category. But by adopting the term "*anake*," the militants took up the tasks of warriors, now not for hunting and defense of cattle herds but for the struggle against British colonialism.

The *Anake wa 40* were part of a generation that no longer had secure access to land. Members' main objective was to reestablish land rights. In doing so, they chose to defy elder nationalists' authority and take a different approach to the resolution of their grievances. They reconfigured the meaning and use of the term *anake* and introduced a "paramilitary dimension" to the independence struggle. In this light, the *Anake wa 40* could be understood to be attempting to re-create and complete the customary generational handover ceremony that was begun in the 1930 but was never completed (for one discussion of the interrupted *ituika* ceremony, see Cagnolo 1933:121). This handover ceremony customarily involved the succession of control over the central decision-making bodies of the society, including councils and courts, from one moiety to another. This was not a strictly generational handover, from elders to youth. Rather, each moiety represented one half of the male population, including members of every age group.

One reading of the allegedly aborted 1930 handover ceremony can be summarized as follows: the moiety that should have handed over power in the 1930s ceremony had taken power during the previous handover ceremony between 1895 and 1902 (Middleton and Kershaw 1953/1972:29-

32). Because it was convenient for the British to choose as chiefs men who had some standing in their communities, it is likely that many of the men who became prominent in the colonial hierarchy were of this ruling moiety. As noted in the previous chapter, the customary handover involved the cancellation of all new laws passed by the retiring moiety. It also required the settlement of all land and other kinds of legal claims. Neither of these was possible in the 1930s. For the colonial chiefs, whether or not they were from the actual ruling moiety, had made agreements and enforced laws that the British would not allow to be rescinded or renegotiated by a new ruling Kikuyu moiety. The British banned the ceremony, backed their loyal chiefs and thereby protected their own hold on African land and labor.

In 1930 the Kikuyu moiety system was not intact in its old precolonial form. The community was no longer so strictly organized into two basically equal halves that alternated rule. Rather, it was divided by class into a minority group of large landowners, many of whom were protected by their ties with the British government, and the majority, the gendered commoners, who continued to live within the shrinking space of customary land-tenure relations, or lived landless in rural or urban squatter settlements.

By the 1950s inequality among the Kikuyu was even more pronounced than in 1930. When the *Anake wa 40* revisited the issue of the incomplete handover ceremony, and sought to complete that handover, this did not necessarily involve a handover from the ruling moiety to the alternate moiety, as in days past. Rather, the *Anake wa 40*, and the Mau Mau battalions they inspired, sought to seize power from the British and the loyalist chiefs. The handover was to take place between the ruling minority and the commoning majority, who sought a return to the principles and practices of universal access to land. Chiefs and commoners had such strongly opposing interests, that this kind of handover could never have taken place without a major confrontation.

The differing manner in which land was used by chiefs and commoners underpinned their conflicting interests. As late as the 1950s European scholars wrote that the Kikuyu retained a highly sophisticated set of social mechanisms for allocating land and negotiating its uses (Prins 1953/1970). This was the case even though many chiefs and other large landholders, such as Kenyatta, were making increasingly exclusionary claims to land (Lonsdale 1997). In the quest to privatize land and get title deeds, the landed elite had begun to exclude those who customarily were welcomed by large landowners, such as *ahoi* (tenants). As we have seen, many wealthy landowners evicted their tenants because they might later lay customary claim to the land and therein prejudice the landowners' progress toward a title deed.

The kind of African land relations that suited the British were those that supported the authority and wealth of the chiefs. At the same time the British consistently withheld title deeds, despite African pleas and petitions to the various land commissions. As noted in Chapter Four, the Kenya Land Commission decreed that only those who could demonstrate exclusive use of land could be awarded titles. So the most wealthy land-owners typically reduced the use of complex customary land relations in order to maximize their private use of land.

It was the land-poor majority in the reserves who were likely to engage in the widest array of customary, indigenous land relations. It was peasant women who predominated in the rural areas, who produced foodstuffs on a customary basis, and who defended indigenous knowledge, farming and social practices most vocally and tenaciously over the first 50 years of colonial rule. In the absence of exclusionary claims to any one piece of land sufficient for survival, peasant women sought to share the land of family members and others. As such they retained the old land-sharing customs and reconfigured new practices. One such practice was that of "strip" farming. Farmers obtained from different relatives and friends any number of strips of land in different ecological niches (on river banks, for instance). There they planted different crops according to the ecological conditions prevailing. In this way gendered commoners built bonds of community by sharing land among themselves. Many also struggled in courts and customary councils of elders to resolve disputes over land. As noted earlier the land that wealthy Africans had appropriated from famine refugees during the 1890s was a matter that some clans sought to rectify as late as the 1950s (Kershaw 1997:61).

Without women's militant resistance, as in the cases analyzed in previous chapters, the Mau Mau war could not have been launched. But, equally, without the alliance between exploited and resisting women and men, the anticolonial movement could not have evolved into the Mau Mau struggle. The members of *Anake wa 40* were central to a new gendered and generational politics of alliance that informed the militancy of Mau Mau. The *Anake* supported the women's terracing strike in Murang'a in 1947, popularized the oathing of women and called up the spirits of the old politics of men's customary rule. In calling up these spirits, the *Anake* also fundamentally changed the character of the handover these spirits were meant to oversee. The new ruling moiety was united not by birth or circumcision set. It was united, instead, by the common experience of exploitation in the colonial circuits of capital. If the Mau Mau land reappropriation were successful, the new ruling set would be composed of women and men; it would consist of the majority, who were landless and exploited. The many political innovations of Mau Mau included this broad reconfiguration of indigenous institutions, meant to support the struggle for land and freedom *for all.*

Let us now turn to a consideration of the instances of resistance within which some of this organizational reconfiguration was taking place.

## SOCIAL ORGANIZATION OF THE 1950 GENERAL STRIKE

In 1950 a nine-day general strike coordinated by a network of trade unions and trade union congresses involved over 100,000 people. Waged and unwaged workers in the informal and formal sectors united to demand improved wages and working conditions and an end to forced labor. For some years the militants at Olenguruone and peasant militants across the colony had been calling for complete independence. Now, for the first time in a union context, demands for the complete independence of Kenya and all of East Africa were made. This chapter considers what enabled the wide range of participants in the strike to act together to close down the major towns of the colony to press their far-reaching demands.

During the May 16-25, 1950 general strike, African women farmers and traders exercised their powers to both withdraw their agricultural products from commercial markets and to divert these products into the direct, day-to-day sustenance of the striking workers. These actions by unwaged women took place against a backdrop of rising European racism in Kenya. Some Kenyan white settlers had themselves come from South Africa, where apartheid was imposed in 1947. Many other white settlers admired the apartheid system and sought to impose a similar regime of rule in Kenya. In a September 1949 meeting of the Electors' Union, Kenyan white settlers proposed "the creation of a new British East African Dominion under European leadership." Dutch settlers who fled South Africa after the Boer War (1899-1904) wished to duplicate South Africa's openly racist apartheid policies in Kenya. White self-government in Rhodesia (later Zimbabwe) was another model that the Kenyan whites sought to emulate. The Electors' Union demanded from the Colonial Office an assurance of the permanency of the white settlement in Kenya, the paramountcy of Europeans, and the "restraint of political advancement for the African until such time as he attains a sense of civic responsibility" (Singh 1969:239).

Soon after the Electors' Union meeting, Eliud Mathu, an African nationalist member of the Local Native Council, wrote to the editor of the *East African Standard* that the "Electors' Union's endeavor to curb political advancement of the African would be tantamount to a declaration of political war" (*East African Standard*, October 6, 1949, cited in Singh 1969:240). The Kenya African Union organized a petition to the British government opposing the "paramountcy of Europeans" in Kenya. Mbiyu Koinange carried it personally to London in late 1949.

Taxi drivers and others in the Transport and Allied Workers Union staged a 16-day strike in October-November 1949 to protest new bylaws that would revoke licenses from drivers who were illiterate, under five feet tall or without a letter of good conduct from the police. Several other strikes were staged in different parts of the country in the months before the May 1950 general strike. The unions were soon to unite with unwaged workers to take coordinated action.

The Labor Department reported at the end of 1949 that

> the steady growth of the working population, its development in sophistication, the increasing number of employers, and the wide variety of occupations all go to make the work of the Department responsible for peace in the industry anxious and exacting. This anxiety is not diminished by the steady progress made in the field of the subversive and anti-British element developing in a part of the trade union movement (Labor Department Report 1949:35, cited in Singh 1969:246-247).

Rumors of imminent boycotts were rife. Trade unions joined with unemployed workers to campaign against the government's forced labor legislation, the Ordinance for the Employment of Voluntarily Unemployed Persons of January 1950. A large union meeting in Nairobi on January 15, 1950, the day the Ordinance was to go into effect, attracted nonunion members who were also opposed to the forced labor legislation. The meeting participants immediately donated money and resolved to send cables to both the United Nations' secretary general in New York and the secretary for the colonies in London. The cables called the ordinance a "slave labor law" and urged the authorities to direct the Kenya government to repeal the law.

In January 1950 the Legislative Council also published a new bill, the Essential Services (Arbitration) Ordinance, which outlawed strikes in water, electricity, health, hospital, sanitation, transport services (including public transport by road, rail and port) and dock services including stevedoring and lightering, loading and unloading of cargo and dispatch of cargo to its destination. The Ordinance was passed in May 1950.

In February 1950 the government announced that the king of England had granted a charter to raise the status of Nairobi to that of a "city." The Nairobi Municipal Council planned a week-long celebration of the city's charter, which was to be presented to the mayor by the duke of Gloucester on March 30, 1950. The news was met with consternation by the trade unions and other organizations. They saw no reason that honors should be given to the mayor when so many workers lived in squalid conditions without services or security. Trade unions boycotted the celebrations. The *Daily Chronicle* of March 7, 1950, reported that

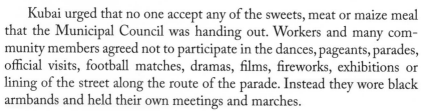

> the boycott was voted following a vigorous speech by Mr. Fred Kubai who described the celebrations as "a mere propaganda trick" designed to make it appear to the outside world that democracy was on the march in this country. "We see no change in our status," declared Mr. Kubai, adding that housing for the worker was still expensive, wages were low and even so basic a need as water was not available to him in adequate quantities. How could the workers under such conditions honestly join in the celebrations? (*Daily Chronicle* March 7, 1950, cited in Singh 1969:252).

Kubai urged that no one accept any of the sweets, meat or maize meal that the Municipal Council was handing out. Workers and many community members agreed not to participate in the dances, pageants, parades, official visits, football matches, dramas, films, fireworks, exhibitions or lining of the street along the route of the parade. Instead they wore black armbands and held their own meetings and marches.

In further detailing the reasons behind the widespread rejection of the city's charter, the East African Trade Union Congress issued a statement. It argued that the boycott arose "from the indignation of the workers and the trade union movement against the antiworking class, antitrade union, antidemocratic and racial politics and practices of the Nairobi Municipal Council and the Kenya Government" (Singh 1969:253). The Congress' statement noted that most workers could not vote. Africans' living conditions in the city were appalling. Education and health facilities were inadequate. And there were, the Trade Union Congress pointed out, plans under way to expropriate more African land to enlarge the new city's boundaries. The boycott also targeted the colonial administration's refusal to repeal the forced labor law or rescind the Essential Services Ordinance. The boycott of the "city celebrations" was almost total. Among those who did attend the celebrations there was, according to the settler paper, the *Kenya Weekly News*, a "lack of enthusiasm" (Singh 1969:256).

Then, on May 12, 1950, 39 squatter laborers on a Naivasha farm were arrested for being members of a secret organization with the aim of overthrowing the colonial government. This led to the first of many Mau Mau trials in the 1950s. Charges against 20 of the workers were dropped. But 15 men and four women were sentenced to seven years in jail. Mau Mau, as it was now publicly called, was banned in August 1950.

On May 16, 1950, the general strike began. On the same day the government published an extraordinary issue of the *Official Gazette* and added to the no-strike "Schedule of Essential Services" the following: supply and distribution of food, fuel, petrol, oil, power and light, and production and distribution of milk, telecommunications, posts and telegraphs (Singh 1969:271). The amendments made illegal the activities of a very large section of the striking workers, who joined from the formal and informal sectors to stop all activities in the city of Nairobi and other major towns around Kenya.

The banning of strikes in the supply and distribution of food and milk, in particular, was an admission on the government's part that Africans' participation in feeding the cities and towns was essential to the colonial economy. This was one measure of the women farmers' and traders' power, a power comparable to that of workers across the range of essential economic services. Despite the orders, the strike continued. For informal traders, participating in the strike meant not only closing markets and depriving Europeans and others of food, but also supplying meals to the strikers. The women who supplied food closed down markets. They collected and prepared food for thousands of workers. They transported the food via the striking taxi drivers or by head carriage. At the same time, public transport stopped, waged workers picketed and strikers held meetings and rallies. Police arrested hundreds and beat many picketers. The independent supply of food meant that the 100,000 African and Asian workers were able to stay away from work for the nine days of this historic strike.

The other activity central to the remarkable duration of the strike was the collection of money for the strikers' fund. This collection was carried out by unions but also by women traders' networks. Without these critical sources of food and money, the strikers' efforts could not have been so widespread, enduring or effective. The alliance between women and men suggested that the coalescing movement for liberation embraced the potential for a far-reaching social transformation.

What had drawn together the interests and actions of the waged, unionized, mainly male workers and the unwaged, nonunionized mainly female food producers and traders? The background to these gendered class alliances and the power of African women traders lay in the unity of producers in autonomous regional trade networks that women had maintained and strengthened during the Second World War. Though nonunionized, women farmers and traders were not unorganized. Women had long been reputed to be "very tenacious of their rights. ...they realize most fully what they are entitled to, and will show themselves more tenacious in holding to their rights than will the men" (Orde-Browne 1925/1970:76).

The contours of wartime colonial capitalism itself had organized food producers and traders into networks that were then marshaled in support of the strike. This creative power, wrought from colonial circuits but shaped by peasant women into a subsistence resurgence, was a major source of the organizational strength of the waged workers, united across trade lines, during the nine-day general strike in May 1950. Further, those who closed the markets and diverted food and money to the support of the strikers used their unity not only to *resist* but to begin to *replace* the commodified colonial political economy with a parallel, producer-controlled, renewed subsistence political economy. This move echoed the well-established independent school movement through which the Kikuyu had asserted their autonomy from colonial authority.

For food-producing women, the 1950 strike was a dress rehearsal for the feeding of the Kenya Land Freedom Army. It was an exercise in replacing service to the colony with the work of provisioning the liberation movement. The strike established a new organizational plateau in Kenyan struggles that featured solidarity across gendered lines and the lines of waged and unwaged. These urban-rural transformational gendered class relations of solidarity would be elaborated during the 1952 to 1960 war for independence. More fundamentally, the Mau Mau insurgency was the male expression of the coordinated regional network that sprang to life in Mekatilili's uprising in 1913 and Mary Muthoni Nyajiru's curse of nakedness mobilization in 1922.

One of the key social outcomes of the work stoppage and demonstrations of May 16-25, 1950, was that those who participated saw and recognized each other, their unity and their power (Brownhill 1994). Expressed clearly in song and debated at open meetings, this recognition was likened to "having one's eyes opened" to each other's struggles and to collective power (First Woman interview, Ruth Wangari wa Thung'u, July 24, 1996). This "awakening" was nascent in the 1947 and 1948 convergence of women's uprisings against terracing throughout Central Province and in Olenguruone.

In the July 1996 interview, Ruth Wangari wa Thung'u spoke of her involvement in politics in the lead-up to the Mau Mau war. She stated that during the Second World War when men were conscripted into military service,

> people did not think anything was wrong about this, because the eyes of the African person had not been open to see the evils of the white man, but as I was saying this is the time that people started realizing what was going on, the eyes of the people started opening, they saw that now the white man is exploiting us to the point of using us for his own selfish interests. And now from the years of 1947 onwards that African set out to stop the oppression of the white man, they set out to stop the misuse of the African by the white man, and as a result that is how the African revolution against the white man started.

In 1950 thousands were to be "awakened" as oath administrators broadened their reach to include large numbers of poor and dispossessed people in a campaign to enlist all the Kikuyu, Embu and Meru in the independence movement, along with members of other ethnic groups. Significant among the new recruits were prostitutes, who were to become crucial suppliers of guns, money and urban hideouts during the early years of the liberation war (White 1990a), and the taxi drivers of Nairobi, who had skills crucial to the operations of the anticolonial mobilization (Singh 1969).

## WOMEN'S RESISTANCE AGAINST "DIPPING DISEASE" IN 1951

The 1951 Murang'a women's anti-inoculation campaign is an example of one of the many struggles that were networked into coordinated regional resistance in the buildup to the Mau Mau war.

In the White Highlands, settlers continued to use the Resident Native Labor Ordinance of 1937 to justify the confiscation, or "culling," of squatters' cattle. This was an outright attempt to reduce the laborers' independent sources of income and security. Talk of the "dangers" of livestock diseases from Africans' cattle was shown to be a cover for efforts to make laborers more dependent; for many of the cattle that were confiscated were appropriated by the settlers themselves.

In a 1998 interview, Rachel Waragu Karutu explained how as a child she herded her squatter parents' cattle. When she was a bit older she left herding to cultivate a small plot of land. She cooperated with a group of girls to complete the tasks in each others' homes and gardens. Her brothers took up the work of caring for the livestock. She remembers that Mau Mau rose up after white men stole the Africans' cattle:

> After the [Second World] War ended there was a change
> in the country as the Europeans looked for ways to stop
> the Africans from looking after cattle. At this time, many
> Europeans entered in the country and they started to
> cultivate land. They employed Africans in their big farms
> and they used to make them work for long hours. ... I
> started hearing about the Mau Mau when the white man
> started to raid people's cattle and say that they should rear
> a small amount of cattle. People started by saying that
> they want to chase the white man away. But they used
> to discuss it secretly and declared that they had to take
> an oath (First Woman Interview, Rachel Waragu Karutu,
> July 28, 1998).

In 1951 in the Kikuyu reserves, it was cattle dipping that led women to rise up. Murang'a peasants' cattle herds were forcibly "dipped" by government veterinarians. The British had subjected Irish cattle to the same treatment: both cattle and Irish people died. The cows were run through a "cattle crush" which funneled them into a large pool of water. The water was laced with a trial vaccine against rinderpest. It was applied in such concentrations that cattle died *en masse* of what the Irish had dubbed "dipping disease." Why did the government compel Africans to dip their cattle? What were the consequences of the cattle's deaths?

Maina wa Kinyatti provides insight into the cattle dip campaign:

> In early 1951 the British gave orders for Africans' cattle in
> Central Kenya to be inoculated against what they called
> "rinderpest disease." The result was that the cattle inoculated
> began dying en masse. In response, the peasants organized
> antiinoculation demonstrations. Thousands of women from
> Murang'a stormed the inoculation centers – they burned
> down the cattle crushes and pens and chased away the
> inoculation operators. In retaliation, the forces of colonial-
> ism arrested more than 500 women and many others were

143

hospitalized with serious injuries from the police beatings. According to James Beauttah who was the KAU leader in Murang'a, the British were using the Africans' cattle as guinea-pigs to test their new vaccine. "When we sent the vaccine secretly to London to be tested," Beauttah explains, "it was discovered that it was poisonous and could kill both cattle and people" (wa Kinyatti 1980:60).

Women's perspective on the 1951 events and their demands for the protection of the indigenous political economy were recorded in the songs such as "Women of Murang'a":

We, the women of Murang'a, were arrested
For refusing to have our goats and cattle poisoned.
And because we rejected such colonial laws
We were thrown into prison cells...
*We beseech you, our Ngai,*
*Take us away from this slavery...*

We were taken to Nairobi after being fingerprinted
And on the way they kept asking us:
"Do you belong to this conspiracy,
Fighting for Liberation?"
And our children continued wailing
Because they had no milk to drink (wa Kinyatti 1980:60-61)

The colonial policies that led, in the reserves and in the highlands, to massive loss of Kikuyu cattle provoked various acts of local resistance. Because, as in the Murang'a case, the women acted so publicly, so loudly, so militantly and in such large numbers, it was impossible for the event to remain "local." The news of widespread arrests of women sped through the communications networks of the colonists as well as through the resistance songs of the women themselves. Livestock were of deep significance to the indigenous people as sources of food and nutrition, as forms of security against crop failure or other hardship, and as necessities in a great range of cultural transactions including marriage. The Murang'a women's defense of their cattle was, consistent with earlier eruptions, a matter of the fundamental rejection of the colonial economy and the defense of an indigenous alternative. As serious as this case was, experimenting with Africans' cattle was not the gravest of offenses the British settlers' sons were to visit upon the Kikuyu, as the next section attests.

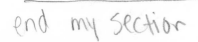
end my section

144

# THE MAU MAU RISE, 1952

Throughout the early months of 1952 women and men who had taken the oath of unity engaged in a campaign of sabotage against the white settlers. To the thousands of acts of everyday resistance in the form of labor slowdowns and derisive songs were now added increasingly coordinated acts of violence against chiefs, settlers and their property. This included arson in Nanyuki, cattle maiming in Timau and the assassinations of several African police informants. On October 3, 1952, white settler Mrs. A.M. Wright was stabbed to death near her Thika farm. Settlers were outraged and called for the declaration of a state of emergency.

Four days later, on October 7, 1952, the prominent Christian loyalist Senior Chief Waruhiu was summoned to the village of Gachie by the district commissioner to hear a land case (interview with Sam Waruhiu in Elkins 2005:381, fn1). Waruhiu was infamous for his part in forcing the women of his location to dig terraces. On his way there, his car was stopped by Mau Mau disguised in police uniforms. Some say the four were women, dressed in men's uniforms. Waruhiu was shot four times in the head. The driver and other occupants were left unharmed. With the assassination in broad daylight of one of the colonialists' staunchest supporters, Mau Mau made it clear that the struggle for independence was to be fought both against the settlers and against Africans who collaborated with the colonial regime.

The newly arrived governor, Evelyn Baring, moved troops into place and drafted emergency legislation. On October 20, 1952, he declared a state of emergency. The government asserted "special powers" to deal with the apparent rising in the colony. Baring, along with most men in the administration as well as most white settlers, believed that the counterinsurgency would have the colony "under control" within three months. They vastly underestimated the strength of the organization of resistance. It was eight years before the Emergency powers were lifted in 1960.

John Nottingham was a colonial official in Kenya during the 1950s. He expressed strong disagreement with many colonial policies in his seminal 1966 book on Mau Mau with Carl Rosberg. They noted that the emergency declaration

> did not head off an incipient mass revolution, but rather precipitated further mobilization for small-scale, violent resistance in the rural areas, along with increased violence in Nairobi. In this respect, much of the violence that occurred during the Emergency was not simply a

continuation of either pre-Emergency political tactics or the Government's security measures but derived from the conditions of the Emergency itself. The deployment of British and East African troops and the strengthening of the police introduced a new element of violence into the situation (Rosberg and Nottingham 1966:277).

"Operation Jock Scott" commenced on October 21, 1952 immediately following the emergency declaration. This was a sweep to arrest all known political leaders and activists. Over 180 Kikuyu activists, including Jomo Kenyatta, were captured in this sweep. Some in the government believed, incorrectly, that Mau Mau was a movement headed by Jomo Kenyatta and other Kikuyu politicians. With the arrest and removal of these "leaders" from the political scene, Governor Baring thought that the movement would fade away. Rosberg and Nottingham stated that for Baring,

> no political changes were considered necessary. It would be sufficient to bring about stricter control of the masses by reasserting "tribal" discipline through the Government chiefs and headmen, who would be given strong support. The economic problems would be investigated within an East African context by a Royal Commission. But within six months, the implementation of this policy, as the Security Forces slowly invested the Kikuyu rural areas, helped to bring about violence on an increasingly large scale (Rosberg and Nottingham 1966:280).

Instead of quelling Mau Mau, the emergency had removed the moderate elements of the nationalist movement. Harsh repression of the Kikuyu yielded new sites and necessities for organizing among the new generation of anticolonial activists.

Through the last months of 1952 Mau Mau strengthened the organization of their regiments and supply lines. Among the new generation of activists that emerged in force after Operation Jock Scott were the *Anake wa 40*, discussed above. Stanley Mathenge, who was to become one of the central commanders of forest fighters, was part of this group. Many of the men of the *Anake wa 40* had joined the radical trade union movement by the early 1950s. Their operations constituted one aspect of the multidimensional movement known as Mau Mau.

Mau Mau was highly diverse. It contained so many loosely coordinated and separate groups within its official and unofficial ranks, that it is useful to conceive of there having been many Mau Maus with many different goals, demands and agendas. Debates and some serious divisions between Field Marshal Dedan Kimathi and General Stanley Mathenge (and their respective battalions) suggest that the Mau Mau of the 1950s was a "many-headed hydra." Many Mau Maus emerged, melded and diverged during the struggle for independence.

The *Anake wa 40* adopted indigenous social forms to strengthen the anticolonial fight. Adriaan Prins, a Norwegian scholar who conducted research in the early 1950s under the guidance of H. E. Lambert, described the Kikuyu precolonial "territorial army" as well as other Kikuyu indigenous social forms that were adopted in part by the Kenya Land Freedom Army. Age-sets, or "regiments," in the precolonial days were organized on a territorial scale. Much of Kikuyu territory is geographically marked by the high ridges and deep intervening valleys that make up the foothills of Mt. Kenya. Different ridges had their own regiments and each regiment had its own captain. The captains belonged to an overall war council (*njama ya ita*), which operated on a consensus basis over a very wide territory to mobilize warriors, decide on strategy and discuss tactics (Prins 1953/1970:106-108).

The Kenya Land Freedom Army was constructed in part of modified precolonial forms such as those described by Prins. Like the original "territorial army" of the precolonial Kikuyu, Mau Mau relied upon seers, both male and female, who advised on the best times for attacks. Mau Mau regiments appointed captains and other leaders who devised strategies and tactics in war council meetings in the forests, just as precolonial *anake* had done. Men and women of a given territory – a ridge, a village, a white settler enclave or other unit – organized together on the basis of their geographical proximity or their sociopolitical association rather than, as in days of old, only on the basis of age-grades. Work-related organizations, from labor gangs to unions, provided new combinations of Kikuyu and others who often carried the unity of the workplace into the forest camps. Among those so organized were ex-soldiers, farm laborers, squatters, communal workers conscripted for forced labor, evictees, refugees and settlement-scheme residents. Walter Rodney noted that Mau Mau in Arusha was based in the settlements of Kikuyu economic and political refugees who had sought safety in Tanzania (Rodney 1973a). All of these groupings created by the settlers and administration were transformed into sites of collective work for the liberation of the colony and the East African region.

The very name Mau Mau has its own precolonial history. As noted earlier, Kershaw reported that the term Mau Mau was first used by the Kikuyu in the time of the Ruraya Famine, 1895-1900. The Mau Mau of the 1890s were young men who lived in the forest and attacked government food caravans. They were also known to have stolen from famine refugees as they fled their villages (Kershaw 1997:74, fn83).

In appropriating the experiences of the Second World War and of the British forces in Kenya, the Kenya Land Freedom Army borrowed military titles from the imperialists. They took on such titles as "General," "Major," "Colonel," Field Marshall" and even "Knight Commander." Some regiments used bugle calls to announce the commencement of their attacks.

As Marx observed of people intent on "making their own history," in periods of "revolutionary crisis they anxiously conjure up the spirits of the past to their service and borrow from them names, battle cries and costumes in order to present the new scene of world history in this time-honoured disguise and this borrowed language" (Marx 1852/1975:15). In this manner both indigenous and colonial social forms were called on in the organic emergence of guerrilla regiments in the forests and supply committees in the reserves and towns.

Guerrilla commanders Dedan Kimathi, Stanley Mathenge and Waruhiu Itote (who was known as "General China" before his capture and collaboration with the British), organized dozens of sophisticated forest camps, some of which housed up to 5,000 soldiers. Guerrillas coordinated across several regions. There were, however, great geographical and some political distances between the regiments. There were isolated units in the White Highlands and near reserves that had little contact with the semi-centralized structures such as the Kenya Parliament and war council organized by Field Marshal Dedan Kimathi. Many of the forest regiments had more contact via their supply lines with militants in Nairobi and the rural areas than they had with one another. The many heads of the Mau Mau hydra were fully apparent in this loosely coordinated and widely decentralized army. As in precolonial days, when the Kikuyu society itself was organized territorially, on a relatively egalitarian basis around the stewardship of the commons, so too did the Kenya Land Freedom Army take on these contours and organizational themes: autonomy, wide geographic dispersion and a shared commitment to the central goal of the reappropriation of Africans' land and freedom.

# CONCLUSION

Much has been written about what the Mau Mau were against. But what were they for? What kinds of social relations were embraced in the "land and freedom" they sought? Did the Mau Mau simply want "the deserving" to get access to pieces of land that could be theirs by virtue of title deeds and private ownership? Did they want "equality" with the British who secured their land through private individual tenure?

One significant indication of the extent to which many Mau Mau struggled for *universal* land rights is the general absence of demands for title deeds and individual security of tenure. Although Mau Mau declarations and songs record much of what the freedom fighters fought for, demands for title deeds appear to be completely absent. Songs did make frequent reference to land as a "birthright" of all Kikuyu, and all Africans. As such, everyone had a right to the lands customarily occupied by their own peoples. Equally common and carrying a similar significance were the references in songs, oaths, ceremonies, declarations and everyday speech to "Mumbi and Gikuyu," the founders of the Kikuyu people; the parents of the nine daughters who in turn originated the full nine clans of the Kikuyu. These parents of the Kikuyu people had left the land to *all Kikuyu*. To struggle for the return of their land meant to get the land back for *all*.

A further indication of the kind of political economy that the Mau Mau fought for is found in the popular boycott of European products that began in the early 1950s. Immediately after the Second World War, goods including beverages (especially bottled beer), cigarettes, biscuits and shoes were for the first time widely available to Africans in markets and small shops throughout the urban and rural areas (Cowen 1983:199). The items required the expenditure of cash and were a force in pulling people into waged employment.

By 1952, many Mau Mau vowed to boycott the use of European products including beer and cigarettes. Local brews and locally produced snuff and cigarettes were manufactured as an alternative to the imported commodities. Instead of using metal cooking pots and packaged cooking fat, Mau Mau encouraged a return to indigenous clay pots and the fats drawn from locally slaughtered sheep. These boycotts valorized the indigenous political economy. Indigenous beer, pots and cooking fats were produced and used by women. Boycotting the imported products meant at the same time fighting to patronize and defend the resources at the heart of women's subsistence work, market activities, collectivity and land.

The use of indigenous alternatives valorized the indigenous political economy. The small-scale indigenous industries that Mau Mau promoted during the boycott were to reemerge on a massive scale in the independence period. Elaborations of local technologies were again to appear both as a form of resistance against low-waged labor and as fallback alternatives for the increasing numbers of landless and jobless people. The demand for privatization of land was antithetical to the principle of universal access because it relied on the *exclusive* ownership of land by named individuals.

Moreover it was alienable. Universal access, or the return to some form of commoning, had always required the operation of *nonexclusive, overlapping* bundles of entitlements. Some Mau Mau songs attested to the desire for land for *all*. In the song, "The Kaloleni Meeting," we hear:

Pray and fight hard all you,
Children of African people,
So that we can seize our freedom.
We shall rejoice, all of us African people,
When the land is returned to us (wa Kinyatti 1980:36)

Significant in delineating the centrality of *land for all* in the Mau Mau struggle are some of the gendered class alliances that held together the insurgency. Hundreds of thousands of women actively engaged in this struggle. They did so because they themselves wanted the land back. The Kenya Land Freedom Army planned to provide widows and orphans with financial assistance and land after the war (wa Kinyatti 1986:38). Such priorities addressed women's rights to land through an extension of customary practices that allowed widows to have access. It was a demand voiced by Field Marshall Dedan Kimathi, the chief guerrilla commander, and by very many insurgents. Additional evidence confirms the fact that the Mau Mau vision of liberation prioritized *universal access* to land.

Tens of thousands of Mau Mau women and men refused to surrender to the British. The surrenders engineered by the British in prisons and detention camps involved a trade-off: give up the fight and betray others in order to preserve your own life and gain a claim to a piece of land. This trade-off and the refusal of many to accept it highlight the contrast between transformational land relations that many Mau Mau aspired to and the individualistic, exclusive property rights that the British sought to preserve and extend.

Perhaps the most eloquent indication of the fight for *land for all* was voiced by one woman who grew up as a child of Mau Mau. In an interview conducted in 1997, Mary Wambui, a squatter living next to Kamiti prison on the outskirts of Nairobi, described the commitment to the land that helped her and others live through the hardships of concentration camps, imprisonment and harassment by Home Guards. She recalled that

when a Mau Mau was killed, she took a handful of soil
in one hand and raised her other fist to the sky to say
that she was dying for this soil and for *all the generations*

who would live on this soil (First Woman interview, Mary Wambui, May 26, 1997).

This chapter has considered the ways in which colonial policies and practices in the early 1950s ironically contributed to Africans' coordination of large- and small-scale acts of resistance, including the general strike of 1950, the cattle dip protest of 1951 and the outbreak of armed struggle after the declaration of a state of emergency in 1952. In these instances, large numbers of women and men united to engage in increasingly effective action. Demands ranged from wage hikes to total liberation of the East African colonies. Old customs of generational or moiety handover ceremonies (*ituika*) provided one indigenous footing for the unity that emerged in Mau Mau. This unity drew together a new kind of moiety, one that consisted of all exploited women and men. This new moiety sought the reappropriation of the land, the settlement of all claims and the abolition of the laws that some from the previous moiety had negotiated with the British colonizers. In this way, Mau Mau expressed a striking new amalgam of indigenous and exogenous social forms, including moieties and generations on the one hand and workplaces, governing hierarchies, markets and the enclosed commons on the other hand.

During the 1950 strike, women and men, waged and unwaged, experienced their collective capacity to bring the colonial economy to a halt and, importantly, to divert their energies, labors and products into the support of their own autonomous networks and organizations. In this sense the general strike signaled the latent potential for an even larger-scale action through which the colonial system as a whole was challenged and finally brought down. The total refusal to terrace by Murang'a women in 1951, the year following the general strike, was a further indication that there existed the capacity and the willingness on the part of the colonized to join together, defy the law and defend their land and livelihoods. Finally, as Mau Mau launched the armed liberation struggle in 1952, they focused on colonial functionaries, white settlers and African loyalist male dealers who were together responsible for the expropriation of Africans' subsistence resources and the exploitation of African labor.

~ CHAPTER SEVEN ↜

# COMMODIFICATION AS COUNTERINSURGENCY: BRITISH AND HOMEGUARD RESPONSES TO MAU MAU, 1953 TO 1956

## INTRODUCTION

C hapter Seven begins with a review of key Mau Mau military actions in the 1953 to 1956 period and an analysis of women's engagement in the Kenya Land Freedom Army. It considers the unity and alliances that women and men constructed for the armed struggle and for survival under the harsh conditions of war. The chapter goes on to examine two means through which the British sought to break the unity of Mau Mau men and women during these hot years of the war for independence: (1) concentration camps and (2) the Swynnerton Plan. The chapter argues that these two policies were designed to commodify Kikuyu subsistence land and labor relations and that this commodification was central to the British counterinsurgency measures.

The British administration held over 1 million Kikuyu in concentration camps during the 1953 to 1960 period. The program was officially called "villagization" or the encampment of the Kikuyu in "protected villages." But the aims of the concentration camps were (1) to break the supply lines between Mau Mau civilians and guerrilla fighters; (2) to visit collective punishment upon the Kikuyu and (3) to destroy relations of collectivity that were key to both Mau Mau resistance and the subsistence alternative for which the Mau Mau fought. This system of colonial control of the entire Kikuyu civilian population simultaneously paved the way for the Swynnerton Plan.

In 1954 colonial official Roger Swynnerton devised a plan to reorganize African land relations and farming toward exclusive, private, male ownership and export cash crop production. The Swynnerton Plan involved a massive redistribution of land. Redistribution, or what the British called "consolidation" of land, was also used as collective punishment and furthered the colonial efforts to break up collectivity among the Kikuyu. The Plan entrenched the power of African loyalists, protected the settler political economy and laid the foundation for the postcolonial integration of Kenya into global agro-industrial circuits.

# MAU MAU WOMEN AND THE DEFENSE OF SUBSISTENCE

By late 1952, thousands of Mau Mau fighters had established bases in the forests of Central Kenya and the Rift Valley. The guerrillas' first major attacks came in late 1952 and early 1953. Two Mau Mau offensives on March 26, 1953 exemplified the coordination and militant capacities of the Kenya Land Freedom Army. In the first attack, 80 women and men raided the Naivasha police station and effected a dramatic jailbreak. They carried weapons and civilian clothing for the prisoners they intended to liberate. They freed 200 Mau Mau prisoners and "drove away a truck containing ammunition, rifles, and automatic weapons" (Rosberg and Nottingham 1966:286).

The second attack, at Lari, requires a brief introduction. In the late 1940s the government had alienated the original lands of some 600 Kikuyu in an area called Tigoni. The settlers wanted the Tigoni land for a sports club. The administration offered the Tigoni residents land in Lari as compensation. Many refused to move and were eventually forcibly evicted. Luka Wakahangare, who had at one time been chief in Tigoni, agreed to move to Lari. He engineered the allocation of large portions of Lari land to his own extended family. His machinations entailed leaving up to one-third of the Tigoni residents landless (Anderson 2005:142-150). The Lari area had also been a site of refuge for some of the many squatters who were being evicted from the White Highlands at the time. The struggle to control the Lari land consequently concerned many more people than the 600 original Tigoni residents. For those dispossessed, Luka Wakahangare was "the root and symbol of all their troubles" (Rosberg and Nottingham

1966:290). Luka was clearly against the Mau Mau. In 1953 he supported the siting of a Homeguard police post in Lari, one of the first such posts in Kiambu District.

On the same day that the Naivasha jailbreak was being executed, Mau Mau coordinated an attack on loyalist ex-chief Luka Wakahangare and the village of Lari. Mau Mau fighters, most of whom were from the Lari area, killed 97 people including Wakahangare, his family and other loyalist chiefs. After the attack, British and Africans soldiers and local police officers launched a reprisal attack and massacred over 400 Mau Mau fighters and civilians in the area (Elkins 2005:45).

While not even an inquiry was made into the reprisal attacks on civilians after Lari, on April 13, 1953, the committal proceedings for the first Lari suspects began. Trials were held at a new courthouse constructed on the site of the demolished Githinguri Teachers' Training College. Barbedwire holding pens were constructed to contain the prisoners. Gallows were built on the College grounds. Nineteen trials were held; 309 women and men were accused of murder; 136 were convicted and 71 men were hung at the gallows at Githinguri between October 1953 and June 1954. Governor Baring was "embarrassed" by the figures: they were too low. He reportedly "did his best to avoid publicizing them for fear of renewed criticism of Kenya. He had hoped for *more hangings*, and seemed disappointed that the legal machinery had not managed to *achieve better results*" (Anderson 2005:175, emphasis added). The Naivasha jail break and the Lari massacre in 1953 took place just as Jomo Kenyatta's trial was wrapping up in the remote town of Kapenguria. Kenyatta was one of the "Kapenguria Six" who were charged with being leaders of Mau Mau with the intent of overthrowing the lawful government of Kenya. But as discussed in earlier chapters, Kenyatta was a politically moderate reformer. He sought a smooth transition to an independent Kenya in which an African elite ruled, owned the large farms and benefited from the cheap labor of the majority of peasants and landless people.

Witnesses against Kenyatta were bribed to testify that he had spoken widely about armed insurrection. Some later confessed their perjuries (Delf 1961:191). Evelyn Baring's biographer claimed in 1978 that Governor Baring himself had taken £20,000 from his emergency fund to bribe Judge Thacker, who was flown in from England for the trial (Douglas-Home 1978, cited in Elkins 2005:40). In truth, Kenyatta opposed the *Anake wa 40* and the Mau Mau, as he repeatedly said in public (Kenyatta 1968:61-62). In his closing remarks Kenyatta's defense counsel, Dennis Lowell Pritt, revealed how far Kenyatta was from the armed militancy of Mau Mau:

You have to prove something grave and terrible, that the accused participated in a terrorist organization, whereas there is very substantial evidence that the body in which they [Kenyatta and the co-accused] are most prominent – the Kenya African Union – is a plain and outspoken enemy of that organization [Mau Mau] (cited in Kenyatta 1968:60).

On April 8, 1953, Judge Thacker delivered a guilty verdict and sentenced the "Kapenguria Six" to the maximum sentence, exile in a remote spot in Kenya for life plus seven years hard labor. Rosberg and Nottingham noted that

just as the previous generation of administrators had hoped that the judgment of the [1934] Kenya Land Commission would produce a final and permanent settlement of the land question, so too their successors hoped that by directly attributing responsibility to these six there would be a final and permanent settlement of the "Mau Mau" question. It could be proved, so the Administration argued, that a small coterie of desperadoes had attempted to pervert Kikuyu traditions for their own criminal ends (1966:281).

Kenyatta was safely out of the way. He was kept in British custody until he was needed to be the moderating force in negotiations for independence in 1960 and 1961. After Kenyatta's arrest Mau Mau only grew stronger. The power of Mau Mau lay in the unity of hundreds of thousands of guerrilla and civilian freedom fighters who had sworn to fight to the death. This unity was sealed by oaths, which, along with age-grades, trade relations and kinship, were important sources of social cohesion.

But not all age-grades or kin networks united in Mau Mau. In fact, many families were divided. Many Homeguard husbands had Mau Mau wives. Roise Wanjiru spoke of her own experience in a 1998 interview:

We used to cook food to take to the forest. When we were informed that the Mau Mau were in the vicinity we would prepare food. This used to be done by those people who were working with the Mau Mau. We used to prepare food and give it to someone who would carry it secretly up to the forest. If one did not want the other members of the family to know that she was associated with the Mau Mau, she had to take the food which she had prepared secretly to the people for delivery to the forest (First Woman interview, Roise Wanjiru, August 8, 1998).

Wanjiru's husband did not support the freedom fight: "he did not belong to it and I belonged to it, but he was not aware. He discovered this later." Wanjiru's husband "observed that those people who were associated with Mau Mau were too [very] friendly to me and we used to talk a lot and I used to be on their side in a discussion." In 1958, when he discovered her sympathies, Wanjiru's husband divorced her. She moved to Kamae, a squatter village situated on Jomo Kenyatta's massive land holding in Kiambu, where she still lived when interviewed in 1998. Life was especially precarious for such women. We shall revisit Roise Wanjiru in Chapter Ten to see how many Mau Mau women persevered in continuing the struggle for land and freedom throughout the postcolonial period.

Colonial social forms also lent themselves to the unity forged among the Mau Mau. The labor gangs on white settler plantations and in the reserves exemplify the ways in which the colonialists drew groups of Kikuyu together into one organization to work in unity for one purpose. Many laborers, so organized, turned this unity toward another purpose: Kenyan independence through armed struggle.

The British responded with ultimate force. General George Erskine began in May 1953 to reorganize the armed forces for an all-out assault on the Mau Mau. The troops arrayed under Erskine's command included three British battalions, six battalions of King's African Rifles, the Kenya Regiment (a volunteer force of several thousand white settlers), an artillery battery, an armored car squadron, Royal Air Force squadrons of Vampire jets and heavy Lincoln bombers, a Homeguard force of some 20,000 armed African men, the Kenya Police Reserves and the police Special Branch (Anderson 2005; Elkins 2005).

A comprehensive list of the battles that took place during the Mau Mau war has not here been reconstructed from the massive literature describing the details of the fighting (Kinyatti 1986; Wanjau 1983/1988; Odhiambo and Lonsdale 2003; Itote 1967; Likimani 1985; Njama 1966; W. Otieno 1998; Furedi 1989). In summary, however, it can be noted that through 1953, the Kenya Land Freedom Army launched hundreds of attacks on Homeguard posts, police stations, settler farms and loyalist targets throughout the country. In Murang'a especially at the end of 1953, Mau Mau assailed Homeguard posts on an almost daily basis.

In 1954 Operation Anvil and the concentration camps, both detailed below, had the effect of virtually cutting Mau Mau's urban supply lines. Erskine's men began to make more frequent and more deadly counterattacks against the forest fighters. By October 1954, Erskine's forces were killing an average of 600 Mau Mau a month (Anderson 2005:269). The Homeguards, police and other counterinsurgent forces also launched frequent attacks on the civilian population. Sometimes these attacks came in the form of outright massacres, such as the killing of over 100 people in Kiruara in November 1952, hundreds in Mununga in 1953, several hundred more in Kandara, and 27 in Nyeri in 1954 (Elkins 2005:51, 72-73, 79). At other times, collective punishment was employed, such as the confiscation of livestock or the imposition of hard labor in the concentration camps (Anderson 2005).

At a Kenya Regiment headquarters in Thigio in southern Kiambu, women detainees were forced to bury those Mau Mau suspects who had been tortured to death or executed. Beatrice Gatonye described the burial detail she endured: "In Thigio, trenchlike graves were dug in rows, and dead bodies would be laid in them. When one was full, it would be covered, and we would go on to the next" (Gatonye interview August 9, 2003, in Elkins 2005:255). At the nearby Ruthigiti Homeguard post, Mau Mau suspects from the concentration camps were rounded up and tortured. Esther Muchiri was one of many arrested one day in 1954. She was brought to Ruthigiti and stripped naked.

We were beaten the whole day until evening, when we were separated from the men, who were ordered to sit a distance away with their hands cuffed together. Then the interrogators started to squeeze their private parts with a pair of pliers. There was only a short distance between where they were and ourselves. I even saw one of them being hit on the face, a blow that sent him sprawling down unconscious. A whole bucket of water had to be poured on his body to revive him. The same evening, the men were loaded onto a vehicle and driven away. We were to learn the following morning that all of them had been executed. That night all of the women including myself were divided among the Home Guards and raped. Even this lady who was eight months pregnant was not spared. We were raped throughout the night. The following morning we were anxious to know the fate of the men. I remember asking the same pregnant woman what happened to our men after they were castrated. She pointed to a vehicle which was a short distance away. The bodies of our men lay inside. They had already been killed (Muchiri interview, August 13, 2003, in Elkins 2005:256-257).

Esther and the other women were then ordered to bury the men. Homeguards constantly harassed, arrested, detained, tortured and raped civilian Mau Mau suspects in the concentration camps. Rape by Homeguards was pervasive (Elkins 2005:254). Hundreds of women were forcibly married to Homeguards. In a 1998 interview, Muthoni wa Gakuhe remembered that

> the Homeguards forced women to marry them. There were many rapes. Some women even voluntarily married Homeguards in order to escape being beaten and being forced into communal labor. But most were forced marriages. Other women ran away to escape marrying Homeguards (First Woman interview, Muthoni wa Gakuhe, April 23, 1998).

Muthoni added:

> After the emergency most of these marriages broke. Only a few remained. Many had had children. So most left and remarried later. Some went back to their original husbands, because they had already been married before the Emergency. But then, many of these marriages broke too.

To continue and exacerbate this torture, some Homeguards visited men's prisons to make announcements over the public address system to the effect that so-and-so's wife was pregnant with loyalist's blood (Wanjau 1983/1988). Under these siege conditions in the concentration camps, which lasted for some eight years, Mau Mau women's steadfast work in supplying and pursuing the war against the British and the Homeguards was astonishing and heroic.

About 50,000 men joined the guerrilla fighting forces in the forests, with thousands more ready to join when called up. An estimated 2,500 women also went to the forest. While the Homeguards used nakedness as part of their torture regime against Mau Mau suspects, the freedom fighters also employed nakedness in their insurgency. Contrary to the humiliation associated with Homeguards' stripping of suspects, Mau Mau used nakedness as a strength and as a symbol of their total commitment to the liberation of the country. One Mau Mau pledge asserted:

> On my honour, and before *Ngai* [God] and many witnesses
> – some of whom are now dead – I stood naked, held soil
> in my right hand, and bit the chest of a ram seven times.
> I swore by Githathi, and by the names of our ancestors,
> Gikuyu *na* Mumbi, that I would be in the service of my
> compatriots and country until I die (Kinyatti 1986:112).

Ruth Wangari wa Thung'u stated that during Mau Mau, nakedness was used "as a disguise":

> We would remove our clothes, so that in the dark, you could
> not be seen because you are dark and you have removed
> your clothes and therefore you were able to move a very
> long distance before the colonialists or security forces saw
> you. Even passing in their camps with your naked body,
> you would be carrying your clothes, maybe one person
> would be carrying them; nobody would notice you (First
> Woman interview, July 16, 1994).

Tens of thousands of Mau Mau women risked arrest, torture and execution by engaging in action from inside the concentration camps. A Mau Mau woman interviewed by Maina wa Kinyatti in 1978 stated that

> the entire success of the Mau Mau struggle depended
> heavily on the peasant women. They provided food, stra-
> tegic information, as well as guns and ammunition (which
> they stole from the enemy soldiers) to the guerrilla fight-
> ers. It was also their main duty and responsibility to trans-
> port all supplies to the front (Kinyatti 1986:125).

The landless were more likely than the landed to side with Mau Mau. Those with large landholdings to protect often joined the Homeguard. Some who did not have land placed their bets on a British victory and joined the Homeguards as well. But the majority of Kikuyu joined Mau Mau and in their different ways engaged in the struggle. Children learned early how to keep their parents' secrets and how to use coded language to pass messages (First Woman interview, Gakuhe wa Kinyatti, April 23, 1998; First Woman interview, Mary Wambui, May 26, 1997). Some elders, especially women, were seers who provided the fighters with spiritual guidance. Many more elders cared for children whose parents were in prison, in the forest or dead. They watched carefully the movements of Homeguards and troops and passed on this intelligence via the supply lines to the forests. The elders were also keepers and users of cultural and historical knowledge – clan and lineage information – oral histories, songs, prayers, myths and riddles. Such elders were highly revered by many Mau Mau.

To the 34,000 or more women who were imprisoned in the 1950s we must add the 500,000 or more who survived within the concentration camps for up to eight years (Elkins 2005). Many of these women engaged in supplying the forest fighting forces. Without their supplies, the war would not have been possible. Mau Mau formed women's committees for the prosecution of the war. They constructed the committees on the basis of customary women's councils, or *kiamas* (Hobley 1929/1970:274). A Mau Mau woman from Nyeri described how these committees organized the delivery of supplies to the forest:

> In every ridge or village, a prominent, able, committed and trustworthy woman or man was appointed to be the KLFA [Kenya Land Freedom Army] representative in the village. She would be authorized to organize a Mau Mau village committee to help her coordinate the activities of the movement in that ridge. In particular, the committee was responsible for supplying guerrillas with food, clothing, medicines, weapons, ammunition and strategic information ...
>
> After the food was prepared, a few trusted women, usually unmarried young women who had taken the Batuni Oath [fighting oath], were selected to carry the supplies to a strategic point where other women would be waiting. They would give these items to the new group of women, and then return to their village. The other group would transport these items to another strategic point where they would be relieved by another group, until the items reached the front. It was a risky task, but it was our duty to support the movement (Kinyatti 1986:126).

Presley reported the testimonies of women who drew a similar picture of women's work in the Mau Mau war:

Women did, indeed, provide a backbone for Mau Mau. Since the women's chain of command had been established as early as the 1940s, the leadership in the hierarchy knew the degree of commitment of women in the entire district and had an efficient means of increasing the numbers of women who were associated with Mau Mau. They were also able to acquire necessary items quickly. When the freedom fighters took to the forests, this network was already in full operation. The funnelling of supplies and the arrangement of safe hiding places became women's responsibility *because of their superior organization.* Former women activists explained the operation of the network in great detail. Each district had a central committee that was responsible for arranging safe places and smuggling supplies. One woman was chosen to be responsible for the coordination of women's activities, it was she who was contacted by the central committee and told when supplies were needed. She would then contact her division leaders and they obtained whatever was required from women under their commands (Presley 1992:131, emphasis added).

Women had organized previously for customary rites, for labor both waged and unwaged, for regional subsistence trade, for the raising of funds to build the Githinguri girls' dormitory, for the operation of the independent school system and for protests and strikes. Now in the 1950s women were explicitly organized into the *colony-wide* Mau Mau networks. As noted above, women were seers (Kinyatti 1986:49). Women fought in the forests. Many escaped from the concentration camps, where they were abused by the Homeguards. Others fled forced marriages to Homeguards. In 1953 Wanja wa Gitonga wrote to Dedan Kimathi to explain why she had come to the forest:

This is exactly what happened: a Homeguard called Muhindi sent his brother, Karangui wa Kariuki, to try and persuade me to marry him, but I refused because I didn't know him. I was also not in love with him. After I rejected his marriage proposal, Muhindi wrote a letter to my father telling him that we had agreed to marry, which was a lie. When they finally met, my father agreed to receive dowry from Muhindi despite my strong objection. He was given shs. 2,000. I decided to come to the forest in protest. I had resolutely decided not to be married to my enemy, the enemy of my country. I entered the forest on 25 September 1953 (Kinyatti 1980:90).

Kimathi wrote a letter of recommendation that Hannah Wamuyu be allowed to join the armed forces:

Hannah Wamuyu is an educated and intelligent girl. She loves her country and people very much. Although many educated women cannot be trusted nowadays, Wamuyu can be. She is a committed and serious patriot. She is a trained nurse; so she can help in reorganizing our hospitals. She can also type. I am therefore recommending that she be allowed to join the Liberation Army (Kinyatti 1980:76).

Literate fighters were especially prized. Kimathi set up a complex archive of Mau Mau documents. Mau Mau field secretaries would write down who was killed, wounded or maimed and the events of the war in order to compensate and reward those who fought when victory was achieved. The field secretaries kept records of the items taken from peasants so that they could also be compensated after the war (Kinyatti 1986:24-25). The Mau Mau forest archives were captured and destroyed by the British. The Mau Mau songs collected by wa Kinyatti were from archives that were not destroyed: the participants' memories.

The district administration called women who engaged in radical politics "prostitutes." Describing a rally in Nyeri on July 26, 1952 the district commissioner wrote: "Over 20,000 men, women and children attended. KAU insinuated over 40 bus loads of Nairobi thugs and prostitutes, who were clearly under instructions to excite the crowd" (cited in Corfield 1960:136-137). Many prostitutes did join Mau Mau; but most of the tens of thousands of Mau Mau women active during the 1950s were not prostitutes. Most colonial officials and many scholars uncritically repeated the characterization of Mau Mau women as prostitutes, or as somehow depraved and in need of psychological "rehabilitation." Many African men took this stance as well, from the nationalist groups that stripped (and continue in the 21st century to strip) urban women accused of being prostitutes, to the queen's representatives in the reserves and the cities, the chiefs and senior chiefs (White 1990a; Elkins 2005). In contrast, it is among the Mau Mau that one finds men who instead related to their "sisters-in-arms" as providers of necessary food, information, medicine and sometimes ammunition and transport (White 1990a; Kinyatti 1980, 1986, 1991; Presley 1988, 1992).

Urban guerrillas, including prostitutes, were important sources of crucial supplies and services for the forest fighters. Monica Njeri remembered in a 1996 interview that women who lived in Nairobi:

> supplied Mau Mau with food, medicine, clothing, guns and bullets. I do not know them by name, but I have ever heard about them. There was coordination between the women in town and in rural areas and the Mau Mau in the forest. Some women would be sent from the village to Nairobi to get those things. Or women in Nairobi would come to the village and bring these things to the women in the village. The women in the village knew how to get to the Mau Mau in the forest so the city women would deliver supplies to village women and the village women would pass them on to the forest. That is how the coordination worked (First Woman Interview, Monica Njeri, August 25, 1996).

Many Mau Mau who were not yet deployed to the forests bided their time in the city. There they undertook assassinations, the collection of funds and other activities until such time as they were called up for active forest fighting. Other jobs performed in the cities included forging documents, counterfeiting money, communicating abroad, supplying arms or the materials needed for the manufacture of arms, stockpiling imported items, medicines and stationery supplies and delivering all these items to the forest camps. When men and women in the city were called up, they entered into a secretive journey to the forest, assisted by prostitutes, taxi drivers, railway workers and peasant women in the villages who hid them and escorted them to the forests' edge. For the Mau Mau, Nairobi was the heartbeat of the enemy. There was a certain proximal intimacy between enemies in this concentrated urban space. This intimacy was to be torn apart by Operation Anvil.

## OPERATION ANVIL AND THE SWEEP OF NAIROBI

On April 24, 954, some 20,000 British and African troops and Homeguards sealed off Nairobi. The city was besieged, with every road blocked, barbed wire enclosures erected and machine gunners positioned on rooftops. For a month Nairobi residents were subjected to arrests, detention, searches, harassment, rapes, beatings, deportations, repatriations and imprisonment. Every Kikuyu in the city was screened or interrogated. By May 26, 1954, when Operation Anvil ended, 24,100 Kikuyu men, nearly half the Kikuyu population of Nairobi, were detained, in effect imprisoned without trial. Some 10,000 women and children, most of them "waifs," were repatriated to the rural reserves (Anderson 2005:205-205).

Many Nairobi workers and residents were sent to Manyani and MacKinnon Road detention camps (Kinyatti 1980:103). It was hard for a Kikuyu to avoid arrest in Nairobi in 1954. Each Kikuyu was required to carry five identity documents at all times: "an employment registration card; a card setting out his history of employment; an identity card; a poll-tax receipt; and a Kikuyu Special Tax receipt. Failure to produce any one of these documents was grounds for suspicion" (Anderson 2005:201). Muthoni Likimani's 1985 book, *Passbook Number F.47927: Women and Mau Mau in Kenya,* reports that Kikuyu women were subjected to random searches and imprisonment if the correct documents were not produced.

By mid-1954 over 70,000 men and women were incarcerated in the dozens of prisons and detention centers newly built or converted for use to hold the growing numbers of Mau Mau suspects and convicts. White settlers who were determined to stop Mau Mau found ample outlets in the Kenya Police Reserves, in prison and detention camps and in the interrogation centers that became infamous for torture. The administration did not openly condone torture. But administrators turned a blind eye to the white settlers and soldiers who tortured Africans.

The British threw a secretive veil over much of what they did in the 1950s. The "top-secret" Operation Anvil was so secret that, though General Erskine planned it for months, not even military commanders knew about it until they were actually carrying out their orders. In addition, the identity of African informers was kept secret. These informers, who came to be called *gikunia,* wore gunny sacks which covered their entire bodies, with holes cut out for the eyes. Those who were arrested were lined up and forced to file past the *gikunia.* The informers sat silently at a table and nodded or whispered to the white officers to designate a Mau Mau. Once pointed out by these men, the accused were sent immediately to detention or to an interrogation center.

Between 1953 and 1959 this veil of secrecy became silent complicity with settlers' and officers' torture, rape, enslavement and murder of tens of thousands of Kikuyu. European settlers ran rogue interrogation centers. Less than a decade earlier many Kenyan whites had been fighting Hitler's fascism in Germany. By 1953 they had dubbed the colony's police Special

Branch "Kenya's SS" (Elkins 2005:86). Boer and British prison warders, policemen and detention camp officers routinely oversaw or engaged in torture of Kikuyu prisoners that was so extreme that colonists called it "Gestapo stuff" (PRO, CO 822/489/1, letter from Inspector H.A. Cross, March 1, 1953, cited in Elkins 2005:86). The British press compared Kenya's detention centers to "Russian prison camps" ("No More White-wash," *The Observer*, London June 17, 1956, cited in Elkins 2005: 292). In a logical extension of the "top-secret" nature of operations carried out against the Kenyan population, the colonial administration kept hidden from the public in Europe most of the violent actions that the anti-Mau Mau forces perpetrated on a daily basis for almost a decade.

There was also, despite their cooperation in crimes against the Kikuyu, a distinct parting of ways between settlers and administration. The Colonial Office gave little money to the fight against Mau Mau. The British Home Office could not justify the expense of a war against colonial subjects. On the contrary Britain depended on colonies such as Kenya to provide revenues with which to repay postwar reconstruction debts owed to the United States government. The Kenya administration fought its counter-insurgency war on a shoestring. It paid African soldiers poorly. The prison departments and detention camps minimized expenditures by keeping the hundreds of thousands of inmates on starvation rations over the course of the decade.

Forced labor not only served as punishment to hundreds of thousands of militant detainees, prisoners and concentration camp inmates. In addi-tion the administration exploited unwaged labor to lessen the expense of the construction of a vast infrastructure including roads and terraces. Roads gave military vehicles easy access to rural areas. More roads and terraces meant more coffee and tea could be grown and exported to gener-ate revenue for European settlers and the colonial authorities. The forced labor of tens of thousands of Kenyans who were worked and starved to death built by hand the capitalist infrastructure of neocolonial indepen-dent Kenya.

# THE CONCENTRATION CAMPS OF RURAL KENYA

The "governing" of rural populations in Mau Mau areas of activity was carried out through the Kenyan state's adoption of the same counterinsur-gency tactics used by the British in Malaysia in the late 1940s. Euphemis-tically called the "villagization scheme," the construction of concentration camps to hold Kikuyu civilians was begun in 1954 and began to be phased out only in 1958. Over 1 million Kikuyu had their homes destroyed and were forced to construct the 854 concentration camps that contained civilians between 1954 and 1960. If guerrilla fighters were like "fish" swimming in a civilian "sea," then the concentration camps were an effort to contain and control the sea itself. Gakuhe wa Kinyatti, a child during the Emergency, remembered that

> all the people in the area were taken to the villages, which were surrounded by moats. Our original homes were burnt. The Homeguards and British were actually beating people and herding them into the villages. It was not voluntary, it was mandatory. As such, it was conducted with a lot of violence. We were in fact forced to burn our own houses and to construct the new ones inside the villages (First Woman interview, April 23, 1998).

More than 1 million Kikuyu were incarcerated in these camps. At least 17,000 squatters who were ejected from the Rift Valley by settler farmers joined them (KNA, KCP, AAD, CP, AR 1955:35,51). The concentration camps were surrounded by barbed-wire fences, and sometimes six-foot-deep moats with sharpened poles along the bottom to injure or kill any Mau Mau who tried to jump over the ditch. Mau Mau quickly adapted to the new situation and placed logs across the moats to enter the camps for supplies.

Women were given a few hours a day to farm and collect firewood and water outside of the camp walls. Homeguards followed them and guarded them against contact with the forest fighters. Many camps had a 4:00 p.m. curfew. Following attacks on Homeguards posts or upon suspicion that inmates were consorting with the guerrillas, the police would call a 23-hour-a-day curfew. Hunger, malnutrition and disease were rife. By 1955 Homeguards used threats of the confiscation of land to wear down the resolve of the Mau Mau in the concentration camps, in the prisons and in the forests. One elderly woman from Murang'a remembered in a 1998 interview:

> Women were chased, beaten, tortured and harassed. A Homeguard might tell all the women to come out of the village and run to a place far away, for instance, near where Gakuhe lives [about 2 kilometres]. All the way, the Homeguards would be chasing us, whipping us and shouting obscenities at us. When we reached the place, there would

be other Homeguards who would tell us to turn around,
then they would chase us and beat us all the way back to
the village (First Woman interview, April 23, 1998).

Concentration camps threw together a vast diversity of people including reserve residents, city dwellers evicted from Nairobi and ex-squatters
evicted from the White Highlands in one of the many sweeps of farm
laborers. White settler agriculture was semi-industrial. Therefore the
women and children who lived and worked in this production system were
experienced in industrial time rhythm, production under supervision, collective socialized work and piecework. All these capacities were immediately translated into survival skills in the larger industrial machine that was
the concentration camp.

The exchange of experience was two-way. The concentration camps
were located in the reserve areas. Outside the camp walls and moats were
the fields, forests and rivers, the sacred grounds and the pathways of the
communities from which some inmates were drawn. Their geographical
knowledge and the gathering and processing of foods and other necessities
was shared by local reserve women with their age-grade sisters, mothers
and daughters from the towns and the white farms. The population of the
concentration camps shared survival tactics. Squatters added their experience under industrial agriculture to the reserve women's survival tactics
that had grown out of the peasant economy in the quasi-autonomy of the
central Kenyan farmlands. In addition city women contributed the fierce
vigilance that had allowed them to survive urban slum life.

This organizational syncretism of the autonomous woman peasant,
the urban woman and the agroindustrial laborer produced a different kind
of women's collectivity, a new expression of the customary women's work
group, with a number of particular features. These were very big groups;
they emphasized loyalty to each other, secrecy and discretion.

Many women have testified to a sense of existential freedom at that
time. Was this the result of staring death in the eye? Was this fearlessness in the face of death? There are many instances of how this existential
freedom was used. One expression of defiance was the construction of
new forms of unity, such as in the case of Kaara wa Macharia. He was an
infant when his mother was made to pull rocks out of a river as part of the
daily forced labor in a concentration camp near Murang'a. Many other
women worked with her. She and several of them had their infants tied to
their backs as they worked. The women would periodically stop to feed the
babies, or comfort them as they cried.

One day when six or seven women stopped to nurse their infants, the officers in charge screamed at the women and demanded that they get back to work. When they did not comply quickly enough, the men rushed at the women and one by one grabbed their babies and threw them into the river. Macharia himself was also thrown into the water. The mothers tried to retrieve the children, but only Macharia survived. As an indication of the unity that women forged through their shared tragedy, each of the mothers who lost her child that day took on Macharia as her own son; all called him "my son" and shared an interest in his progress for the rest of his life (First Woman interview, Kaara wa Macharia, April 17, 1997).

Survival in the concentration camps necessitated cooperation among women in the caring for elders and children, the collection of firewood and water, the harvesting of crops and the preparation of meals. The camp conditions sometimes hindered togetherness, but more often they fostered greater levels of unity and love among the Mau Mau. Those women who survived the harsh conditions did so through hard work, collectivity and chance. The twofold character of women's unity involved defiance of injustice and solidarity for the preservation of life. The organization of the camps themselves thereby forged a new kind of subsistence actor, a new kind of subsistence political economy and a new collectivity based on love and solidarity as the conditions of survival. The well-being of "all" suddenly included a huge number of sophisticated people thrown together in the camps and struggling together for life, land and freedom.

The creation of new forms of women's unity and solidarity was clearly not the intention of the Community Development Department, which devised, implemented and ran the concentration camps ("protected villages"). On the contrary, much of the Department's annual budget of £250,000 was spent on the "rehabilitation" of women:

> In view of the large numbers of women and children to be found in these villages whose husbands are either serving sentences, detained, working in the Homeguard, operating in the forests or living in the towns, the accent of rehabilitation must be on the women (KNA, KCP, CDD, AR 1955:31).

The content and some of the implications of this "rehabilitation" are taken up in greater detail in Chapter Eight. The concentration camp policy worked to enclose Kikuyu land and labor. It was a corrosive, coercive form of colonial counterinsurgency meant to destroy the unity of villagers who supported and supplied Mau Mau. While the camps physically impeded communications, Mau Mau women continued to supply the forest fighters despite the grave dangers involved. Mau Mau women maintained and elaborated their unity in the face of tremendous violence against them. With the introduction of the Swynnerton Plan in 1954, Mau Mau women also had to deal with the processes and impacts of major adverse changes in land relations facilitated by the enclosure of the Kikuyu population within the concentration camps.

# THE 1954 SWYNNERTON PLAN FOR THE INTENSIFICATION OF AFRICAN AGRICULTURE

In 1954 the colonial administration trained and sent out thousands of European and African agricultural officers to institute a new production regime and property system among the detainees. It was no coincidence that the reorganization of African farming began in the Kikuyu concentration camps. The Swynnerton Plan for the Intensification of African Agriculture was a counterinsurgency tactic based on the reward of loyalists with land titles, loans and export crop production licenses and the punishment of Mau Mau hard core by the confiscation of land.

In March 1954 the Kenyan administration passed into law the Forfeiture of Lands Bill, which allowed for the formal confiscation of land from known Mau Mau. The law was limited in that it allowed only the confiscation of land that was individually occupied by the suspect. By June 1955, the government had taken some 270 acres from 23 Mau Mau, including 11 acres from Kimathi and 1.4 acres occupied by the family of Stanley Mathenge. The administration later strengthened its hand by amending the law to allow for the confiscation of clan land to which Mau Mau had claims. A deadline of July 11, 1955 was attached, with the proviso that any guerrilla remaining in the forest after this date would lose his claim to land. When the deadline expired, the Homeguards who controlled the land board began to identify the land of Mau Mau and demarcate it for confiscation. Then began a massive grab. Another 3,471 Mau Mau had their lands, an estimated total of 7,000 acres, confiscated in this way (Anderson 2005:272).

Since the entire Kikuyu population had already been removed from their farms and forced to live in concentration camps, it was relatively easy for the administration to redraw the boundaries of the farms and to hand land out to loyalists. A few thousand Mau Mau suspects' lands were confiscated. But the Swynnerton Plan promised a more far-reaching redistribution of land. It called for the "consolidation and enclosure" of all the land; meaning that the boundaries to every farm were to be redrawn. Fencing in was encouraged and title deeds were issued to male heads of households. Ghai and McAuslan noted that

> by authorizing the round up and detention of thousands of Africans, mainly Kikuyu, by requiring those that remained in the Central and Rift Valley Provinces to be grouped together in fortified villages, by restricting movement, by forfeiting the land of those who joined the rebels, and by increasing the use of forced labor, all actions taken in order to meet the challenge of Mau Mau, the administration at the same time gave itself the opportunity of replanning the holdings, and remoulding the tenure system of much of Central Province on a scale which could not have been, indeed was not by the EARC [East Africa Royal Commission[1]], envisaged for in normal conditions (Ghai and McAuslan 1970:117).

Chiefs, headmen and other loyalists took part in the land redistribution exercise by indicating the boundaries of their land and others' land. They had every opportunity to allocate larger portions of land to themselves and their family members and smaller portions to others. The customary system of land use involving the cultivation of several strips of land located in different ecological niches in the area was repudiated in the process. Instead single blocks of "consolidated" land were surveyed and registered. Consolidation facilitated mechanized moncropping systems and involved the total reorganization of the geography of indigenous settlements. The land of many more Mau Mau militants was confiscated and allocated to loyalists in this way. Consolidation of land had long been used by English colonists. In Ireland in the 1840s, Irish tenant farmers in the south were evicted in order to consolidate their many holdings into large plantations. Consolidation in this case contributed to starvation during the ensuing potato famine. Many were either landless or they were semiserf farm laborers who had no control over the vegetable crops they did produce, which were exported to Britain throughout the famine years.

In Kenya in the 1940s, the British extended to certain "loyal" Africans the right to grow and export coffee. This was one means through which colonial officials orchestrated a mass buy-off of male peasants. Many Mau Mau men were persuaded to stop fighting and settle for the rights to produce and market high-value crops on small private plots of land. The Swynnerton Plan stipulated that all coffee trees were to be planted on terraces (Ruthenberg 1966). Therefore the forced labor regime within the concentration camps was directed toward such infrastructural projects as would facilitate the commodification of African agriculture in the years to come. The terracing labor that Murang'a and Olenguruone women had refused to do in the 1940s was forced upon them at the point of a gun in the 1950s.

The Swynnerton Plan was backed by a £5 million government fund. The changes it effected in the reserves included the loss of customary land rights of the *ahoi* (tenants) and the handing out of title deeds only to men, and therefore the creation of greater insecurity in women's land rights. The Plan left large numbers of people landless and unemployed. This was expected by Swynnerton himself, who saw landlessness as a normal part of the "modernization" process. Ruthenberg characterized land redistribution as a "beneficial consequence" of the Emergency (1966:8). He never identified exactly who the beneficiaries were, but their identity was no mystery. The goals of the land consolidation and enclosure process, which was still going on when Ruthenberg wrote in 1966, were to create a landed class that could employ and thereby "absorb surplus population and thus reduce the pressure of unemployment in towns." By creating a "prosperous middle-class society of farmers, firmly established on the land," the Plan aspired "to exercise a stabilising influence on politics in Kenya" (Ruthenberg 1966:14). This approach came to characterize the programs supported by the World Bank across Africa in the 1950s and 1960s. The myth of the heroic yeoman farmer was born out of this counterinsurgency strategy.

The administration, and eventually the white settler community, supported the Swynnerton Plan insofar as it protected the settlers' economy. It was hoped that "the development of the vast potential of the Non-Scheduled areas [native reserves] would lessen the desire for land in the Scheduled areas [White Highlands] and would thus give long-term stability to the large farm economy" (Ruthenberg 1966:14). Consistent with the policies of the colonial administration throughout its years in Kenya, the Swynnerton Plan disrupted Africans' subsistence political economy to better secure the property rights and commodity production regime of Europeans and their African allies. The Plan's focus on cash cropping led to a flight from food production in the reserves. By the mid-1960s, food shortages and hunger resulted from this overemphasis on cash crops.

Swynnerton himself thought that the enclosure of land and handing out of title deeds in the Kikuyu land unit would take from 15 to 20 years. But because it was used by the administration as a counterinsurgency weapon, planners undertook the redistribution of Kikuyu land at a very rapid pace. The agricultural staff of the colonial regime completed the entire exercise within six years. Enthusiastic planners worked to beat the clock as they hastily measured out the new boundaries of properties. The end of the Emergency in 1960 would send thousands of Mau Mau back into the villages. They would oppose the theft of their land, at which point it would become very difficult to demarcate and redistribute land without renewed conflict. Ruthenberg noted that

> the Emergency, furthermore, made it easier for the British to enforce those measures thought to be appropriate. The need for drastic changes was evident. One no longer feared to push aside traditional customs. The British were – at least in Central Province – in a position of absolute authority and thus able to carry out and control development measures with hardly anybody in a position to object (Ruthenberg 1966:9).

Indeed custom was "pushed aside" but it is hardly true that "nobody was in a position to object." Gakuhe wa Kinyatti remembers that "There was a lot of confrontation, in fact. From 1956 to 1960 during the time of demarcation, tensions were very high, to the point that people would get into fist fights and even kill each other" (First Woman interview, April 23, 1998). Okoth-Ogendo argued that the land reform program began as a "counter-revolutionary measure" of rewarding Homeguards and punishing Mau Mau. As the "security situation improved, however, this original scheme was abandoned in favour of a broader political objective, ie. the creation of a stable *peasantry*" which could quiet the general clamor for land and produce high value crops for export (Okoth-Ogendo 1978:163). He spelled out some of the consequences of the land reform process carried out in Kikuyuland in the 1950s and in other areas of the country throughout the 1960s:

> The very narrow view taken on land rights in the statutes made it virtually impossible to bring to the register all the multiple rights claimable under customary law. In almost all communities public grazing lands disappeared as people moved in to claim every bit of land under the rubric of cultivation. ... Those who were most directly affected were people such as women and children, both of whom had actual or potential rights of access to the use of the land, but were without the power of ultimate control over it (Okoth-Ogendo1978:177-178).

The dual policies of concentration camps and land consolidation negatively impacted the subsistence options of hundreds of thousands of Kikuyu for generations to come. The land consolidation program was carried into the reserves of other ethnic groups in the 1960s. As the cash economy could not possibly employ or sustain all of those made landless during the land privatization exercise, a process leading to a general crisis of subsistence was set in motion.

# CONCLUSION

By 1952 hundreds of thousands of African peasant women were directly exploited on white settler farms. Tens of thousands engaged in demonstrations, strikes, protest marches, direct action and organizational networking. Kikuyu women's entitlements to land were premised on communal access and negotiated use. With the breakdown and redrawing of the lines of communities, women's rights were narrowed and insecure. The erosion of many of women's community-based powers had already taken place largely through the deep rifts the colonialists created between loyal chiefs and the majority over whom they ruled. The concentration camps and Swynnerton Plan were meant to further dissolve the community.

Divide and rule was long established through the colonial manipulation of custom to suit the profit-making process and extract work and wealth from those engaged in the "mere" production of social life. Due to the tight relation between community and women's entitlement to land, any colonial attacks on or threats to the customs of the people that were seen to erode community life were understood by women as direct threats to their own rights of access to land. Such divisions fostered conflicts over land, especially when one side of the divide was supported by the government against the other. The government consistently throughout its entire 75 years in Kenya gave land as a reward for loyalty to the Crown and took it as a punishment for disloyalty. If the 1934 Kenya Land Commission had occasioned such cleavages, the Emergency was to multiply these cleavages a thousandfold.

Chapter Seven has examined the concerted efforts made by the colonial regime to break the gendered class alliances emerging in Kenyan resistance movements. The concentration camps and the Swynnerton Plan were implemented in combination to divide, terrorize and control the entire Kikuyu people. Both relied on the support and participation of African men, Homeguards and chiefs; who, as we have seen, were rewarded with special privileges and, above all, greater shares of land in the redistribution initiative. Commodification took on a new imperative for the British colonialists in the 1950s. It was no longer only a matter of increasing cash incomes for the white settlers and tax revenues for the government. Commodification became a central pillar of the fight against the revolutionary Mau Mau.

Despite the curfews, barbed wire, and threats to the land rights of Mau Mau militants, most of the women and men of the liberation struggle maintained their commitments and their connections with one another. Mau Mau strengthened and used the regional network of resistance built during earlier periods of struggle to launch their coordinated attack on colonial rule. Militarily, the Mau Mau were overwhelmed. They relied on a small cache of arms they had manufactured or stolen from the enemy. Supplies were difficult to obtain and the armed forces began to fracture in 1956, especially as land confiscation proceeded and thousands of Mau Mau men deserted. But the freedom fighters had forced the hand of the British. The liberation war was to be a qualified win for the freedom fighters. Though they were to win independence, it was not to be obtained on the subsistence terms that most Mau Mau demanded. The next chapter considers how the British prepared the besieged population for an independence most friendly to settler and Homeguard interests. The forced commodification of land and labor reviewed in this chapter was only the beginning of colonial efforts to save the white settler estates from the reappropriation that Mau Mau promised.

## *Note*

1.    A body set up in 1953 to consider how to "develop" land in East Africa. Similar to the Kenya Land Commission of 1934.

## ∼ CHAPTER EIGHT ∽

# A WAR FOR SUBSISTENCE: MAU MAU ON THE GLOBAL STAGE, 1957-1960

## INTRODUCTION

Chapter Eight considers the final years of the state of emergency from 1957 to 1960. The chapter analyzes British colonialists' attempts to force African men to submit to colonial rule and to make African women submit to their husbands' authority as well. The British administration tried to reshape social relations with and among Africans through rigorous discipline and "training" in (1) prisons and (2) *Maendeleo ya Wanawake* or "Progress for Women" groups in the rural concentration camps. Here colonialists worked to create compliant workers for expanding global agroindustries. Prisoners constructed roads, canals and airports. Prison warders tried to pry men and women away from the freedom struggle through torture and confiscation of property. Progress for Women clubs were intended to lay the foundation for peasant women's acceptance of "housewifization" and the accompanying commodification of agriculture. The clubs were meant to divert women from the fight for land and freedom and train them to be dispossessed, subordinate housewives.

This chapter also examines the ways in which Mau Mau women and men turned the organization of their repression into opportunities for resistance. Many incarcerated Mau Mau used the factory-like prison milieu to form new relations of solidarity, organize strikes and continue the Mau Mau struggle inside the prison walls. Some smuggled letters out of prison to alert the world to the ill-treatment and human rights abuses of the incarcerated prisoners of war. With allies throughout Kenya, in Britain and in other countries, inmates in Kenya's gulags raised the specter of an international campaign and thus struck a damaging blow against British colonialism.

Mau Mau women also used the infrastructure created by the colonial Progress for Women clubs to expand their local autonomous organizations into networks that had international dimensions. In these ways many Mau Mau elaborated practices of collectivity that subverted imperial enclosures. Collectivity in turn moderated the process of agricultural commodification by sustaining social relations conducive to the expansion of a life-centered subsistence political economy.

# "WE DECIDED NOT TO DO ANY WORK"[1] MAU MAU PRISONERS AND DETAINEES

Some 200,000 women and men were imprisoned and detained for violations of the Emergency Regulations in Kenya from 1952 to 1959 (Elkins 2005:xiii). Thousands were "repeat offenders," and many were listed as *maisha*, or "lifers." "Consorting with terrorists," that is, talking to a member of the Kenya Land Freedom Army, was a capital offense in Kenya in the 1950s.

In 1954 a young British social worker, Eileen Fletcher, was hired by Tom Askwith of the newly established Community Development Department to design and implement a rehabilitation program for women and girls in Kamiti prison. She worked under prison warder Katherine Warren-Gash, a white settler's daughter who became an infamous torturer in Kenya (Elkins 2005:222-223). After a tour of the colony's detention camps, interrogation centers and prisons and eight months of work at Kamiti, Fletcher resigned in protest against the brutality prison staff meted out to prisoners and detainees (Presley 1992:144-145). In 1956 Fletcher published a three-part exposé in the U.K. Quaker publication, *Peace News: The International Pacifist Weekly*. In the same year the British-based Movement for Colonial Freedom published her pamphlet, *Truth About Kenya: An Eyewitness Account*.

In May 1956 Eileen Fletcher testified before members of the House of Commons in London about the inhumane conditions and abuse of women and girls by officials at Kamiti prison. Fletcher revealed that girls as young as 11 were being detained, imprisoned for life, held in solitary confinement for up to 16 days at a time and being regularly abused, tortured, harassed and malnourished. The colonial secretary and Kenya governor collaborated to cover up what they came to call the "Fletcher affair."

The only positive action taken by the British government was to order an official inquiry. Many other accusations and eyewitness accounts were to be lodged in the years ahead, including further revelations by British ex-prison staff, petitions from churches that had their missionaries "in the field," and letters to London officials written by detainees in Mwea and other camps throughout the colony. The inquiry into the prison conditions at Kamiti dismissed Fletcher's charges as unfounded. It claimed that there had merely been a number of "careless clerical errors" in the prison records: that the girls in question were in fact over 14 years old and therefore not "underage." The committee of inquiry recommended that the prison department write an annual report on conditions within the facility and dismiss staff for any maltreatment of inmates. The committee of inquiry, the Colonial Office and the governor gave little attention to the fact that the treatment to which prisoners of all ages were subjected was inhumane and *illegal*.

The British government was then scandalized when, in the course of heated debate in the House of Commons, it was discovered that these were not "clerical errors" as the committee of inquiry had reported, but rather, that the prison records had been altered (Presley 1992:146). The colonial secretary's office admitted that the Kenyan administration had broken the penal code by subjecting prisoners to long periods of solitary confinement and handing out life sentences to girls under age 14. The government tried to legitimize its illegal actions by charging that the imprisoned girls "of whom we are talking as if they were juveniles in the strict sense of the term have themselves played a terrifying role in the Mau Mau conspiracy" (Tribune [London], November 16, 1956, cited in Presley 1992:146).

Annual reports on prison conditions did not end the abuse. Nor did the torture and beatings stop the resistance of Mau Mau prisoners and detainees. That many Mau Mau women were fearless in the face of death is illustrated by the actions of "hardcore" Mau Mau women in Kamiti prison. The "hardcore" were Mau Mau who refused to confess or to renounce their allegiance to the liberation struggle despite beatings and torture. Mau Mau activist and publisher Gakaara wa Wanjau visited his wife in Kamiti prison in 1957. His description offers rare insight into the militancy of Kenya's Mau Mau women:

Sometimes men detainees would travel from Athi River
[a detention camp where many of the inmates had con-
fessed] to Kamiti to see and talk to their wives who were
still holding out against making a confession. Some of the
women exhibited a single-minded determination which

put many men to shame. Some women would refuse to talk to their husbands for the reason that these men had sold out by making a confession. Others would insist that their husbands, who had already confessed, should only talk about domestic affairs and should by no means discuss matters relating to detention. One woman told her husband point blank that she would have no dealings with the sellouts and traitors from Athi River. The response of the women taught me that when women really set their mind to a cause they are capable of a remarkably single-minded commitment (Wanjau 1983/1988:194).

This kind of commitment was confirmed by Mau Mau fighter, Mwende wa Irungu, in a 1994 interview:

I wonder if, today, people were to fight, whether people would be able to go to that sacrifice. But, no woman ever surrendered, only men surrendered. In spite of all these problems, no woman surrendered. No woman showed any weakness. The men were the first to surrender. I guarantee you, no woman surrendered. Ask anybody else. No woman surrendered. We were beaten and thrown in a hole that had safari ants at Kangema [prison], but no woman surrendered, only men. Even if you hear these men saying that "Muci na mundumuka ni ta muci na kihii" [Kikuyu = "Stealing with a woman is like stealing with an uncircumcised boy," meaning 'a woman is not reliable, especially with secrets'], these men don't beat us in anything. They don't beat us in intelligence or in keeping secrets, neither in moral courage. These men are good for nothing (First Woman interview, May 1, 1994).

The hardcore women of Kamiti were indomitable in the face of prison guards' violence and intimidation. Wanjau stated that

just adjacent to the Women's Detention Camp was the great Women's Prison, where women who had been tried in courts of law and convicted were imprisoned. Some of the prisoners had been women soldiers in the national-ist Mau Mau army. Those who were captured bearing weapons of war were tried, convicted and sentenced to life imprisonment. Some of these "*maisha*," "life," people were Wanjira wa Kimiti, Wambui Gacanja, Wanjiru Kimiti and Muthoni, wife of W. Gakuru. Some of the work they had to do in prison was to bury the bodies of Mau Mau people who had been condemned to death by hanging. They would bury the bodies with the heads facing Mount Kenya on whose magnificent top God dwelled. Guards would try to thwart the carrying out of these burials of honour and would subject these women to brutal beatings; but the women were adamant and no amount of beatings would thwart them. Eventually the guards left them alone - to bury the corpses of their own people as they chose (Wanjau 1983/1988:194).

Elkins noted that burial detail was "considered the worst punishment at Kamiti. ... The dead were men and women, old and young. Some had been shot, others visibly tortured, and some emaciated from starvation." According to Mary Nyambura, who had been imprisoned at Kamiti, "It was terrible; sometimes a woman would recognize [the corpse of] someone she knew, and she could not do anything. If she started weeping, the *askaris* [guards] would just start beating her." Nyambura's baby died in Kamiti while she carried the child on her back (interview December 16, 1998, cited in Elkins 2005:226-227).

One of the most widespread forms of resistance by detainees, some of whom spent up to six years in detention without trial, was to collectively refuse to perform forced labor. Thousands of people in the system simply refused to do any work in the camps, sometimes arguing that since they were detainees, and not prisoners, they were not required to carry out punishing labor (Wanjau 1983/1988). One elderly man from Githima, Molo, in the Rift Valley stated that he had been imprisoned for five years and detained for three more years. During his imprisonment he spent some years at Embakasi where he and others did stone-crushing and road-building for the Embakasi [now Jomo Kenyatta International] Airport. Of his subsequent detention in Kajiado in 1958, he said,

We organised there. We discussed so much and we decided not to do any work. We demanded that the Magistrate be brought here and prosecute us from here so that we could be sentenced, but we were not going to work (First Woman interview, May 26, 1996).

In 1957 Tom Askwith found that the authority of his Community Development Department was being undermined within the prisons and detention centers. "Rehabilitation" was being taken over by prison warders and guards. Askwith was alarmed by the "techniques" he witnessed in Mwea detention center, which included beating detainees senseless to extract confessions. He wrote several reports to his superiors warning that the kind of violent treatment to which detainees were subjected "might well by misfortune lead to death or serious injury" (Memorandum from T.G. Askwith to the chief secretary, "Rehabilitation," December 16, 1957, cited in Elkins 2005:327). Askwith was fired, his warning went unheeded and the violence continued. Two years later in Hola, Askwith's prediction proved accurate.

In 1958, the administration established the Hola Closed Camp specifically for "exiled detainees who persisted in rejecting all other kinds of work - except cooking their meals - while still in colonial detention" (Wanjau 1983/1988:200). Gakaara wa Wanjau was detained at Hola from May 2, 1958 to August 19, 1959. He described the events leading up to the March 3, 1959 massacre of detainees by prison guards. After a white officer was beaten by some insubordinate Mau Mau detainees, the Hola camp commandant, G. M. Sullivan,

> requisitioned a special platoon to come and intimidate these people to work in digging a huge water canal; should they resist they should be beaten without pity. On 3 March 1959 more than 100 soldiers of the special platoon invaded Hola Closed Camp. They were armed with guns, hoe handles, clubs and they carried iron shields and wore iron helmets. They confronted about 85 detainees who were sworn to rejection of work. They set on them and subjected them to brutal assault, hitting at the detainees' bodies and heads indiscriminately, until they had driven the detainees out of their quarters (Wanjau 1983/1988:200-201).

Eleven Hola inmates were beaten to death and dozens more were sent to hospital with serious permanent injuries. Wanjau continued:

> Those of us who were working on our farms, about three miles away from Hola Closed Camp, learned about one hour later about the massacre. So we trooped to the hospital with heavy hearts and the women wept and wailed

when they saw the battered bodies of our people. The injured men lay in a mass with bandages covering their broken limbs, skulls and ribs. Well might they weep with springs of bitterness bursting in flow at the realisation that the act of hateful carnage had been perpetrated not by white colonialists but by our Black brothers. For the white imperialist is uncannily adept at using ignorant Black stooges to oppress and destroy their own people. And our heroic people who had been battered into a mass of broken limbs and ribs also carried injured psyches, for these stooges had beaten them and subjected them to verbal abuse and insults. "What kind of freedom do people like you demand, you ignoramuses!" they had shouted. "Stupid people like you: how can you ever hope to put a case for a return of land?" (Wanjau 1983/1988:201).

The camp authorities claimed that the men had died after drinking contaminated water. But letters from the injured were smuggled out, and the autopsies clearly showed that the cause of death was beating. Though camp commandant Sullivan was dismissed, he maintained his benefits and pension. The director of prisons in Kenya quietly retired. Despite debate and discussion in the House of Commons in London, no independent inquiry or prosecution ensued.

But the scandal finally brought to an end the detention and "pipeline" systems (Presley 1992:147; Rosberg and Nottingham 1966:335-344). The "pipeline" was a system of rehabilitation through which detainees were assessed for their compliance with prison and colonial rule and finally released once all traces of militancy for the freedom struggle were erased. Much violence was used in pushing prisoners and detainees through this pipeline. Indeed, the whole colonial project was thrown into question by the Hola massacre and the scandals it raised. With other colonies already being granted independence, and the financial and political costs of maintaining the Kenyan colony escalating, the Hola massacre marked, for the Colonial Office, the opening pages of the final chapter in its brutal catalog of rule in East Africa.

By 1959 the Emergency was coming to and end. Independence was three years away and prisons and detention camps were releasing their inmates. White settlers maintained a grip on their property and on the government. Land entitlements in the reserves were seriously skewed in favor of the loyalists and those Mau Mau men who surrendered earliest in the war. Women's rights to land depended more than ever on their relations to husbands. The colonialists had done what they could to retain power. It was clear that their time was drawing to an end. They did not take any chances with the security of their property. The British tried to maintain their control over the export economy even after they handed government power to Jomo Kenyatta in 1963.

For the Mau Mau, the 1960s were to unfold with a new array of land relations within which, against all odds, a new subsistence political economy was forged. The unity that prisoners and concentration camp inmates had elaborated during the emergency between 1952 and 1960 contributed to a postcolonial explosion of renewed collectivity. In addition to this unity, the divisions between Mau Mau and Homeguards were carried into the independence period. These divisions were deeply engraved in the land by the newly drawn boundaries of Homeguards' privatized farms. Homeguards appropriated much of this land from Mau Mau. The divisions between Mau Mau and Homeguards over land and other resources continue to inform many Kenyan social movements' continued pursuit of justice in the 21st century.

Unity among the Mau Mau was forged through oaths as well as through the formation of battalions, supply lines, recruitment drives and Mau Mau committees in towns and concentration camps. As the war progressed, British counterinsurgency introduced new forms of organization and control via the prison-industrial complex and the factory-like concentration camps within which Kikuyu were "rehabilitated" and "reeducated" with violence and procolonial propaganda. It was within these new strictures that insurgents were drawn into the emerging global relations of postcolonial neoimperialism as small producers and landless low-waged laborers.

# HOUSEWIFIZATION THROUGH *MAENDELEO YA WANAWAKE* WOMEN'S CLUBS

In 1954 the British undertook the massive campaign of privatizing land in African reserves. Kikuyu territories were the first to be targeted in what would later be a colony-wide strategy of commodification. The extension of commodification into the newly privatized lands required the reshaping of household relations of production. Many men used their title deeds to immediately secure loans for the purchase of seedlings and the necessary inputs for production of coffee and other cash crops. While Africans had always worked on Europeans' coffee and tea estates, who would do the work of weeding and harvesting Africans' crops? The answer, in short, was the landowners' wives and children.

As with many women worldwide in the 1950s, Kikuyu women were exposed to propaganda and state-sponsored social welfare programs aimed at producing good housewives. The housewife was to be a woman with no land or other independent means of production. She was wageless and depended for money on a husband (Rogers 1980; Mies 1986:103). Housewifization, then, was the process through which women lost access to self-directed and organized subsistence livelihoods and were encouraged to submit to often unwaged work under the control of a man who, in turn, was incorporated into relations of commodified exploitation.

As we saw earlier in Chapter Five, in Kenya during the Second World War, African women were encouraged to grow food for the supply of the military and prisons. This policy was reversed a decade later. By the 1950s, government policies of enforced landlessness and "domestic education" promoted housewifization as a way to draw women away from independent farming livelihoods and deter them from participation in Mau Mau. A concerted effort was made to redirect women's efforts in the direction of the care of husband, house and home (Koeune 1952/1983).

This process of housewifization was instituted by a Community Development Department program called *Maendeleo ya Wanawake*, or Progress for Women clubs. The clubs were crucial forerunners of the subsequent "women in development" projects instituted by imperial planners on a global level in bilateral and multilateral development programs.

Kikuyu women were known by many colonial officials to be militants in the fight for land during Mau Mau (Rosberg and Nottingham 1966). Askwith devised what for public relations purposes in Britain were called "social welfare programs" for women in the "protected villages." He argued that within the concentration camps,

> it will be necessary to cleanse the women in the same way as the men before they are permitted to rejoin them, as there is evidence that wives have in many cases persuaded their husbands to take the oath and are often very militant. They are also said to be bringing up their children to follow the Mau Mau creed. It is therefore more important to rehabilitate the women than the men if the next generation is to be saved (PRO, CO 822/794/1, "Rehabilitation," January 6, 1954, cited in Elkins 2005:109-110).

A women's club was to be the vehicle through which such rehabilitation could be delivered. *Maendeleo wa Wanawake* was launched in the late 1940s but did not enjoy a wide appeal among Kenyan African women. Settlers and administrators' wives ran the clubs and taught African members domestic skills such as crocheting and European cooking.

As a compliment to the land theft and redistribution program of the Swynnerton Plan, a relatively few women who were dispossessed of land were "trained" to become attractive mates for the emerging class of large-landholding loyalists. But the landless majority was drawn into global corporate supply chains as the cheap or unwaged producers of primary agricultural products. The Community Development Department's other programs included forced labor and limited religious and educational activities in detention centers and prisons designed to draw support away from the liberation struggle.

During the Emergency years *Maendeleo ya Wanawake* membership in the three Kikuyu districts of Nyeri, Murang'a and Kiambu rose dramatically from some 200 to over 18,000 women by 1954 (Presley 1992:166-167). This was read by the Community Development Department as a sign that women really did want to crochet doilies rather than fight for the return of their land. Some women who aspired to be wives of wealthy Homeguard men joined *Maenedeleo* clubs to learn European cooking, cleaning and decorating methods. A more practical consideration was at play for many women in the concentration camps. Thousands joined *Maendeleo ya Wanawake* in order to gain access to the food rations available to members. Sometimes women would get a break from forced labor by joining the clubs (Presley 1992).

The *Maendeleo* clubs ran a very few day nurseries, made and distributed soup, distributed milk to members' children and cared for orphans. These services were particularly important in 1955 and 1956 when famine struck. At the same time that children were dying of starvation, the British were confiscating their parents' cattle in very large numbers as a form of collective punishment (Anderson 2005:355). *Maendeleo* membership was also used to aid the security forces. Presley notes that some *Maendeleo* club members

> gathered information about Mau Mau activities and tried to persuade Mau Mau adherents to abandon the movement. Women were told that they had to become allied with the Government rather than with Mau Mau. If they chose to remain publicly sympathetic to Mau Mau, they lost access to the services which the clubs offered (KCP, CDD, AR 1955:7 in Presley 1992).

Some have described the administration's use of "community development" in general and *Maendeleo ya Wanawake* clubs in particular as an
attempt to win Africans'"hearts and minds"(Robertson 1997; Elkins 2005).
While this may have been the case, there were more fundamental matters
at stake. "Development" in the shape of Swynnerton's private land title
and cash cropping regime was designed to move Africans away from the
indigenous political economy and more completely into the commodified
global market economy. Loyalist chiefs and Homeguards got titles to land,
professional salaries, loans and commodity licences. The Swynnerton Plan
saw to that. The vast majority of women got none of this. Via *Maendeleo*
clubs, they were instead required to make themselves as "attractive,""Euro-
peanized" and "presentable" as possible as potential monogamous wives for
this new class of men. Hardcore Mau Mau women would form the low
waged labor gangs on the new bourgeoisie's farms.

A *Maendeleo* trainer in Molo told me of her work with the organization beginning in 1956:

> We used to train the Mau Mau women on things like
> agriculture. We also used to train them how to wash cloths
> for their husbands, how they would cook all kind of food
> for the husband apart from the traditional food. We used
> to train them how to cook the white man's food, biscuits
> and even how to make soup, even if it is bean soup, meat
> soup and even brown stew and everything in general that
> could be cooked. We trained them on how to make jam,
> how even they could make soap from the very small pieces
> that are left over when the soap is finished, how they could
> put together the small pieces and make a soap out of that
> (First Woman interview, Name Withheld, July 10, 1997).

She also described the kinds of marriages such women could look forward to:

> It is true that when a lady or a woman goes through the
> *Maendeleo* training, there is a very big difference in her
> cooking because her food is different from the traditional
> food or food that is cooked on daily basis. We were even
> training them to make the traditional food but in a better
> way such that they were able to make the normal kind of
> food but with a difference because they now had a train-
> ing and they knew how to make it better than they were
> making initially before they joined the training. So it is

true that any woman who has gone through this kind of the training would get married to an influential person. I mean she would not just be married to any kind of person. She would be married by the elite of the society, because they were being associated with development and they were presentable, anybody would just like them. So it is true that they were being married by the people from the government.

Despite the small number of African women who were to serve as counterparts to this embryonic bourgeoisie, the colonialists were eager to ensure that such housewifized women were available. As early as 1939, a number of Kenyan men had already received university degrees abroad and returned to Kenya with more education than most of the white settlers of the colony. The government saw a need to educate African women to be proper wives for such men. Governor Henry Robert Brooke-Popham wrote in 1939 that indeed, African women's education was a serious mission which could divert husbands from political "disaffection." He wrote that women

> must receive education not only in cooking food and looking after babies, both of which I admit are very important, but also sufficient to be able to read native books and papers so they shall be able to talk on an equal footing with their menfolk. I believe the African who takes quite an intelligent interest in European affairs, gets fed up when he goes back to his hut and finds his wife can think and talk of nothing but maize, manure, and goats. Thereupon he goes off to his counterpart of the club ... which may become a sort of talking shop, and possibly a center of disaffection (Henry Robert Brooke-Popham to Sir Henry Moore, CO, October 24, 1939, Brooke-Popham letters, RH MSS Afr.s. 1120/2, ff. 3/9, cited in White 1990a:142).

The effort to educate African women to partner with educated African men may have been motivated in part by racist dislike of the fact that several Kenyan men had returned from abroad with educated European wives. Kenyatta married (and later divorced) a British woman and C.M.G. Argwings-Kodhek, Kenya's first African lawyer, married an Irish woman.

With the privatization of land, men of all classes were to have much more significant individual control over family farm decisions than they had had within customary land relations. The new land dispensation consisted of a new hierarchy of ethnicized gendered class relations. Peasant women were on the "ground level," literally digging the soil that would produce global commodities. The cash crop regimen placed African men on the bottom rungs of a global corporate ladder. Male landowners were the first crucial link in a global circuit that connected the rural woman farm producer to the multinational food conglomerates via state marketing bodies.

In addition, in the early years of the development of African coffee production, European agricultural officers closely regulated every stage of production on the Kikuyus' new cash crop plots. These men oversaw the construction and maintenance of terraces, recommended the type of crops planted, calculated the number and spacing of the plants, the amount and timing of inputs such as fertilizers and pesticides, the extent of intercropping and the rhythm of weeding, harvesting and processing of the crop. This system brought colonial officials into the homes of rural Africans through a paternalistic system of supervision, backed by the threat of repression. A seven-year prison sentence awaited those convicted of neglecting a coffee tree.

The Department of Agriculture Annual Report of 1954 spelled out the importance of socializing women for the new political economy of export cash crop production and consumerism:

> It is believed that the most promising focal point for attack is the women and the home. It is the woman who must be educated to want a better home and a better life for her children. A man needs encouragement and pressure for sustained effort and the most potent driving force is woman. [British] women agricultural officers are unsatisfactory employees in many ways; they get married, they need escorts. African women agricultural instructors are employed in large numbers and they perform a most useful function in our approach to the true tillers of the soil, the women, but some more subtle approach, possibly through the medium of Women Social Welfare Workers seems desirable. This approach is being used to a limited extent but the aim merits the employment of selected, well-educated African women whose object should be *to create in their particular parish a body of women who will not*

*be content with their present lot* (Agri 4/116 Department of
Agriculture Annual Report 1954:3-4, cited in Robertson
1997:248, *emphasis added*).

To "want a better home and a better life for her children" was, for the
administration, to want a cash income and an approximation of a middle-
class Victorian home life. Cash cropping and export marketing were promoted as a means for African women who were not "content with their
present lot" (subsistence) to achieve a "better life" (of consumerism which
required greater involvement in the cash economy).

This reorganization of agricultural work affected the majority of
women, not only those whose husbands had large holdings. If *Maendeleo*
was aimed at producing wives for the more wealthy "yeoman" farmers, the
concentration camp setting itself was to prepare the majority of women
and children for their new lives. Many were to live the rest of their lives in
slums or squatter settlements that in many ways resembled the cramped
conditions of the concentration camps, with little privacy and few amenities in an alienated community with little secure access to any land at
all. The rigid discipline of the concentration camp was echoed in many
women's post-Emergency lives in the shape of subordination to men and
exploitation as unwaged producers for the corporate global market.

*Maendeleo ya Wanwake* club leaders were keen to instill a self-image
in selected Kenyan women of an updated Victorian middle-class gentil-
ity. This was not only to suit the needs of a bourgeois husband. It was
an identity to be consciously contrasted to the indigenous 'everywoman,'
especially the Mau Mau woman. The *Maendeleo* ideal had as its negation a
denigration of indigenous Kikuyu womanhood and, indeed, African womanhood. The nature of the colonialists' and loyalists' effort to housewifize
and control African women's labor can be garnered from the type of households *Maendeleo* promoted among Africans: square (not round) houses, tea
parties, cakes, crocheted doilies on the couches, centerpieces on the tables
and pictures hung at eye level on the (flat, not curved) walls. In this way,
the "tradition versus modernity" trope was at the center of the capitalist nation-building project. This was a project of building self-hatred and
breaking social solidarity and identification with one's people. Although
many women joined *Maendeleo*, few were to accept these changes. Fewer
still were in a position to afford the Victorian homes and cuisine that
*Maendeleo* championed.

During the 1950s *Maendeleo ya Wanawake* had a clear agenda of counterinsurgency. The clubs distributed propaganda that "stressed the positive
benefits of colonialism for Kenya and the evils of Mau Mau" (Presley 1992:

166). Members were encouraged to be informants. Many were enlisted into propagandizing about the "benefits of colonialism." Meanwhile, women who refused to join *Maendeleo* were compelled to fortify the concentration camps against the Mau Mau by digging trenches, building fences and cutting the tall grasses around the internment centers that might provide cover to forest fighters. In 1958, when the war was winding down and the government no longer required the cooperation of women informants, the administration withdrew funding for the *Maendeleo ya Wanawake* clubs and dismissed European staff members. Some African women continued to meet on a limited scale, while others became volunteer leaders of *Maendeleo* clubs.

By imprisoning rural women in concentration camps the British established a significant physical break between the women and the forest fighters. But at the same time, the camps, like the prisons, provided a constrained space within which new collectivities emerged. Mau Mau women's committees in the camps spread the word about the liberation struggle and deepened the consciousness of unity through mutual support and continued oathing. Committee members became adept at avoiding detection by security forces while they carried out the work of supplying the forest fighters with food and other necessities. With song and prayer, Mau Mau women maintained the morale of their compatriots, children, elders and others around them. The *Maendeleo ya Wanawake* clubs tried to counter the unity of the Mau Mau women's committees. But the Community Development Department's efforts to break Mau Mau in this way only strengthened the determination of Mau Mau women and further delineated two distinct perspectives on Kenyan women's future. Mau Mau fought for land while *Maendeleo* created housewives.

Landlessness among East African women was not recognized as a problem by the colonial administration or the anticolonial groupings of the 1930s and 1940s. Women themselves pursued struggles against land alienation and labor exploitation because they were exposed to the worst effects of each and because their organizations enabled them to exercise power. Women's forced labor and colonial interference in female genital mutilation (and therefore in community land relations) repeatedly became political *cause célèbres*. And these political causes that were centered on women's concerns often grew into whole movements, such as the independent school and church movements.

Yet most male nationalists failed to articulate a position in favor of women's access to land. For the most part, the anticolonial movement appeared to be a contest between African and European men for control over land and African women's labor. This changed in the 1950s. When large landholding men such as Kenyatta were imprisoned, the poorer, more exploited elements of the anticolonial movement came to the fore to define whose interests would be defended in the struggle for liberation. The landless, the unionists, the male and female impoverished peasants all contributed to defining a way forward that was much more inclusive and universalist than were the narrowly focused aims of Kenyatta's Kenya African Union. *Maendeleo ya Wanawake* promoters tried to undermine both the unity and the inclusive demands of the revolutionary Mau Mau.

Landlessness was created among African women with the advent of colonialism. Women who had no possibility of surviving from the land relations of old escaped to missions or into trading or prostitution in settler towns and railway camps. Urban women were more visible to the colonial administration as "public health menaces" than as "landless." Some were acknowledged as useful in providing male migrant workers with "the comforts of home" (White 1990a). The colonial administration intervened periodically against urban women with arrests, "public health" campaigns and demolition of slums. But mainly it ignored them as unfortunate but culpable misfits. Insofar as women's landlessness was seen as a problem by the male dealers who created it, there were easy solutions found in prison, waged employment, public works and slum existence.

Mau Mau women themselves defended their own land rights and entitlements. They did so by building the independent school movement in the 1930s and 1940s. In the 1950s, Mau Mau women directly confronted colonial power, took and administered oaths of unity and, finally, took up arms and sustained the struggle for liberation. In the 1950s Mary Wambui was interned with her mother and siblings in a concentration camp in Gatundu, Kaimbu. She stated that there were more women than men involved in the Mau Mau:

> There were many cases where women were in the Mau Mau and husbands were Homeguards. There were many cases of this kind. Many of the men were very violent and ended up chasing away the woman if they knew of her involvement with the Mau Mau. It can be assessed that more women tended to support the Mau Mau than men (First Woman interview, May 26, 1997).

The British had instrumentalized women's work groups in the 1940s to do forced terracing. Peasant women fiercely resisted this slave system for the building of infrastructure for capitalist agriculture. The British response to this resistance was to force over a million women and men into concentration camps, detention camps and prisons. With guns and whips, the British worked them to death building roads for the transport of tea and coffee; irrigation canals for rice; hydrological systems for provision of water to urban areas; quarrying of rock for building of official residences and offices; and even the manual construction of airport runways.

Forced labor was used to build up the entire infrastructure of a postwar capitalist Kenya, which then became the model for the World Bank's vision of independent nations in Africa. *Maendeleo ya Wanawake* was the social service aspect that tried to put a human face on Kenya's counterinsurgency program. The women's clubs were also to be pivotal to the vision of globalizing capital. They were an instrument for winning women over to the project of commodification. The events of the 1960s, however, illustrate clearly the countervailing power of women's autonomous collectivity.

# CONCLUSION: "WE HAVE TO CONTINUE TO CAUSE MORE TROUBLE"[2]

The colonial armed forces concentrated on militarily engaging with the forest fighters while Tom Askwith's Community Development Department ran the prisons, detention centers and the concentration camps that cut the connection between the armed regiments and their civilian supply and support systems. Over a million Kikuyu women, children and elders encamped in concentrated villages were subject to harassment, rape, forced marriages, arrests, detentions, fines, confiscation of property, sexualized torture, enslavement and the targeted killing of children.

At the hands of the Home Guards and British military forces, an estimated 300,000 Africans died during the eight-year Emergency (Elkins 2005:89). Insanity for the perpetrators was one of the results of the dehumanizing action these men engaged in.[3] Reports of massacres of African prisoners of war and civilians, compiled at the time and since, leave no doubt about the extraordinary level of violence colonialists and home guards used to quell the Mau Mau insurgency.

In the terror of colonial counterinsurgency those Mau Mau men who would not give up were decimated. Those who lived to see independence were left landless, maimed or both. Tens of thousands of Mau Mau women came out of prison, detention and concentration camps to find their access to land more dependent than before upon husbands. Widows were particularly vulnerable to landlessness. The numbers of Mau Mau widows continued to grow well into the independence period as many Mau Mau men succumbed to the injuries they received during interrogation or at other points in the war.

As the colonial government undertook its war against the Kikuyu, it also loosened restrictions on other ethnic groups' political activities to try to avoid the spread of Mau Mau on a more generalized scale. But in giving concessions to other groups, the British underestimated the depth of anticolonial feeling in the colony by the mid-1950s. To contain these sentiments among the waged workforce the British quickly replaced the East African Trade Union Congress, coordinated by Makhan Singh and Dennis Akumu, with the more moderate pro-U.S.A. trade union, the Kenya Federation of Labor, under the leadership of Tom Mboya. Although it was possible for the British to suppress the Congress, it was politically impossible for them to completely forbid trade unionism. The liberal capitalism that the United States government fostered world wide in the mid-1950s used "business unionism" as a mechanism for disciplining labor and increasing productivity.

While the East African Trade Union Congress had made waged workers' demands just one part of a comprehensive political platform, Mboya's Federation muted political discussion and channeled union activities toward increasing productivity and wages. Whereas the Congress had fought for peasants' rights and land justice, Mboya's Federation focused narrowly on labor-management disputes. Through the McCarthy years and Mau Mau, and into the independence period, the Kenya Federation of Labor maintained ties with the anticommunist AFL-CIO and the CIA-controlled International Confederation of Free Trade Unions. At the same time the Kenyan colonial administration moved away from the protection of the white settler economy and toward an open door policy for transnational, and especially U.S. capital. Mboya also entered the Legislative Council and was later a key figure in KANU, the Kenya African National Union, which, under Kenyatta, became the ruling party at independence in 1963.[4]

Many non-Kikuyus were of the view that the government's tolerance of the new trade unions and its wage concessions to the expanding industrial labor force were direct results of the Mau Mau struggle. In 1955 a police informant recorded the following contribution from a man in the crowd at a *baraza* (public meeting) at which Governor Baring had spoken:

> He [the Governor] said that Mau Mau are bad people, and we know perfect well that Mau Mau brought something good to us because before Mau Mau started people were getting low salary, and when Mau Mau started to fight with the Europeans the African are getting much more money than they used to get in early day ... We have

to continue to cause more trouble with the Europeans
until they would tire with us and to understand that this
country is not belong to them at all and they are strangers in this country (KNA/DC/TN 3/1, "Secret report of
William Wanyoni, police informer," November 28, 1955,
cited in Berman 1990: 398).

Between 1957 and 1960, the government expanded the representation
of Africans in the legislature. Oginga Odinga was among the new African
elected officers of the Legislative Council who orchestrated "from within"
the near-collapse of the Kenyan colonial government. Odinga and other
anticolonialists staged walkouts and boycotted legislative proceedings.
In 1958 inside the legislative chambers, Odinga shocked the European
members by calling for the release of Jomo Kenyatta and the establishment
of an African majority government (Berman 1990:399-400). He then
went "above the heads" of the settlers and administrators in Kenya and
appealed to the Colonial Office to secure the revision of the constitution.
A constitutional conference began in London's Lancaster House in 1960.

If Mau Mau was a coordinated regional uprising mainly among the
Kikuyu with important participation by Maasai, Luo, Asian, Indian and
other anticolonialists, it was also a movement that promoted Pan-African
unity (Kinyatti 1980:76-77). Mau Mau sang in "Song of Africa:"

We shall be very happy
When all Black people come together
So that we forge in unity
One Pan-African state.

Mau Mau has consistently, to date, inspired struggles against imperialism throughout the world. Mau Mau was one of the first "global stories."
Kenyan guerrillas winning a war against British forces had the ingredients
of a drama that captured the interest of millions of people. Would Africans reclaim Africa's other white colonies through armed struggle? Would
Algerians evict the French? Would the Viet Cong vanquish the French
(and later the U.S.) invaders? The coincidence of the timing of Mau Mau
was also a factor in the circulation of images. The dreadlocked Mau Mau
were ushered onto the world stage just at the moment that television took
to the air. In 1953 *Life* magazine carried full-page color photographs of
Mau Mau guerrilla fighters. Many public figures spoke of Mau Mau. Pan-
Africanist George Padmore witnessed and wrote of Mau Mau's power;

Malcolm X spoke on public platforms; C.L.R. James spoke and published internationally. Padmore described the Mau Mau war as

> a full-scale military operation - the biggest colonial war in Africa since the Boer war. Over thirty thousand British troops have been assembled to assist the local police force, the Kenya Regiment recruited exclusively from among the European male population, the Kikuyu Home Guards, and the King's African Rifles are in open warfare against what the Africans call the Kenya Land Liberation Army (1953:254).

On St. Valentine's Day, February 14, 1965, Malcolm X told a Detroit crowd at Ford Auditorium, that

> the Mau Mau played a major role in bringing about freedom for Kenya, and not only for Kenya but other African countries. Because what the Mau Mau did fright-ened the white man so much in other countries until he said, "Well I better get this thing straight before some of them pop up here" (X February 14, 1965 http://www.malcolm-x.org/speeches/spc_021465.htm).

For C.L.R. James the movements of Mau Mau, Rastafari, Black Muslims and white beatniks in the 1950s and 1960s were all manifesta-tions of "a universal feature of contemporary life." All these social move-ments expressed the complete "rejection of the life to which we are all submitted" (James 1984:164).

The Kenya Land Freedom Army inspired the invocation of Mau Mau in other movements locally, regionally and globally. This emulation has persisted for 50 years. Mau Mau themes have taken on a life of their own, in the global arena, in debates in popular culture and in the academy. In 2002, the British Broadcasting Corporation produced a one-hour docu-mentary film called *Kenya: White Terror*, which exposed British atrocities in Kenya in the 1950s. In 2005 Kenya's Mau Mau veterans launched a legal challenge that sought to prosecute the British government for crimes against humanity.

The trancripts of documents of the 1960 U.S. FBI Counterintelligence Program (COINTELPRO) obtained by author Brian Glick under the Freedom of Information Act reveal that counter-insurgency is another glo-balized dimension of Mau Mau. On March 4, 1968, J. Edgar Hoover issued a top-secret communique to FBI agents in the United States. It spelled out the FBI's Counterintelligence Program against U.S. black nationalists:

> For maximum effectiveness of the Counterintelligence Program, and to prevent wasted effort, long-range goals are being set.
> 1. Prevent the COALITION of militant black nationalist groups. In unity there is strength; a truism that is no less valid for all its triteness. An effective coalition of black nationalist groups might be the first step toward a real "Mau Mau" in America, the beginning of a true black revolution (J. Edgar Hoover, cited in Glick 1989).

The "protected village" program that Askwith studied in Malaysia and further developed in Kenya became a model for U.S. counterinsurgency in Vietnam. There is widespread contemporary evidence of the further globalization of the torture that characterized the anti-Mau Mau prison system, not least in U.S. prisons in Abu Ghraib (Iraq) and Guantanamo (Cuba) under George Bush.

When news of the 1959 Hola massacre hit the world press, the British Colonial Office may have seen the writing on the wall. But neither the administration nor the settlers would admit defeat. The administration maintained the appearance of having everything under control in Kenya to avoid the appearance that Mau Mau had won. The false posture was also meant to assuage the fears of white settlers who were poised to invest in the country. A financial collapse would have weakened the administration's bargaining powers. The settlers invested £5.9 million in their large farms in 1960 alone (Ruthenberg 1966:8). But by 1960, sorely strapped for cash, the administration and the Colonial Office in London concluded that they could not afford to maintain the Kenyan colony. Britain was still in debt to the United States government. U.S. agencies and corporations took a new interest in development of ex-colonies' minerals and agricultural exports, notably coffee and tea. Colonial protectionism and restrictions on the origin of foreign investments in Kenya were increasingly difficult to sustain.

In addition to financial pressures, it was no longer politically tenable for the British to remain in direct control of East Africa. Sudan (1956), Ghana (1957), Nigeria (1960) and Somalia (1960) had all gained their independence from Britain by the time of the 1960 Lancaster House talks in London on the decolonization of Kenya. Tanzania (1961) and Uganda (1961) would secure independence before Kenya. The large white settler population mobilized "kith and kin" lobbyists to resist pressure on

Whitehall to release Kenya from colonial control. For many Europeans in London and in Nairobi the question was how to decolonize without losing their investments in the country. British partnerships with the large Kenyan Asian bourgeoisie provided some answers. Other answers were found in green revolution plans to rapidly increase peasants' export commodity production and thereby make room for corporate investment in the marketing of farming inputs and products.

The key decolonization condition was the sacrosanct status of private property. There was to be no free land. When Kenyatta accepted the "willing seller-willing buyer" approach to decolonization, he fulfilled the desires and demands of those who had opposed Mau Mau's fight for land for all. These included, centrally, the white settlers who were compensated for the land they had originally expropriated, and those loyalists and African businessmen who could afford to purchase plantations in the former White Highlands. Those Europeans willing to sell their land were given fair market prices. Only buyers willing to pay market price were able to acquire land after independence. Land reappropriation, central to revolutionary Mau Mau demands, was shelved by Kenyatta. The demand is still being made in the early 21$^{st}$ century.

Land was not to be handed out to Africans. European settlers were not required to vacate the land they occupied. Their titles were to be respected by the independent Kenyan government. Kenyatta's compromise with settler capital tolerated the continued landlessness of hundreds of thousands of Africans. It seemed, at least in official rhetoric, that the sacrifice represented by the Hola detainees and the Kamiti women was to be forgotten. Kenyatta initiated a reconciliation campaign after independence in which he urged Kenyans to "forgive and forget" the conflicts of the 1950s. But among the Mau Mau, their children and new generations of landless Kenyans, the fight for land and the memories of Mau Mau were not so easily forgotten. Nor were the perpetrators of brutalities against them so easily forgiven.

The outright male deals between chiefs and British administrators were no longer functional for capital in late colonial Kenya. The British spent nearly a decade in armed conflict with Mau Mau before sealing a decolonization deal in Whitehall and Nairobi. The colonialists did not negotiate independence with any of their hand-picked chiefs. Nor did they debate the terms of surrender with Mau Mau Generals Dedan Kimathi or Stanley Mathenge. Rather they turned to a rehabilitated Jomo Kenyatta. George Delf's 1961 book, *Jomo Kenyatta: Towards Truth About the Light of Kenya*, was part of the campaign to restore the acceptability of Kenyatta who was transformed, in a matter of months, from a terrorist to the only African statesman who could unite Kenyans.

The relations of collaboration between the British government and the Kenyatta regime constituted the beginnings of a new type of male deal appropriate to global capitalist relations of the 1960s: the *corporate* or *peasant cash crop male deal*. The government was advised to encourage export cash crop production by rural small farmers and to move toward industrialization and integration into global markets. A 1963 study produced for the World Bank noted that "Africans in increasing numbers are acquiring advanced skills and entering the money economy - and indeed a speeding-up of this process should figure largely in future public policy" (World Bank 1963:1). The World Bank mission specifically recommended "a program devoted mainly to land consolidation, enclosure, and the development of cash production in the nonscheduled areas [the native reserves]" (1963:301). Further, they advised:

> Efforts should first be directed toward replacing subsistence farming with modern methods of production and developing those farms already producing for the market. The transformation of African agriculture that has already been achieved since the introduction of the Swynnerton Plan in the mid-1950s has been remarkable. The pattern for development has been established. The task of the next few years will be to continue the progress which has already been made (1963:2).

The end of the Mau Mau war marked the end of the British empire in Kenya and in most of the world. But through counterinsurgency strategies in prisons and concentration camps, including redistribution of land through the Swynnerton Plan, the colonial administration laid the groundwork for maintaining corporate control over resources in the country even after decolonization. Fundamental to preparing for a transition to independence that would protect white settler and multinational interests was the land privatization program discussed in Chapter Seven. Prisoners built the infrastructure required for new agroindustries. Tens of thousands of rural women were subjected to efforts to create subservient housewives for husbands who would be either owners of or laborers on export crop farms. Hundreds of thousands more rural women were subjected to brutal concentration camp conditions that were replicated in the urban slums to which many thousands were consigned after 1963.

Decolonization, for the British, represented a major reorientation of the organization of capital. Land privatization and housewifization in Kenya went a long ways toward securing British (and U.S.) corporate interests in the region as well as perpetuating, and even deepening, Africa's exploitation by foreign capital. The establishment of the World Bank and the United Nations assured the financing and the corporate market-oriented policy frameworks that defined the direction of postcolonial development. The characters were new. The cloak under which capitalist exploitation advanced was new. But the line of argument was old. The commodification forced upon Kenyans in the 1950s was intensified in the name of development and modernization beginning in the 1960s. Kenyatta's willing-seller willing-buyer land compromise of independence served to delineate and protect the private property of both the reconstituted Kenyan bourgeoisie (African, Asian and European settlers) and its international partners.

By the early 1960s Mau Mau was known globally. The central organizational feature of Mau Mau that appeared as a threat to people such as U.S. FBI Director J. Edgar Hoover was its constitution as a "network of networks" or a "movement of social movements." In Kenya this organizational form was the special arena of anticolonial women activists. They had developed this kind of movement of social movements by amalgamating colonial social organizations such as the church and school with their indigenous kin and age-grade based trade and work groups. Anticolonial networking was articulated in the independent school movement and the Olenguruone struggle. It was adapted for war during Mau Mau. And dispossessed rural and urban women, in particular, were to reappropriate this social form in the 1960s to create an indigenous women's movement focused on securing land and subsistence life goods for their families and entire communities.

J. Edgar Hoover's 1968 warning about the possibility of the emergence of a "coalition of militant black nationalist groups" in the United States was a confirmation of the power of this form of organizing when it was turned toward the struggle for subsistence. It was also a prescient vision of the development of just such a global movement of social movements by the end of the 20th century.

## Notes

1. The quote in the subheading is from First Woman interview, Githima, Molo, May 26, 1996.

2. The quote from the subheading is from KNA/DC/TN 3/1, "Secret report of William Wanyoni, police informer," November 28, 1955, cited in Berman 1990:398.

3. For example, in the early 1990s I met a young Canadian man who told me of his father's experience as a British soldier in Kenya during Mau Mau.

His father had kept a dairy at the time that recorded atrocities his regiment committed against Mau Mau. His father later suffered from insanity.

4.  Tom Mboya was assassinated in Nairobi in 1969. At the time of his death he was minister for economic planning and secretary-general of the Kenya African National Union.

# PART IV

# WINNING THE FIGHT FOR FERTILITY, 1960 TO 2007

~ CHAPTER NINE ⌐

# KENYAN WOMEN'S GROUPS AND THE STRUGGLE FOR SUBSISTENCE, 1960 TO 1979

## INTRODUCTION

In this chapter I trace the resurgence of subsistence in the 1960s and 1970s, in particular, as expressed in the proliferation of Kenyan women's groups. I show how small peasants, land-poor and landless women used the solidarity they had shaped in the Mau Mau war to build a powerful "movement of social movements" on the foundation of a regional network of women's groups.

"Solidarity" here refers to "working together for the commons." Sometimes this working together takes the form of a "gendered class alliance," as in an action-oriented agreement between independent women's collectivities and men who support the women's demands. Men in these alliances are often young men and men with no claim to land or other property. The men may join alliances with women individually or in groups, as they did in 1992 in the Freedom Corner action.

A "movement of social movements" refers to the growing coalition of different kinds of organizations that unite, maintain their autonomy and at the same time share strategies, carry out joint campaigns and generally support each others' initiatives. In the 1960s and 1970s Kenyan women's organizations and the movement they generated made major contributions to food security and community-building. These contributions were made in the context of increasing globalization of both popular and corporate activity. In 1961, Kenyans sang about Zaire's Patrice Lumumba as "a fierce lion against the European colonialists," reflecting the extent to which "African political consciousness" had reached a "continental level" (Owino-Ombudo 1972:40).

Multinational corporations were, in the same period, increasing their activity in agriculture, tourism and related industries in Kenya as elsewhere in Africa, including development programs and projects. This chapter considers how Kenya's peasants reconstructed and expanded the gendered commons for the benefit of all. In a march back onto the land after independence, and against capitalist development plans, thousands of peasant women in urban and rural areas reinvented customary land use for the purposes of survival and elaborated life-centered social relations. These subsistence social relations included trade and self-help networks among women's groups and links between women's groups and other community, church and labor organizations.

Subsistence relations proliferated in Kenya in the post-1963 independence period. Especially widespread were rural peasant women's relations of collective farming and cooperative labor. Against the backdrop of the corporatization of the Kenyan economy in the 1960s appeared thousands, and then tens of thousands, of small- and large-scale women's organizations that worked in, against and outside of the commodified system to enable the elaboration and resurgence of subsistence social relations and land use practices. Rural and urban Kenyan women in large numbers joined together to create a network of women's groups focused on sustaining members' families and communities. Trade, kinship and friendship brought women together into groups and connected groups to each other. This Kenyan women's movement was built on Mau Mau women's organizing for the freedom struggle. But the movement took a new departure: women organized themselves autonomously. They fully determined the priorities of their groups themselves.

Urban areas contained working and dispossessed people from across Kenya and East Africa. There, women's groups were ethnically heterogeneous. Women's savings groups, or "merry-go-rounds," were characterized by a certain level of class homogeneity. This was because women typically joined with others who could afford to contribute about the same amount to the weekly or monthly pot. Rural women's groups were more ethnically homogenous, but many had ties with groups in other areas of the country. As women built up and expanded their network of groups, they forged wide relations of solidarity and collectivity across ethnic and gender lines. The network soon embraced groups that included some men.

Organized in networks of collective work and trade groups, peasant women, in particular, fought for and won some control over land and their own fertility. They wielded significant power to reshape subsistence social relations and garner resources for the life needs of all. The networks of women's groups also provided a platform for the elaboration of a host of new social movements for the gendered commons. By the end of the 1970s this movement of social movements included thousands of women's groups and numerous expressions of the *harambee* [Kiswahili = Let's all pull together] movement. Despite, or perhaps because of, the insecurity of women's land rights, hundreds of thousands of Kenya's women built and engaged in broad social movements that contributed to laying the foundations for further organizational innovations in the subsequent decades.

This chapter explains how the Kenyan women's movement created the *harambee* movement that came to characterize a particularly Kenyan form of indigenous-led development. *Harambees*, like the women's work groups of the colonial period, were subject to capture by the Kenyan state. That is, Jomo Kenyatta sought to use *harambee* like the colonialists used the women's groups of the colonial era; he took a community organizational form and directed it toward the support of political elites and projects that profited individuals at the expense of the peasant population (Ajulu 2000). Out of the women's groups movement, and contestation over the direction of *harambees*, emerged new coordinated efforts among social movements aimed at securing access to life goods.

In Kenya's rural areas peasant women accessed land through marriage, other customary means, land-buying collectives or land allocations from their menfolk. In the 1960s and 1970s, many peasant and landless women concentrated on food production for consumption, usually on one- to four-acre farms, and for sale in rural and urban markets. Very small farms were the most likely to be operated by women, *de facto* heads of households. Since their plots were too small to maintain an entire family, it was among such small-holders that the men were most frequently absent and for longer periods of time compared to holders of larger plots. Local food markets were, in turn, operated largely by single, divorced and widowed landless women who had bonds of solidarity, friendship and exchange with peasant food producers, as well as connections with urban waged working populations who purchased their food at formal and informal markets (Robertson 1997).

After securing access to land through formal and informal arrangements, peasant women employed indigenous methods to organize labor collectively. Most focused on low-input indigenous crops as well as the maize that the colonialists had made a staple of the African diet. Access to land facilitated collective food production and trade, and in turn, collective initiatives strengthened women's claims to land and their capacity to defend their claims. Perhaps the most significant measures of the subsistence resurgence were women's groups' explicit campaigns for the expansion of life-centerd peasant commoning.

# BRITISH ENCLOSURES AND WOMEN'S GROUP EXPANSION

As we saw in Chapter Eight, Kikuyu women emerged from the last of the Emergency-era concentration camps in 1960 to encounter a new set of land relations. The Swynnerton Plan was in full effect, with lands in Kikuyu territory being subjected to private ownership, with communal ownership rights extinguished, in policy if not fully in practice. As noted in Chapter Seven, privatization of common lands under the Swynnerton Plan was also taking place in the late 1950s and early 1960s in much of the rest of Kenya. In 1968, the independent government of Kenya introduced acts to streamline what was a piecemeal, or reserve-by-reserve approach to land privatization under the Swynnerton Plan. The Land Consolidation and Land Adjudication Acts of 1968 involved "the wholesale transferal of land from a jurisdiction governed by customary rights to one governed by private rights" (Bates 1981/2005: 53).

Many rural and urban dispossessed and peasant women met the new land hierarchy by reorganizing customary land relations and collective work, savings mechanisms and social-economic groups. Many peasant women and their daughters formed self-help organizations. These organizations were in the main small-scale, locally based groups of 10 to 20 women, but were sometimes as large as several hundred women. Groups concentrated on the work of food production, local trade and casual labor picking tea and coffee to earn an income for school fees and other necessities.

The main activities of women's self-help groups can be categorized as *social welfare activities*, or the improvement of living conditions in members' households and the community; and *commercial activities*, whereby women jointly invest in a maize mill, a minibus service, a trade partnership or another project to generate income for group members. Commercial ventures were most commonly found in areas in which cash crop or waged employment were already well-established such that women had some access to cash with which to initiate their commercial activity. Social welfare groups predominated (Pala et al. 1978:80-82). The two most common social welfare activities were the collective work group and the merry-go-round or rotating loan society.

At each merry-go-round group meeting (weekly, biweekly or monthly), members contributed a set small sum of money, the equivalent of three or four dollars. About once a month, or at any agreed interval, one member in rotation would get the whole pot. Most groups had conventions about what could be bought with the funds raised in the merry-go-round. In Maragua, a coffee-growing region of Murang'a, women in one landless womens' group forbade members to spend the pot on school fees. The group would put pressure on a member if her husband forced her to hand over the money or to spend it on something that group members had defined as his responsibility, including school fees.

Land-buying cooperatives, shared work groups and *mabati* [Kiswahili = galvanized, corrugated iron sheets] groups or "roofing societies" were all, in fact, versions of the merry-go-round concept and often involved joint savings as a way for women to self-fund larger projects. Some groups organized transport cooperatives to facilitate marketing of rural produce, although in many cases men took over these projects. Others bought or constructed buildings as sources of rental income. Women's groups in addition focused on education and other social reproduction activities. Trade was a major concern, as was support for the ill, elderly, infants and postpartum mothers. The groups engaged in the organization of weddings, circumcisions and funerals; and in targeted tasks such as beer-brewing and house building (Stamp 1986).

The social and physical reconstruction that was necessary after the 1950s war for independence required the mobilization of enormous energies. The huge, articulated network of women's groups that emerged to address this reconstruction was a heritage of the Mau Mau period. Women's collective energies were now released to sustain life itself in peacetime. Mau Mau women, many of whom had been armed in the 1950s, returned to farming in the 1960s. They protected themselves and their claims to land by uniting as women to defend customary entitlements. They used their collective power to produce and to exert pressure on any man who challenged their claims. They tried to realize in practice what they had risked dying for in the 1950s: land and freedom for all.

The unity among women in evidence in precolonial days had been strengthened in Mau Mau. It had not been destroyed during the British counterinsurgency of the 1950s. Monica Njeri of Sagana, who experienced the horrors of the concentration camps in the 1950s, spoke of the strong value placed on unity when she was growing up in the 1940s:

> Since we were brought up, we were taught to stay in unity
> and how to farm and herd animals. We grew doing that

until we got married doing that. After the whites came and made us farm in their land, we were taught to plant maize, we were taught to plant coffee and even taught to breed different types of goats and different types of sheep. We used the knowledge we got from these places for our own economic and social needs. First and foremost, from childhood we were taught to work together in unity with love. It meant that even a person who has nothing, must get assistance from those who have something (First Woman interview, August 25, 1996).

In the independence period, cash crop production was taken up by many farm families, but most continued to dedicate the greater part of their land to food crops (Leys 1971). Even after the colonial agricultural officers had departed, the key decisions involved in export crop production (notably coffee and tea) were almost completely outside the control of the producers. Local marketing boards, the Nairobi auction house and corporate buyers determined prices and farm families' incomes.

But many peasants escaped these controls in the 1960s and 1970s. Swynnerton had stipulated in 1954 that only plots of four or more acres were eligible for coffee production licenses. Immediately this excluded almost half of Central Kenya's farmers. In the 1960s, small landowners, mainly male peasants who wanted cash incomes from the land, had succeeded in putting enough pressure on the Kenyatta government through local Members of Parliament to extend coffee farming to farmers on just two acres (Kershaw 1997:259). Even with the increase in numbers who took up coffee farming, the primary focus remained subsistence food production and local trade. This prioritization reflected women's provision of most agricultural labor and, to an extent, their power in decision-making on family farms.

Whereas family labor and hired hands were used to cultivate cash crops, the collective labor of women was primarily applied to food crop production. By sharing the work of each other's farms, women farmers made very efficient use of their small plots and maintained the social basis for a diverse array of collective works. Private tenure became just another one of many "bundles of entitlements" that was absorbed into the customary practices of overlapping, nonexclusive rights of access. Not until World Bank structural adjustment programs were introduced in the 1980s, and peasants' intensified need for cash led to their expansion of cash cropping, did private ownership begin to usurp customary rights.

The continuing predominance of indigenous land use practices favored the maintenance of women's solidarity and collective work organizations. Many rural women's groups appropriated part of the wealth created within commodified social relations and used it for the strengthening of subsistence social relations. For instance, women whose husbands grew coffee diverted some of the money earned from the sale of the crop into merry-go-round activities that focused on the provision of galvanized iron roofs, household utensils or the purchase of a goat or a cow. These items contributed to women's production in the household and community including in schools.

On a massive scale, women rapidly constructed a network of women's groups that spanned the country and the East African region. In 1975, thousands of women, including many Kenyans, celebrated the United Nations International Women's Year. By 1976, the Kenyan government's Department of Social Services had formed a Women's Bureau as part of government responses internationally to a burgeoning global women's movement. The Women's Bureau registered over 4,300 Kenyan women's groups with a membership of 156,892. Within eight years, by 1984, the number of registered women's groups nearly quadrupled to 16,500 with a membership of 630,000 (Wamalwa 1991:247). By the end of the 1980s there were some 23,000 registered women's groups with over 1 million members (Robertson 1997:249). Hundreds or perhaps thousands more groups remained unregistered because they operated intermittently or so informally that registration was not deemed necessary. In addition many groups had official members who had paid their dues, and many more unofficial participants and supporters.

Kenyan women's groups operated at two levels: first, the thousands of small-scale organizations of women worked at a local level and addressed immediate concerns of their members. Second, many of these small-scale organizations networked with others often but not exclusively via one of the two national women's congresses, *Maendeleo ya Wanawake* and the National Council of Women of Kenya. Most women's groups were independent and members formed their own networks of solidarity among themselves. These networks of women's groups emerged simultaneously with other women's movements globally.

As stated in Chapter Eight, *Maendeleo ya Wanawake* gained a large membership during the Emergency (1952-1960). Many were attracted to the time off from hard labor, the free milk program and other social services the clubs offered during the hard years in these concentration camps. But members soon departed and formed their own informal associations once the Emergency regulations were lifted. *Maendeleo* began anew to gain a membership base during independence once African women were trained and appointed as leaders and facilitators. Its agenda of housewifization remained unchanged however, and many women preferred to organize independently or to join groups organized under the umbrella of the "more politically militant" National Council of Women of Kenya, which formed in 1964 (Robertson 1997:249). Pala stated that

> the *Maendeleo ya Wanawake* organization was preceded by and co-existed with a large number of more local-level groups which formed an integral part of indigenous social institutions in various parts of the country. These local-level solidarity groups, being more closely linked with processes in their societies, were and are able to play a far more active and substantial role at the local level than the national organization. The *ngwatio* among the Kikuyu, the *risaga* among the Gusii and *saga* among the Luo are historically all groups associated with mutual aid efforts in the spheres of agriculture and home community improvements and welfare (1978:74).

The independent Kenyan government, as had the colonial regime before it, intervened in concerted attempts to instrumentalize the autonomous women's groups for the strengthening of the commodified political economy. For example, *Maendeleo ya Wanawake* continued its housewifization programs and eventually, in 1987, became the official women's wing of the ruling party, Kenya African National Union (KANU) (Robertson 1997:249). This absorption is itself the tip of the iceberg of a complex gendered class struggle whereby the state again tried but failed to use *Maendeleo ya Wanawake* as a mechanism for the control of women and the commodification of their labor. Women's groups were enlisted to sing at KANU events and campaign for KANU candidates. Rural candidates often appealed to women's group leaders and contributed money to women's fund-raisers in order to capture the peasants' votes. *Maendeleo ya Wanawake* also participated in the commodification of women's group activities by encouraging donor-funded income generation projects. *Maendeleo* officials engaged with international donors in the provision of the infamously exploitative microcredit schemes for small enterprises (Isla 2001).

*Maendeleo* leaders were among the most visible new "female male dealers." Like their male counterparts, they acted as intermediaries between exploited women and corporate and sometimes state bodies. They channeled women's labor and resources from the subsistence to the commodified realm. For instance, some *Maendeleo* group leaders encouraged rural women to make baskets, which were later sold in boutiques internationally, with very little money reaching the producers.

Even before KANU's absorption of *Maendeleo ya Wanawake*, women's groups were commonly featured in public political meetings. It has been noted that such meetings in Kenya would typically open with songs and dances by costumed women. Public performances of songs and dances had often been staged by hundreds of women. Some of these performances had customarily celebrated subsistence relations or censured those who offended the women. Women's songs of praise were transposed into the political arena of KANU rallies and election campaigns. Women's groups were co-opted to sing the praises of the elite male politicians. At the same time their prominence in these public performances indicated a new level of women's influence in local and national politics.

Singing was not the only activity of women's groups in election processes. Wamalwa argued that in the 1980s,

> in electoral campaigns in some constituencies, their [women's groups'] support, or lack of it, can mean the success or failure of a candidate. For example, in Kiambu, where women form a significant majority, their votes are obviously important and more so when their votes are organized. These groups can empower women to participate in public life by giving them collective confidence, bargaining power and pooled resources (Wamalwa 1991:249).

Women's singing groups persisted in using the customary power of derisive songs to shame leaders. Roise Wanjiru was a freedom fighter in the 1950s. When her Homeguard husband found out that she was a Mau Mau, he divorced her in 1958. She then became a squatter in the village of Kamae on one of the huge farms of the Kenyatta family, just outside of Kamiti prison. She recalled in a 1998 interview that the insecurity of this squatter community's hold on land led her Kamae women's group to sing a protest song to *Mzee* Kenyatta in the 1970s at a public event at his Gatundu residence (*Mzee* is Kiswahili for "old man," and was commonly used as a term of endearment for Kenyatta). He responded with a sexist diatribe that centered on men's prerogative to define and direct development in Kenya. Roise Wanjiru stated that

> the women formed themselves into a group. This was the time people used to go and sing for Kenyatta. After we

formed ourselves into a group, we composed a song that we would sing for him. We agreed that he [had to give either] food or land to cultivate. We were not able to grow food in Kamae because the Army men were complaining that we were using their football field [as a garden]. So we agreed that we were going to compose a song that would communicate our message to Kenyatta.

Now when the day came for the event, we went. The song that we had composed said, "Kenyatta go around your country and see that there are those people who are sleeping on '*managu*'" (a kind of wild, bitter, leafy vegetable) [sleeping hungry].

[while laughing] We used to sing like this:

Kenyatta, walk around Kenya and see for yourself
that there are those people who are sleeping with a plate
of *managu*,
sleeping with *managu*,
which they have cooked with urine from Kamiti.
Kenyatta walk around Kenya
and see there those who are sleeping on *managu*.

When he heard this, he paused. At that time Mburu was the Provincial Commissioner of Nairobi. Kenyatta asked him "Mburu, what did you hear?" Mburu told Kenyatta that he had heard what Kenyatta too had heard. Kenyatta laughed and let us finish the song as it was. After the song was over he called Mburu again and told him "Mburu, after I was born by Wambui, I never went back to my mother's womb. An arrow shot at night is usually answered back by shooting back from where it came through."

He abused us. He really abused us. In fact some of the leaders [present at the meeting] hid and went home. We were left without even a vehicle to take us home. ... After abusing us, he used very obscene words that I cannot even mention. [amid laughter] Can I say?

This is what he told us: "And you say that you sleep on *managu*? Look at these vaginas, whose buttocks are as fat as those of hippopotamus, and you say that you sleep on *managu*? Can I cut for you my penis to walk around Kenya with it and develop where I have failed?"

> When the leaders heard that, they all ran away. We
> could not even tell where the vehicle that had taken us
> there went. He then told us, "That place that you are
> picking the wild vegetable, if you planted maize or beans,
> would they not grow? I don't want to ever hear that you
> are sleeping on *managu*" (First Woman interview, Roise
> Wanjiru, August 8, 1998).

She continued that even though he was angry at the women for
abusing him, he gave in to their plea for a secure piece of land. He did not
give the squatters title deeds, but he stopped others from trying to remove
them from the land they occupied in Kamae:

> So when we came back [to Kamae], each of us got a piece
> of land. From then on we never saw anyone coming to
> claim the land. Even the Kenya Army vehicles stopped
> coming. And that is how we have been living. *Mzee* had
> also said that those people in Kamae belonged to him and
> unless he had somewhere to re-settle them nobody should
> remove them from Kamae. Whoever will remove them
> there should go and settle them elsewhere, but if he has no
> place to settle them he should leave them there. So up to
> now we have been waiting to be given land. Then it came
> a time when we were told that we were going to be given
> a piece of this land [with a title deed]. People from the
> college came, as they claimed that this land belonged to
> them. They came and counted the houses that were here.
> They counted the houses, which numbered 675. They then
> set aside a piece of land.

The song Wanjiru composed and sang for Kenyatta about land problems and hunger was incisive. His reaction was cruel. The singers threatened
him with the curse of nakedness, or he perceived their song as a threat,
as can be judged from his reaction. Kenyatta suggested that women may
give birth to children through their vaginas, but that it is men, with their
penises, who "develop" the country, control land and direct the economy.
He claimed creativity, fertility and potency for men. At the same time, he
distinctly avoided pushing these women to the point that they might challenge his claim to power and creativity by cursing him with nakedness. It
is almost as if he spoke the words "vagina," "buttocks" and "penis" in order

to neutralize any plan the women may have had to actually disrobe and expose their vaginas against him.

Kenyatta explicitly spoke against the curse by claiming that he had never gone back into his mother's womb: "after I was born by Wambui, I never went back to my mother's womb." The curse of nakedness revokes life. Kenyatta preempted the power of the curse, and the surprise element of the curse, by speaking of it before it happened, and suggesting that he would not be affected in any case. He would not "climb back into the womb." He would not have his life revoked or reversed by these women. Nonetheless, he was not immune from the threats of just such a curse and the potential collective power of women's claims. That is why he ensured that the women were safe from others' claim to the land in Kamae.

Though he verbally castigated them, he also made sure that these, "his women," were secure on their land. This was a preventative measure on his part, preventing the women from cursing him, as implied in the song, and no doubt in the dance the women performed. Kenyatta preempted action by the women against him and avoided the danger of their mobilizing others to do the same. The typical pattern of powerful men and large landowners giving consideration to the land needs of the poor is apparent in Kenyatta's granting of use rights to the women of Kamae. Kenyatta's *tha*, or blessings in land, extended only so far, however. He did not ensure the women had legally secure access to their land. The struggle for Kamae land was to continue into the 21st century.

Access to land and the reemergence of customary land and labor-sharing practices after the war for independence laid the groundwork for the expansion of women's collectivities. Women's collectivities, in turn, built the organizational framework for the emergence and expansion of a uniquely Kenyan social initiative: the *Harambee* movement.

## HARAMBEE!

The collectivity of women's work groups, or the "women's group movement," entered into official policy in the form of a self-help movement called *harambee*. *Harambee*, as already mentioned, is a Kiswahili term meaning "Let's all pull together." In Kenya it also refers to both a method of fund-raising and the event at which the fund-raising takes place. Jomo Kenyatta used the term in his early addresses after independence to characterize the kind of effort required to build the infrastructure of the country. The call of *"Harambee!"* often punctuated Kenyatta's speeches and it quickly became the national motto. "Let all the people of our country roll up their sleeves in a spirit of self-help to create the true fruits of *Uhuru* [freedom]. This is what we mean by *Harambee*" (Kenyatta 1965).

Communities were urged to pull together, to combine efforts and resources to construct nursery schools, primary schools, secondary schools, health clinics, cattle dips and water projects. Often people donated labor or materials in lieu of cash. People were also encouraged to join together in mutual assistance groups and production groups. It was this kind of self-help, undertaken in what Kenyatta called the "*harambee* spirit," that would allow the newly independent country to provide the services and amenities that the government would otherwise not be able to afford.

Rok Ajulu builds on Joel Barkan's (1994) analysis to show how Kenyatta used the *harambee* as "an extra-parliamentary institution to facilitate bargaining among politicians" (Ajulu 2000:136). Jennifer Widner explained that "Kenyatta employed a unique extra-parliamentary bargaining system, *harambee*, and a loosely defined political party to focus attention of politicians on local issues and on the formation of alliances across communities" (Widner 1992:73, cited in Ajulu 2000:137). In a review of Jennifer Widner's work, *From Harambee to Nyayo*, Rok Ajulu suggests that Kenyatta's "genius" lay

> in building the institution of *harambee*, as a mechanism for forcing compromise and alliance between spokesmen for different communal groups, and for rewarding politicians whose constituents lost share in the allocation of public funds – an essential tool for facilitating compromise and encouraging politicians to limit their bids for control of party offices and platforms. *Harambee*, according to Widner, allowed bargaining between ethnic elites to take place. In order for local elites to establish or maintain their local clienteles, they not only had to procure funding from the center for *harambee* projects, they were obliged to supplement this personally. Such large demands were often met through an appeal for sponsorship to senior politicians with different ethno-regional identification (Widner 1992:62-63; Ajulu 2000:137).

Having noted how elites used and manipulated *harambee* for their own pursuit of power and profit, let us now return to the popular origins of *harambee*, and examine how rural people themselves used the institution.

Mbithi and Rasmmusson traced the early uses of the term harambee to the Mau Mau period. They showed how Omolo Ongiro, a Luo activist in the 1950s,

> used the word Harambee as a keyword at meetings in 1955 protesting against British-led land registration that was perceived to deprive poor peasants of their land. This created great unity and stopped a registration process that benefitted only so-called progressive [wealthy, loyalist] farmers (Mbithi and Rasmmusson 1977:146).

An earlier study by Owino-Ombudo, *Harambee: It's Origins and Use* (1972), further notes that the Luo activist Ongiro had himself lost his land in the British land consolidation exercises ongoing in Western Kenya in the mid-1950s. He became an anti-consolidation activist and was called upon to mobilize others who were likewise opposed to the enclosure program, but who were themselves unlikely to speak up to the colonial authorities (Owino-Ombudo 1972:36). At one meeting in the mid-1950s, Ongiro was asked to help show the European District Commissioner (D.C.) that the majority were opposed to the enclosures entailed in the land consolidation program.

> The Chief and the Headman, anxious to flatter and impress their master – the D.C. – told him at the Baraza [public meeting] that the people supported land consolidation wholeheartedly. At this point Omolo shouted "Harambee" and the people sang back in chorus:
>
> "Waywagie lowo;
> lowoo, lopwa ma Wasungu kawo."
>
> Meaning: "Let's bemoan our land, our land which Europeans are snatching away from us." Many people therefore showed by approval [of Omolo's mobilizing call] that they were against land consolidation.... The chorus at this crucial meeting went on like this:
>
> "Omolo: Harambee!
> Chorus: *Eeeeeeee!*
> Omolo: Harambee!
> Chorus: *Eeeeeeee!*

Omolo: Harambee!
Chorus: *Eeeeeee!*
Omolo: Harambee!
Chorus: *Eeeeeee!*
All: Rudisha Mashamba Yetu!"

Meaning: Return our land to its rightful owners (Owino-Ombudo 1972:36-37).

Barkan and Holmquist point out that after independence in 1963 *harambee* or self-help "was initially encouraged by and given the official blessing of the Kenyan government in order to shift the cost of providing social services to the peasantry. The net result, however, has been a greater transfer of resources from the center than would have occurred had the movement never grown to its present size" (1989:374). The transfer of government resources to communities came in various forms. Often when a community built a *harambee* school through donated supplies and labor, they would apply for government assistance in the employment of teachers. The government did supply teachers and curriculum to many *harambee* schools. But school-building projects proliferated at such a fast tempo that they outpaced the government's capacity to provide teachers. For instance by 1978, the government aided 380 secondary schools, while another 600 *harambee* schools operated solely through community contributions (Keller 1978:228).

The main activities of the *harambee* self-help movement overlapped with the key foci of women's groups. In fact, *harambees* used as their organizational template the same indigenous self-taxation system that lay at the root of women's merry-go-rounds. As noted above, the origins of the women's group movement in Kenya lay in *ngwatio* and other indigenous collective work groups. Mbithi and Rasmusson stated that harambee "is grounded firmly in existing social ties, rights and duties which have existed and will exist beyond the requirements of a specific project. ... Harambee is founded on the various forms of reciprocal work groups such as 'ngwataniro,' 'mwethya,' 'mwilaso,' 'ielo,' and other associations such as 'mbari,' 'nthuku,' 'ngolano'" (Mbithi and Rasmusson 1977:147).

The Kikuyu *ngwatio*, and its equivalent expressions in other communities, is a form of extra-household labor organization. According to Mackenzie,

both women and men could call together small work groups, *ngwatio*, of their own sex, generally numbering under five people. Such arrangements were reciprocal and involved kin, affines, friends or neighbours in an *itura* (pl. *matura*) [a homestead group]. Frequently, for a woman, they involved "riikamates" [members of the same age grade]. As one woman remarked in 1984, "You can't stop until you have worked for everyone. It's like a debt" (MacKenzie 1998:43).

In precolonial and early colonial days, these very common work arrangements were made for the completion of various types of jobs including clearing land, hoeing, planting, weeding, harvesting, building terraces, cutting thatching grass and making beer (Mackenzie 1997:43).

Kikuyu women had a special option in the process of organizing *ngwatio* that was not open to men. They could call on the help of people from both their parents' home area and from their husbands' locations. This provided for women a wide network of support for their endeavors. It also showed that they had the independence with which to organize collective work on their own farms and to pay back the labor debts not only in their husbands' home areas but also in the places of their birth. Women, more than men, maintained the labor practices of *ngwatio* as the colonial period wore on. Jean Fisher noted in 1954 that "women seem to be more willing to co-operate in garden work than men" (Fisher 1954:234).

As land poverty increased, and men migrated to find enough resources with which to pay taxes and to secure household necessities, women discovered that they required each others' help more than ever. Kershaw noted that, by the late 1940s,

women in poor households, with husbands in migrant labor, became more dependent on their female kin, and, as they did so, they created a (probably new) female social and economic group. It provided care of children and land, in *ngwatio* [extra-household collective labor organization] and sickness. It provided more labor, more income, and companionship when husbands were absent. It gave a psychological refuge: though aging women had the right to live in the homestead of their sons, they often would rather depend on and receive help from daughters than be beholden to daughters-in-law. Women who, for whatever reason, did not or could not stay with a husband, might have found their sisters more accepting of their presence than their fathers and brothers, who had to return the brideprice (Kershaw 1997:156).

Communal work was democratically dynamic and had been highly refined by women in Kenya. They made collective work part of the most highly esteemed kind of participation in the social relations of community among women. Fisher noted that women shared work both formally, such as with *ngwatio* and other forms of labor-sharing; but also very informally as a part of everyday interaction: "Often in the hoeing and planting season a woman is given a brief respite from her labors by other women who are passing by; they go into the garden, take the *icembe* [hoe] or *panga* [machete] from her, and proceed to work for perhaps ten or fifteen minutes. Women who are strangers to one another will sometimes act thus after exchanging greetings" (Fisher 1954:234).

With the introduction of the cash economy on an ever-widening scale as the postindependence decades progressed, women incorporated money resources into the shared-work principle and practice to develop an innovative new social form. They extended *ngwatio,* or the rotating labor group, to include the collection of money to be used by each member in a rotating loan group (Robertson 1996). This was the women's merry-go-round, mentioned above.

Another expression of the incorporation of money into indigenous collective social forms was a kind of community self-taxation to raise funds for such projects as the anticolonial 1930s and 1940s independent schools. In 1913 Mekatilili similarly organized with Giryama women to collect a fee of five rupees per elder and three rupees per young man for the support of their movement against British forced labor, tax and trade policies (Brantley 1986). *Ngwatio* fed into the merry-go-rounds. The merry-go-round was expanded into community fund-raising which was, after independence, the *harambee.* It is in this sense that women's indigenous work practices shaped and generated the most important aspect of Kenya's postcolonial community-building practice.

Wamalwa showed that the government took a hands-off approach to women's concerns by accepting that women were capable of raising their own funds and managing their own projects through *harambee* efforts in their communities.

> *Harambee,* as an "alternative" approach to development, becomes important in a country such as Kenya because of the inadequacies of the prevailing institutional mechanisms for generating growth and development. *Harambee* cannot, however, be expected to replace these institutional mechanisms. And in most cases it does not – except when it comes to women. In this case it can be seen that although

policy holds that the economic position and status of the Kenyan woman has to be improved, it must not be done at the expense of groups that have already attained some degree of prosperity or status. Policy has accordingly placed emphasis on that which the women can undertake together, in groups, on their own initiative, with little or only token assistance (Wamalwa 1991:250-251).

Wamalwa showed that the politicians' use of *harambee* limited the capacities of participants to target projects for the benefit *of all*. She assessed the potential of Kenyan women's groups to act as a "channel for the development of women." She argued that

women's groups are viable institutions for women at the local level. They offer members opportunities which can only be obtained when resources are pooled. At this level, women through such groups can even be an important part of the equation in the local politics of development. They can be the backbone of Kenya's *harambee* self-help movement, and hence catalysts for rural development (Wamalwa 1991:251-252).

Wamalwa critiqued the Daniel arap Moi state's inadequate "institutional mechanisms," but did not question the logic of the capitalist "growth and development" agenda. It was "prosperity and status" that marked "development" for elite urban men, at least. But was this what the women of Kenya's women's group movement sought? Did communities organize *harambees* in order to achieve prosperity and status? For Wamalwa, *harambees* were an "alternative" form of development because communities, not the government, funded such initiatives. I would suggest, however, that the women's group movement and *harambees*, independent of manipulation from male dealer politicians and entrepreneurs, were alternative forms of development because many within the communities that participated sought a different kind of development altogether. Women's groups activities and *harambees* served all. The prosperity they fostered was measured not in commodified terms but rather in measures of social belonging and well-being, such as food security and universal access to education, health care and clean water.

Members of Kenyatta's government promoted women's organizational efforts insofar as these contributed to the state's capitalist development policies. Praise of women often came couched in terms of the production of proper housewives. In the lead-up to independence in 1963 Tom Mboya, conservative unionist who was to become a high-level government official, wrote that

> there is room for a mass movement of women, not as a separate political entity, but as an enormous pressure-group for advancement in a certain field. ... I found the tales of Mary Mukasa, the schoolteacher's wife, who looked after four young children, kept her house spotless and put on a clean dress before her husband returned home, and who pleaded with him at budget sessions for an increase in the milk vote, both charming and worthwhile. I would agree with the description of her coined by her husband Augustine – "Flower in the Home." If there were many such Flowers in East Africa, we could revolutionize the homes of twenty-five million people. I hope it may still be possible to form a mass movement of women, who will challenge the government and the men in each district to give them greater facilities, and who will seek out every woman in a gigantic campaign for literacy and self-improvement. That will be the best preparation of all for consolidating independence (Mboya 1963/1986:161-162).

Mboya hoped for millions of housewifized "flowers." There was no room for women's right to access what they needed directly. Rather they were expected to access the resources they needed through the generosity of men. The government seemed content to deny women's land rights, to prejudice them in inheritance and divorce and to construct necessary facilities only when women had organized enough pressure to make the cost of not providing those facilities greater than the cost of providing them. While the government allocated land to men, women were left to their own devices, to organize and pressure the government and their husbands for what was rightfully theirs.

Wamalwa noted that the government's hands-off approach left women to organize self-help initiatives that were, in the end, an inadequate tool for the enormous task of securing sufficient resources for community health and well-being. However, the women's groups were not intrinsically inadequate organizational forms. Rather, women's groups had to compete with powerful local and foreign corporate interests for control over the same land, markets and other resources. According to Wamalwa, the implication, then, is that the women of Kenya are gaining very little from the formal economic sector which they help to build through their productive and reproductive efforts. They are therefore being shunted into an alternative form of development which should and can only assist institutionalised official avenues, not replace them (Wamalwa 1991:252).

While the indigenous social forms of shared labor and shared land use contributed to the emergence of the women's group movement and the *harambee* movement, other critical social forces were at play. Foreign investment and the increase of peasant cash crop production had unevenly and selectively insinuated a vast network of capitalist marketing throughout Kenya. The government focus on investing in infrastructural development that supported the export of cash crops left the construction of social facilities and the provision of social services largely to the communities, that is, the women themselves (Mackenzie 1998:293).

What was the mechanism through which millions mobilized to produce and struggled to retain their products within the subsistence political economy? The *combination* of the indigenous social forms used by women for food gardening and community-building projects, on the one hand, and the capitalist organizational template disciplining peasants' small-scale or cooperative-based export crop production, on the other hand, was the mechanism through which millions organized this self-help movement. Women's merry-go-round lending groups and community self-taxation practices established groundings in the rural political economy for the dynamic elaboration of community fund-rasing in the *harambee* movements of the 1960s and 1970s. Through involvement in *harambees*, women and men, wealthy and poor, cooperated to quickly fund the construction of necessary social amenities such as schools, clinics and other common life goods. These amenities were meant to improve the educational, health and social situations of rural dwellers and to diversify income possibilities for the next generation, especially since so many had so little land to pass on to their children.

# CONCLUSION

Women's groups of every description proliferated in Kenya in the first decades of independence. Many women's groups developed self-help organizational methods that were taken up in the well-known *harambee* movement, which involved both women and men in fund-raising for community undertakings, especially educational projects.

This chapter has argued that the large numbers of African women who took to the land after independence reestablished subsistence relations on a widening scale. Despite the privatization of almost 100 percent of holdings in central Kenya in the hands of about 10 percent of the population by the 1960s, private land title did not, in practice, extinguish widespread customary claims to and uses of land (C. Leys 1971:318). Women were the clear majority of the rural population in both the reserves and in the new settlement areas of the White Highlands, where most subsistence agriculture was taking root. The women and men residing in the rural areas related to the land as squatters, small landholders, settlement scheme plot-owners, tenant farmers, casual agricultural laborers, managers of agricultural laborers, absentee farmers and landlords.

In the 1970s a few hundred large farms and plantations were outnumbered by tens of thousands of smaller plots of under seven acres each. These were occupied and used in various customary adaptations of land-sharing and succession. Hundreds of thousands of Kikuyu women asserted customary claims to land. Many were successful in these assertions in the reserves and White highland farms during the 1960s and 1970s. Those who did not succeed in attaining access to land through customary means joined land-buying groups or made claims in urban areas, where they lived in squatter slums. The legal status of most women as landowners had been largely nullified by the Homeguards' 1950s application of British land law to indigenous common lands. Widows' and single mothers' customary claims were then much easier for men to ignore. This was because neither the colonial nor the postcolonial governments gave the same legal standing to the customary laws as they gave to the British-imposed land laws centered on the issue of private title deeds. Widows who persisted in defending their own claims to their deceased husbands' land risked being persecuted as witches (Federici 2004; Abwunza 1997).

A process of indigenous peasantization accelerated after independence. It was characterized by an expansion of the numbers of peasant holdings and farmers' priority focus on food crop cultivation for consumption and local trade. However, critical land problems persisted. These problems included the large numbers of farms that were subeconomic or too small to support a family and to divide among children as an inheritance. This led in turn to an increasing incidence of landlessness. Many settlement schemes meant for peasants were located on marginal lands in distant corners of the White Highlands (Jones 1965). Marketing, communications and road networks built from the 1950s through the 1970s, with international loans and local, low-waged (or unwaged) labor, were almost exclusively designed to facilitate the export of crops such as coffee, tea and pyrethrum. Peasant-dominated areas lacked infrastructure and services.

While settlement of peasants onto small plots of land continued into the 1980s, landlessness was simultaneously on the increase. Contrary to some development specialists' assessments that poverty was rooted in lack of access to waged employment and consumer spending power (Seavoy 2000), poverty in Kenya resulted from inadequate access to subsistence resources and relations. While millions of peasants made it clear that they could live without 99 percent of the commodities that filled store shelves, they did need adequate land of sufficient quality, along with the networks of communications, transport and markets dedicated to their economic activities.

Peasant export crop production also boomed after independence. Many channeled their earnings into community-building activities. Although development planners had intended to increase consumption of commodities through the increasing involvement of peasants in cash-generating agriculture, much of what peasants earned was invested back into the community itself. For instance, such activities as merry-go-rounds and *harambees* often focused on raising money for some community member's foreign university fees. This money went not into consumption items per se, but into investments that were expected to yield benefits for the community in the future, for example in the form of educated advocates for rural interests and concerns.

The extensive network of self-help organizations in Kenya in the postcolonial era, including women's groups and the *harambee* movement, drew organizationally on indigenous practice of *ngwatio* or reciprocal work groups. Self-help groups also drew on networks of cooperatives, both producer-controlled and government-sponsored, which emerged in the period to facilitate the channeling of commodities from producers to the global corporate market.

In the colonial period the corporate structure of multinational capital had insinuated itself unevenly throughout the countryside to coordinate the production, harvesting, processing, transport and final export of cash crops such as coffee, tea and pyrethrum. This corporate framework provided many of the lines of communication and organization that were to facilitate the oppositional actions of peasant women in cash crop producing regions, especially in the 1980s. As coffee producers turned the proceeds of their labor toward community-building projects that strengthened subsistence, corporate capital began to take significant steps to more tightly control production and more directly engage peasants in commodity consumption.

The country-wide self-help efforts of Kenyan women's groups produced the *harambee* movement and inspired further organizing in the 1980s. The

Kenyan women's movement facilitated the emergence of a movement of social movements that was to be elaborated by activists in the 21$^{st}$ century. For example, hundreds of autonomous groups around the country began to affiliate with one another in a powerful democracy movement that emerged in the 1990s and continued its creative activities into the 2000s.

An important outcome of the activities of women's organizational networks was the construction, operation and maintenance of a *harambee* school system that included nursery, primary and secondary schools serving several million children. In addition to mobilizing the resources for the physical infrastructure and much of the recurrent expenditures of this school system, the self-help practices and principles of the independence period were reflected in educational approaches that combined academic subjects, vocational training and indigenous education. Adult education and literacy training contributed to the conscientization of thousands of men and women. The syllabi, as Ngugi wa Thiong'o lamented, took years to begin to reflect African, not European society (Thiong'o 1986/1994). "Africanization" of education was a struggle, as wa Thiong'o saw it, against cultural imperialism. But was education simply a route out of peasant society or was it a means of securing a hold on land?

In Chapter Five I addressed the "passionate demand" for education as expressed through the independent school movement of the 1930s and 1940s. Mau Mau songs of resistance and mobilization from the 1950s praised education as a tool in the struggle for land and freedom. In the 1960s *harambee* appeared as a new expression of the indigenous community self-taxation system.

Through the popularity of *harambee* activities, community fundraising was co-opted and elevated to a national practice, over which the highest officeholders in government sometimes officiated. The *harambee* schools, like those of the independent school movement, were mobilizations for something relatively new: the ability to read and write. But the organizational form of the mobilization was not new. And in this combination of the colonial education system and the indigenous fund-raising for African-run schools, the *harambee* movement appeared as a creative amalgam of old and new, indigenous and capitalist cultures. This amalgam was used to strengthen peasants' access to and capacities on the land, to diversify their families' income options that would allow land to be purchased in the last event and to resist separation from the land. As Monica Njeri of Sagana stated, "we used the knowledge we got from these places [of the colonialists] for our own economic and social needs" (First Woman interview, August 25, 1996). In other words peasants' "passionate demand" for education rested in part on their desire to strengthen and elaborate the subsistence political economy through the infusion of new ideas and the resources that an education might provide.

This was not, of course, the educational agenda of the colonial or the independent government. Edmond Keller noted that in Kenya, "the school is expected to produce hard-working, resourceful, loyal, and responsible young citizens who are cognizant of the significance of their future roles in the development of the country; this in spite of the fact that the school does not engage in systematic and manifest civic training" (1978:227). Drawing on the text of various government reports, Keller showed that "responsible young citizens" were expected to be "future-oriented, coopera-tive, progressive, egalitarian, disposed to self-help *only when it does not go counter to national development objectives* and above all, he or she is loyal to the political system as a whole" (1978:230, *emphasis added*). Keller found that both *harambee* and government-run schools inculcated values of egalitarianism and constructive social change, but were "not so influential in insuring loyalty to the political system" (1978:248). Criticism of the land policies of the government were widespread, and constituted, in some assessments, "disloyalty to the political system." Opposition to growing landlessness was especially incisive during the 1960s.

~ CHAPTER TEN ~

# GLOBALIZATION FROM BELOW AND KENYAN SUBSISTENCE MOVEMENTS, 1980 TO 2007

## INTRODUCTION: NEOLIBERAL "DEVELOPMENT"

Kenyans' widespread opposition to the capitalist development agenda was only one of the problems faced by the Kenyatta regime. By the end of the 1970s the entire commodified political economy was threatened by a collapse of both the price of coffee on the international market and the collapse of international coffee price agreements. The second global oil crisis of 1979 also had a severe impact on Kenyan export-oriented agriculture, which was heavily reliant on imported petroleum and petrochemical products. The Kenyan government, with others in the majority world, sank into intractable debt, as interest rates shot through the roof at the same time that costs rose and incomes fell. The commodi-fied global market system reached its tentacles into the remotest villages of Kenya, where export crops had been showcased as the savior of the economy just a few years before.

If it were not for the massive investment of the majority of small farmers in subsistence food production and trade, the impact of this eco-nomic crisis would no doubt have been more severe. In the event, there was enough to eat for most, for the time being. But many men decided to plant more coffee trees in the food plots of their wives to try to make up for the decline in coffee prices. This phenomenon was repeated through the coffee-growing regions of Kenya, Africa and the world. Other cash crops were similarly expanded in response to price reductions in global markets reinforced by structural adjustment dictates in the early 1980s. Global markets were glutted and prices collapsed. The results were reaped in a great famine that by 1984 had devastated much of East Africa, in particular Ethiopia and the Sudan (Davis 2001; Rau 1991; Lawrence 1986).

The previous chapter dealt with the resurgence of commoning in the development epoch of the postcolonial period in Kenya. By the end of the 1970s a new era for leading corporations had dawned. Expansion to a global level in several sectors was imperative if major corporations were to survive takeovers. Neoliberal policies and agencies were organized at the behest of corporate organs, notably the International Chamber of Commerce, and leading Organization for Economic Cooperation and Development (OECD) governments. The Washington Consensus that emerged was premised on the dogma that "there is no alternative" to private corporate sovereignty. Chief justification of this dogma is "the invisible hand" – the magical faith in the "free" markets' supposed capacity to balance supply and demand and thereby generate the greatest good for the greatest number. Analysts have exhaustively exposed, rebutted and repudiated this neoliberal dogma (McMurtry 1998a, 1999; Miles 2001; Chossudovsky 2003; Nitzan and Bichler 2002; Stiglitz 2002; Palast 2001). However, the practical projections of power by large corporations have continued, although with decreasing legitimacy. This chapter treats the delegitimization of corporate rule and its new male deal in Kenya. But in order to grasp the new challenges faced by the dispossessed, and especially by women, it is necessary to provide a selective and brief description of the package of private capitalist trade and investment (and speculation) policies that constitute neoliberalism.

Neoliberalism refers to policies and practices that promote corporate trade and investment "free" of government restrictions. National state sovereignty is reduced and international corporate sovereignty is increased. Beginning in the early 1980s, neoliberalism was expressed through World Bank and International Monetary Fund (IMF) structural adjustment programs, or what Michel Chossudovsky calls "market colonialism" (2003:20). Countries were forced to accede to structural adjustment programs in order to receive loans required for debt repayment.

Structural adjustment programs (SAPs) purported to manage debt by imposing neoliberal conditions. SAPs required state prioritization of export growth and foreign corporate profit opportunities to generate foreign exchange to repay debt. This was achieved through mandated restrictions in social expenditures, especially on health, education and infrastructure, elimination of many public-sector jobs; removal of price subsidies on essential commodities and services; reduction of wages; the privatization of state assets (for example, forests, water and land, publicly owned companies) and public service provision; and, overall, the removal of protection from national economic activities along with the freeing of financial transactions.

As a result, economies became much more open to global corporate activity. Crucial policy areas and instruments were no longer under government control. Instead, global corporations gained a virtually free hand in extending enclosure of previously public and common resources, and especially in speculating on currencies. Foreign firms have taken full advantage of the opportunities to buy businesses, exploit resources and purchase debt and other valued options at bargain basement prices. With the creation of the World Trade Organization in 1994, these opportunities and the neoliberal policies expressed through structural adjustment programs were formalized on a multilateral basis.

The social consequences of neoliberalism include rapid impoverishment of the majority of the population and an expansion of the income gap between the wealthiest 20 percent of the population and the poorest 20 percent. Social unrest has, predictably, followed. Joseph Stiglitz, ex-chief economist at the World Bank, has stated that the authors of structural adjustment in fact expected popular protest (2002). The emergence in the 1980s of "new social movements" was largely a response to neoliberalism's policy impositions and the negative results for the poor, rural and urban, and for the small business class.

These social movements are grounded in local affirmations of public control over common assets. Local affirmations have grown into national campaigns against structural adjustment. By the late 1990s many "commoning" organizations were connected across national borders. Global corporate enclosure was met, in the World Trade Organization meeting in Seattle in November-December 1999, with global popular resistance that shut it down. In the new millennium both corporate and popular claims on labor and resources have intensified. The result is a face-off between an increasingly militarized corporate campaign for control and a popular reassertion of democratic entitlements. At the same time it is important to recognize that both sides in this face-off contain infinite divisions and complexities. Of central interest here are the gendered complexities of actions in defense of the commons in Kenya. Also of interest is the process by which national defense against intensified corporate enclosures extended into the international arena. We now turn to the growth of gendered class struggle in Kenya and the world in the context of neoliberal impositions in the years between 1980 and 2006.

# NEOLIBERALISM IN THE KENYAN CONTEXT

Despite relentless state and foreign programs to commodify and industrialize agricultural production in Kenya, the predominant pattern of land use in 1980 still favored small-scale peasant farming. Women were the majority in most rural areas of the country. Rural and urban dispossessed peasant women were subsistence-oriented; food production for local consumption was firmly in their hands within a huge variety of collectivities and networks. By the 2000s Kenyan women farmers produced 80 to 90 percent of the food crops (Kenya Land Alliance 2004:6).

In the 1980s the export of agricultural products continued to be the source of most of Kenya's foreign exchange. Women predominated among cash crop farmers as well, producing more than 70 percent of all cash crops (Kenya Land Alliance 2004:6), although their husbands owned the land. Some women and men worked for wages on the coffee, tea and sisal plantations of transnational firms. But most of the coffee and tea, the country's most important sources of foreign exchange, was produced by unwaged wives and children of male peasant landowners. As noted in Chapter Nine, many rural farm families channelled the income from export crops into community-building activities, thus redistributing the money benefits of cash crop production to all. Women's groups were central to this process, as were *harambees*, as discussed in Chapter Nine. While commodity production was widespread on rural farms, the cash it generated for farmers was largely used to support subsistence activities. Many peasants and urban landless, for instance, spent much of their incomes on foodstuffs in regional subsistence markets and trade networks.

In the 1980s structural adjustment raised the cost of living overall and thereby eroded the capacities of the landless and customary land claimants to get by without cash. New global actors entered into relationships with the local Kenyan and Asian bourgeoisies. Corporate bankers and investment advisors replaced the old ex-colonial administrators and white settlers who had predominated in the 1960s and 1970s. The male deals of structural adjustment used the "carrot" of cash income to entice men to grow more coffee, and also the "stick" of higher costs of living, which required the increasing family incomes.

The rising cost of living also pressured landowners to forego their customary obligations to tenants and kin. They instead turned the land over to income-generating activities including agriculture and subdivision and sale of land. By thus destabilizing and undermining subsistence relations around the use of land, structural adjustment programs edged more rural farmers toward export crop production.

On the ground, this meant explicit dispossession of many customary tenants. On the farms of those who remained on the land, husbands often plowed under their wives' food gardens and planted more coffee bushes. Peasant coffee-farming men were also expected to discipline female family labor in order to increase productivity. A high degree of control over an essentially unwaged female workforce was possible only through the extension of male deals to the large numbers of peasant men and others engaged in commercial farming. The cash crop male deal of the 1960s was further entrenched in the 1980s structural adjustment programs. These male deals relied upon husbands' control over wives' labor. At the same time, they fostered a new vulnerability confronting transnational capital: these cash crop deals were readily interrupted by wives' demands and actions for family food security.

The enforcement of the corporate agenda of structural adjustment continued through the 1990s and into the new millennium. But the efforts of what John McMurtry (2001) calls "corporate male gangs" abroad and within Kenya to enforce private land relations were met everywhere with the resistance of a rural population which fiercely defended customary tenure. The Zapatistas' January 1, 1994 uprising in Chiapas, Mexico was perhaps the most dramatic instance of the new expressions of peasant resistance to global capital.

Corporate globalization generated new technologies and social organizations that tied Kenyan producers more closely into global markets. Within these circuits, Kenya's movement of social movements, or network of coordinated local organizations, began to engage more actively in a range of international networks of resistance. Repressive policies and state violence in the late 1970s and throughout the 1980s and 1990s led to the exile of thousands of Kenyan intellectuals, activists and others. They in turn constituted yet another set of circuits for global social movement organizing. Many of those who went into exile in the 1980s maintained connections with Kenyan social movements. Others established links with international organizations such as Amnesty International, which further engaged in the coordination of activities with Kenyan networks. This process of "globalization from below" involved the integration of Kenyan subsistence capacities into a global movement of social movements for the commons.

This chapter assesses the process of globalization from below in three instances of resistance against dictatorship and corporate enclosures during the era of neo-liberal corporate globalization: (1) the Freedom Corner hunger strike and vigil in 1992; (2) the upsurge since 1999 of an extensive wave of decentralized, autonomous actions for land reappropriation; and (3) new expressions of the 1990s democracy movement in the 21st century, including protests at the Cancun, Mexico meeting of the World Trade Organization and the struggle for a new Kenyan constitution.

The chapter shows that as Kenyan social movement activists resisted corporate globalization from above, they simultaneously engaged in a process of popular globalization from below. It further argues that peasant women's rootedness in subsistence networks provided a key organizational milieu within which resistance to corporate rule was pursued on an ever-widening scale. The chapter ends by examining aspects of the ongoing processes of globalization from below in Kenya in the new millennium.

By the mid-1980s, thousands of East African farmers, women in particular, resisted the continued pressure to expand export crop production. They diverted their energies from export crops to food crops. In the 1990s the Kenyan state used staggering levels of violence to enforce commodification. At the same time the 1990s social movements were characterized by a new scale of resistance. They attacked the Kenyan state and corporate rule by devising new subsistence social relations capable of replacing the commodified corporate model of export-oriented agriculture. The stories of women's resistance to cash crop production in Maragua and Mwea, and the activities of women in the Green Belt Movement offer illustrations of this struggle and provide important background to the analysis of the 1992 Freedom Corner hunger strike presented below.

# RURAL WOMEN'S ORGANIZING IN THE ERA OF STRUCTURAL ADJUSTMENT

In previous studies of rural women's resistance to cash crop expansion in Kenya, my coresearchers and I identified relations among key actors in the struggle of small-scale peasant coffee farmers in Maragua, Central Kenya (Brownhill, Kaara and Turner 1997). Here I briefly review the findings of our study of Maragua and Mwea women's rejection of cash crop expansion imposed in the 1980s in the context of global structural adjustment and the simultaneous emergence of global peasant resistance. I also outline a short history of the Green Belt Movement in order to introduce some of the organizational initiatives that form a backdrop to women's action at Freedom Corner in 1992.

State corruption, a surge in the price of petroleum-based agricultural inputs and a 70 percent drop in real international prices for Africa's coffee exports in the 1980s contributed to Maragua coffee farmers' increasing impoverishment (World Bank 1994). By 1986 increasing most Kenyan peasant women received virtually nothing from their husbands' government-issued coffee payments (First Woman interview, Rev. Samwel Waithaka, January 2, 1997).

By 1987 many Maragua coffee wives began to plant vegetables among the coffee trees. It was against agricultural regulations to intercrop with coffee. But hunger forced women to break this regulation. When failed incomes led to hunger in some of East Africa's richest farmlands in the mid-1980s, peasant women took further action. Although it was illegal to damage a coffee tree, women in Maragua and elsewhere in Kenya and East Africa uprooted the trees and used them for firewood. One woman stated that it was on the way home from a church service that she and her friends made a pact to destroy all the coffee trees on their farms that day. They did so, and helped each other plant food gardens in their place (First Woman interview, Monica Njeri, April 19, 1997).

Soon many more women began uprooting coffee. It was so widespread as to be unstoppable. Maragua women in effect repudiated the law by direct action. They rejected World Bank development because it did not work as a livelihood strategy. Maragua women returned to subsistence and fed themselves. Women's reassertion of economic autonomy over even a relatively few acres of coffee land became a direct challenge to the authority of Daniel arap Moi, whose friends controlled and benefitted corruptly from coffee revenues.

The Maragua women's coffee strike lent economic power to a growing anti-Moi mobilization that had begun to gather force. Their power was three-fold. They had withdrawn labor from global coffee supply chains. They immediately reduced the Kenyan government's revenues. And, most creatively, they turned their land and labor towards the rebuilding of relations of subsistence commoning.

Over the 1990s this pattern of coffee wives rejecting structural adjustment policies and strengthening subsistence political economies was repeated with varying intensity throughout the East and Central African region. In the Maragua case, by shifting their energy and land to food production, women kept and enjoyed the benefits of their labor. They did so by cooperating with kith and kin within and beyond their local communities.

Mwea is a state-run rice irrigation scheme located in Kirinyaga District some 100 kilometers northeast of Nairobi. In 1953 the colonial government began using the captive labor of Mau Mau detainees to dig irrigation canals by hand at what was then Mwea detention camp (Njihia 1984:1). In 1961 the Mwea detention camp became the Mwea Irrigation

Scheme. Many of the detainees had lost their land during the war and had no alternative but to remain in the detention camp, now not as detainees but as tenants. The National Irrigation Board (NIB) was established to sell milling and marketing services and inputs to the tenant farmers. The NIB also enforced strict production regulations.

It was more difficult for Mwea farmers to challenge the repressive commodified agricultural production regime than it was for the coffee women of Maragua, owing to the fact that the rice producers were tenants, not landowners in the state-run Mwea settlement scheme. Tenants were threatened with eviction should they fail to produce adequate quantities of rice. Nevertheless, Mwea women did initiate resistance to government pressures to produce more rice, especially after structural adjustment opened the market to rice imports, which undercut prices of locally produced paddy. Mwea's women were at the forefront of resistance. They gained the support of many men in Mwea in diverting water from rice irrigation channels to grow vegetables instead, for their families and for the local subsistence market.

A host of social problems accompanied the exploitative production regime in Mwea in the 1980s and 1990s. Rice production declined 13 percent in the decade ending in 1995 while actual deliveries to the government purchasing body declined much more as farmers sold their rice at higher prices on the parallel market (National Irrigation Board 1996; Kamau 1996). Child survival in Mwea had "deteriorated." There were high incidences of alcoholism, "marital problems" and child neglect (Republic of Kenya, *Kirinyaga* 1993:70). Violence against women in Mwea was rampant. Single mothers' groups gained members by the month, as abused women fled their husbands (First Woman interview, Carolyn Wamarua, 10 October 1996). Many young women in Mwea refused to marry at all. Instead they moved straight into appropriating land and planting tomatoes and rice for sale on their own account (First Woman interview, Mwea, July 23, 1998).

Farming women of both Maragua and Mwea defied their husbands, confronted the state and rejected the commodification policies of the corporations. They began by refusing the discipline meted out by husbands who sought money gains from the crops women produce. While the International Monetary Fund and World Bank stepped up pressure to privatize state assets, including coffee and rice marketing boards, women producers created an alternative to corporate takeover. Many revived customary women's work groups. Through these self-organized groups they continued to reconstruct an autonomous regional subsistence production and trade system. These women took command of their own labor and other resources by spurning often violent discipline by husbands, defying state policies, and resisting their own incorporation into global markets on capital's terms. Maragua farmers, in their refusal to produce export crops, in effect repudiated the debt, which was being repaid in part from the foreign exchange earned by exports of Kenyan AAA coffee.

In resisting cash crop agriculture women in Maragua and Mwea expanded the terrain for a much more sustainable, ecologically sound, life-focused indigenous subsistence agriculture. Women were at the forefront of many forms of resistance to structural adjustment in Kenya in the 1980s and 1990s. They were joined by a growing number of men who declined to be overseers of their wives' production on behalf of the state and capital.

The Green Belt Movement was another women-led initiative committed to enhancing food security by conserving forests, water sources and indigenous seeds. Dr. Wangari Maathai founded the Green Belt Movement in 1977 under the auspices of the National Council of Women of Kenya. The Movement addressed the decline of both ecological resources and principles of stewardship that Maathai observed to be coinciding with the advance of commodity production in farming areas.

In 1992 Maathai spoke to the U.S. Sierra Club of how she returned to Kenya after some years of education abroad to find that ancient fig trees were being felled throughout her home area. These trees were customarily never cut down. They were sacred (see Beech 1913) and even the twigs were not picked up from the ground or burned as kindling. These trees were sacred because they acted as protectors of the vital water catchment areas. With the expansion of tea plantations in the 1960s and 1970s, the fig trees were sacrificed. Desiccation of the soil quickly followed (Women's International News Gathering Service 1991). In one sense the reforestation of the old Kikuyu reserves by Maathai's Green Belt Movement was a process of healing the land that had been bombed and burned by British and Homeguard counterinsurgency in the 1950s and denuded by the export crop development that intensified from the 1960s onward.

With minimal funding and through self-help efforts, the Green Belt Movement began to establish branches, first throughout Central Kenya and then more broadly. Women's groups were encouraged to plant trees. They were educated in seminars held in rural areas about how trees might be planted along boundaries and in different sites within the homestead. The types of trees planted might be chosen for their fruit-bearing capacity, medicinal qualities, ritual purposes, firewood-producing capability, water catchment protection or for their decorative appeal. Trees were also planted on public land: school compounds, church yards, public squares, road verges and other common lands. This beautifying of public, common social space was a prelude to its popular defense from elite land-grabbers in the 1990s. Through advocacy and a massive educational campaign, the Green Belt Movement branches built on traditional ecological knowledge and encouraged the return to indigenous seeds and cultivation techniques that raised soil fertility and slowed desertification. Its branches were also sites for seed exchange among women farmers.

In an important respect, women's tree-planting activity was an innovation on custom. Temporary crops were always women's domain while permanent crops, and particularly trees, were customarily men's domain because men had more permanent rights to the land itself. When women planted trees, they also strengthened their claims to the land. Women's tree-planting activities were partially based in customary practices that devolved responsibility for food provision to women. Hobley wrote in 1929 that among the Kikuyu, "old women, past the child-bearing age, can participate in sacrificial ceremonies at the sacred trees. This is due to the fact that the growth of cereal and other vegetable food falls to the woman, and they alone are responsible for the food of the family" (1929/1976:275).

In organizing the reforestation campaign, rural women's organizations expressed a new form of social power as they drew on aspects of customary practice. While running tree nurseries and reforesting public areas may or may not have been customary practices, women in large numbers did apply customary organizational techniques and indigenous environmental knowledge to the carrying out of these formalized activities. These aspects of customary practice augmented the success of Green Belt ventures and laid the groundwork for the expression of a new form of women's power: the power to heal the heavily damaged ecology, first of the Kikuyu reserve lands and later across the country and the continent. This power to heal the earth was recognized by officials and citizens alike. This recognition was accorded in part because of the obvious improvement in all indicators of environmental well-being, and in part due to the rejuvenation of indigenous knowledge and practices which went along with the women's engagement in the cultivation of trees.

An educational component of the Green Belt Movement was aimed at school children who were recruited to plant trees in their school compounds, their homes and further afield. Both women and children were instructed not only in planting but also in the care and maintenance of the trees. In this way, hundreds of thousands of rural Kenyans assumed and defended their rights to control and protect land on which, by the new millennium, they had planted some 20 million trees.

The establishment of green belts of forests was a response to the historical and continuing expansion of the colonial "white belt" of European settler capitalist occupation that had begun the deforestation of millions of acres of land early in the 20th century. The Green Belt Movement used tree planting as an entry point into wider discussions and actions in five areas: food security, the negative impacts of petrochemical-based agricultural systems on health and environment, genetically modified seeds, civic education and voter registration. Tree planting and associated activities were adopted by hundreds of women's groups, many of which continued to engage in other types of activities such as merry-go-rounds and shared work on each others' farms. The environmental activism of Green Belt injected into the rural women's group movement a new focus and a new source of support. Indigenous food production techniques, for instance, were validated not only as familiar, affordable and in line with women's skills and needs; but also as ecologically restorative practices which contributed to the overall health of the environment and the community (Wane 2000:65).

The production and sale of tree seedlings became a commercial aspect of the Green Belt Movement. Many women's groups ran nurseries. Although the Green Belt activities addressed soil erosion, food insecurity and income-generation needs of the rural people, Maathai herself was vilified by President Moi in the 1980s. Why did the activities of this ecological movement raise the ire of businessmen and others in the government? The land on which women planted and defended their trees was clearly land not available for mechanized plantation-style cash crop production. Women were becoming more and more adamant about the need to limit plantation agriculture and return land to indigenous uses. The subsistence uses of the land that peasant farm women pursued were, however, direct challenges to private interests who wished to buy forest land, clear it and either develop or subdivide and sell it. For the land speculator or plantation owner, the Green Belt Movement was an impediment to trade.

The standoff took on a national and international character in 1991 and 1992, when Maathai campaigned against the destruction of Uhuru Park. The Moi regime had secured a World Bank loan to build a skyscraper, to be the tallest building in Africa. The site chosen was Uhuru Park, the largest open green space in Nairobi. Maathai opposed the plan and coordinated an international campaign against World Bank funding of what was widely regarded as a prestige project for the president. It was also a potential ecological nightmare for Nairobi. Maathai was successful in stopping the construction plans. Her victory fed directly into the Freedom Corner women's hunger strike, which began in February 1992. By this stage, the conflict between rural women's land concerns and global corporate interests was central to the agendas of many Kenyan movements for democracy and human rights.

## ON TO THE DEMOCRACY MOVEMENT: FREEDOM CORNER 1992

The farmers' protests reviewed above were among the first of many peasants' and unwaged workers' acts of resistance that began to engulf the entire society in the era of structural adjustment. A three-day general strike began on July 7, 1990. This developed into a mass rally for democracy that defied the dictatorial regime of Daniel arap Moi. The "Saba Saba" rally, as it came to be called, was organized by market women, transport workers, secondary school and university students, street vendors and the urban unemployed. "Saba Saba" translates from Kiswahili to "Seven Seven," and it stood for the date of the beginning of the strike, July 7.

The strikers demanded the reintroduction of multiparty democracy. They protested police killings three months earlier during the contested attempts by the state to demolish Nairobi's downtown Muruoto slum. They decried high prices of food, transport, school fees and other necessities. The nationally effective strike and demonstrations continued for three days, during which time police killed some 20 protestors (Human Rights Watch 1993; Kenya Human Rights Commission 1993, 1994).

It was in the context of an international democracy movement that women held a national conference in Nairobi in February 1992 (Brownhill and Turner, 2002). It was on the first day of this conference that Moi abandoned his plans to build Africa's tallest skyscraper. When the announcement that the building plans had been cancelled was made during the women's conference, Maathai mobilized women to march immediately to Uhuru Park. They placed a wreath on a tree near the now-abandoned building site. In a brief celebratory ceremony, the women renamed the site "Freedom Square."

It was at this same women's conference that the mothers of political prisoners began to publically discuss the actions they planned to undertake in an effort to secure the release of their sons who were languishing in Kenyan jails. Maathai and others had formed a group called "Release Political Prisoners" to lobby for the men's release. Two mothers, Monica Wamwere and Ruth Wangari Wa Thung'u, spoke to the women at the conference about their ordeals. Wa Thung'u made an impassioned plea for solidarity and announced that she would go on hunger strike to pressure the government to release her son (First Woman interview, Wahu Kaara, April 29, 1996).

Within the week, on February 28, 1992, 12 Release Political Prisoners (RPP) women delivered a letter to the attorney general demanding the release of their loved ones. The attorney general promised to take the matter under advisement. From his office, the women marched the four blocks to Uhuru Park to the location where they had hung a wreath some days earlier. The women set up camp and began their hunger strike. Those refusing to eat ranged in age from the mid-20s to mid-70s. Some had been Mau Mau fighters in the 1950s. They occupied the most public corner of Nairobi's Uhuru Park, the place that had a week earlier been christened "Freedom Square," and renamed it Freedom Corner.

Within hours, over 10,000 people had joined the women's protest. A gathering of this many people was unprecedented in Moi's repressive era. A police permit was required to legally assemble with more than three people at a time. Four Asian youth showed up on the second day to erect a tent to shelter the women. Activists of a number of organizations provided a volunteer security cordon around the hunger strikers. Someone anonymously donated a public address system. Members of the public from barefoot street beggars to African statesman, Oginga Odinga, spoke freely of their grievances and demands over the public address system. Dozens more mothers of political prisoners came forward and asked that their children's names be added to the list. The president was reportedly afraid to drive past the corner on his way to Parliament.

On the fourth day of the hunger strike, March 3, President Moi sent police to break up the protest. By 3:00 pm, several hundred policemen had surrounded the site. They broke the protestors' security cordon with truncheons. General Service Unit soldiers threw tear gas into the hunger strikers' tent. Policemen indiscriminately battered the old women. They beat Wangari Maathai unconscious. She was rushed to the hospital where she recovered. It was after the tear gas had immobilized most of the protestors that hunger striker and Mau Mau fighter Ruth Wangari observed police brutalizing a protestor. Wangari recalled:

> We were attacked with tear gas, clubs, and the whole area was sealed off by policemen and security officials. But me, because of the experience I had in the forest during the Mau Mau war when we were assaulted with tear gas and faced with other problems, we had been taught how to defend ourselves. I took a blanket and soaked it in water and covered my head....
>
> After all this, I tried to think what I would do next. I then stripped my clothes and remained stark naked and

started fighting with the policemen, because I saw a young man called Kanene, who was one of us in Release Political Prisoners, struggling with a policeman who wanted to shoot him. I came in between them and stripped off my clothes (First Woman interview, May 29, 1996).

Ruth Wangari's action, so similar to that taken by Mary Muthoni Nyanjiru 70 years earlier, stopped the police in their tracks. The protestors fled, the police walked away and the imminent bloodbath was defused. Because they were old women, they raised the immediate interest and sympathy of the public at large. Kenyans typically call women of an advanced age "my grandmother." Similarly, the elders may speak as if they had "given birth" to the entire generation of younger people: not only those of their own ethnic group, but *all* young people. All men of a particular age become "my sons." Likewise, all women of a particular age can be referred to as "my mothers." These are contemporary expressions of the indigenous age-grade systems.

By exposing her naked body, Wangari drew on these deep-seated relations to curse the men who dared to defy their mother. In this single act, Ruth Wangari established the mothers of Freedom Corner as the mothers of a whole generation of Kenyans. Newspaper photos of her defiant "curse of nakedness" galvanized people throughout the region. Rural women, who best understood the call to action implied in Wangari's act, were especially aware that a new stage in the democracy movement had been reached. International news coverage of the police brutality and Ruth Wangari's nakedness prompted an outpouring of support for the women's cause.

Hunger striker Wahu Kaara secured permission from the Rector of the nearby All Saints Cathedral to continue the women's vigil there. Within 24 hours, without telephones or broadcast media, all of the hunger strikers had reconvened at the Cathedral, where they hosted an interfaith prayer meeting with representatives from the Catholic, Protestant and Muslim communities. Hundreds of visitors came to the Cathedral during the women's one-year encampment there. They included ordinary Kenyans who came to thank the mothers for their courage, as well as victims of the rural land clearances, representatives of Amnesty International and other international human rights organizations, and the ambassadors of several European and North American countries. The police defied orders and refused to interfere with the mothers because they feared the nakedness curse and, perhaps, because some police were in sympathy with the mothers' cause.

At the end of February 1993 after a full year the women left the refuge of the church. By then the government had released from prison 51 of the 52 men whose liberation the mothers had demanded. The 52nd political prisoner, James Apiny Adhiambo, was released on November 14, 1997, after a five-year international campaign coordinated by the mothers' Release Political Prisoners group.

The Freedom Corner women broke through the wall of repressive silence that had contained dispossessed Kenyans for the three decades since the Mau Mau insurgency. They brought together issues of freedom for political prisoners and a host of other concerns, including land rights, democracy, debt repudiation, reparations and other women's rights. The curse of nakedness tapped into the collective historical memory of millions of Africans. The power of the women's actions was rooted in their collectivity and their prioritization of life over profit. At its core, the struggle for democracy in Kenya was a struggle for land. Moi was characterized as "undemocratic" not only because he outlawed all political parties besides the ruling KANU party. The policies of KANU, which incorporated structural adjustment corporate dictates, denied and overrode the demands and interests of the majority of citizens. It was in this context of citizens' dispossession, hunger and alienation, and corporations' increasing wealth and power, that Kenya's democracy movement gathered force. Democracy was not as much about the political pluralism that U.S. Agency for International Development and other international organizations championed in the early 1990s as it was about expanding the majority's security of access to life goods and community well-being.

The Freedom Corner protest demonstrates the expansion of the scale, scope and integration of Kenyan social movements in the period. Beginning with 12 women who were members of a small new organization called Release Political Prisoners, the Freedom Corner protestors demanded the release, initially, of some two dozen men from prison. The women did not speak for political parties or other organized groups. They did not advertise their protest. They quietly sat at the corner of a city park with signs listing their demands. Ten thousand people immediately stood with them.

The explosion of support was accompanied by a massive expansion of demands. These ranged from protection from the violence of politically motivated land clearances (what the government labeled "ethnic clashes"), to employment, health care, food, land, electricity, running water, freedom from police harassment and brutality and a long list of other specific and overarching demands. The momentum built up at Freedom Corner, and the incipient "movement of social movements" it embraced, were carried into the struggle for the rewriting of Kenya's colonial-era constitution, analyzed later in this chapter.

How were the thousands of people who engaged in the four-day demonstration at Freedom Corner and the year-long vigil at All Saints

Cathedral connected with one another? This question is especially pertinent to an examination of the organization of resistance because so many people came together in so short a time without prior planning. There were in Nairobi in 1992 a large number of informal organizations including Release Political Prisoners, Tent of the Living God, *Mungiki* [Congress or Multitudes], and the slumdwellers' organization *Muungano wa Wanavijiji* [Kiswahili = Organization of Villagers]. Since the successful stand of Muruoto women against the police in March 1990 and the Saba Saba strike of July 1990, there had developed a keen interest among many of Nairobi's residents to organize, to defy the police and state, to demonstrate and to mobilize large numbers of people. But there were few opportunities to mobilize mass protests because police brutality was almost guaranteed. Women were particularly vulnerable to rape by security forces.

News of the elderly women's hunger strike spread rapidly by word of mouth, via market women and thousands of commuters who passed Freedom Corner daily on their way to work, and via transport workers who have a history of engagement in protest politics in Kenya. As they stopped for traffic signals or alighted from public transit, the people encountered banners and the elderly protestors themselves. The elders were strategically camped near the university, where students, prone to demonstrations of their own, were in session.

When the people of Nairobi who were already organized into their own small groups saw the stand that their "grandmothers" were taking, many were eager to lend support. Thus organizations converged at Freedom Corner to support the women and to add their own demands to the public outcry. The Freedom Corner protest had a particular draw because it was generally the case that police would avoid beating or raping elderly women. To do so could invite wrath and even the curse of nakedness from one's own grandmother. The women were seen as simultaneously vulnerable and courageous. While they were apparently weak, the elderly women also offered protection to the others who joined them. In addition, the sentiment seems to have been, "If our grandmothers can take a stand, why can't we?"

A general strike was looming. The urban crowd was massing and could easily shut the capital down. International media were intensely active. Global communications effectively broke the censorship of the Moi regime. Faxes and email alerts circulated the globe and quickly mobilized human rights activists, feminists and environmentalists. For instance Wangari Maathai's Green Belt Movement was well-known internationally. Beginning in 1991 Maathai used various ecological activists' internet lists to disseminate information and action alerts concerning the first "ethnic clashes," or violent state sponsored land-grabs.

At least four organizational forms came together at Freedom Corner. These established the return of the ordinary woman and man to public, open resistance politics. First, the involvement of Mau Mau women evoked memories of the armed struggle as well as the wisdom inherent in subsistence social forms, such as the curse of nakedness which drew on age-grade formations (First Woman interview, Wahu Kaara, April 24, 1997). Second, Green Belt Movement founder Wangari Maathai's involvement in the founding and activities of Release Political Prisoners brought to the mix the politics of women's groups' environmentalism and connections to international ecological, women's and human rights movements. Third, the involvement of women who participated in the clandestine MwaKenya politics of the late 1970s and early 1980s brought forward the lessons of that difficult time.[1] And fourth, the new peasant politics of direct action for food security and subsistence livelihoods, exemplified by the protests in Maragua and Mwea, informed each of these other overlapping experiences.

Freedom Corner was an important turning point in Kenya's movement for globalization from below. By the early 1990s Kenyan commoners had built up a widespread matrix of resistance. This matrix included links with global movements in defense of political prisoners, women, the environment, democratization, debt repudiation, land to the landless and peace. The histories of dispossessed peoples' militancy in Kenya demonstrate that the alternatives to corporate globalization were being reinvented on the ground. Peasant women were integral to the articulation of these subsistence alternatives.

## THE GENDERED COMMONS: CORPORATE ENCLOSURES AND POPULAR REAPPROPRIATION

World Bank structural adjustment programs created conditions within which the Kenyan state orchestrated and supported violent rural land clearances between 1991 and 1998. SAPs required the privatization of state properties. Kenyan male dealer politicians were loath to privatize state corporations if it meant that foreigners would come to own the major industries. Throughout the late 1980s and early 1990s, politicians in league with the president allocated to themselves ownership of all kinds of government properties. It was agricultural land, however, that presented the biggest prize in the land-grabbing frenzy that structural adjustment privatization programs had ignited.

The problem for the men who coveted the land was that it was occupied by hundreds of thousands of peasants living in mixed-farming subsistence communities. Some were producing small quantities of cash crops for the domestic and export markets. By 1991 various spokespeople for the democracy movement in Kenya were sufficiently well-connected to make their own direct appeals to the World Bank. They pressured the Bank to withhold funds from President Moi until he reversed land-grabbing, reverted to multiparty democracy and ceased the use of violent repression against political opponents. The Bank did withhold the funds, and Moi did (formally) reintroduce multiparty politics in December 1991. But his land-grabbing and tactics of violent repression did not end. In fact they increased dramatically in 1992, the year of the first multiparty general election since 1982 when Kenya became a single-party state.

Kenyan male dealers devised their own project of privatization. They dispossessed thousands of peasants who lived on state, cooperative and common lands and tried to make it their own private property. State officials with the sanction of the president turned to outright violence to force hundreds of thousands of peasants to vacate their land completely. Mercenaries and thugs were promised plots of land, but the bulk of the farmland thus cleared was earmarked for large-scale plantations for a handful of well-connected and well-protected politician-businessmen (Human Rights Watch 1993, 1997). Government officials organized the training of paramilitary squads and the importation of weapons, such as flaming arrows from Korea (First Woman interview, Muriithi Nduthu, June 11, 1997). The government restricted media, medical, religious and relief access and interventions.

These violent enclosures, called "ethnic clashes" by the government-controlled press, dispossessed peasants who insisted on growing food. Many thousands who were on strike against export crop production were murdered. Over the 1991 to 1998 period the land clearances left some 30,000 dead, 300,000 homeless and millions living in fear of the next attacks (Human Rights Watch 1993, 1997).

The clearances appear to have had two main aims. First, those political incumbents responsible accumulated a large amount of property. The land might buy them political support, as it could be handed out in small or large parcels. The land was also an investment for the politician who might soon lose access to the power that had allowed him to grab other peoples' property with impunity. Second, the land clearances were an effective means by which the entrenched elite could fight against those who were likely to vote for the opposition in the general elections, or punish those communities in which support for the opposition was strongest. By killing, raping and dispossessing some half million people, many of whom were thought to be supporters of the opposition, the politicians in government ensured their own victories at the polls.

Moi's violent land clearances persisted through the late 1990s. State-sanctioned mass murder was concentrated especially around the times of the 1992 and 1997 general elections. Moi-style privatization in the shape of landgrabs and "clashes" wreaked havoc on the subsistence political economy. The Kenyan democracy movement had succeeded in forcing a return to multiparty politics. By the end of the 1990s a dense network of formal and informal organizations was intensely engaged in social trans-formation to make democracy real on the ground, especially with regard to land, food production, regional trade and respect for human rights. They did so in a context of murderous land clearances aimed at enforcing priva-tization and other commercial policies (Seavoy 2000:113).

In the context of Moi's repression and the World Bank's structural adjustment programs, a highly networked democracy movement arose. The network was characterized by the loose affiliation of autonomous groups that arose in the hundreds after Freedom Corner in 1993. Kenyans were organized, in the course of their daily lives, in trade and transport associa-tions, agricultural and land-buying cooperatives, parent-teacher commit-tees, churches and other kinds of work, school and religious organizations. These were the old organizations, or those that were permitted to operate under the more or less strict supervision of members of the local, district or provincial administration. Few of these organizations were independent. When coffee farmers and minibus drivers tried to form independent asso-ciations in the late 1980s, their efforts were squashed by the police.

These old organizations had been formed between 1960 and 1990, in the initial independence period. After Freedom Corner, new groupings took shape. The Freedom Corner women's lobby group Release Political Prisoners is illustrative of the new organizations arising in the 1990s. It was founded by citizens concerned with human rights abuses. It was not government controlled. On the contrary, it was strictly opposed to the gov-ernment and its policies. Its activities were originally aimed at disseminat-ing information to Kenyans and the international community and building support for the demands made of the government; in this case the release of political prisoners.

Of all the old organizations (i.e., unions, cooperatives, churches), churches were most active in the democracy movement. It was from the pulpit that public calls for democracy were most frequently voiced before 1992. The church was a safe haven, as we saw in the case of Freedom Corner. All of the other organizations were ultimately controlled by the administration, via the chief or other official appointed to manage the organizations' affairs, and often their finances. It was therefore difficult for ordinary people to use the power of their unity in these organizations to influence political decisions. This fact is reflected in the actions of the Maragua coffee wives, who acted autonomously outside of their coffee cooperative to protest the low price for coffee and the plowing-under of their food gardens when their husbands' planted more coffee trees.

The country had also suffered under a decade of structural adjustment between 1980 and 1990. The decade saw the destruction of the local and export agricultural markets, and thus the weakening of the cooperatives that managed farmers' crops. The state began to engage in the violent enclosure of cooperatively held farm land in 1991. Politicians fomented violence, distrust and division among peoples who had shared land and thus destroyed their land-buying and crop cooperatives. School fees introduced by the World Bank meant more pressure on parents, more problems for teachers and the general decline of the capacity of teacher-parent committees to operate with dwindling funds and resources. As these organizations crumbled, it was difficult for others to arise to replace them, as there was little freedom of association in the country under Moi. It was only after Freedom Corner that it was politically possible for people to organize in public. This they did immediately and in large numbers (Brownhill and Turner 2004).

The Freedom Corner hunger strike and year-long vigil brought together a huge number and range of organizations and individuals, including thousands of street children made homeless by structural adjustment, AIDS and the "ethnic clashes." In turn, the protest spurred the activities of many new organizations such as *Muungano wa Wanavijiji, Mungiki* and Release Political Prisoners. The women of Freedom Corner, because of their age, inspired others to take up the task of struggling for democracy.

Because of the public status of the church in which the Freedom Corner women kept vigil, the All Saints Cathedral in Nairobi became a hub for the coming together of an increasingly diverse array of organizations. The network of rural and urban groups that grew out of the year-long mobilization at Freedom Corner focused on issues ranging from cultural preservation to women's rights, the fight against HIV/AIDS and the defense and reappropriation of land against land grabbers, privatizers and developers. Over the course of the 1990s, Kenyan social movement participants succeeded in asserting their rights to organize, to agitate for their rights, and in that process, to engage in international networking for the protection of organizations' members and for the dissemination of the demands and information that organizations generated. Women's direct action at Freedom

Corner in this way set the stage for the land reappropriations of 2000 and thereafter. Concerns, demands and organizations themselves had moved, between 1960 and 2000, from the national to the global level.

In December 2002, in the third multiparty election since Freedom Corner in 1992, Daniel arap Moi was defeated at the polls. Mwai Kibaki, a former vice president under Moi, was elected president. His platform rested on the promises to finalize the drafting and implementation of a new constitution, to end corruption and to reintroduce free universal primary education. In January 2003, when the new school year began, thousands of eager mothers and grandmothers arrived at schools across the country ready to enrol their children and themselves. The problem of overcrowded and undersupplied classrooms was exacerbated by the infrequent payment of teachers. The expectation of a newly invigorated democracy induced thousands to stand up against landlessness and land-grabbing.

In July 2003 the new government of Mwai Kibaki made the remarkable revelation that "almost all public land and property have been grabbed by undeserving individuals"(*Daily Nation* July 2, 2003). These "undeserving individuals" included both corrupt private developers and public officials of the Moi regime (many of whom retained their government positions after the December 2002 change of presidents). Their grabbing of public and common land and property, which reached a frenzied pace in the late 1980s and early 1990s, was life-threatening especially to landless women. By 1985, 100,000 people constituted an army of urban gardeners in Nairobi. Two-thirds of them were women. Almost all of these gardeners occupied public, open spaces of the city (Freeman 1991: xiii, 82). When politicians and developers grabbed "almost all public land," they also evicted these occupants and destroyed their subsistence livelihoods. This is one important reason why women initiated and were the majority in Nairobi's 21st-century social movements. It also underlines a key historical continuity: the gendered commons, most central to women's productive activities and relations, had been the target of capitalist enclosures since the 1800s.

As their parents resisted the commodification of farming, many rural and urban youth of the late 20th century addressed another set of problems. Thousands were graduating from school with no hopes for employment and no access to arable land. Their parents' generation had fought for land, yet they were landless. Many began to come together to question and propose alternatives to the government's repressive neoliberal policies. In 1999 the diverse social movements in Kenya began to include groups directly occupying land as a defense against land-grabbing, violent state enclosures and International Monetary Fund and World Bank austerity measures. The landless and land-poor began to assert their claims to land, not for investment, plantation agriculture or real estate speculation, but for subsistence livelihoods and relations of commoning.

It was Maasai cattle herders who engaged in the first recorded instances of land reappropriation in September and October 1999. This was an especially rainless season. River beds were dry and pastures were parched throughout large swaths of Maasailand. Maasai herders moved thousands of head of cattle onto private ranchers' still-green pastures. The ranchers complained that their own herds would suffer, but the Maasai refused to move. Armed security personnel and the return of the rains ended the standoff in late October 1999. Such confrontations over land provided the context for the Maasai community to launch legal challenges over the following years. The first, in 2001, concerned deaths and injuries suffered by Maasai due to British army land mines. After it was settled successfully out of court, the land mine prosecution was followed by a subsequent suit brought by over 600 Maasai women who charged that British soldiers had raped them during military training exercises in the Dol Dol area (Walter 2003:23).

In early 2000 it was apparent that new Kenyan social movements for land reappropriation had emerged (Brown 2000). In April 2000, workers and squatters autonomously organized in the Taveta Welfare Society occupied part of a 96,000-acre plantation seized from them during the colonial era. In a public statement the Society's chairperson, Ruth Lelewu said that "the solution to the matter is for the government to buy the land and settle thousands of Taveta squatters. The community will not allow any other individual to buy the land" (Mutonya 2001).

In May 2000 Marakwet squatters occupied the 14,500-acre state-run Cherangany experimental agriculture station. In the same month, Ogiek forest dwellers went to court to protect their forest land from enclosure and destruction (*Daily Nation* June 21, 2003). This spurred international campaigns, several local nongovernmental organizations and continued activism for Ogiek indigenous forest land rights.

After the General Election of December 2002, a new wave of land occupations began. Throughout 2003 peasants and others initiated dozens of other occupations across the country (*Daily Nation* January 22, 2003; Agutu 2003; Oketch and Ringa 2003). These peasant actions for land spurred the militancy of waged workers. On January 20, 2003, 10,000 women workers in the Athi River Export Processing Zone destroyed 16 textile plants, raided a near-by shopping center that charged workers exorbitant prices, looted shops and battled contingents of antiriot police. Tear gas prevented them from trashing a second shopping center. The strikers' demands included an end to sexual exploitation and harassment, a medical scheme, transport at night and overtime pay (Mulaa and Githaiga 2003).

A month later, some 5,000 squatters in Kilifi occupied 2,700 acres of prime coastal farm and pasture land. A spokesperson said the takeover was autonomous, with "no politician behind it." The squatters said they "had no leaders." They instead "had a committee since July 2002 to coordinate the land occupation" (Kithi and Mwandoto 2003). This autonomous and nonhierarchical organizational form was duplicated in Nyeri, where on February 10, 2003, some 500 traders stormed the Soko-Huru market, from whence they had been evicted the previous year. They "sub-divided the plots among themselves and prepared to start selling their wares" (Ogutu 2003).

The following types of property were all targets of occupation, defense and reappropriation from land-grabbers: playgrounds, settlement schemes, forests, stadiums, urban neighborhood land, cemeteries, public farm research centers, public utility plots, markets, private ranches, game reserves, dump grounds, bus terminals, road reserves, school grounds, the National Cereals and Produce Board property, hospital compounds, parking areas, fire stations, council clinics, weather stations, loading zones, open air markets, public gardens, social halls, public toilets, housing estates, open spaces, parks, alms houses for the old and the poor, rivers, lakes, the grounds of courthouses and government houses.

The social forces engaged in the array of land defenses and occupations were similarly diverse. Those most affected by the particular case of land-grabbing were the ones who organized the reappropriations. Students and parents reappropriated school grounds. Traders defended markets. Women street hawkers occupied and rehabilitated public toilets. Residents defended open spaces in their neighborhoods. In public buses, passengers stopped policemen from taking bribes from the bus conductors; they also stopped drivers from speeding. Throughout the society citizens rose to defend and reclaim the public spaces that government officials and private developers had previously milked for their own profit. This was a prelude to a citizens' renegotiation of citizenship itself through the ongoing democracy movement, reviewed below.

As the numbers of activist organizations grew, so did the range of actions they undertook. Organizations began to relate to one another in what had become, by 2000, a multicentered movement of social movements. Massive demonstrations against corporate globalization in the Americas, Europe and worldwide signalled to social movements in Kenya that they were not alone in their dispossession or in their resistance (Bassey 2002). Kenyans joined demonstrations in Seattle in 1999 against the World Trade Organization, in Washington in 2001 against the World Bank (Osoro 2001), in Genoa in 2001 against the Group of Eight. Autonomous slum-dwellers' organizations such as *Muungano wa Wanavijiji* raised funds from among their members to send several members to South Africa to network with the Landless Peoples' Movement there (First Woman interview, July 25, 1998). Kenyans participated in the African Social Forums and the World Social Forums held in various cities around the world and hosted the 2007 Forum in Nairobi. "Land for the landless" was the theme that brought Kenyans together with international activists in these fora.

Over the period 1999 to 2008 thousands of organizations involving millions of Kenyans demonstrated their intentions to reestablish aspects of a producer-controlled, life-centered society. They employed the familiar, highly decentralized, autonomous organizational forms that had character-ized Kenyan social movements for a century. Those involved in the occupa-tions rejected exploitation on plantations and in factories. They demanded their own land for their own production. Local defensive actions in one area encouraged land defenses and reappropriations elsewhere. The land occupa-tion movement was an elaboration of the democracy movement of the early 1990s, which culminated in the drafting of a new constitution in March 2004. Social movements for land broadened support for changes to the country's colonial-era laws. The land occupation movement also mobilized the popula-tion to take up the most pressing issue for the majority of citizens: land.

## *UIGUANO WA MUMBI* WOMEN'S GROUP AND THE STRUGGLE FOR MURENGAI FARM

Marata Muthoni Gatundu spoke at a First Woman Workshop, "Land, Food, Freedom," in July 2004 of the inspiration she drew from Mau Mau in the continued struggle for land in Murengai, Nanyuki:

> Personally, I fought for Mau Mau. At that time, a police-man could come for you and that policeman could aim [a gun] at your back but this didn't worry me, because I knew even if the policeman shot at me from the back I would die but my kids, our kids, the next generation would live in harmony, would live in peace and enjoy the freedom that we had fought for. And this gives me hope and strength to fight for our land (First Woman interview, Marata Muthoni Gatundu, July 7, 2004).

What follows is a summary of the complex history of intertwined sets of claims to the Murengai farm. The Murengai farm consists of two very desirable parcels of land of approximately 296 acres located outside of the white settler town of Nanyuki in Laikipia District in the Rift Valley Province. The fertile plateau offers a spectacular view of Mount Kenya, the home of the Kikuyu god, *Ngai*. The British alienated the land from the Maasai in a 1904 treaty. White settlers occupied the fertile land for many years. In the 1970s, by the time this land conflict began, Mahmood Ali Guleid owned the farm.

Guleid sold the land to Paolo Bindi in 1978, but later challenged the sale in court on a technicality. Before the court challenge, however, Bindi had sold the parcels to the *Uiguano wa Mumbi* women's group. Guleid's legal challenge eventually led to the eviction of Bindi. In regard to the second party, the *Uiguano wa Mumbi* women's group, Guleid "proved" he still owned the land by showing the women his title deed. *Uiguano wa Mumbi* translates from the Gikuyu to "Mumbi's Sweat" and Mumbi is the founding mother of the Gikuyu people. The women who established this women's group acknowledged, through the choice of their name, that they improved the well-being of their community through hard work. In the face of the legal challenge, the women then undertook court proceedings to get their money back from Bindi. Meanwhile, they purchased the land again, from Guleid this time. Guleid took payment from them but did not undertake any legal paperwork, nor did he transfer the title deed to the women. He convinced the women that since he was tied up in court with Bindi, he would need to hold onto the title deed until the case was settled.

Guleid swore customary oaths, holding soil in his hand, in ceremonies to transfer the land to the women. He argued that it was best to use "the traditional Agikuyu custom of land buying since a formal receipt and a legal transaction would raise Paolo's [Bindi's] objection" (Laikipia 2004:4). Guleid "carried out some solemn traditional rituals" with the women of *Uiguano wa Mumbi* and "vowed using the soil of the land that he would hand them the entire land and the title deed once he kicked Paolo out of the farm" (Laikipia 2004:4). Having sworn customary oaths on the land, the women were convinced of the security of their claim. They established their villages, planted gardens and trees, buried their dead elders and children and established communal amenities.

It was only some ten years later, in 1994, that Bindi and his family finally vacated their portion of the land due to an eviction order and threats and harassment by Guleid. Helena Wamuyu Gitichi recalled that

> Mahmood [Guleid] told us not to take our goats to graze
> on the upper side because he will bring the police to arrest
> Paolo. And he went from house to house telling us not to
> graze our goats on the upper part of the land. And he said

"Because I don't want you to lose your property, I don't want you to take your goats to the upper part." And we did obey (First Woman interview, Helena Wamuyu Gitichi, July 7, 2004).

Soon thereafter, in 1995, Bindi died. In 1997 the original owner, Guleid, also died. His wife insisted that the women's group, which had occupied the land for some twenty years, pay her for the land yet again. In fear of eviction, the women paid. The secretary of the organization this time kept the receipts. Widow Guleid sent out a surveyor to measure the land. In July 1999 the women's group also sought the involvement of the district commissioner for a formal transfer of the landownership. Widow Guleid refused to enter into a formal agreement. The same month, she passed away. Her daughter Halima Ali almost immediately began eviction proceedings against the *Uiguano* women's group. In May 2000 Ali threatened to sue the women if they did not vacate. In March 2001 she resurrected the 1994 eviction order against Bindi. In the order, Ali claimed that the women of *Uiguano wa Mumbi* were agents and servants of Bindi and that they, like he, should vacate the land. The women questioned the validity of the order and refused to comply.

On December 13, 2001, Ali arrived at Murengai farm, which was now home to some 500 members of *Uiguano wa Mumbi* and their families. Armed administrative police and hired men accompanied her. They demolished some homes and destroyed property. The residents pleaded with the police to stop. The police warned the residents that they had one week to vacate the land. However, the following morning, Ali returned with reinforcements and burned down all of the houses. The fire destroyed all of the residents' property, including livestock and the receipts for the payments made to Ali's mother for the land.

The Murengai farmers sought help from their local member of parliament, Mwangi Kiunjuri. Murengai resident Martha Wangari Muturi recalled that

after the [eviction] order, as a village we sat in a meeting to consult on the next step to take. And we decided out of the meeting that we should go see our Member of Parliament to seek help. Our MP came over and he told us to build by the roadside, which we did, so that we could put pressure while we are there. At that time, no one had food, blankets or even clothing, because everything was burnt in the fire. Our MP left and after some time we thought we should get a lawyer so that we take the case to court. We wanted justice to be done, because we had given money to Halima [Ali] for the piece of land. We had bought the land already and we wanted justice to be done. The treatment was inhuman. We didn't have anything (First Woman interview, Martha Wangari Muturi, July 7, 2004).

From December 2001 to 2006, some 20 elderly women and men of *Uiguano wa Mumbi* camped by the roadside in makeshift shelters to maintain a presence at the disputed land. Their "homes" were made of grass, sticks, rusty tin and plastic sheets. They had no electricity, no running water. Halima Ali blocked their access to the closest stream, so they had to walk three kilometers to reach water. Ali plowed over the residents' gravesites and planted wheat. She cut down the groves of trees that the women had planted and used the timber to make fence posts to keep the women off of their own land.

Helena Wamuyu Gitichi explained the origins of her women's land buying group in the 1970s:

We had formed a women's group and our main objective as women was to buy a piece of land for our kids. We had agreed that we needed a piece of land, and that is why we formed this group. We have come this far, we contributed that money. By then it was not 800,000, it was very cheap. But now what did we see in return? After having formed the group many years ago we went on contributing the money. And in return what we saw was Halima [Guleid's daughter] coming down to burn down our makeshift houses (First Woman interview, Helena Wamuyu Gitichi, July 7, 2004).

Murengai resident Marata Muthoni Gatundui stated that "Halima's husband comes in his helicopter and it really destroys our makeshift huts. When originally the land was ours, we had developed and allocated some space for a football pitch and a tennis court. And that is where Halima's husband's helicopter lands, on the football pitch" (First Woman interview, Marata Muthoni Gatundui, July 7, 2004). Ali has also on several occasions had police arrest everyone on the farm, including women in their 90s and disabled elderly men. Numerous bogus charges of trespassing, forced entry, malicious damage to property and robbery keep the Murengai women tied up with expensive and time-consuming court cases. Halima Ali has sent the police several times to burn down the makeshift shelters the women have built. According to one displaced peasant woman,

> now what is defeating us most is this lady who just came and really didn't dialogue with us to ask if this land is really ours. What Halima [Ali] does, is just comes up and burns our makeshift houses. So where we need a lot of assistance is to get clearance [to return to the land] and some light shed on us (First Woman interview, Helena Wamuyu Gitichi, July 7, 2004).

The Murengai farm women's struggle continues on many levels. They have pooled money to hire lawyers, who have consistently allowed the case to drag on for years. The women continue to mobilize support by inviting human rights, legal and women's organizations to visit the farm and join the defense. Adult children of the original women's group members have taken up the cause by forming the Laikipia Human Rights Forum and linking with human rights groups across the country. The Forum seeks to build a political campaign for the resolution of the case, as the legal route has so far been less than fruitful.

To make matters more complex, when Kenya's new government took office in January 2003, the family of Bindi returned to pursue their own claim to the land. The Bindis and the women's group decided to work together to seek redress. Their case is pending.

The Murengai case is typical, outside of its specific details, of thousands of instances in which land has been fraudulently sold to more than one party at a time, often leaving the defrauded parties to fight among themselves. The case illustrates both (a) the continued use and saliency of customary land transactions and (b) the general legal bias against such transactions as seen in Halima Ali's capacity to call upon law enforcement officials to defend her "ownership" based on her possession of the title deed, despite her father's solemn oaths taken in the process of the sale of the land to the women's group and the receipts they had at one time.

The coming together of a range of organizations and informal squatters' associations to defend the Murengai women's claims illustrates the kinds of networks of loosely affiliated organizations that characterize Kenya's movement of land occupation and defense. Although they were networked with many different kinds of organizations, the Murengai women acted autonomously and of their own accord. This, too, is characteristic of the land occupation movement: it combines many distinct actions and groups.

With the emergence of the land occupation movement in Kenya, the numbers of people engaged in social action against enclosure again increased dramatically. Demands centered on land rights and the freedom to carry out local subsistence trade and global fair trade. But the priority was land. As one Murengai resident stated in 2004:

> Our first declaration at this workshop should not be how to market our products. It should be to fight for those people who do not have land, the squatters in this country. That is our first declaration in this workshop. Because if we fight for how we will market our products and we do not have a place to live, how is that? We have first to fight for a place to live in and then we fight for how we market our products (First Woman interview, Helena Wamuyu Gitichi, July 8, 2004).

In the meantime, the Murengai women continue to engage in the struggle at the level of their daily occupation of the land, in their pursuit of a legal (and political) victory and in their campaign to link the struggle for a new Kenyan constitution with the capacity to defend subsistence land rights. As one Murengai commoner observed in 2004:

> We shall put pressure on our government to give us a new constitution which will cater for our needs. Once that constitution is in place, then we are assured of getting our land back. Here in Kenya, we have two tribes, and when I say two tribes, I mean the haves and the have-nots, the poor and the rich. And what I am saying is that the gap is widening. But once we have a new constitution in place then the needs of the poor will be taken care of in the new constitution. Those people who have chunks and chunks of land will have their land taken by the government and given to the poor. That is my plea (First Woman interview, Martha Wangari Muturi, July 8, 2004).

The chapter now turns to an examination of the integration of Kenyan social movements for land, food and freedom into global social movement networks. It reviews the Kenyan contribution to the collapse of the World Trade Organization meeting in Cancun, Mexico, and the Kenyan constitutional struggle. Both instances of resistance, one at the global level and one at the national level, have important implications for Kenya's gendered commoners' fight for control over fertility and the life ground of subsistence.

## THE COLLAPSE AT CANCUN

Vandana Shiva wrote of the September 14, 2003 World Trade Organization (WTO) "failure at Cancun" that it

> is a failure for the unfair and undemocratic agenda of W.T.O. and the rich countries. It is a victory for democracy and equality and it gives a chance to fair trade which guarantees farmers' survival. ... The Cancun ministerial took place in the shadow of the martyrdom of a Korean farmer, Lee Kyung-Hae, who took his life at the barricades during the farmers protest on 10th September, the first day of the meeting. Lee was the former president of the Korean Advanced Farmers Federation and identified the unfair W.T.O. rules with the crisis faced by him and small farmers world wide. He made visible the crisis millions of Indian farmers are facing which has pushed thousands to commit suicide. ... What the U.S./E.U. wanted in Cancun was to continue the right to dump, to continue unfair trade by supporting their agribusiness interests to take over world markets ... [and] ... to destroy small producers (Shiva 2003).

Kenyan social movements for the commons contributed to the collapse of the World Trade Organization at Cancun in September 2003. This brief account illustrates some of the channels through which the local struggles of ordinary Kenyans, like those of the Korean farmers, emerged in Cancun as powerful forces against corporate globalization. The subsistence content of social movements' demands in Kenya set the stage for 21$^{st}$-century gendered class struggles at the global level (Turner and Brownhill 2004).

As noted above, in December 2002 the government of Daniel arap Moi was voted out of power. Mwai Kibaki became president. Several women and men who had engaged in the democracy struggle of the 1990s were elected. These included Wangari Maathai, Mirugi Kariuki and Mutisya Kituyi. Trade minister Mutisya Kituyi led the walkout of the G-21 majority world governments' from the World Trade Organization negotiations in Cancun on September 14, 2003. Kituyi was a long-time supporter of the women's led democracy movement. In Cancun, he was convinced that the agreement under discussion would set back the Kenyan struggle for a more just economy and society. One participant in the celebratory marches outside the Cancun meeting place observed that "the Kenyan delegate to the WTO slapped his hand on the table and announced, 'This meeting is over. We have our second Seattle!'"(Mooney 2004).

On September 14, 2003 while Kituyi anticipated the walkout, an array of international nongovernmental organizations rallied outside. Korean farmers attended in the hundreds. As Shiva reported above, their leader committed suicide outside the conference center to protest the agricultural policy of the WTO. Protestors came from the Americas, Europe, Africa and Asia. South African women demolished the chain-link fence surrounding the WTO meeting venue. One participant wrote that

> thousands of resisters descended on the newly fortified security barrier near kilometer zero. Like the initial structure, this fortification was pulverized by the collective action of the demonstration. A couple of hundred women first massed along the fence and set about it with heavy bolt cutters. Mountains of wire were cut free and discarded by supporters as the women went into the 10 foot deep no man's land, thousands of riot police pressing at the other side. Bolts and chains which locked the wall together disappeared in a Fordist destruction line, the chains worn around the necks of the African women as trophies (Writers Bloc 2003).

Before Kituyi led the walkout, Bryan Ashley, from South Africa's Alternative Information and Development Center, reported that

> Kenya is one of the stronger countries resisting what is being put forward by the major countries pushing liberalization – the U.S., E.U., Canada, and Japan. A stalemate in the WTO negotiations ... will give the social movements time to build stronger coalitions and louder protests in order to put "the WTO to bed and corporate globalization policies to bed with it" (cited in Truglia 2003).

Yao Graham of Third World Network-Africa observed further that

> African countries represent the single largest continental bloc in the WTO. African people have a strategic respon-

sibility to their compatriots around the globe so that their governments do not contribute to selling out the interests of the world's people (cited in Truglia 2003).

The collapse at Cancun showed that the power of social movements for the commons to turn the tide against corporate enclosures was greater than ever. A substantial power lay behind the stark "NO!" message Kituyi and others sent. A network of social movements in East Africa, focused on subsistence, had this direct impact on the outcome of major world trade meetings. Kenyan insurgency is an exemplar of anti-WTO mobilizations. The insurgency was threefold. First, Kenyan networks joined a global movement of social movements. Second, popular resistance to corporate rule directly shaped Kenyan government policy as expressed in the WTO forum of member states. Third, Kenyans of all walks of life continued to creatively reconstruct a new subsistence world based on their own experience and knowledge. From gardening to a new constitution, Kenyans struggled to realize their commoning plans and demands. Shiva observed that

> the paradigm of trade liberalization has been dealt a severe blow in Cancun. It is time to give concrete shape to a fair trade paradigm that builds on robust local and national economies. It is time to put people before profits. It is time to put domestic production before international trade. ... The ball is now in the court of our domestic economy and national democracy. Democracy won in Cancun. Explicit consent in the domestic sphere is the foundation for recovery of national sovereignty and economic democracy. This is the real challenge after Cancun (Shiva 2003).

Kenyans' resistance at the Cancun meeting was guided by the demands of social movements at home, especially those of rural Kenyan women. After the collapse, Kenyan resistance continued. At a February 2004 protest outside of a subsequent WTO meeting in Mombasa, a dozen arrests were made. This was followed in March 2004 by the final acceptance by Kenyan Constitutional Conference of the popular "Bomas Draft" of the country's new constitution. The constitution was an assertion of sovereignty in the face of a global regime of corporate rule.

# FROM BOMAS TO THE REFERENDUM: THE STRUGGLE FOR A NEW CONSTITUTION

The constitution that Kenya inherited at independence in 1963 was a colonial creation. Since 1963, presidents Kenyatta and Moi had amended the constitution some 27 times to concentrate power in the office of the executive. Moi finally relented to overwhelming internal and external pressure to reintroduce multiparty democracy in 1991 by repealing Section 2(a) of the constitution, which had outlawed all opposition political parties. Multiparty democracy brought few changes. Moi rigged the 1992 election and, even so, only narrowly won the 1997 contest. But popular mobilization continued and in 1997 Moi finally convened a constitutional conference to deliberate the content of a new constitution (First Woman interview, Wahu Kaara, July 3, 2004).

In December 2002 Mwai Kibaki was elected president mainly on the basis of his promises to finalize the constitutional drafting process and reintroduce free universal primary education. Kibaki had been a member of parliament since independence in 1963. He helped draft the original constitution of Kenya between 1960 and 1963. Between 1978 and 1988, he served as Moi's vice president. With the return of multiparty democracy in 1991, he founded the Democratic Party and served as an opposition member. He was defeated in both the 1992 and 1997 presidential elections before joining with other parties in a "Rainbow Alliance" and winning the presidency in December 2002. Kibaki's election promises to voters were accompanied by little-publicized plans to negotiate new loans with the International Monetary Fund.

Kenya's constitutional conference, which wrapped up its work in 2004, consisted of 621 voting delegates, including all members of parliament and some 400 women and men who were members of community organizations, notably churches and NGOs. The constitution-drafting process involved extensive consultations across the country, the writing of each chapter and then the final voting on each clause. The terms of reference specified that each clause had to be approved by a two-thirds majority or it was bracketed as "contentious." Such "contentious issues" would then be subject to further negotiation and revision until they secured more than two-thirds of the total delegates' support. The process was referred to as the "Bomas conference" after the conference hall at which it was held, Bomas of Kenya. The document produced there was called the "Bomas Draft." Interestingly, the Kenyan press dubbed the Bomas Draft the "Wanjiku Draft." Wanjiku is a common Kikuyu women's name. This nickname referred to the fact that the draft constitution reflected the needs and demands of the most exploited people in the society, ordinary African women. In this way the Wanjiku Draft constitution was canonized as the distillation of Kenyan women's reassertion of their Mau Mau legacy of struggle for land and freedom.

By March 15, 2004, every chapter of the Bomas or Wanjiku Draft had been passed by a two-thirds majority. Yet a faction of Kibaki's government staged a literal walkout from the conference hall and vowed to block the adoption of the new constitution. President Kibaki had promised to have the new draft constitution ratified by Parliament and in effect by June 30, 2004. Instead he challenged the legality of the constitution-drafting process. He reshuffled his cabinet on June 30 to reinforce support for his position. He claimed that the peoples' constitution was "unwieldy" and that there had been too many outstanding "contentious issues." The conferees had not, in fact, identified any contentious issues during their deliberations. Why, then, did the president and a minority of Parliamentarians walk out on the process?

Central to the March 2004 draft constitution was the abolition of the colonial system of chiefs, subchiefs and headmen, and the creation of an alternative in the form of democratically elected local, regional and district councils. This crucial provision formalized the repudiation of this particular male deal. Citizens were empowered to recall councilors with whom they were unsatisfied. Of the ten seats on the local councils, three were reserved for women. Vital economic matters were placed within the jurisdiction of these local and regional councils. All physical resources were under the councils' control. Such councils could, for example, prioritize subsistence food production over development projects focused on export crops, tourism or mining. Environmental management of forests, water sources and land use were also placed within the jurisdiction of these regional and local councils. In a separate clause, women's legal rights to inherit property were strengthened.

Significantly, the new constitution stipulated that Parliament had to consent to and formally approve any IMF and World Bank loans, conditionalities and repayment schedules. The IMF and World Bank objected that this provision was "unwieldy" and would lead to "inefficiency." But delegates to the constitutional conference and many ordinary people saw the provision as a significant step toward a repudiation of all debts and a call for reparations.

The new constitution was created with the full involvement of all sectors of Kenyan society, most notably women, rural and urban poor people, the disabled and the dispossessed. It redistributed power in significant ways. It raised the ire of international financial institutions and the elite within government that had much land, property and power to lose if the draft were to be adopted. At a rally on July 3, 2004, some 10,000 people in the cities of Nairobi and Kisumu protested the government's illegal obstructionism. Delegates and others formed "Bomas Katiba Watch" [Kiwahili = Bomas Constitution Watch] and continued through 2005 to demand the implementation of the March 2004 Draft. Meanwhile, the multiparty cabinet was generating a very different draft constitution behind closed doors. By late 2005, Kibaki presented this new draft constitution to the public and scheduled a November 21, 2005 referendum. Voters turned out in large numbers to vote against the government's very different version. Of the 6 million votes cast, 57 percent voted to reject the government's proposed constitution (Kadida and Mugonyi 2005).

The struggle for a new constitution was a culmination of the gendered class struggles for land, food and freedom in the period 1980 to 2005. The Wanjiku Draft brought the needs and demands of the landless into the legal framework governing the society as a whole. The regime's obstructionism was also consistent with long-standing male deal relations between the local Kenyan elite and the regime of corporate rulers operating from the World Bank and the World Trade Organization. One very valuable aspect of the ongoing constitutional struggle is that Kenyans have had the experience of determining the kinds of relations and institutions that would best support their struggle to build a new society. This decade of experience involved (1) insisting on securing the right to devise a new constitution; (2) holding public discussion throughout the country to ascertain citizens' views on the governing framework of the society; (3) debating the hundreds of clauses making up the new constitution at the "Bomas" conference center over a seven-year period, and (4) rejecting the regime's attempt to impose its alternative constitution through demonstrations, campaigns and ultimately through a "No vote" in the November 2005 referendum. Kenyans were able to vote "No!" because they had already worked out an alternative that better addressed their needs. The "No" vote for Kibaki's draft was also a "Yes" vote for the redistribution of wealth and power that was locked into the Bomas (Wanjiku) Draft.

This analysis requires further elaboration given the disastrous fallout of the December 2007 presidential election. In reaching a political settlement to the election standoff, the new government promised to settle the question of land use and to draft and implement a new constitution. In mid-2008, the shape of this settlement and its impact on ordinary Kenyans has yet to be fully determined.

The concluding chapter turns to a brief review of the changes in the organization of capitalist exploitation, through the introduction of successive male deals in three periods. The conclusion also outlines the feminist subsistence orientation of organizations involved in struggles against enclosures in Kenya over the long 20th century.

## Note

1. MwaKenya was an underground political movement originating among revolutionary intellectuals in the late 1970s. Members published and distributed leaflets and newsletters detailing critiques of the neocolonial state and advocating a transformation toward socialism. MwaKenya's organizational form rested upon secret "cells" coordinated by a central committee. The organization was destroyed in the early 1980s by the arrest, assassination and exile of the MwaKenya members. Some reorganized abroad, but the immediate connection of the original members to the ordinary people of rural and urban areas appears to have been broken.

~ CHAPTER ELEVEN ~

# CONCLUSION: OVERCOMING THE MALE DEAL

The organization of capital in Kenya over the "long 20th century" (1870-2007) was premised upon the construction of male deals that facilitated colonial exploitation of African land and labor. Three types of male deals – or cross-class, cross-race agreements among capitalist and exploited men for their mutual but unequal benefit – were successively introduced, coincident with successive waves of corporate amalgamation. Each wave of amalgamation required new male deals which would enlarge the scope of corporate control over Kenya's gendered commons.

Male deals expanded to include first African *traders*, then British-appointed *chiefs* and finally corporate-controlled peasant *cash crop farmers*. *Traders* organized the supply of goods to European caravans from among local African hunters and farmers between 1870 and 1929. *Chiefs* worked on a regional or national scale to formalize colonial rule, especially in the years 1930 to 1959. And *cash crop farmers* and parties in the developmentalist state linked Kenyan farm families directly into global commodity markets in the years between 1960 and 2007. Thus the geographical scope of the organization of Kenyans' exploitation widened, in waves, over the century.

Early 20th century social movements culminated in the Mau Mau war of 1952 to 1960. Although Mau Mau brought independence to Kenya, corporations did not stop their efforts to commodify Kenya's rich resource base. A newly pervasive form of the male deal was introduced in the postcolonial era that tied Kenyan peasant farmers directly to the global corporate market. Cash crop contracts spelled out the content of these new cash crop farmers' male deals, through which peasant men channelled the labor and products of nature and of their unwaged wives and children into overseas marketplaces in return for access to cash incomes. The postcolonial era in Kenya embraces two of Nitzan and Bichler's (2002) "waves," which took corporate amalgamations through the national and onto the global stage. In the 1960s and 1970s Kenya's cash crop farmer, in particular the coffee farmer, was held up by the World Bank (with the complicity of many academics) as the development model for all of Africa. By the mid-1980s, neoliberal structural adjustment programs had turned the coffee boom to bust and had ended the era of national development in favor of the closer integration of Kenyan peasants into global circuits of capital.

The 20$^{th}$ century's waves of capitalist enclosure – accomplished with the collaboration of first traders, then chiefs and finally cash crop farmers – had their counterparts in the organization of antienclosure movements. Simultaneous with the waves outlined above, subsistence struggles in Kenya moved from *local defensive* actions to *regional and national resistance* to a *global movement of social movements* focused on defending and extending life-centered subsistence social relations. In the instances of resistance against enclosure analyzed here, peasant women were at the forefront. The social relations of resistance were characterized by gendered class alliances between men who rejected their own exploitation and women fighting against the enclosure of the commons. Central among the findings of this study is that these gendered class alliances, constructed in the course of the struggle for the commons in Kenya, have the power to interrupt the male deals that bind Kenyan commoners into global circuits of capital. These alliances have also provided the solidarity required for the protection, expansion and elaboration of subsistence social relations.

Kenyan social movements were vibrant and innovative in the national realm during the 1960s and 1970s. Women's organizing, in particular, was effective and a harbinger. In contrast to the private wealth accumulation promoted by cash crop development, women's groups and the *harambee* self-help movement focused on collective action to serve the needs of all. In the 1980s, as structural adjustment bound ever-more people into the web of the corporate market, social movements in Kenya leapt into global social movement networks. This leap was facilitated by the dispersal throughout the society of new information and communication technologies, which were originally intended to facilitate the global operations of corporate and other nonstate actors. Beginning around 1990, corporations moved from foreign investment to transnational *ownership* of assets in countries around the world (Nitzan and Bichler 2002: 274-275). By the 2000s, Kenyans were at the forefront of global struggles for the formation of subsistence alternatives to the global regime of corporate rule.

This book has sought to demonstrate how capital has organized, disciplined and united the exploited, both waged and unwaged, to resist their exploitation. Who resists? How? And with what have they sought to replace capitalist relations of exploitation? A brief review of the arguments in each chapter helps to answer these questions.

Chapter One detailed the study's key conceptual framework of gendered, ethnicized class analysis. Within this framework, the conceptual category of the exploited class is shown to include both waged and unwaged labor. This framing allowed a focus on the social relations through which capital organized the exploitation of unwaged women. Finally, the framing also emphasized the transformational, subsistence, life-centered capabilities of the unwaged, who continued to organize within a cooperative form of labor, which in turn contributed to their capacity to both challenge exploitative relations and to replace them with life-centered social relations.

Chapter Two illustrated the centrality of women to the indigenous precolonial political economy and, in turn, the importance of land rights to women's customary powers over food, fertility and environmental endowments. The traders' male deal constituted the central mechanism through which women's fertility and the life goods of the community as a whole were channeled into the colonial political economy in late-19th-century Kenya.

Chapter Three examined the extent to which colonialism reconfigured relations among African men and women, wealthy and poor, in the first three decades of the 20th century. While new taxes, forced labor and land alienation imposed by colonists decomposed some indigenous collectivities, subsistence actors also drew upon kin and trade networks of the past to survive, resist and transform the colonial commodified political economy. Mekatilili and Mary Muthoni Nyanjiru were among the prominent women who worked to adapt, maintain and reinvent life-centered activities for the purpose of resisting enclosure and strengthening the life economy of the gendered commons.

Chapter Four analyzed the labor and population policies of the 1930s and 1940s to show how women's fertility lay at the heart of colonial processes of enclosure.

Chapter Five delineated three instances of resistance against these and other kinds of attacks on Africans' fertility-related concerns, endowments and relations. In organizing against colonial enclosures, Kenyans first mobilized popular support for an independent school movement. In 1946, unity for a wider independence struggle was built and supported by Olenguruone oaths and widespread resistance against women's forced labor in the government terracing program. Women were, for the first time, included in community-wide customary oaths. This reconfiguration of custom was deepened, as women became leading recruiters and oath-administrators for the armed independence struggle.

Chapters Six, Seven and Eight detailed gendered, ethnicized class struggle in the Mau Mau war. Colonial policies contributed to the coordination of anticolonial resistance by providing common conditions of exploitation and dispossession, while also supplying new collectivities within which resistance was nurtured on a regional scale. Old customs of generational handover ceremonies provided one indigenous footing for the unity that emerged in Mau Mau. This unity drew together a new kind of moiety, one that consisted of all exploited women and men. This new moiety sought the reappropriation of the land, the settlement of all claims and the abolition of the laws that the previous moiety had negotiated with the British colonizers. In this way, Mau Mau expressed a striking new amalgam of indigenous and exogenous social forms, including moieties and generations on the one hand and workplaces, governing hierarchies, markets and the enclosed commons on the other.

Resistance in the Mau Mau war involved the formation of widespread gendered class alliances aimed at securing land and freedom for all by breaking relations of collaboration between the colonists and the African chiefs and Homeguards. The concentration camps and the Swynnerton Plan implemented in the 1950s as counterinsurgency measures were to have a long-lasting impact on the shape of the postcolonial political economy. Mau Mau won independence, but not the land and freedom for all for which they had sacrificed so much. Because independence was achieved, but universal land rights were not part of the deal, the fear among the political and business elite was that Mau Mau would reemerge to complete the unfinished business of the 1950s. A new guerrilla struggle was preempted by the construction of the corporate or cash crop farmers' male deal. Poverty and landlessness among the most committed Mau Mau fighters dampened their capacity to organize. Political freedoms were curtailed, as were many of the Emergency-era regulations. These remained on the books well into the independence years.

Chapter Nine shows, however, that the women's groups of every description that proliferated in Kenya in the first decades of independence focused on securing land and organizing for the production of life-goods for all. Many women's groups developed self-help organizational methods that were taken up in the well-known *harambee* movement, which involved both women and men in fund-raising for community undertakings, especially educational projects. Large numbers of African women reestablished subsistence relations on a widening scale. The collective work groups

Kenyan women had mobilized into a movement of social movements by the 1980s provided a solid foundation for collective action against hunger and landlessness in the coming years.

Chapter Ten provides an analysis of the social movements that have effectively drawn Kenyan struggles into the international arena. These social movements have shown that the subsistence concerns of Kenyans are paralleled in the movements of peoples worldwide. The chapter's gendered class analysis of the struggles of rice and coffee farmers indicated the very great extent to which land poor and landless Kenyans, especially women, rejected their dispossession and took matters into their own hands to reestablish life-centered social relations and uses of land. A consideration of the Freedom Corner protest illustrated the coming together of a wide array of demands and social forces focused on the reassertion of commoners' control over the life ground of subsistence. An examination of the land occupation movement of 1999 to 2005 showed how gendered class alliances for the civil commons have suffused Kenyan struggles as these movements merged with others in a process of globalization from below.

Local and regional Kenyan organizations for social and ecological justice increasingly coordinated with continental and international movements during the period 1980 to 2006. At the same time distinctly Kenyan social forms persisted. Three major continuities in indigenous social institutions characterized the period 1980 to 2006. First, self-help associations, including women's groups, community groups and welfare societies, were a major source of continuing organizational strength. Second, cultural expressions such as song, dance, popular theatre and oaths continued to provide important focal points for mobilization. Finally, the overall pattern of a loosely coordinated network of autonomous organizations echoed the common indigenous egalitarianism through which many of Kenya's social groups have historically organized. The horizontal integration of equals was deeply rooted and widely practiced in Kenya by the turn of the 21$^{st}$ century.

Perhaps the most important contribution that Kenyan peasant women have made to social movements both within Kenya and at the global level is their persistent focus on the skills, resources, relations and organizations necessary for the subsistence of all. While many poverty-alleviation programs and gender and development initiatives are individualistically focused on commercializing agriculture (Spring 2000), Kenyan women are among the very vocal proponents of strategies that focus on elaborating the subsistence systems that ensure

the survival and well-being *of all*. There is no doubt that there are major obstacles to the construction of a life-centered political economy that prioritizes food, a healthy environment and harmonious social relations. Commercial policies are chief among these barriers. The exclusion of the majority from access to the means of production constitutes a major assault on this majority's capacity to survive. Yet despite the fact that a century or more of commercializing policies has gravely worsened the situation for millions of people, neoliberal polemicists continue to argue in favor of increased commodification (Sachs 2005; Seavoy 2000).

In light of the hegemonic power of the commodifying regime, the actually existing alternatives reflected in peasant social movements in Kenya provide important lessons for global social movement actors. By maintaining and transforming the practices that allow peasants to live outside the commodity-cash nexus, Kenyan peasant women in dynamic social movements stand with one foot already planted in a postcapitalist world. And with their propensity for incorporating aspects of exogenous social forms as a means of strengthening indigenous capacities, there can be no question about Kenya's subsistence social movements aiming to "drag society back into the Stone Age," a charge often leveled against proponents of subsistence (Bennholdt-Thomson and Mies 1999:14). The cell phone and palm pilot are used in current mobilizations in Kenya. Solar panels power rural televisions to keep peasants up to date with breaking news. One need go no further than the drafting of the new constitution to recognize Kenyan commoners' capacities to bring subsistence priorities successfully into the institutional framework represented by the constitution.

This study has offered an analysis of social movements for subsistence over the long 20th century in just one country. But the resurgence of subsistence is not a feature unique to Kenyan commoners' movements. It can be found elsewhere. Among Korean farmers, Brazilian slum dwellers, Nigerian villagers and indigenous peoples everywhere are many who are engaged in movements that similarly prioritize subsistence as a solution to the problems of capitalist exploitation and the destruction of the gendered commons.

For over a century, peasant women have creatively initiated and sustained the major social movements to defend, reappropriate and redefine subsistence social relations in Kenya. This should not be surprising. Peasant women are the unwaged producers whose survival and well-being depend directly upon the commons and the cooperative, life-centered orientation of indigenous farming, animal care and trade relations. These same women are at the heart of that system that supports, through the production and distribution of food, the waged and unwaged workers, the children and elders who populate the rural areas and, especially, the urban neighborhoods and slums. Peasant women's capacities to survive without a wage and their importance to the sustenance of waged workers constitute the double source of their power in social movements and in everyday relations. The cases analyzed in this study demonstrate the power of Kenyan women's subsistence-oriented organizations to unite the waged and unwaged against capital and provide the knowledge and experience necessary for the construction of a society beyond capital.

~ APPENDIX ~

# "GENDERED ETHNICIZED CLASS ANALYSIS" AND THE METHODOLOGY OF THE STUDY

## INTRODUCTION

I have learned of the history and political economy of Kenya through a feminist rereading of a wide selection of studies on Kenya's particular struggles and, for more recent history, through direct observation, oral history collection and participatory action research. I drew in this study on a wide range of sources including explorers' diaries and memoirs, government documents, internet archives, scholarly articles, media reports, reports from nongovernmental organizations and historical material from the Kenyan National Archives. The information collected included qualitative and quantitative published findings relevant to the processes of popular mobilization. Colonial, anticolonial, neocolonial and postcolonial writers have produced a massive literature about the history, cultures, revolutionary uprisings and social movements of Kenya. In addition to an array of court statements, government documents, observers' diaries, missionary chronicles, press reports and analyses of these records by scholars, there exists a rich collection of published and unpublished Kenyan oral narratives, oral histories, songs and stories. Many of these popular sources contain remembrances of indigenous subsistence lifeways and stories of the anticolonial struggle. These records and repositories of popular culture have served as especially important sources of insight and information.

<?> Many historical, ethnographic and anthropological analyses of Kenyan peoples provide rich accounts of ethnic communities' customs, social

relations and economic practices (Middleton and Kershaw 1953/1972; Orde-Browne 1925/1970; Thomson 1885). Most analysts, however, frame these customary lifeways as archaic and inevitably giving way under the pressures of a modern capitalist political economy (Fisher 1954; Kournossoff 1959; O'Connor 1966; Orde-Browne 1925/1970; Thomson 1885). Other scholars studied indigenous social organization in order to more effectively employ customary norms in enforcing colonial and corporate rule (Lambert 1947, 1956/1965; Leakey, 1952; Perham 1967; Prins 1970; Routledge 1910/1968).

Much of the literature focusssing on Kenyan women is similarly imbued with the assumption that subsistence political economies are being and should be replaced by fuller engagement in global commodity markets (Spring 2000; Kanogo 1987, 2005; Pala et al. 1978). Finally, most authors of the vast literature on the Mau Mau war fail to acknowledge women's and communities' subsistence interests, demands and activities (Askwith 1995; Barnett and Njama 1966; Cooper 1988; Furedi 1989; Maloba 1993; Throup 1988). Most writers are virtually silent about women and gender relations in Mau Mau. Those who do write of women, typically do so in the "add-on" mode (Anderson 2005; Berman 1990; Berman and Lonsdale 1992; Elkins 2005; Kanogo 1987; Odhiambo and Lonsdale 2003; Rosberg and Nottingham 1966). Among scholars who do analyze Kikuyu women's activism, none, with the important exception of Claire Robertson (1996, 1997), has identified the defining continuity of women's subsistence-focused demands and actions. Nor have earlier analysts centrally considered the dynamic changes in the social relations through which Kenyan women and men have organized and defended their subsistence activities.

For many the word "subsistence" means mere survival. In contrast, as noted in Chapter One, the present analysis understands subsistence to be life support in the fullest sense, including trade, for both rural and urban peoples. Using this understanding, the study confirms the global relevance of the feminist subsistence perspectives of Maria Mies and Vandana Shiva (1993), as well as Claudia Von Werlhof, Farida Akhter and Veronika Bennholdt-Thomsen (all in Bennholdt-Thomson et al. 2001). In this study I analyze the subsistence relations among Kenyan peoples who remain steeped in relations of reciprocity and commoning. The analysis suggests that peasant women's fight against structural adjustment in the late 20th century was the beginning of the reemergence of a century-long struggle to defend life-centered relations of production, trade and ecological stewardship.

Fiona Mackenzie's 1998 study, *Land, Ecology and Resistance in Kenya 1880-1952*, offers further valuable insight into the strengths of indigenous agricultural practices. Most relevant to this study's focus was Mackenzie's elaborated analysis of women and men's collective responsibilities for food sufficiency and the stewardship of the environment. My study builds on these observations to examine the ways that indigenous commoning practices have been at the heart of resistance movements.

The present examination of Kenyan women's engagement in social movements also draws on the work of June Nash. Her 1994 article on "Global Integration and Subsistence Insecurity" analyzed subsistence-oriented social movements in the Americas. Nash reiterates Rosa Luxemburg's insistence that the theft of the wealth of subsistence political economies is essential to the process of capital accumulation. In a comparison of social movements in Mexico, Bolivia and the United States, Nash found that "the poor of Third World countries seem to have a stronger basis for avoiding demoralization in the face of economic decline" (1994:23). She explains this resilience with reference to the fact that impoverished Mexicans and Bolivians had a stronger footing on the land and in relationships of reciprocity than did the poor of the United States. The Third World poor had access to collective means of survival and the social networks already attuned to collective needs.

In terms of oral history methodology, this study benefits from Paul Thompson's popularization of the use of oral history as a means of reaching into communities to understand micro and macro process of gendered and generational social change. Thompson wrote that "oral history gives history back to the people in their own words. And in giving a past, it also helps them towards a future of their own making" (Thompson 1978/1988:265). Ardra Cole and Gary Knowles' attention to the intimate details, emotions and experiences that make up "life history" (2001) has also been influential to my approach. The oral histories I have collected provide knowledge of everyday life that Dorothy Smith foregrounded in her emphasis on "situated knowledge" (1987).

Several volumes have been published containing East African women's life histories (Adagala and Kabira 1985; Davison 1989; Mirza and Strobel 1989; W. Otieno 1998; Romero 1988). Marcia Wright's (1993) publication of East African women's oral narratives from the 19th and early 20th centuries has been a particularly strong inspiration to me. In addition to providing accounts of colonial history from European and African women's perspectives, Wright's book aptly delineates the reciprocity between the personal and the political.

# BACKGROUND

This account of peasant women's struggle for the gendered commons begins in the decade immediately prior to European incursion into central

Kenya, circa 1870. I draw upon the social histories of peoples over a wide area of East Africa, especially the integrated ethnic communities of the Giriama, Kamba, Embu, Meru, Maasai and Kikuyu living in the area between the coastal plains and the central highlands. This wide lens is necessary to encompass the breadth of the regional economy within which agriculturalists, pastoralists, forest dwellers and others operated to sustain their own "subsistence niches" and to maintain relations of reciprocity with other communities.

A useful perspective on Kenyan ethnic groups is provided by Kershaw's conception of "ethnicity." According to Kikuyu elders' oral histories, collected by Kershaw in the 1950s and 1960s, "tribe" was an unknown organizational concept in Kenya before the mid-19th century (Kershaw 1997). Peoples distinguished one another according to the primary means of subsistence each pursued. Kenyans shared distinctive but often overlapping political economies directed toward the support of life in general. That is, subsistence supported not only the life of the individual producer of food or some other life requirement, but also the lives of everyone in the group or community, and even beyond the group, into other groups and communities. Geographic locations as well as shared needs linked them together in subsistence communities. Insofar as peoples in different geographic regions intermarried, traded and shared resources, they were also united in larger-scale regional relations of solidarity, kinship and trade. This perspective on ethnicity clearly reveals actually existing histories of precolonial cooperation and reciprocity within and across ethnic groups. These cohesive social relations among Kenya's peoples were dismantled through colonial divide and rule practices that eroded relations of cooperation. Ethnic groups became labor pools under colonial stewardship, and so ethnic groups were set against one another, as competitors and sometimes as outright enemies. The results of the colonial reengineering of ethnic relations in Kenya still strongly influences ethnic interactions in the 21st century.

I begin with a wide lens in order to frame the regional character of the East African subsistence political economy. However, the specific circumstances of the Kikuyu ethnic group require a more focused examination. In most of this book, I address social relations among the Kikuyu of central Kenya. I do not write of them as if they are a monolithic people. Rather, I recognize "multiple, contested and constructed historicities" and therein examine solidarities, differences and diversities within the community (Clifford 1992:101). I focus especially but not exclusively on social movements among the Kikuyu people for six reasons.

*First*, the Kikuyu, the largest ethnic group in Kenya,[1] were prominent in almost all major anticolonial struggles in Kenya over the long 20th century.

Moreover, in almost every struggle examined here, Kikuyu women were protagonists; when not, their fertility-related concerns were central.

*Second*, the subsistence political economy of the Kikuyu is particularly vibrant in the 21st century. Like all peoples of central Kenya, the precolonial Kikuyu were integrated with and protected by peoples who had fought off slave traders for hundreds of years. The Giriama, Maasai, Nandi and, in Uganda, the Nyabingi, kept slave dealers out of central Kenya. As a result the subsistence society of the Kikuyu was relatively unscathed by slave raiding. There were instances of slave raids and of the pawning of women and children during famine, but not on the large scale seen in Southern and West Africa. In the late 1800s Kikuyu indigenous society was strongly rooted, autonomous and integrated with surrounding subsistence societies. It was also under threat and suffered sever consequences from colonial incursion including massive losses of life during several periods of famine. There also developed internal conflicts among neighbouring ethnic groups (Rosberg and Nottingham 1966). Famines weakened communities and scattered families from around Mt. Kenya into a diaspora in the plains, forests and hills of the surrounding areas. This process broke up established networks of production, trade and kinship and undermined critical subsistence entitlements. Land theft and social breakdown facilitated the colonial introduction of hierarchical relations of rule.

*Third*, the colonialists alienated a greater proportion of land (relative to the population) from the Kikuyu than from any other indigenous group in Kenya.[2] The Kikuyu were plagued with landlessness to a greater extent than others. They have actively defended their land and indigenous political economy and adapted exogenous social forms to serve the purposes of anticapitalist resistance.

*Fourth*, white settlers hired men from many ethnic groups, including the Luo, Kamba and Kikuyu, to reside and work on Europeans' farms in the White Highlands. However it was only Kikuyu men who brought their families and livestock with them. Many Kikuyu saw the Highlands not as a temporary site of migrant labor opportunity but as a frontier to which they could make permanent claim. This embedded among the Kikuyu more than other resident laborers a feeling of entitlement and eventually a conviction that they possessed rights of occupancy. This conviction contributed to a particular militancy among Kikuyu laborers resident on the white settler farms of the Rift Valley and White Highlands.

*Fifth*, the Kikuyu predominated among those who took oaths of unity from 1946 onward, joined the Kenya Land Freedom Army and engaged at one level or another in the Mau Mau war between 1952 and 1960. The British confined over 1 million Kikuyu civilians to concentrations camps and another 300,000 in prisons and detention centeres (Elkins 2005). The Kikuyu were the first Kenyans to have their land subjected to consolidation and the assignment of private title deeds during the 1950s. This process reconfigured ownership to reward African men loyal to the British (Seavoy 2000:142) and to punish Mau Mau, tens of thousands of whom were left landless after the war. A similar land titling program was implemented in other areas of the country in the subsequent decades.

*Sixth*, multiethnic and multinational popular struggles between 1980 and 2007 have important roots in the Kikuyu experiences of resistance in the 1950s. Even in the thoroughly multiethnic slum-dwellers' organization, *Muungano wa Wanavijiji*, which arose in the 1990s, participants conceive of themselves as "following the footsteps of the Mau Mau" (First Woman interview, Livingstone Gachamo, July 24, 1998).

In order to maintain a cohesive story line and historical method of analysis, I focused on social movements that arose out of the particular, shared, evolving circumstances of the Kikuyu, a widespread, diverse community with its own complex interethnic networks. This study of primary and secondary sources in Kenyan history has therefore been weighted in favor of the anticolonial politics and social relations of the Kikuyu. I have also spent more time in Kikuyu-dominated areas of Nairobi, Central Province and the Rift Valley than elsewhere. Kikuyu women's life histories feature prominently in the interviews I have conducted and collected.

However, this analysis is not restricted to Kikuyu women's struggles. It is also informed by the different and much smaller literature on the struggles of the Luo of Western Kenya, the Turkana and Samburu of Northern Kenya, the Maasai of Southern Kenya and the Mijikenda and Swahili of the coast. All Kenyans faced British enclosures and all groups engaged in building solidarity and undertaking acts of resistance. Had my focus been on labor struggles in Kenya, the book necessarily would have examined more deeply the multiethnic alliances that characterize that history of organizing among waged workers. The history of Kenyan anticolonial and subsistence struggle is, in important ways, best understood as a multiethnic history.

# RESEARCH HISTORY

In the late 1980s as an undergraduate, I began to study and write with Terisa E. Turner who was then teaching at the University of Massachusetts. In 1988 and 1989 we published two collectively edited books of students' essays on grandmothers' lives and revolutionary popular culture in the 20th century. Thus began my interest in oral history. Our cooperation in research and scholarship in East Africa has continued since then.

This study is indebted to our continuing conversations and writing about Kenyan women's history and the global political economy.

My research experience in Kenya includes direct observation, oral history collection and participatory action research. I first traveled to East Africa for eight months as an undergraduate in 1989 to conduct an independent study on women's livelihoods. I was committed to learning Kiswahili. I attended classes in Lamu, an Indian Ocean island rich in Swahili culture and poetry. I made a second trip to Kenya for ten months in 1990. During this time I volunteered as a teacher at a small rural high school on Lake Victoria. I turned my attention to a more systematic study of social movements in Kenya. I focused in a Master of Arts program on rural Kenyan women's resistance to the British in the 1940s and early 1950s (Brownhill 1994). My academic interest in *subsistence political economies* was sparked by observing and participating in Kenyan women's practical work. This work encompassed a wide range of subsistence practices, including gardening, water and firewood collection, child care, herding, fish processing, craft production, domestic chores, community service and trade.

In April 1994 I attended the Pan-African Congress in Kampala, Uganda, with Terisa Turner. We were introduced to Wahu Kaara, a teacher and historian. She is an orator and actor, skilled with language. Ms. Kaara was one of the hunger strikers of Freedom Corner in 1992, where she met and organized with some of the elderly women whose stories appear in this book. Together we founded an informal research network, *First Woman: The East and Southern African Women's Oral History and Indigenous Knowledge Network*. Our main objective was to make video- and audiotape recordings of the accounts of women who were directly engaged in the Mau Mau war to expel the British in the 1950s. During these visits to Kenya, I spoke Kiswahili with many of the younger women I met in urban areas. However, I quickly discovered that few of the elderly and rural Kenyan women with whom I began to work in 1994 spoke Kiswahili. Almost all were Gikuyu speakers and preferred to discuss their life histories in their mother tongue. Wahu Kaara organized most of the initial oral history interviews. She also translated to English for us and translated any of our questions into Gikuyu for the interviewees.

Since 1994 First Woman has grown to include some 30 researchers, most of whom are young Kikuyu women and men involved in social movement organizing in Nairobi. The group has collected the oral histories of approximately 300 elderly women and men. These many tapes are being transcribed and reproduced on more permanent media, such as digital storage, after which they will be made available to the public through the Kenya National Archives in Nairobi and the Mau Mau Archive in Brooklyn, New York. Over the years, only a few women have indicated that they would prefer that their names not be mentioned in the record of their oral histories. Women we spoke to in Molo in 1998 related to us their experience with the 1991 and 1992 ethnic clashes, and explicitly wanted their stories heard. They did not want their names divulged. Tensions in the area continued to flare at the time, as they still do a decade later, and these women chose not to reveal their identities because they fear direct persecution.

All interviews were carried out in Gikuyu, often with simultaneous English translations by the Kenyan researchers. Audio tapes of Gikuyu interviews were later fully translated into English and the translations then double-checked by Wahu Kaara. Through a process of trial and error, we came to identify the most skilled translators in the group and relied upon them for this important stage of the work. Though I am not fluent in Gikuyu, I did come to understand much of what was being said in interviews. I developed a definite rapport with the interviewees based on my keen interest in their stories, my appreciation of their involvement in the oral history project and my respect for their continuing struggles. An important aspect of my future work in Kenya includes developing my fluency in Gikuyu, the *lingua franca* of those I have worked with for over a decade.

First Woman researchers who acted as translators in the collection of the oral histories did more than translate the words being spoken. They also mediated the cultural intersection between me, as a foriegn researcher, and the rural African women interviewees. Often, the meaning of what was being said went far beyond the literal translation of the words spoken; it involved the interpretation of proverbs and the negotiation of specific cultural and historical references. I did not approach the interviewees simply out of an academic interest. They were engaged in social movement networks in which I also participated. My Kenyan research associates were fellow activists. We met our elderly interviewees as senior participants in a common struggle. Because of this affiliation, and because of the age of the translators, the interviewees often spoke to the Kenyan researchers as if they were grandchildren. Customarily, Kikuyu children are named after their grandparents and this encourages an especially close relationship. In the research setting, then, this intergenerational dialogue facilitated an easy interchange between the Kenyan researchers and the elderly interviewees.

Most of the elders interviewed were contacted through the personal friendships and social movement networks of the Kenyan researchers and activists of First Woman. These elders, in turn, introduced us to their friends and acquaintances, many of whom were also interested in speaking about their lives and their involvement in Mau Mau and subsequent struggles.

During the period, I was not alone in researching the indigenous political economies of the recent Kikuyu past. I joined a virtual movement of students of Kenyan history, which included some four generations of Kenyan intellectuals, writers and activists. Jomo Kenyatta, Ralph Bunche and Mbui Koinange are among the eldest set, and were more politically conservative than many in the next set. These include the peoples' scholars Yash Ghai, Makhan Singh, Godfrey Muriuki, Micere Mugo, Maina wa Kinyatti, Ngugi wa Thiong'o, Karim Abdelraheem, Koigi wa Wamwere and Peter Anyang' Nyango among others. Some of their most accomplished students, the next generation, became my personal friends and co-researchers. They include Wahu Kaara, Kaara wa Macharia, Josephine Nyamwere and others.

At the 7th Pan-African Congress in Kampala, Uganda, in 1994, I was introduced to three young Kenyans who ran the offices of Release Political Prisoners lobby group in Nairobi. Karimi Nduthu, Tirop Kitur and Kang'ethe Mungai suffered for seven years as political prisoners and were released only when their mothers staged a hunger strike and employed the curse of nakedness at Freedom Corner in 1992. These men were among those who were released from jail and worked to carry on the work of Freedom Corner after the mothers' year-long hunger strike and vigil had ended in early 1993. Release Political Prisoners was founded by the mothers of Freedom Corner. After some years, the lobby group had the resources for an office for human rights educational efforts and other lobbying activities.

Yet a fourth generation of young scholars and activists from Kenya has influenced my thinking and informed the direction of my research. These were the activists, like Maryanne Wanjiru Kahiga and Muriithi Nduthu, who worked within the RPP organization in the mid-1990s. Many of them had had their education cut short by imprisonment, exile and the general economic downturn precipitated by World Bank structural adjustment programs. I was involved with some of the RPP youth and others in First Woman. Because Mau Mau women were so closely associated with RPP, youthful members of the organization became natural allies in the gathering of interviews from the elders. My interest in the gendered class dynamics of Kenya's revolutionary anticolonial struggle intersected with my Kenyan agemates' interest in rectifying long-standing social inequalities as well as the colonial distortions of the historical record of Mau Mau. At the same time, other groups pursued their own interests in learning from their elders. In organizations such as *Mungiki* [The Congress, or The Multitudes], a generation of jobless, landless and mobilized Kenyans approached their elders and asked them to relate their own histories to the youth. *Mungiki* members in particular sought to defend those villagers who were being targeted in the early 1990s land clearances. They looked to their elders for advice.[3] First Woman's collection of interviews with Mau Mau women, along with RPP's diverse educational programs, became part of this wider, popular intergenerational dialogue.

I undertook data collection in Kenya for this book between June and August 2004. My doctoral research builds on and extends the work I did independently and in First Woman over the previous17 years. Although First Woman had collected hundreds of oral histories, we had not yet had the opportunity to bring interviewees together to discuss common concerns. In July 2004 First Woman organized a five-day workshop that brought together 10 elderly women engaged in land and human rights struggles.

A research team of 20 women and men worked together to facilitate and organize the workshop. On the First Woman team were members of several other organizations working in the areas of popular theatre for human rights, HIV/AIDS awareness and civic education. The inclusion of these professional grassroots actors and performers was fortuitous in that the daily schedule of workshop activities always included rejuvenating songs, skits and role playing. This enhanced the learning and sharing experience by drawing people together across the generations on emotional, spiritual and social planes. Members of *Mulika*, a media and democracy organization based in Nairobi, also participated in all stages of the workshop from planning to logistics. *Mulika's* director, Ndungi Githuku, hosted the event at his family's farm in Mwimuto, outside of Nairobi.

Workshop participants came from five different locations in the country (Mwimuto, Kamae, Nyeri, Nanyuki and Eldoret). We specially invited women with whom we had long-standing friendships through First Woman and other networks. They invited some of their friends. And a member of the research team involved in human rights campaigns invited women who were engaged in an ongoing land occupation in his home area of Nanyuki. All participants volunteered to attend the five-day event to present and record their oral histories or to elaborate on their earlier testimonies. Participants involved themselves mainly out of an interest in documenting the history of their struggles from their own perspectives. They sought to learn from and connect more closely with other women in struggle and in building capacity to pursue social justice activities. They also sought to set down their own stories in the historical record, and therefore consented and actively sought to have their real names used in published accounts including this study.

The Mwimuto workshop was organized around the three themes of enclosure, resistance and subsistence. Small-group sessions and plenaries stimulated energetic discussions of the women's particular experiences and allowed for sharing, comparison and strategizing among the women from different communities. Discussions and follow-up interviews, almost all in Gikuyu, were tape recorded and in many cases also video recorded. Translations of the tapes took place in the evenings and were finalized after the workshop ended. Wahu Kaara continuously updated us with summaries of the proceedings while note-takers made detailed accounts in English of each session.

After the workshop I followed up with visits to women in three of the five communities from which the workshop participants were drawn (Kamae, Nanyuki and Nyeri). I recorded interviewees' stories of their lives with special attention to the circumstances and details pertinent to the social justice activity in which they participated. These activities included the Mau Mau war for independence in the 1950s, the struggle against political repression in the 1980s and the ongoing struggle against land expropriations in the 2000s. Again, interviews were tape recorded and translated by First Woman researchers.

After the Mwimuto workshop, the First Woman research team conducted some 20 further interviews with activists engaged in the struggle for a new people-driven constitution and against the World Trade Organization. I also interviewed six activists in various local organizations engaged in work pertinent to this study, such as members of the "Peoples' Parliament," an informal grassroots network whose participants meet daily in Jivanjee Gardens, a public park in Nairobi, to debate matters of national and international policy.

## ANALYSIS OF THE DATA

The study brings a subsistence perspective to the gendered ethnicized class analysis of 15 major instances of Kenyan resistance between 1913 and 2007. These range from two-day demonstrations, to long-term social movements, to the decade-long Mau Mau guerrilla struggle. I chose these 15 instances of resistance from a larger set of struggles, revolts and protests because they constitute the major Kenyan uprisings of the long 20th century. I have given different weight to their analyses because of the varied intensity of these struggles. For example, three chapters are devoted to the study of the instance of the Mau Mau war. However, an understanding of each of these cases requires an analysis of the entire gendered social world out of which it arose. I analyze popular uprisings not in isolated instances, but rather as part of an unfolding history of gendered, ethnicized class struggle. A multiethnic convergence is highlighted, for instance, in my analysis of the 1960s women's groups and *harambee* movements and in the analysis of the 1990s land occupation movement and the struggle for a new constitution.

As noted above this research draws on interviews gathered in earlier periods of study as well as the oral histories generated in 2004 at a major workshop focused on the theme of this doctoral research. Most of the women interviewed chose to share particular memories that they believed would guide those engaged in contemporary struggles. Many who spoke of the past connected their experiences explicitly with the current period. They compared the Mau Mau war to the 1990s ethnic clashes or armed attacks on ethnic minorities or immigrant communities. One mother spoke of a daughter who took up arms against the land raiders in 1992. This mother had taken the oath during the 1950s (First Woman interview, Molo South, July 9, 1998). She had fought for land with arms in the 1950s and succeeded in securing her land in Molo through cooperative effort in the 1960s. For these Mau Mau women and many others, the struggle for land and freedom in Kenya has continued quite viscerally into the 21$^{st}$ century.

For this study, I analysed and reviewed the data from the oral histories and other sources in order to:

*First*, (a) register peasants' experiences of the life economy, including the social relations associated with a variety of expressions of subsistence; (b) examine respondents' knowledge of and experience within particular instances of struggle; and (c) identify commonalities and differences in the processes and social relations of struggle in 15 instances of crisis and transformation across the long 20$^{th}$ century.

*Second*, assess each instance of resistance in terms of its (a) scale (number of people involved); (b) scope (with respect to revolutionary versus reform-ist objectives); and (c) integration (extent of networking and links with other social movements).

*Third*, address the ways in which Kenyan activists organized their struggles by examining the extent to which social movement participants drew on and amalgamated aspects of indigenous and exogenous social forms in the process of struggle.

This three-pronged analysis of the data enabled me to identify emerg-ing and changing forms of social movements' organization in tandem with the process by which large corporations expanded the scale of their opera-tions. More can be said about the connections between local and global processes of capitalist production and gendered commoners' resistance. The analysis focused on the creative impulses within Kenyan social movements, beginning with Mekatilili's 1913 uprising in Giriamaland in coastal Kenya and ending with the multiethnic convergence of gendered commoners and "strange eruptions from below" that have brought the unfinished business of the 1950s Mau Mau war into the 21$^{st}$ century.

## Notes

1.  According to 1989 census data, the 4,455,865 Kikuyu made up some 21 percent of the Kenyan population. The Kikuyu are by far the largest single ethnic group in the country (Bhushan, 1997-1998).
2.  The British alienated almost all of the Maasai people's original territory and inadequately compensated them with land elsewhere. The British forestalled Maasai rebellion by making a lasting peace pact with the customary indigenous religious and political leader of the Maasai, the *laibon* (Mungeam 1966b). The Kikuyu and most other Kenyan peoples had no such pre-existing indigenous authorities with whom the British could make such convenient peace agreements. In the 1990s and 2000s, the Maasai began to engage on a large scale in a variety of efforts to recuperate land and other rights. These efforts include the successful Maasai land mines compensation case and the Maasai women's mass rape (war crimes) case.
3.  *Mungiki* contains several strands, some of which have engaged in gang-like behavior and the open enforcement of female circumcision among women members of the group. These controversial aspects of the organization have limited the capacity of the group to work in many social movement networks in Kenya and further afield.

# ❧ BIBLIOGRAPHY

Abantu for Development, *The Other Side of Prison: The Role of the Women Left Behind*, Nairobi: Abantu for Development, 2004, http://www.abantu.org.

Abwao, Peter, "Food crisis: Kenya needs urgent overhaul," *Kenya Times*, Nairobi, July 16, 1996, p.16.

Abwunza, Judith, *Women's Voices, Women's Power: Dialogues of Resistance from East Africa*, Peterborough, Ont.: Broadview Press, 1997.

Achieng', Judith, "Protests against Land Reforms in Kenya," Inter Press Service, "The African Portal," December 9, 2000, http://www.afrol.com/News/ken008_landreform2.htm

Achieng', Judith, "Rice Farmers Battle For Their Rights," InterPress Service, Third World News Agency, March 20, 2000, www.hartford-hwp.com/archives/36/154.html.

Adagala, Kavetsa and Wanjiku Mukabi Kabira (eds.), *Kenyan Oral Narratives: A Selection*, Nairobi: Heinemann, 1985.

Africa Confidential, "Moi Versus the Economy," *Africa Confidential*, Vol. 42, No. 18, September 14, 2001, pp. 1-3.

Africa Watch, *Kenya: Taking Liberties*, New York: Africa Watch, 1991.

Agutu, Mark, "70 families made homeless," *Daily Nation* (Nairobi), January 28, 2003.

Ahlberg, Beth Maina, *Women, Sexuality, and the Changing Social Order: The Impact of Government Policies on Reproductive Behavior in Kenya*, Langhorne, PA: Gordon and Breach, 1991.

Ajulu, Rok, "Thinking Through the Crisis of Democratisation in Kenya: A Response to Adar and Murunga," *African Sociological Review*, Vol. 4, No. 2, 2000, pp. 133-157.

Ajulu, Rok, "What Was Mau Mau? A Controversy Revisited," book review of *Mau Mau and Kenya: An Analysis of A Peasant Revolt*, by Wunyabari O. Maloba, in *Review of African Political Economy*, No. 6, 1994, pp. 226-233.

Akhter, Farida, "Resisting 'Technology' and Defending Subsistence in Bangladesh: Nayakrishi Andolon and the Movement for a Happy Life," in Veronika Bennholdt-Thomsen, Nicholas Faraclas and Claudia Von Werlhof (eds.), *There Is an Alternative: Subsistence and Worldwide Resistance to Corporate Globalization*, London, Zed, 2001, pp. 167-177.

Akolo, Judith, "Kanu loses KICC to Narc government," *Daily Nation* (Nairobi), February 11, 2003.

Alport, C.J.M., "Kenya's Answer to the Mau Mau Challenge," *African Affairs*, Vol. 53, No. 212, July 1954, pp. 241-248.

Ambler, Charles H., *Kenyan Communities in the Age of Imperialism: The Central Region in the Late Nineteenth Century*, New Haven, CT: Yale University Press, 1988.

Anderson, David, *Eroding the Commons: The Politics of Ecology in Baringo, Kenya, 1890-1963*, Oxford: James Currey, 2002.

Anderson, David, *Histories of the Hanged: The Dirty War in Kenya and the End of Empire*, New York: W.W. Norton, 2005.

Anderson, David M. and David Killingray (eds.), *Policing the Empire: Government, Authority, and Control, 1830-1940*, Manchester, UK: Manchester University Press, 1991.

Antrobus, Peggy, *The Global Women's Movement: Origins, Issues and Strategies*, London: Zed, 2004.

Apologetics Index, "Mungiki," http://www.gospelcom.net/apologeticsindex/index.html.

Arrighi, Giovanni, *The Long Twentieth Century: Money, Power, and the Origins of Our Times*, London and New York: Verso, 1994.

Arrighi, Giovanni and John S. Saul, *Essays on the Political Economy of Africa*, New York: Monthly Review Press, 1973.

Askwith, Tom G., *Kenya's Progress*, Nairobi: East African Literature Bureau, 1958.

Askwith, Tom, edited by Joanna Lewis, *From Mau Mau to Harambee*, Cambridge African Monograph Series No. 17, 1995.

Barnett, Donald L. and Karari Njama, *Mau Mau from Within*, New York: Monthly Review Press, 1966.

Barkan, Joel D., *Beyond Capitalism Vs. Socialism in Kenya and Tanzania*, Boulder, CO: Lynne Rienner, 1994.

Barkan, Joel D. and Frank Holmquist, "Peasant-State Relations and the Social Base of Self-Help in Kenya," *World Politics*, Vol. 41, No. 3, April, 1989, pp. 359-380.

Bassey, Nimmo, "What Peace in the World Today?" Lecture at a conference marking the *International Day of Peace*, Benin City, Nigeria, September 21, 2002.

Bates, Robert H., *Markets and States in Tropical Africa: The Political Basis of Agricultural Policies*, Berkeley: University of California Press, 1981/2005.

Bates, Robert H., *Beyond the Miracle of the Market: The Political Economy of Agrarian Development in Kenya*, Cambridge: Cambridge University Press, 1989.

Beech, Mervyn H., "The Sacred Fig Tree of the A-Kikuyu of East Africa," *Man*, Vol. 13, 1913, pp. 4-6.

Beech, Mervyn H., "Slavery on the East Coast of Africa," *Journal of the Royal African Society*, Vol. 15, No. 58, January 1916, pp. 145-149.

Beech, Mervyn H., "Kikuyu System of Land Tenure," *Journal of the Royal African Society*, Vol. 17, No. 65, October 1917, pp. 46-59.

Beech, Mervyn H., "Kikuyu System of Land Tenure (Continued)," *Journal of the Royal African Society*, Vol. 17, No. 66, January 1918, pp. 136-144.

Benjamin, Craig S. and Terisa E. Turner, "Counterplanning from the Commons: Labour, Capital and the 'New Social Movements,'" *Labour, Capital and Society*, Vol. 25, No. 2, November 1992, pp. 218-248.

Bennett, George, "Kenyatta and the Kikuyu: Review Article," *International Affairs*, Vol. 37, No. 4, October 1961, pp. 477-482.

Bennholdt-Thomsen, Veronika, "What Really Keeps Our Cities Alive, Money or Subsistence?" in Veronika Bennholdt-Thomsen, Nicholas Faraclas and Claudia Von Werlhof (eds.), *There Is an Alternative: Subsistence and Worldwide Resistance to Corporate Globalization*, London, Zed, 2001, pp. 217-231.

Bennholdt-Thomsen, Veronika, Nicholas Faraclas and Claudia Von Werlhof (eds.), *There Is an Alternative: Subsistence and Worldwide Resistance to Corporate Globalization*, London, Zed, 2001.

Bennholdt-Thompsen, Veronika and Maria Mies, *The Subsistence Perspective: Beyond the Globalised Economy*, London: Zed Books, 1999.

Berman, Bruce, *Control and Crisis in Colonial Kenya: The Dialectic of Domination*, London: James Currey, 1990.

Berman, Bruce and John Lonsdale, *Unhappy Valley: Conflict in Kenya & Africa*, London: James Currey; Nairobi: Heinemann; Athens: Ohio University Press, 1992.

Berry, Sara, "Social Institutions and Access to Resources," *Africa*, Vol. 59, No. 1, 1989, pp. 41-55.

Bhushan, Kul, *Kenya Factbook*, 15th ed., Nairobi: Newspread International, 1997-1998.

Blackledge, Catherine, *The Story of V: Opening Pandora's Box*, London: Weidenfield & Nicolson, 2003.

Bond, Patrick, "Johannesburg's Resurgent Social Movements," in Nigel C. Gibson (ed.), *Challenging Hegemony: Social Movements and the Quest for a New Humanism in Post-Apartheid South Africa*, Trenton, N.J.: Africa World Press, 2005, pp. 103-128.

Bowden, Gary, "Reconstructing Colonialism: Graphic Layout and Design, and the Construction of Ideology," *The Canadian Review of Sociology and Anthropology*, Vol 41, No. 2., May 2004, pp. 217-240.

Boyes, John, edited by C. W. L. Bulpett, *John Boyes, King of the Wa-Kikuyu: A True Story of Travel and Adventure in Africa*, London: Methuen & Co., 1911.

Bragg, Billy, "World Turned Upside Down," music recording, words by Leon Rosselson, music by Billy Bragg, *Back to Basics*, London: Cooking Vinyl, 1985/1993, http://www.billybragg.co.uk/releases/albums/index.html.

Brantley, Cynthia, "Mekatilili and the Role of Women in Giriama Resistance," in Donald Crummey (ed.), *Banditry, Rebellion, and Social Protest in Africa*, London: James Currey, 1986, pp. 333-350.

Brown, Donal, "Kenyan Farm Take-overs Spotlight Plight of Landless Poor," Pacific News Service, June 7, 2000, http://www.ncmonline.com/in-depth/2000-06-09/kenyan.html.

Brownhill, Leigh S., "Struggle for the Soil: Mau Mau and the British War Against Women 1939-1956," unpublished Major Paper, Master of Arts Programme, Department of Sociology and Anthropology, International Development Studies, Guelph, ON: University of Guelph, December 1994.

Brownhill, Leigh S., Wahu M. Kaara and Terisa E. Turner, "Gender Relations and Sustainable Agriculture: Rural Women's Resistance to Structural Adjustment in Kenya," *Canadian Woman Studies/Les Cahiers de la Femme*, Vol. 17, No. 2, Spring, 1997, pp. 40-44.

Brownhill, Leigh S. and Terisa E. Turner, "Feminism in the Mau Mau Resurgence," *Journal of Asian and African Studies*, Special Issue on Africa and Globalization, Vol. 39, Issues 2/3, March 2004, pp. 95-117.

Bryceson, D.F., "African Women Hoe Cultivators: Speculative Origins and Current Enigmas," in D.F. Bryceson (ed), *Women Wielding the*

*Hoe: Lessons for Feminist Theory and Development Practice.* Oxford: Berg Publishers, 1995 (typescript), pp. 2-20.

Bryceson quotes R. Swynnerton, "Interview with Sir Roger Swynnerton Concerning his Work in the Tanganyika Colonial Agricultural Service," By D.F. Bryceson. Rhodes House Library, Oxford, England, April 1985.

Buell, Raymond Leslie, *The Native Problem in Africa*, London: Frank Cass & Co., 1928/1965.

Bunche, Ralph, "The Irua Ceremony among the Kikuyu of Kiambu District, Kenya," *Journal of Negro History*, Vol. 26, No. 1, January 1941, pp. 46-65.

Bush, Barbara, *Imperialism, Race and Resistance: Africa and Britain, 1919-1945*, New York: Routledge, 1999.

Caffentzis, George and Silvia Federici, "Modern Land Wars and the Myth of the High-Tech Economy," in Cindy Duffy and Craig Benjamin (eds), *The World Transformed: Gender, Labour and International Solidarity in the Era of Free Trade, Structural Adjustment and GATT*, Guelph, ON: RhiZone, 1994, pp. 21-30.

Cagnolo, Father C., *The Akikuyu, Their Customs, Traditions and Folklore*, Nyeri, Kenya: Akikuyu Mission Printing School, 1933.

Caine, Sydney, minute, April 23, 1946, Andrew Cohen, minute, May 6, 1946, Colonial Office, 852/1003/3.

Campbell, Horace, *Reclaiming Zimbabwe: The Exhaustion of the Patriarchal Model of Liberation*, Trenton, NJ: Africa World Press, 2003.

Carey, Walter Julius, *Crisis in Kenya: Christian Common Sense on Mau Mau and the Colour-Bar*, London: Mowbray, 1953.

CESNUR: Centre for Study of New Religions, "Mungiki Movement (Kenya): 2001 Updates," http://www.cesnur.org/testi/mungiki_001.htm.

Chambers, Robert, *Settlement Schemes in Tropical Africa: A Study of Organizations and Development*, London: Routledge & Kegan Paul, 1969.

Chambers, Robert and J. Morris, (eds.), *Mwea: An Irrigated Rice Settlement in Kenya*, Munich: Weltforum Verlag, 1973.

Chanler, William Astor, *Through Jungle and Desert; Travels in Eastern Africa*, New York: Macmillan, 1896.

Chisika, Eliud, "Court summons police chief over Mungiki man's arrest," *East African Standard* (Nairobi), November 23, 2001.

Chossudovsky, Michel, "Famine generated by global food surplus," *Kenya Times*, Nairobi, July 15, 1996, p.12.

Chossudovsky, Michel, *The Globalization of Poverty and the New World Order*, London: Zed, 1998/2003.

Clark, C.M., "Land and Food, Women and Power in 19th Century Kikuyu," *Africa*, Vol. 50, No. 4, 1980, pp. 357-370.

Clarke, Tony, "How to take advantage of the WTO's 'crisis of legitimacy,'" *The CCPA Monitor*, Vol. 7, No. 2, June 2000, pp. 1/6.

Cleaver, Harry, "Technology as Political Weaponry" in Robert Anderson (ed.), *Science, Politics and the Agricultural Revolution in Asia*, Boulder, CO: Westview Press, 1981, pp. 261-76.

Clifford, J., "Travelling Cultures," in L. Grossberg, C. Nelson and P. Treichler (eds), *Cultural Studies*, London: Routledge, 1992, pp. 96-116.

Clough, Marshall, *Fighting Two Sides: Kenyan Chiefs and Politicians, 1918-1940*, Niwot, CO: University Press of Colorado, 1990.

Cole, Ardra L. and J. Gary Knowles, *Lives in Context: The Art of Life History Research*, Walnut Creek, CA: AltaMira Press, 2001.

Colony and Protectorate of Kenya, *Native Land Tenure in Kikuyu Province* (Chairman G.V. Maxwell), Nairobi: Government Printer, 1929.

Colson, Elizabeth, "The Impact of the Colonial Period on the Definition of Land Rights," in Victor Turner, (ed.), *Colonialism in Africa, 1870-1960, Volume 3: Profile of Change: African Society and Colonial Rule*, Cambridge: Cambridge University Press, 1971, pp. 193-215.

Concerned City Askari, "Nairobi street wars will only get worse," Letter to Editor, *Daily Nation* (Nairobi), October 9, 2001, p. 19.

Cooper, Frederick, *From Slaves to Squatters: Plantation Labour and Agriculture in Zanzibar and Coastal Kenya, 1890-1925*, Nairobi: Kenya Literature Bureau, 1980.

Cooper, Frederick, "Peasants, Capitalists, and Historians: A Review Article," *Journal of Southern African Studies*, Vol. 7, No. 2, April 1981, pp. 284-314.

Cooper, Frederick, "Review Article: Mau Mau and the Discourses of Decolonization," *Journal of African History*, Vol. 29, 1988, p. 313-320.

Coquery-Vidrovitch, Catherine, *African Women: A Modern History*, Boulder, CO: Westview Press, 1997.

Corfield, D.F., *The Origins and Growth of Mau Mau: An Historical Survey*, Nairobi: Government Printer, 1960.

COSATU (Congress of South African Trade Unions), www.cosatu.org.za.

Cowen, Michael P., "The Commercialization of Food Production in Kenya after 1945," in Robert I. Rotberg (ed), *Imperialism, Colonialism and Hunger: East and Central Africa*, Lexington, MA: Lexington Books, 1983, pp. 199-224.

Crosby, Alfred W., *Ecological Imperialism: The Biological Expansion of Europe, 900-1900*, Cambridge: Cambridge University Press, 1986.

Crummey, Donald (ed.), *Banditry, Rebellion, and Social Protest in Africa*, London: James Currey, 1986.

Crummey, Donald and C.C. Stewart (eds.), *Modes of Production in Africa: The Precolonial Era*, Beverly Hills, CA: Sage Publications, 1981.

*Daily Nation*, "Invasion calls scare investors, says envoy," May 17, 2000.

*Daily Nation*, "Row over Criticos land sale," June 8, 2001.

*Daily Nation*, "Chaos rocks EPZ firms: Textile companies forced to close as workers damage property and battle anti-riot police in wave of strikes," January 21, 2003.

*Daily Nation*, "Police foil bid to repossess," January 22, 2003.

*Daily Nation*, "17 arrested after houses are burnt on disputed farm," January 27, 2003.

*Daily Nation*, "300 city EPZ workers sacked as row persists," February 4, 2003.

*Daily Nation*, "Traders storm disputed Soko-Huru," February 11, 2003.

*Daily Nation*, "All land owners to get new title deeds," March 14, 2003.

*Daily Nation*, "Dzoro rules out land for Mau Mau kin," March 26, 2003.

*Daily Nation*, "Slum dwellers merit titles," June 14, 2003.

*Daily Nation*, "Nine seized in row over Biwott farm," June 21, 2003.

*Daily Nation*, "Yes, probe land allocations," July 2, 2003.

Dalla Costa, Mariarosa and Giovanna F. Dalla Costa (eds.), *Paying the Price: Women and the Politics of International Economic Strategy*, London: Zed Books, 1995.

Dalla Costa, Mariarosa and Giovanna F. Dalla Costa (eds.), *Women, Development and Labor of Reproduction: Struggles and Movements*, Trenton, NJ: Africa World Press, 1999.

Dauda, Carol L., "'Yan Tatsine and the Male Deal: Islam, Gender and Class Struggle in Northern Nigeria," unpublished MA thesis, University of Guelph, Department of Political Studies, Guelph, ON: 1992.

Davis, Mike, *Late Victorian Holocausts: El Nino Famines and the Making of the Third World*, London: Verso, 2001.

Davison, Jean, *Voices from Mutira: Lives of Rural Gikuyu Women*, Boulder, CO: Lynne Rienner, 1989.

Delf, George, *Jomo Kenyatta: Towards Truth About the Light of Kenya*, London: Victor Gollancz, 1961.

Digital Freedom Network, "Supporting the rights of a Kenyan indigenous group," www.ogiek.org, 2000-2002.

Douglas-Home, Charles, *Evelyn Baring: The Last Proconsul*, London: Collins, 1978.

Drillbits & Tailings, "What You Can Do: Follow up Action: Stop Titanium Mining in Kenya," *Drillbits & Tailings*, Vol. 6, No. 2, February 28, 2001, www.globalresponse.org.

Dyer-Witheford, Nick, *Cyber-Marx: Cycles and Circuits of Struggle in High-Technology Capitalism*, Urbana and Chicago: University of Illinois Press, 1999.

East African Standard, "The battle for matatu turf in the city," *Special Report, East African Standard* (Nairobi), November 18, 2001.

Elkins, Caroline, *Imperial Reckoning: The Untold Story of Britain's Gulag in Kenya*, New York: Henry Holt and Company, 2005.

El Sadaawi, Nawaal, *The Hidden Face of Eve*, London: Zed Press, 1980.

Federici, Silvia, *Caliban and the Witch*, New York: Autonomedia, 2004.

Federici, Silvia, "The Great Witch Hunt," *Maine Scholar*, Vol. 1, No. 1, Autumn 1988, pp. 31-52.

Federici, Silvia, "Women, Globalization and the International Women's Movement," *Gender, Feminism and the Civil Commons*, Special Issue of the *Canadian Journal of Development Studies*, Vol. 22, 2001, pp.1025-1036.

Feierman, S., *Peasant Intellectuals: Anthropology and History in Tanzania*, Madison: University of Wisconsin Press, 1990.

Feldman, Rayah, "Women's Groups and Women's Subordination: An Analysis of Policies Toward Rural Women in Kenya," *Review of African Political Economy*, No. 27/28, 1983, pp. 67-85.

First Woman, interviews with Njeri Kabeberi and Ruth Wangari wa Thung'u, Nairobi, July 16, 1994.

First Woman interview, Rahad Nduta Gachoka, May 26, 1994.

First Woman interview, Karimi Nduthu, Nairobi, May 28, 1994.

First Woman interview, Wahu M. Kaara, Nairobi, April 29, 1996.

First Woman Interview, Karen and James Ngugi, Maragua, May 12, 1996.

First Woman interview, Wahu Kaara, Maragua, May 12, 1996.

First Woman interview, name withheld, Githima, Molo, May 26, 1996.

First Woman interview, Ruth Wangari wa Thung'u, Nairobi, May 29, 1996.

First Woman interview, Mwalimu Ben Kaurugo, June 7, 1996.

First Woman interview, Ruth Wangari wa Thung'u, Nairobi, July 24, 1996.

First Woman interview, Monica Njeri, Sagana, August 25, 1996.

First Woman interview, Wanjiru Kahiga, Nairobi, September 4, 1996.

First Woman interview, Zawadi Women's Group, Savings and Loan meeting with Kenya Women's Finance Trust, Sagana, October 7, 1996.

First Woman interview, Carolyn Wamarua, Wanguru, Mwea Division, October 10, 1996.

First Woman interview, Kamene, Alexiah, Maragua, October 12, 1996.

First Woman interview, Reverend Samwel Theuri Waithaka, Tumutumu, January 2,,1997.

First Woman interview, Elizabeth Wanjiru wa Gatenjo, Nairobi, January 15, 1997.

First Woman interview, Dennis Akumu, Nairobi, April 12, 1997.

First Woman interview, Kaara wa Macharia, Nairobi, April 17, 1997.

First Woman interview, Monica Njeri, Sagana, April 19, 1997.

First Woman interview, Wahu Kaara, Nairobi, April 24, 1997.

First Woman interview, Mary Wambui, Gatundu, May 26, 1997.

First Woman interview, Muriithi Nduthu, Nairobi, June 11, 1997.

First Woman interview, Beldina Adhiambo, Nairobi, July 27, 1997.

First Woman interview, Muthoni wa Gakuhe, Mukurwe wa Gathanga, April 23, 1998.

First Woman interview, Gakuhe wa Kinyatti, Mukurwe wa Gathanga, April 23, 1998.

First Woman interview, Name Withheld, Molo, July 9, 1998.

First Woman interview, Name Withheld, Molo, July 10, 1998.

First Woman interview, Men of Mungiki, Nairobi, July 23, 1998.

First Woman interview, Women of Mungiki, Nairobi, July 23, 1998.

First Woman interview, Men and Women of Mwea, Nairobi, July 23, 1998.

First Woman interview, Women elders of Mungiki, Nairobi, July 24, 1998.

First Woman, interview with *Muungano wa Wanavijiji* members: Caroline Atieno, Livingstone Gichamo, Sabina Wanjiku, Nairobi, July 25, 1998.

First Woman interview, Rachel Waragu Karutu, Ol Kalou, July 28, 1998.

First Woman interview, Roise Wanjiru, Kahawa West, August 8, 1998

First Woman interview, Wahu Kaara, Nairobi, July 3, 2004.

First Woman, Mwimuto Workshop Sessions, Nairobi, July 6-10, 2004.

First Woman interview, Marata Muthoni Gatundu, Mwimuto, July 7, 2004.

First Woman interview, Helena Wamuyu Gitichi, Mwimuto, July 7, 2004.

First Woman interview, Martha Wangari Muturi, Mwimuto, July 7, 2004.

First Woman interview, Helena Wamuyu Gitichi, Mwimuto, July 8, 2004.

First Woman interview, Martha Wangari Muturi, Mwimuto, July 8, 2004.

First Woman interview, Marata Muthoni, Nairobi, July 8, 2004.

First Woman interview, Octavia Mutahi, Nairobi, July 8, 2004.

First Woman interview, Hannah Wamuyu, Nairobi, July 8, 2004.

First Woman interview, Margaret Nyambura, Nairobi, July 8, 2004.

First Woman interview, Wahu Kaara, Nairobi, July 9, 2004.

Fisher, Jean, *The Anatomy of Kikuyu Domesticity and Husbandry*, Nairobi and London: Department of Technical Cooperation, 1954.

Fisher, William F. and Thomas Ponniah, *Another World Is Possible: Popular Alternatives to Globalization at the World Social Forum*, London: Zed, 2003.

Fletcher, Eileen, *Truth About Kenya: An Eyewitness Account*, London: Peace News, The Movement for Colonial Freedom, Goodwin Press, 1956.

Foeken, Dick and Nina Tellegen, *Tied to the Land: Household Resources and Living Conditions of Labourers on Large Farms in Trans Nzoia District, Kenya*, Leiden: African Studies Center, 1994.

Freeman, Donald B., *City of Farmers: Informal Urban Agriculture in the Open Spaces of Nairobi, Kenya*, Montreal: McGill-Queen's University Press, 1991.

Furedi, Frank, *The Mau Mau War in Perspective*, London: James Currey, 1989.

Gaitho, Macharia, "Why Kibera slum-dwellers revolted," *Daily Nation* (Nairobi), November 20, 2001.

Gakuo, Kariuki, *Nyumba ya Mumbi: The Gikuyu Creation Myth*, Nairobi: Jacaranda Designs, 1992.

Gatheru, Claire, "Reject US demands, leaders urge Kibaki," *Daily Nation* (Nairobi), June 23, 2003.

Ghai, Yash and J. P. W. B. McAuslan, *Public Law and Political Change in Kenya: A Study of the Legal Framework of Government from Colonial*

*Times to the Present*, Nairobi and New York: Oxford University Press, 1970.

Githongo, John, "Why Does Kenya Hate Its Heroes So Much?," *The East African* (Nairobi), February 28, 2000.

Githongo, John, "Why Won't the State Clip Them Dreadlocks?" *The East African* (Nairobi), November 15, 2000, available at http://www.hartford-hwp.com/archives/36/241.html.

Glick, Brian, *The War At Home: Covert Action Against U.S. Activists and What We Can Do About It*, Boston: South End Press, 1989; see also http://www.whatreallyhappened.com/RANCHO/POLITICS/COINTELPRO/COINTELPRO-FBI.docs.html, accessed May 31, 2005.

Greenidge, Charles Wilton Wood, *Forced Labour*, London: The Anti-Slavery and Aborigines Protection Society, 1943.

Gregory, Robert G., *India and East Africa: A History of Race Relations Within the British Empire, 1890-1939*, Oxford: Clarendon Press, 1971.

Grimshaw, Anna (ed), *The C.L.R. James Reader*, Oxford: Blackwell, 1992.

Gudeman, Stephen, *Economics as Culture: Models and Metaphors of Livelihood*, London: Routledge & Kegan Paul, 1986.

Hanger, J. and Morris, J., "Women and the Household Economy," in Robert Chambers and J. Morris (eds.), *Mwea: An Iirrigated Rice Settlement in Kenya*, Munich: Welforum Verlag, 1973, pp. 45-62.

Hardin, Garrett, "The Tragedy of the Commons," *Science*, No. 162, 1968, pp.1243-1248.

Harris, Paul, "Mau Mau Returns to Kenya," *Sydney Morning Herald*, January 17, 2000, http://www.hartford-hwp.com/archives/36/260.html.

Haugerud, Angelique, *The Culture of Politics in Modern Kenya*, New York: Cambridge University Press, 1995.

Haugerud, Angelique, "Land Tenure and Agrarian Change in Kenya," *Africa*, Vol. 59, No. 1, 1989, pp. 61-90.

Heyer, Judith, J.K. Maitha and W.M. Senga (eds.), *Agricultural Development in Kenya: An Economic Assessment*, Nairobi: Oxford University Press, 1976.

Hobley, Charles William, *Bantu Beliefs and Magic; with Particular Reference to the Kikuyu and Kamba Tribes of Kenya Colony Together with Some Reflections on East Africa after the War*, London: Frank Cass, 1967.

Hobley, Charles William, *Kenya, From Chartered Company to Crown Colony; Thirty Years of Exploration and Administration in British East Africa*, London: Frank Cass, 1929/1970.

Hobley, Charles William, *Ethnology of A-Kamba and Other East African Tribes*, London: Frank Cass & Co., 1910/1971.

Hobsbawm, Eric, *Primitive Rebels: Studies in Archaic Forms of Social Movements in the 19ᵗʰ and 20ᵗʰ Centuries*, New York: WW Norton, 1959.

Hobsbawm, Eric and Terence Ranger, *The Invention of Tradition*, Cambridge: Cambridge University Press, 1983.

Human Rights Watch, "Divide and Rule: State-Sponsored Ethnic Violence in Kenya," New York: Human Rights Watch, November 1993, http://www.hrw.org/pubweb/Webcat-58.htm.

Human Rights Watch, "Failing the Internally Displaced: The UNDP Displaced Persons Program in Kenya," New York: Human Rights Watch, June 1997, http://www.hrw.org/pubweb/Webcat-58.htm.

Human Rights Watch, "Protectors or Pretenders? Government Human Rights Commission in Africa," New York: Human Rights Watch, 2001, http://www.hrw.org/reports/2001/africa/kenya/kenya3.html.

Hunt, Diana, *Impending Crisis in Kenya: The Case for Land Reform*, Aldershot: Gower, 1984.

Hussain, Athar and Keith Tribe, *Marxism and the Agrarian Question Vols.1 and 2*, Atlantic Highlands, NJ: Humanities Press, 1981.

Ikonya, Philo, "Targeting laws that dehumanise women," *Daily Nation* (Nairobi), October 20, 1996, p. 6.

Inter-Church Coalition on Africa, "Kenya in 1999: A Human Rights Report, "Which Way Forward?," Inter-Church Coalition on Africa, Toronto, March, 2000, www.web.net/~iccaf.

International Forum on Globalization, "A Better World Is Possible: Here Are the Ten Basic Principles for Sustainable Societies," *The CCPA (Canadian Centre for Policy Alternatives) Monitor*, Vol. 10, No. 8, February 2004, pp. 19-23.

International Oil Working Group, Interview No. 2 with Nigerian source, August 2, 2003.

Isenberg, Charles William, *Journals of C. W. Isenberg and J. L. Krapf Detailing Their Proceedings in the Kingdom of Shoa and Journeys in Other Parts of Abyssinia in the Years 1839, 1840, 1841 and 1842, to Which Is Prefixed a Geographical Memoir of Abyssinia and South Eastern-Africa 1843*, London: Frank Cass, 1968.

Ishemo, Shubi L., "Forced Labour, *Mussoco* (Taxation), Famine and Migration in Lower Zambezia, Mozambique, 1870-1914," in Abebe Zegeye and Shubi Ishemo (eds.), *Forced Labour and Migration: Patterns of Movement within Africa*, London: Hans Zell Publishers, 1989, pp. 109-158.

Isla, Ana, "Enclosure and Micro-Enterprise as Sustainable Development: The Case of the Canada-Costa Rica Debt-for-Nature Investment," in *Gender, Feminism and the Civil Commons*, Special Issue of the *Canadian Journal of Development Studies*, Vol. 22, 2001, pp. 935-942.

Itote, Waruhiu, *"Mau Mau" General*, Nairobi: East African Publishing House, 1967.

James, C.L.R., *The Black Jacobins, Toussaint L'Ouverture and the San Domingo Revolution*, 2nd ed., New York: Vintage 1938/1989.

James, C.L.R, "Dialectical Materialism and the Fate of Humanity" (original: 1947), in Anna Grimshaw (ed.), *The C.L.R. James Reader*, Oxford: Blackwell, 1992, pp. 153-181.

James, C.L.R.,"Rastafari at home and abroad," in C.L.R. James, *At the Rendevous of Victory*, London: Allison and Busby, 1976/1984, p. 163-165.

James, C.L.R., "Towards the Seventh: The Pan-African Congress - Past, Present and Future," in C.L.R. James, *At the Rendezvous of Victory*, London: Allison and Busby, 1984, pp. 236-250. Origianlly an address delivered at the First Congress of All African Writers in Dakar, Senegal, January 8, 1976.

James, C.L.R. and Terisa E. Turner, Personal communication, 1971.

James, Selma, *Marx and Feminism*, London: Crossroads Books; first published in

Kenneth Leech (ed.), *After Marx, The Jubilee Lent Lectures for 1983*, London: The Jubilee Group, March, 1984; also published in "Marx and the Third World," *Third World Book Review*, Vol. I, No. 6, 1986.

Jones, N.S. Carey, "The Decolonization of the White Highlands of Kenya," *The Geographical Journal*, Vol. 131, No. 2, June 1965, pp. 186-201.

Kabira, Wanjiku Mukabi and Patricia Ngurukie, *Our Mother's Footsteps: Stories of Women in the Struggle for Freedom*, Nairobi: Collaborative Centre on Gender and Development, 1997.

Kadida, Jillo and David Mugonyi, "Orange Victory Vow," *Daily Nation* (Nairobi), November 23, 2005, www.nationmedia.com

Kago, Tony and Mugumo Munene, "Maathai in court over forest excision," *Daily Nation* (Nairobi), November 20, 2001.

Kamau, Munene, "Rice farmers fear for crop," *East African Standard* (Nairobi), June 1, 1996, p.4.

Kanogo, Tabitha, *African Womanhood in Colonial Kenya, 1900-1950*, Oxford: James Currey; Nairobi: EAEP; Athens: Ohio University Press, 2005.

Kanogo, Tabitha, *Squatters and the Roots of Mau Mau*, London: James Currey, 1987.

Kanyinga, Karuti, *Re-Distribution from Above: The Politics of Land Rights and Squatting in Coastal Kenya*, Research Report No. 115, Uppsala: Nordiska Afrikainstitutet, 2000.

Kapoor, Dip, "NGO Partnerships and the Taming of the Grassroots in Rural India," *Development in Practice*, Vol. 15, No. 2, April 2005, pp. 210-215.

Kareithi, Amos, "We're innocent," *East African Standard* (Nairobi), July 2, 1998, p. 18-19.

Kaula, Edna Mason, *Land and People of Kenya*, New York: J.B. Lippincott, 1968.

Keller, Edmond, "The Political Socialization of Adolescents in Contemporary Africa: The Role of the School in Kenya," *Comparative Politics*, Vol. 10, No. 2, January 1978, pp. 227-250.

Kenya, Colony and Protectorate, *Report of the Development Committee*, 2 vols., 1945.

Kenya Human Right Commission, *Independence without Freedom: The Legitimisation of Repressive Laws and Practices in Kenya*, Nairobi: Kenya Human Right Commission, 1994.

Kenya Human Right Commission, *State of Human Rights in Kenya: A Year of Political Harassment*, Nairobi: Kenya Human Right Commission, 1993.

Kenya Land Alliance, *The National Land Policy in Kenya: Critical Gender Issues and Policy Statements*, Nairobi: Kenya Land Alliance, Issue Paper No. 1, 2004.

Kenya Land Commission, *Kenya Land Commission: Report, Evidence and Memoranda*, 3 vols., London: HMSO, 1934.

Kenya News Agency, "Board to Buy Farm Rice," *Daily Nation* (Nairobi), February 2, 2004.

Kenya Times Briefs, "Milk sales up," *Kenya Times* (Nairobi), June 25, 1996, p. 12.

Kenyatta, Jomo, *Facing Mount Kenya: The Tribal Life of the Gikuyu*, London: Secker and Warburg, 1938/1953.

Kenyatta, Jomo, Foreword to Sessional Paper No. 10, "African Socialism and Its Application to Planning in Kenya," Nairobi: Government Printer, May 4, 1965

Kenyatta, Jomo, *Suffering Without Bitterness: The Founding of the Kenya Nation*, Nairobi: East African Publishing House, 1968.

Kershaw, Greet, *Mau Mau from Below*, Oxford: James Currey, 1997.

Khasiani, S.A. and E.I. Njiro (eds.), *The Women's Movement in Kenya*, Nairobi: AAWORD, 1993.

Kihuria, Njonjo, "Is Mungiki a religious sect or political body?" *East African Standard* (Nairobi), November 18, 2001.

Kimemia, Maguta, "Saitoti on SAPs; 'They tap economic potential,'"*Daily Nation* (Nairobi), October 17, 1996, p.15.

Kimenyi, Mwangi S., "Agriculture, Economic Growth and Poverty Reduction," Kenya Institute for Public Policy Research and Analysis (KIPPRA), Occasional Paper No. 3, June 2002.

King, Anne, "The Functionary in Kenya's Colonial System," in B.E. Kipkorir (ed.), *Imperialism and Collaboration in Colonial Kenya*, Nairobi: Kenya Literature Bureau, 1980.

Kinyatti, Maina wa, *Mau Mau: A Revolution Betrayed*, Jamaica, NY: Mau Mau Research Centre, 1991.

Kinyatti, Maina wa, *Kimathi's Letters*, Nairobi: Heinemann Kenya, 1986.

Kinyatti, Maina wa, *Thunder from the Mountains: Mau Mau Patriotic Songs*, London: Zed Press, 1980.

Kiragu, Mwangi, unpublished untitled paper, P.O. Box 40539, Nairobi, Kenya, 1996.

Kisero, Jaindi, "Unrest reflects desire for change," *Daily Nation* (Nairobi), February 19, 2003.

Kithi, Ngumbao and Walker Mwandoto, "Squatter fury on MPs: Leaders ejected from meeting and asked to free suspects," *Daily Nation* (Nairobi), March 18, 2003.

Klein, Naomi, *Fences and Windows: Dispatches from the Front Lines of the Globalization Debate*, Toronto: Vintage, 2002.

KNA AN 32/70 Native Agriculture, Olenguruone, Item 6H, February 1946.

KNA, AN 32/70, November 23, 1946.

KNA, AN 32/70 Native Agriculture, Rift Valley Province, "Olenguruone: Report of a Meeting at the Provincial Commissioner's Office," December 10, 1946.

KNA, Olenguruone Evictions, 1948, Kenya Police, Signals Branch.

KNA, Olenguruone Evictions, 1948, L&O/1/195/48, Office of the District Officer, Olenguruone Settlement, "Demolition of Kikuyu Huts," August 3, 1948.

KNA, KCP, CDD, AR 1954.

KNA, KCP,AAD,CP,AR 1955.

Konchora, Justin, "Briton held, quizzed over Soweto demo," *Daily Nation* (Nairobi) January 14, 1997, p. 4.

Koeune, Esther, *The African Housewife and Her Home*, Nairobi: Kenya Literature Bureau, 1952/1983.

Kournossoff, Gwendolyn Mary, *The Underlying Causes of the 1952 Emergency in Kenya and a Consideration of Some of the Immediate Results*, Master's Thesis, Department of History, University of British Columbia, April 1959.

Kwena, Edmund, "Workers worried over MP's departure," *Daily Nation* (Nairobi), May 16, 2001.

Laikipia Human Rights Forum, *The Long Night of Justice: Report of the Murungai Farm Tussle*, Nanyuki: Laikipia Human Rights Forum, mimeo, March 2004.

Lambert, H.E., *The Use of Indigenous Authorities in Tribal Administration: Studies of the Meru in Kenya Colony*, Communications from the School of African Studies, No. 16, Cape Town: University of Cape Town, 1947.

Lambert, H.E., *Kikuyu Social and Political Institutions*, London: Oxford University Press, 1956/1965.

Land Caucus, "Kenya: Land and Jubilee 2000," presented at the Symposium of Episcopal Conferences of Africa and Madagascar (SECAM), October 1999, http://www.maryknoll.org/.

Lawrence, Peter (ed.), *World Recession and the Food Crisis in Africa*, Boulder, CO: Westview Press, 1986.

Leakey, Louis Seymour Bazett, *Mau Mau and the Kikuyu*, London: Methuen & Co., 1952.

Leakey, Louis Seymour Bazett, *Southern Kikuyu before 1903*, Vol. 3, New York: Academic Press, 1977.

Lenin, V.I., *Imperialism: The Highest Stage of Capitalism*, New York, International Publishers, 1917/1969.

Leo, Christopher, *Land and Class in Kenya*, Toronto: University of Toronto Press, 1984.

Lewan, Todd and Dolores Barclay, "Torn From the Land: AP Documents Land Taken From Blacks Through Trickery, Violence and Murder," *Associated Press*, December 2001, http://wire.ap.org/APpackages/torn/.

Leys, Colin, "Capital Accumulation, Class Formation and Dependency: The Significance of the Kenyan Case," in Ralph Miliband and John Saville (eds.), *The Socialist Register*, London, 1978, pp. 241-266.

Leys, Colin, "Politics in Kenya: The Development of Peasant Society," *British Journal of Political Science*, Vol. 1, No. 3, July 1971, pp. 307-337.

Leys, Colin, *The Rise and Fall of Development Theory*, London: James Currey, 1995.

Leys, Norman, *Kenya*, London: L.&V. Woolf, 1924.

Likimani, Muthoni, *Passbook Number F.47927: Women and Mau Mau in Kenya*, London: Macmillan, 1985.

Linebaugh, Peter and Marcus Rediker, *The Many Headed Hydra: Sailors, Slaves, Commoners, and the Hidden History of the Revolutionary Atlantic*, Boston: Beacon Press, 2000.

Liverpool, Hollis, *Rituals of Power and Rebellion: The Carnival Tradition in Trinidad and Tobago, 1763-1962*, Chicago: Research Associates School Times Publications, 2001.

Lugard, Frederick John Dealtry, *Dual Mandate in British Tropical Africa*, London: Frank Cass, 1965.

Luxemburg, Rosa, *Accumulation of Capital*, translated from the German by Agnes Schwarzschild, New York: Monthly Review Press, 1951/1964.

Maathai, Wangari, "The People Suffer," *Society*, March 29, 1993.

Maathai, Wangari, *The Green Belt Movement: Sharing the Approach and the Experience*, New York: Lantern Books, 2004.

MacDonald, James, R.L., *Soldiering and Surveying in British East Africa, 1891-1894*, London: Dawsons of Pall Mall, 1897/1973.

Macharia, Murigi, Michael Otieno and Warambo Owino, "Looters cause chaos in city," *East African Standard*, March 5, 1992, pp. 1-2.

Mackenzie, A. F. D., *Land, Ecology and Resistance in Kenya, 1880-1952*, Portsmouth, NH: Heinemann, 1998.

Mackenzie, Fiona, "Political Economy of the Environment, Gender, and Resistance under Colonialism: Murang'a District, Kenya, 1910-1950," *Canadian Journal of African Studies*, Vol. 22, No. 4, 1991, pp. 226-256.

Mackenzie, A. Fiona D., "'Without a Woman There Is No Land': Marriage and Land Rights in Small-holder Agriculture, Kenya," *Resources for Feminist Research*, Vol. 19, Nos. 3/4, 1990, pp. 68-73.

Mackinder, H.J. and K. Michael Barbour (eds.), *The First Ascent of Mount Kenya*, London: 1991.

Mair, Lucy, "New Elites in East and West Africa," in Victor Turner (ed.), *Colonialism in Africa, 1870-1960, Volume 3: Profile of Change: African*

*Society and Colonial Rule*, Cambridge: Cambridge University Press, 1971, pp. 167-192.

Makokha, Kwamchetsi, "Kenya should never discover oil," *Daily Nation* (Nairobi), March 21, 2003.

Maloba, Wunyabari, *Mau Mau and Kenya: An Analysis of a Peasant Revolt*, Bloomington: Indiana University Press, 1993.

Mamdani, Mahmood, *Citizen and Subject: Contemporary Africa and the Legacy of Late Colonialism*, Princeton, NJ: Princeton University Press, 1996.

Mango, Caroline, "Tana River clash victims to sue Govt," *East African Standard* (Nairobi), December 4, 2001.

Markovitz, Irving Leonard (ed.), *Studies in Power and Class in Africa*, New York: Oxford University Press, 1987.

Marris, Peter, *African Businessmen: A Study of Entrepreneurship and Development in Kenya*, London: Routledge and Kegan Paul, 1971.

Martin, Esmond Bradley, *The History of Malindi: A Geographical Analysis of an East African Coastal Town from the Portuguese Period to the Present*, Nairobi: East African Literature Bureau, 1973.

Marx, Karl, *Capital, Volume I*, London: Penguin Marx Library, 1867/1976.

Marx, Karl, *The Communist Manifesto*, 1847, www.marxists.org, or www.marxist.com.

Marx, Karl, "First Draft of Letter To Vera Zasulich, March 1881," in *Karl Marx Frederick Engels Collected Works*, Vol. 24, 1874-1883, London: Lawrence & Wishart, 2004, p. 346.

Marx, Karl, *The 18th Brumaire of Louis Bonaparte*, New York: International Publishers, (1852) 1975.

Maryknoll, "Kenya: Nairobi's Urban Land Campaign," August 2000, http://www.maryknoll.org/GLOBAL/NEWSNOTES/xNEWS-NOTES/newsnote08_00/kenyaland.htm.

Matthews, Z.K., "An African View of Indirect Rule in Africa," *Journal of the Royal African Society*, Vol. 36, No. 145, October 1937, pp. 433-437.

Maxwell, G. V., *Native Land Tenure in Kikuyu Province, Report of Committee*, Nairobi: Colony and Protectorate of Kenya, November 1929.

Mbaria, John, "Drive Mungiki out of site," *Daily Nation* (Nairobi), November 15, 2001.

Mbilinyi, Marjorie and A. Mosha, "A gender perspective on environmental policy," paper presented to Gender and Development Seminar Series of the Tanzania Gender Networking Programme (TGNP), PO Box 8921, Dar es Salaam, Tanzania, February 22, 1995.

Mbithi, Philip M. and Rasmus Rasmusson, *Self Reliance in Kenya: The Case of Harambee*, Uppsala: Scandinavian Institute of African Studies, 1977.

Mboya, Tom, *Freedom and After*, Nairobi: Heinemann, 1963/1986.

McGhie, John, "Mau Mau war crime inquiry," *Guardian Weekly* (London), May 22-28, 2003, p. 8.

McMurtry, John, *Unequal Freedoms: The Global Market as an Ethical System*, Toronto: Garamond Press, 1998a.

McMurtry, John, "The Economics of Life and Death," unpublished paper presented at the World Congress of Philosophers Conference, Boston, MA, August, 1998b.

McMurtry, John, *The Cancer Stage of Capitalism*, London: Pluto, 1999.

McMurtry, John, "The Life-Ground, the Civil Commons and the Corporate Male Gang," *Gender, Feminism and the Civil Commons*, Special Issue of the *Canadian Journal of Development Studies*, Vol. 22, 2001, pp. 819-854.

McMurtry, John, *Value Wars: The Global Market Versus the Life Economy*, London: Pluto, 2002.

Merchant, Carolyn, *The Death of Nature: Women, Ecology, and the Scientific Revolution*, San Francisco: Harper & Row, 1980.

Mgendi, Catherine, "Reasons for Decline in Agricultural Production," *Daily Nation* (Nairobi), October 3, 1996, p.1.

Mgendi, Catherine, "Sector Records Negative Growth Rates," *Daily Nation* (Nairobi), December 13, 1996, p. 4.

Middleton, John and Greet Kershaw, *Central Tribes of the North-Eastern Bantu: The Kikuyu, Including Embu, Meru, Mbere, Chuka, Mwimbi, Tharaka, and the Kamba of Kenya*, London: International African Institute, 1953/1972.

Midnight Notes Collective, "Introduction to the New Enclosures," in *The New Enclosures: Midnight Notes*, Fall 1990, pp. 1-9.

Mies, Maria, *Patriarchy and Accumulation on a World Scale: Women in the International Division of Labour*, London: Zed, 1986.

Mies, Maria and Vandana Shiva, *Ecofeminism*, London: Zed, 1993.

Miles, Angela, *Integrative Feminisms: Building Global Visions, 1960s-1990s*, New York: Routledge, 1996.

Miles, Angela, "Women's Work, Nature and Colonial Exploitation: Feminist Struggle for Alternatives to Corporate Globalization," in *Gender,*

*Feminism and the Civil Commons*, Special Issue of the *Canadian Journal of Development Studies*, Vol. 22, 2001, pp. 855-878.

Miller, Charles, *The Lunatic Express: An Entertainment in Imperialism*, New York: Macmillan, 1971.

Miring'uh, Eliud and Martin Masai, "Pastor denounces women's stripping," *East African Standard* (Nairobi), March 5, 1992, pp 1 and 13.

Mirza, Sarah and Margaret Strobel (eds.), *Three Swahili Women: Life Histories from Mombasa, Kenya*, Bloomington: Indiana University Press, 1989.

Mitrany, David, *Marx Against the Peasant: A Study in Social Dogmatism*, New York: Collier Books, 1961.

Monbiot, George, "Beware the bluewash," *Guardian Weekly*, September 4-10, 2003, p. 11.

Mooney, Pat, "Foreword: A Cancun Diary," in Jerry Buckland, *Ploughing Up the Farm: Neo-Liberalism, Modern Technology and the State of the World's Farmers*, London: Zed, and Halifax: Fernwood, 2004, pp. xv-xvii.

Morton, Fred, *Children of Ham: Freed Slaves and Fugitive Slaves on the Kenya Coast, 1873-1907*, Boulder, CO: Westview Press, 1990.

Mosley, Paul, *Settler Economies: Studies in the Economic History of Kenya and Southern Rhodesia, 1900-1963*, Cambridge: Cambridge University Press, 1983.

Mugonyi, David and Kevin Kelly, "Mystery of US base plea to Kenya," *Daily Nation* (Nairobi), June 17, 2003.

Muiruri, Stephen, "Police to fight city transport cartels," *Daily Nation* (Nairobi), November 16, 2001.

Mukaru-Ng'ang'a, D., "Thirty Years Before Mau Mau: A Study in Rural Resistance and Political Organisations, 1920-1952," Institute of African Studies, University of Nairobi, Paper 104, mimeo, n.d.

Mulaa, Adieri and Peterson Githaiga, "Chaos rocks EPZ firms: Textile companies forced to close as workers damage property and battle anti-riot police in wave of strikes," *Daily Nation* (Nairobi), January 21, 2003.

Mulama, Joyce, "Former Freedom Fighters to Sue Britain for Compensation," Inter Press Service News Agency, http://www.ipsnews.net/africa/interna.asp?idnews=20175, September 17, 2003.

Mungeam, G. H., *British Rule in Kenya 1895-1912; The Establishment of Administration in the East African Protectorate*, Oxford: Clarendon Press, 1966a.

Mungeam, G. H., "Kikuyu and Masai Responses to the Establishment of British Administration in the East Protectorate," paper presented at the Social Science Conference, University College, Nairobi, December 1966b.

Munro, J. Forbes, *Colonial Rule and the Kamba: Social Change in the Kenya Highlands, 1889-1939*, London: Oxford University Press, 1975.

Muriuki, Godfrey, *History of the Kikuyu, 1500-1900*, Nairobi, London: Oxford University Press, 1974.

Muriuki, Muriithi, "All land owners to get new title deeds" *Daily Nation* (Nairobi), March 14, 2003.

Museka, Lillian, "Anti-war demonstrators seek poverty alleviation," *Daily Nation* (Nairobi), February 17, 2003.

Mutonya, Njuguna, "Row over Criticos land sale," *Daily Nation* (Nairobi), June 8, 2001.

Mutua, Makau, "Kenyans must reject anti-terrorism bill," *Daily Nation* (Nairobi), July 2, 2003.

Mwai, Muthui, "What makes Mungiki tick?" *Daily Nation* (Nairobi), October 23, 2000.

Mwai, Muthui, "Top names tied to land problem," *Daily Nation* (Nairobi), October 17, 1996, pp. 1 and 16.

MwaKenya, *The Draft Minimum Programme of MwaKenya*, Nairobi: Union of Patriots for the Liberation of Kenya, September 1987.

Mwangi, Mburu, "City hall's land swindle against women," *Daily Nation* (Nairobi), October 8, 2001.

Nash, June, "Global Integration and Subsistence Insecurity," *American Anthropologist*, New Series, Vol. 96, No. 1, March 1994, pp. 7-30.

Nation Correspondent, "Widows: Chief Has Taken Our Land," *Daily Nation* (Nairobi), November 4, 1996, p.16.

Nation Correspondent, "Release Mwea report, commission urged," *Daily Nation* (Nairobi), December 19, 1996, p. 20.

Nation Correspondent, "Villagers lynch demolition man," *Daily Nation* (Nairobi), December 21, 1996, p .5.

Nation Correspondent, "Squad flattened shanty village," *Daily Nation* (Nairobi), December 31, 1996, p.3.

Nation Correspondent, "Invasion calls scare investors, says envoy," *Daily Nation* (Nairobi), May 17, 2000.

Nation Correspondent, "Leaders' woes over Mungiki," *Daily Nation* (Nairobi), December 3, 2000

Nation Correspondent, "Police kill Mungiki member," *Daily Nation* (Nairobi), April 3, 2001.

Nation Correspondent, "6,500 people barred from cultivating disputed land," *Daily Nation* (Nairobi), November 20, 2001.

Nation Reporter, "Government Plans Fundamental Reforms For Agriculture," *Daily Nation* (Nairobi), October 3, 1996, pp.1-2.

Nation Reporter, "Kanu and women's body 'are divorced,'" *Daily Nation* (Nairobi), December 4, 1996, p.16.

Nation Reporter, "Wako warns on land threats," *Daily Nation* (Nairobi), April 19, 2000.

Nation Reporter, "MPs speak out on land feuds," *Daily Nation* (Nairobi), May 21, 2000.

Nation Reporter, "Fury as motion seeking Tiomin probe is halted," *Daily Nation* (Nairobi), November 15, 2001.

National Irrigation Board, "Schemes to be proud of," *East African Standard* (Nairobi), November 22, 1996, p. III.

Natsoulas, Theodore, "The Kenyan Government and the Kikuyu Independent Schools: From Attempted Control to Suppression, 1929-1952," *The Historian*, Vol. 60, Winter 1998a, pp. 289-305.

Natsoulas, Theodore, "The Politicization of the Ban on Female Circumcision and the Rise of the Independent School Movement in Kenya: The KCA, the Missions and Government, 1929-1932," *Journal of Asian and African Studies*, Vol. 33, No. 2, May 1998b, pp. 137-157.

Ng, Roxana, "Freedom for Whom? Globalization and Trade from the Standpoint of Garment Workers," *Canadian Woman Studies*, Vol. 21/22, Spring/Summer 2002, pp. 74-81.

Ngure, Joseph, "Elders reject curse plan over Minister's land row," *Daily Nation* (Nairobi), November 8, 2001.

Nguyo, Wilson, Betty Kaunga and Mesfin Bezuneh, "Alleviating Poverty and Food Insecurity: The Case of Mwea Irrigation Scheme in Kenya," University of Wisconsin-Madison: Broadening Access and Strengthening Input Market Systems (BASIS), basis-me@facstaff.wisc.edu, http://www.wisc.edu/ltc/basis.html, September 2002.

Nitzan, Jonathan and Shimshon Bichler, *The Global Political Economy of Israel*, London: Pluto, 2002.

Njeru, Mugo and David Aduda, "World Bank $5b aid to fight hunger," *Daily Nation* (Nairobi), February 5, 2003.

Njihia, C. M., "Causative factors of rice yield variations and decline at Mwea Irrigation Scheme, Kenya," Irrigation and Drainage Research

Project Report No. 38, Nairobi: Ministry of Agriculture and Livestock Development, July 1984.

Njuguna, Michael, "Factories grounded by cost of servicing," *Daily Nation* (Nairobi), December 3, 1996, p. BW 16.

Norberg-Hodge, Helena, "Local Lifeline: Rejecting Globalization – Embracing Localization," in Veronika Bennholdt-Thomsen, Nicholas Faraclas and Claudia Von Werlhof (eds.), *There Is an Alternative: Subsistence and Worldwide Resistance to Corporate Globalization*, London: Zed, 2001, pp. 178-188.

Northrup, David, *Indentured Labor in the Age of Imperialism, 1834-1922*, Cambridge: Cambridge University Press, 1995.

Nthiga, Silas and George Munene, "MP, policeman hurt in fighting," *Daily Nation* (Nairobi), July 15, 1996, pp. 1-2.

Nuri, Joia Jefferson, "US Troops Move to Africa to Protect Oil Interests," Institute for Policy Studies, July 9, 2003, posted at www.corpwatch. org/bulletins/PBD.jsp?articleid=7449.

Nyagah, Robert, "Slump in tourism blamed on marketing," *Daily Nation* (Nairobi), April 25, 2000.

Nzioki, Elizabeth Akinyi, *Women in Food Production, Their Work and Constraints: A Case Study in Mumbuni Location*, Addis Ababa: Organization for Social Science Research in Eastern Africa, 1991.

Ochieng, Philip, "A US base would be suicidal," *Sunday Nation* (Nairobi), 22 June 2003.

O'Connor, Anthony Michael, *Economic Geography of East Africa*, London: G. Bell and Sons, Ltd, 1966.

Odalo, Bob, "Zone's coffee output drops," *Daily Nation* (Nairobi), November 2, 1996, p.12.

Odhiambo, E.A. Atieno and John Lonsdale (eds.), *Mau Mau and Nationhood: Arms, Authority and Narration*, Oxford: James Currey, 2003.

Odingo, Richard S., *Kenya Highlands: Land Use and Agricultural Development*, Nairobi: East African Publishing House, 1971.

Ogot, Bethwel A. (ed.), *Kenya Before 1900*, Nairobi: East African Publishing House, 1976.

Ogutu, Evelyne, "Traders storm disputed Soko-Huru," *Daily Nation* (Nairobi), February 11, 2003.

Okello, Rosemary, "Women, the Dispossessed Land Tillers," *Daily Nation*, Nairobi, November 4, 1993, p. II, supplement.

Oketch, Willis and Mathias Ringa, "Squatters invade Kilifi farm at dawn," *Sunday Nation* (Nairobi), February 9, 2003.

Okoth-Ogendo, H.W.O., "The Changing System of Land Tenure and the Rights of Women," in AcholaPala, Thelma Awori and Abigail Krystal (eds.), *The Participation of Women in Kenyan Society*, Nairobi: Kenya Literature Bureau, 1978, pp. 132-139.

Okoth-Ogendo, H.W.O., "Some Issues of Theory in the Study of Tenure Relations in African Agriculture," *Africa*, Vol. 59, No. 1, 1989, pp. 6-17.

Onyango-Obbo, Charles, "'Secrets' behind US, UK anti-terror war in Kenya," *Sunday Nation* (Nairobi), June 22, 2003.

Openda, Francis, "Moi: KANU, NDP to Hold Joint Polls," *East African Standard* (Nairobi), November 1, 2001.

Orde-Browne, Granville St. John, *Vanishing Tribes of Kenya; a Description of the Manners & Customs of the Primitive & Interesting Tribes Dwelling on the Vast Southern Slopes of Mount Kenya, & Their Fast Disappearing Native Methods of Life*, Westport, CT: Negro Universities Press, 1925/1970.

Osoro, Jacque, "The Kenyan anti-debt crusader in the US," *Sunday Nation* (Nairobi) June 24, 2001.

Otieno, Jeff, "Yes, slum rents must be cut, says Raila," *Daily Nation* (Nairobi), December 4, 2001.

Otieno, Jeff, " Land boards will be ready in two months," *Daily Nation* (Nairobi), July 5, 2003.

Otieno, Wambui Waiyaki, *Mau Mau Daughter: A Life History*, Boulder, CO: Lynne Rienner, 1998.

Owino-Ombudo, *Harambee: Its Origins and Use*, Nairobi: Vaid Printing Works, 1972.

Oywa, John, "State blamed for high poverty," *Daily Nation* (Nairobi), October 8, 2001.

Padmore, George, *Pan-Africanism or Communism*, London: Dobson, 1953.

Pala, Achola, "The Changing Economic Position of Women in Rural Areas," mimeograph, University of Nairobi: Institute for Development Studies, 1974.

Pala, A., T. Awor and Abigail Krystal (eds.), *The Participation of Women in Kenya Society*, Nairobi: Kenya Literature Bureau, 1978.

Palast, Greg, "The Globalizer Who Came in From the Cold: Joe Stiglitz, Today's Winner of the Nobel Prize in Economics," *The Observer* (United Kingdom), October 10, 2001, http://www.gregpalast.com.

Perham, Margery, "Some Problems of Indirect Rule in Africa," *Journal of the Royal African Society*, Vol. 34, No. 135, April 1935, pp. 1-23.

Perham, Margery Freda, *Colonial Sequence, 1930 to 1949: A Chronological Commentary upon British Colonial Policy Especially in Africa*, London: Methuen, 1967.

Pettifor, Ann (ed.), *Real World Economic Outlook, The Legacy of Globalization: Debt and Deflation*, New York: Palgrave, 2003.

Polyani, Karl, *The Great Transformation*, Boston: Beacon Press, 1944/1964.

Presley, Cora Ann, *Kikuyu Women, the Mau Mau Rebellion, and Social Change in Kenya*, Boulder, CO: Westview Press, 1992.

Presley, Cora Ann, "The Mau Mau Rebellion, Kikuyu Women, and Social Change," *Canadian Journal of African Studies*, Vol. 3, 1988, pp. 502-527.

Prins, Adriaan Hendrik Johan, *East African Age-Class Systems: an Inquiry Into the Social Order of Galla, Kipsigis, and Kikuyu*, Westport, CT: Negro Universities Press, 1953/1970.

Randall, Margaret, *When I Look into the Mirror and See You: Women, Terror, and Resistance*, New Brunswick, NJ: Rutgers University Press, 2003.

Rau, Bill, *From Feast to Famine: Official Cures and Grassroots Remedies to Africa's Food Crisis*, London: Zed Press, 1991.

Reader, John, *Africa: A Biography of a Continent*, London: Penguin, 1997/1998.

Redfield, Robert, *Peasant Society and Culture*, Chicago: University of Chicago Press, 1965.

Republic of Kenya, *Kirinyaga District Development Plan, 1994-1996*, Rural Planning Department: Office of the Vice President and Ministry of Planning and National Development, 1993a.

Republic of Kenya, *Murang'a District Development Plan, 1994-1996*, Rural Planning Department: Office of the Vice President and Ministry of Planning and National Development, 1993b.

Riunge, Muniu, "Ogieks win battle for forest," *Daily Nation* (Nairobi), November 21, 2001.

Robertson, Claire C., "Grassroots in Kenya: Women, Genital Mutilation and Collective Action, 1920-1990," *Signs*, Vol. 21, No. 3, Spring 1996, pp. 615-642.

Robertson, Claire C., *Trouble Showed the Way: Women, Men, and Trade in the Nairobi Area, 1890-1990*, Bloomington: Indiana University Press, 1997.

Rocheleau, Diane, "Gender, Ecology and the Science of Survival: Stories and Lessons from Kenya," *Agriculture and Human Values*, Vol. 8, No. 1, 1991.

Rodney, Walter, *How Europe Underdeveloped Africa*, London: Bogle-L'Ouverture Publications, 1973a.

Rodney, Walter, "A Note on Mau Mau in Tanganyika Territory," paper presented at the Annual Conference of the Historical Association of Kenya, 24-26 August 1973b.

Rogers, Barbara, *The Domestication of Women: Discrimination in Developing Societies*, London: Tavistock, 1980.

Romero, Patricia W. (ed.), *Life Histories of African Women*, London: Ashfield, 1988.

Ronald, Kefa A., "Africa must say NO to GM foods," *Daily Nation* (Nairobi), June 17, 2003.

Rosberg, Carl and John Nottingham, *The Myth of "Mau Mau": Nationalism in Kenya*, Nairobi: East African Publishing House, 1966.

Ross, Marc Howard, *Grass Roots in an African City: Political Behavior in Nairobi*, Cambridge, MA: MIT Press, 1975.

Ross, William McGregor, *Kenya: A Short Political History*, London: Allen & Unwin, 1927.

Rosset, Peter, "World Food Summit Five Years Later: Access to Land: Land Reform and Security of Tenure," Oakland, CA: Food First Institute for Food and Development Policy, 2001, www.foodfirst.org.

Rosset, Peter, "Tides shift on agrarian reform: New movements show the way," *Third World Resurgence*, Vol. 129, No. 130, May/June 2001, pp. 43-48.

Rostow, Walt W., *The Stages of Economic Growth: A Non-Communist Manifesto*, Cambridge: Cambridge University Press, 1960.

Rotberg, Robert I. (ed.), *Imperialism, Colonialism and Hunger: East and Central Africa*, Lexington, MA: Lexington Books, 1983.

Routledge, William Scoresby and Katherine Routledge, *With a Prehistoric People: The Akikuyu of British East Africa: Being Some Account of the Method of Life and Mode of Thought Found Existent Amongst a Nation on its First Contact with European Civilisation*, London: Frank Cass, 1910/1968.

Ruthenberg, Hans, *African Agricultural Production Development Policy in Kenya, 1952-1965*, Berlin: Springer-Verlag, 1966.

Sachs, Jeffrey, *The End of Poverty: Economic Possibilities for Our Time*, New York: Penguin Press, 2005.

Santilli, Kathy, "Kikuyu women in the Mau Mau revolt: a closer look," *Ufahamu*, Vol. 8, No. 1, 1977, pp.143-174.

Seavoy, Ronald E., *Subsistence and Economic Development*, Westport, CT: Praeger, 2000.

Shaffer, John W., *Family and Farm: Agrarian Change and Household Organization in the Loire Valley, 1500-1900*, Albany: State University of New York Press, 1982.

Shah, Anjuna, "Kenyans need foreign experts," *Daily Nation* (Nairobi), October 30, 1996, p.7.

Shah, Wahida Patwa, "Community problem solving for sustainable development: A review of Kenyan grassroots women's initiatives," Kenya Energy and Environment Organization (KENGO), Policy Study Series No.3, Nairobi, 1993.

Shimoli, Eric and Nation Correspondent, "Leaders react to fracas," *Daily Nation* (Nairobi), July 16, 1996, p. 4.

Shiroya, O.J.E., *Kenya and World War II: African Soldiers in the European War*, Nairobi: Kenya Literature Bureau, 1985.

Shiva, Vandana, "The causes and implications of the failure of W.T.O. Ministerial in Cancun," Press Statement, Diverse Women for Diversity, divwomen@vsnl.com, September 18, 2003.

Sibanda, Ruramisai Mary, "If You Are Sexist - You Equate a Racist," *Southern African Feminist Review*, Special Issue on The Gendered Politics of Land, Vol. 1, No. 1, 1995, p. 94.

Singh, Makhan, *History of Kenya's Trade Union Movement to 1952*, Nairobi: East African Publishing House, 1969.

Sisule, Tony, "Now is the time to resolve land question," *Daily Nation* (Nairobi) October 8, 2001.

Smith, Dorothy E., *The Everyday World as Problematic: A Feminist Sociology*, Boston: Northeastern University Press, 1987.

Sorrenson, M. P. K., *Land Reform in the Kikuyu Country: A Study in Government Policy*, Nairobi: Oxford University Press, 1967.

Sorrenson, M. P. K., *Origins of European Settlement in Kenya*, Nairobi and London: Oxford University Press, 1968.

Spear, Thomas T., *Kenya's Past: An Introduction to Historical Method in Africa*, Essex: Longman, 1981.

Spring, Anita (ed.), *Women Farmers and Commercial Ventures: Increasing Food Security in Developing Countries*, Boulder, CO: Lynne Rienner, 2000.

Stamp, Patricia, "Kikuyu Women's Self-Help Groups: Toward an Understanding of the Relations Between Sex-Gender System and Mode of Production in Africa," in Claire Robertson and Iris Berger (eds.), *Women and Class in Africa*, New York: Africana Publishing Co., 1986, pp. 27-46.

Stamp, Patricia, *Technology, Gender and Power in Africa*, Ottawa: International Development Research Centre, 1989.

Standard Correspondent, "Mungiki boss freed," *East African Standard* (Nairobi), December 4, 2001.

Starhawk, "Cancun Update 9/12/03: We did it!" www.starhawk.org and www.utne.com, September 12, 2003.

Stichter, Sharon, *Migrant Labour in Kenya: Capitalism and African Response, 1895-1975*, Essex, UK: Longman, 1982.

Stiglitz, Joseph, *Globalization and Its Discontents*, New York: W.W. Norton, 2002.

Sundstroem, Lars, *Exchange Economy of Pre-Colonial Tropical Africa*, New York: St. Martin's Press 1965/1974.

Sutherland, Bill and Matt Meyer, *Guns and Gandhi in Africa: Pan-African Insights on Nonviolence, Armed Struggle and Liberation*, Trenton, NJ: Africa World Press, 2000.

Swynnerton, R.J.M., *A Plan to Intensify the Development of African Agriculture in Kenya*, Nairobi: Government Printer, 1954.

Swynnerton, R.J.M., "Interview with Sir Roger Swynnerton concerning his work in the Tanganyika Colonial Agricultural Service," by D.F. Bryceson, Oxford: Rhodes House Library, April 1985,

Tamarkin, M., "The Loyalists in Nakuru during the Mau Mau revolt," *Asian and African Studies*, Vol. 12, No. 2, July 1978, pp. 247-261.

Taylor, Peter J., "The New Geography of Global Civil Society," *Globalizations*, Vol. 1, No. 2, December 2004, pp. 265-277.

Thiong'o, Ngugi wa, *Decolonising the Mind, The Politics of Language in African Literature*, Nairobi: East African Educational Publishers, 1986/1994.

Thiong'o, Ngugi wa and Ngugi wa Mirii, *I Will Marry When I Want*, Nairobi and London: Heinemann, 1982.

Thomas, Greg, "Mau Mau Music," *PROUDFLESH: A New Afrikan Journal of Culture, Politics & Consciousness*, Issue 3, 2004, http://www.proudfleshjournal.com/issue3/thomas.htm accessed May 31, 2005.

Thomas, Lynn M., *Politics of the Womb: Women, Reproduction and the State in Kenya*, Berkeley: University of California Press, 2003.

Thompson, Paul, *The Voice of the Past: Oral History*, 2nd Ed. London: Oxford University Press, 19781988.

Thomson, Joseph, *Through Masailand: A Journey of Exploration Among the Snowclad Mountains and Strange Tribes of Eastern Equatorial Africa*, London: Sampson Low, Marston, Searle and Rivington, 1885.

Thornburn, Fraser, "Laying Claim to Zimbabwe's Land," *Guardian Weekly* (London), May 11, 2000, p.13.

Throup, David W., *Economic and Social Origins of Mau Mau, 1945-1953*, London: James Currey, 1988.

Thuku, Wahome, "Slum battle leaves tenants injured," *Daily Nation* (Nairobi), November 29, 2001.

Thuku, Wahome, "Mass exodus from slum after night ordeal," *Daily Nation* (Nairobi), November 30, 2001.

Thuku, Harry, *An Autobiography*, Nairobi: Oxford University Press, 1970.

Tiffen, Mary, M.J. Mortimer and Francis Gichuki, *More People, Less Erosion: Environmental Recovery in Kenya*, New York: John Wiley, 1994.

Tomlinson, Chris, "Africa faces hunger, why can't the continent feed itself?" *East African Standard* (Nairobi), February 10-16, 2003.

Traverso, Enzo, "Nazism's Roots in European Culture: Production Line of Murder," *Le Monde Diplomatique* (Paris), February 2005, http://mondediplo.com/2005/02/15civildiso.

Truglia, Elvira, "Africa Is Not for Sale: The Resistance Continues in Cancun," Indymedia, Mexico, http://cancun.mediosindependientes.org/newswire/display/664/index.php, September 13, 2003.

Turner, Terisa E., "Rastafari and the New Society: East African and Caribbean Feminist Roots of a Popular Movement to Reclaim the Earthly Commons," in Terisa E. Turner (ed.), with B. Ferguson, *Arise Ye Mighty People! Gender, Class and Race in Popular Struggles*, Trenton, NJ: Africa World Press, 1994, pp. 9-58.

Turner, T. E. and C. S. Benjamin, "Not in our nature: The male deal and corporate solutions to the debt-nature crisis," *Review: Journal of the Fernand Braudel Center*, State University of New York, Binghamton, Vol. 18, No. 2, Spring 1995, pp. 209-258.

Turner, Terisa E. and Leigh S. Brownhill, "African Jubilee: Mau Mau Resurgence and the Fight for Fertility in Kenya, 1986-2002," in *Gender, Feminism and the Civil Commons*, Special Issue of the *Canadian Journal of Development Studies*, Vol. 22, 2001a, pp. 1037-1088.

Turner, Terisa E. and Leigh S. Brownhill, "Gender, Feminism and the Civil Commons: Women and the Anti-corporate, Anti-war Movement for Globalization from Below," *Gender, Feminism and the Civil Commons*, Special Issue of the *Canadian Journal of Development Studies*, Vol. 22, 2001b, pp. 805-818.

Turner, Terisa E. and Leigh S. Brownhill, "'Women Never Surrendered:' The Mau Mau and Globalization from Below in Kenya, 1980-2000," in Veronika Bennholdt-Thomsen, Nicholas Faraclas and Claudia

Von Werlhof (eds.), *There Is an Alternative: Subsistence and Worldwide Resistance to Corporate Globalization*, London: Zed, 2001c, p. 106-132.

Turner, Terisa E. and Leigh S. Brownhill, "We Want Our Land Back: Gendered Class Analysis, the Second Contradiction of Capital and Social Movement Theory," *Capitalism, Nature, Socialism*, Vol. 15, No. 4, 2004, pp. 21-40.

Turner, Terisa E., Wahu M. Kaara and Leigh S. Brownhill, "Social Reconstruction in Rural Africa: A Gendered Class Analysis of Women's Resistance to Cash Crop Production in Kenya," *Canadian Journal of Development Studies*, Vol. 18, No. 2, 1997, pp. 213-238.

Turner, Terisa E., Leigh S. Brownhill and Wahu M. Kaara, "Gender, Food Security and Foreign Policy Toward Africa: Women Farmers and the Sustenance Economy in Kenya," in Rosalind Irwin (ed), *Ethics and Security in Canadian Foreign Policy*, Vancouver: University of British Columbia Press, 2001, pp. 145-176.

Van Zwanenberg, Roger, *An Economic History of Kenya and Uganda, 1800-1970*, Atlantic Highlands, NJ: Humanities Press, 1975.

Veltmeyer, Henry and James Petras, "The Social Dynamics of Brazil's Rural Landless Workers' Movement: Ten Hypotheses on Successful Leadership," *The Canadian Review of Sociology and Anthropology*, Vol. 39, No. 1, February 2002, pp. 79-96.

Verma, Ritu, *Gender, Land, and Livelihoods in East Africa: Through Farmers' Eyes*, Ottawa: International Development Research Centre, 2001.

Von Bulow, Dorthe and Anne Sorenson, "Gender and Contract Farming: Tea Outgrower Schemes in Kenya," *Review of African Political Economy*, No. 56, March 1993, pp 38-52.

Wabala, Dominic and Nancy Khisa, "Top Mungiki man arrested," *East African Standard* (Nairobi), November 20, 2001.

Waciuma, Charity, *Daughter of Mumbi*, Nairobi: East African Publishing House, 1969.

Waihenya, Kariuki and Paul Katana, "Traders report low sales," *Sunday Nation* (Nairobi), December 22, 1996, p. 5.

Waihenya, Waithaka, "Where do the Mungiki get confidence from?" *East African Standard* (Nairobi), November 15, 2001.

Wallengren, Maja, "Tanzania seeks to improve its standing on the coffee market," *The East African* (Nairobi), November 4-10, 1996, p. 22.

Waller, David, *Rwanda: Which way now?*, Oxford: Oxfam, 1996.

Wallerstein, Immanuel, "The Three Stages of African Involvement in the World-Economy," in Peter C.W. Gutkind and Immanuel Wallerstein (eds.), *The Political Economy of Contemporary Africa*, Beverly Hills, CA: Sage Publications, 1976, pp. 30-57.

Walsh, Janet, "Double Standards: Women's Property Rights Violations in Kenya," *Human Rights Watch*, Vol. 15, No. 5 (A), March 2003.

Walter, Natasha, "Terror at Dol Dol," *Guardian Weekly* (London), May 29-June 4, 2003, p. 23.

Wamalwa, Betty, "Limits of Women's Groups as a Viable Channel; for the Development of Women in Kenya," in Tina Wallace and Candida March (eds.), *Changing Perceptions: Writings on Gender and Development*, Oxford: Oxfam, 1991, pp. 245-252.

Wamue, Grace Nyatugah, "Revisiting Our Indigenous Shrines Through Mungiki, *African Affairs*, Vol. 100, No. 400, July 2001, pp. 453-467.

Wane, Njoki Nathani, "Indigenous Knowledge: Lessons from the Elders - A Kenyan Case Study," in George Sefa Dei, Bud L. Hall and Dorothy Goldin Rosenberg, *Indigenous Knowledges in Global Contexts: Multiple Readings of Our World*, Toronto: OISE/UT Press, 2000, pp. 54-69.

Wanjau, Gakaara wa, *Mau Mau Author in Detention*, Nairobi: Heinemann Kenya, 1983/1988.

Waring, Marilyn, *Counting for Nothing: What Men Value and What Women Are Worth*, Toronto: University of Toronto Press, 1999.

Welbourn, F. B., "Missionary Stimulus and African Responses," in Victor Turner (ed.), *Colonialism in Africa, 1870-1960, Volume 3: Profile of Change: African Society and Colonial Rule*, Cambridge: Cambridge University Press, 1971, pp. 310-345.

Weru, Gakiha, "Mungiki: Dangerous Subversives?," *Sunday Nation* (Nairobi), June 28, 1998, p. 12-15.

Weru, Gakiha, "It's a lifetime of misery for rice farmers," *Daily Nation* (Nairobi), May 22, 1996, p. VI.

Wharton, Clifton R. (ed.), *Subsistence Agriculture and Economic Development*, Chicago: Aldine Publishing Co., 1969.

White, Luise, *The Comforts of Home: Prostitution in Colonial Nairobi*, Chicago and London: University of Chicago Press, 1990a.

White, Luise, "Separating the Men From the Boys: Constructions of Gender, Sexuality and Terrorism in Central Kenya, 1939-1959," *International Journal of African Historical Studies*, Vol. 23, No. 1, 1990b, pp. 1-26.

White, Luise, Stephan F. Miescher and David William Cohen (eds.), *African Words, African Voices: Critical Practices in Oral History*, Bloomington: Indiana University Press, 2001.

Wipper, Audrey, "Kikuyu Women and the Harry Thuku Disturbances: Some Uniformities of Female Militancy," in *Africa*, Vol. 59, No. 3, 1989, pp. 300-337.

Wipper, Audrey, *Rural Rebels: A Study of Two Protest Movements in Kenya*, London and Nairobi: Oxford University Press, 1977.

Wisner, Ben, "Mwea Irrigation Scheme, Kenya: A Success Story for Whom?" *Anthropological Research Council Newsletter*, Boston, MA, 1982, p. 1-3.

Women's Edge Coalition, "WTO Talks Collapse as Poor Nations Unite Against Rich Nations to Resist Unfair Trade Rules," http://www.womensedge.org/pages/newsandevents/news.jsp?id=152, September 15, 2003.

Women's International News Gathering Service (WINGS), (eds.), "Wangari Maathai on Africa, women and the environment," a speech upon acceptance of a Sierra Club Award, at the World Affairs Council, San Francisco, California, May 1991.

Woodham-Smith, Cecil, *The Great Hunger: Ireland 1845-1849*, New York: Signet, 1962.

World Bank, *The Economic Development of Kenya; Report of a Mission Organized by the International Bank for Reconstruction and Development at the Request of the Governments of Kenya and the United Kingdom*, Baltimore: Johns Hopkins University Press, 1963.

World Bank, *Adjustment in Africa: Reforms, Results and the Road Ahead*, Washington DC: World Bank, March 13, 1994.

World Bank, *Kenya Poverty Assessment*, Washington D.C.: World Bank, 15 March 1995.

World History Archives, History of the Mungiki Movement of Kenya, January-December 2000, http://www.hartford-hwp.com/archives/36/index-bfba.html.

Wright, Marcia, *Strategies of Slaves and Women: Life-Stories from East/Central Africa*, New York: Lillian Barber Press, London: James Currey, 1993.

Writers Bloc, "Report from Cancun: We Are Winning," *Counterpunch*, http://www.counterpunch.org/cancun09152003.html, September 15, 2003.

X, Malcolm, "After the Bombing," a Speech at Ford Auditorium, Detroit, Michigan, February 14, 1965, http://www.malcolm-x.org/speeches/spc_021465.htm accessed May 31, 2005.

X, Malcolm, "Message to the Grass Roots," a speech in Detroit, Michigan, November 10, 1963, http://www.thespeechsite.com/famous/MalcolmX-2.htm accessed May 31, 2005.

Youe, Chris, "Rebellion and Quiescence: Kenyan and Rhodesian Responses to Forced Removals in the 1950s," in, Chris Youe and Timothy Stapleton, *Agency and Action in Colonial Africa: Essays for John E. Flint*, Hampshire, UK: Palgrave, and New York: St. Martin's Press, 2001, pp. 172-194.

Zegeye, Abebe and Shubi Ishemo (eds.), *Forced Labour and Migration: Patterns of Movement within Africa*, London: Hans Zell Publishers, 1989.

Zeleza, Paul Tiyambe, "Labor Coercion and Migration in Early Colonial Kenya," in Abebe Zegeye and Shubi Ishemo (eds.), *Forced Labor and Migration: Patterns of Movement within Africa*, London: Hans Zell Publishers, 1989, pp.159-179.

Zwartz, Hannah, "Mothers try to free political sons," *The Dominion* (New Zealand), May 23, 1992.

# ❧ INDEX